The Narrows

The Narrows

Ann Petry

With an Introduction by Nellie Y. McKay

Beacon Press Boston

Beacon Press
25 Beacon Street
Boston, Massachusetts 02108

Beacon Press books
are published under the auspices of
the Unitarian Universalist Association of Congregations.

95 94 93 92 91 90 89 88   8 7 6 5 4 3 2 1

Library of Congress Cataloging-in-Publication Data

Petry, Ann Lane, 1911–
  The Narrows.
  (Black women writers series)
  Reprint. Originally published: Boston : Houghton
Mifflin, 1953.
  Bibliography: p.
  I. Title.   II. Series.
PS3531.E933N3   1988   813'.54   87-42853
ISBN 0-8070-8303-8

this book is for
Mabel Louise Robinson ●

Introduction

Nellie Y. McKay

● Much of Ann Petry's critical reputation rests on *The Street*, her first novel, published in 1946 — the first by a black woman to have sales of over one million copies.[1] Following the appearance of this book, Petry published two other novels, *Country Place* (1947) and *The Narrows* (1953); a collection of short stories, *Miss Muriel and Other Stories* (1971); and four books for juveniles: *The Drugstore Cat* (1949), *Harriet Tubman: Conductor of the Underground Railroad* (1955), *Tituba of Salem Village* (1964), and *Legends of the Saints* (1971).

Petry's entrance into the world of letters did not go unnoticed by critics and scholars in the field. Her three adult novels were reviewed in several important journals and newspapers including *The New Yorker*, *The Saturday Review of Literature*, *The New York Times Book Review*, *The New Republic*, *The Christian Science Monitor*, and the *New York Herald Tribune Book Review*. But while Petry became the first black woman to receive such prominent literary attention in her own time, her reputation was long overshadowed by the comparisons that several early critics made between her and other "naturalist" writers. In their readings of *The Street*, for example, Robert Bone and Alain Locke argued that Petry had a less effective naturalistic vision than Richard Wright or Chester Himes.[2]

Although it is perhaps easy to understand the vulnerability of

vii

The Street (set in a decaying Harlem ghetto) to unfavorable comparisons with such works as Richard Wright's *Native Son*, a thoughtful reader soon discovers wide discrepancies in the basic philosophies of these texts. Far from being an inadequate imitation of Wright's fiction, Petry's novel expands Wright's boundaries as well as those of much previous black fiction. Indeed, she borrowed heavily from elements in the naturalistic tradition, but her view of the world was significantly less one-dimensional than that of a more lauded peer like Wright. While he intended to prove the almost irreversible damnation that race entailed for black people, she demonstrated that the picture was also complicated by economics, limitation of vision, and gender.

The Street introduces Lutie Johnson, the first black female protagonist in American literature who battles a hostile urban environment, but her life deviates significantly from the naturalistic formula Wright used to create Bigger Thomas. Compared with Bigger, Lutie has a different perception of herself, a different value system, and a different view of the world. While she makes mistakes that contribute to her tragic outcome, Bigger is wholly a victim of fate. Similarly, while she is free from a debilitating fear of white people, that fear dominates Bigger's consciousness. She is proud and self-respecting to a fault; Bigger suffers from internalized low self-esteem. Lutie is confident that she can overcome disadvantages of race and class through hard work and thrift, even if these assumptions are faulty and naïve because she overlooks the complexities of race, class, and gender, and their relationship to social/economic mobility.[3] In other words, while race and environment are undeniably important factors in Lutie's tragic outcome, they are not, as they are in Wright's work, the only causes. Her failure to be more astute concerning the politics of class and gender, and her unexamined acceptance of white middle-class values and concepts of the American Dream, make Lutie an easy prey for the greed, anger, and sexism of the black and white men (like Boots and Junto) who surround her. The fact that Lutie's tragedy comes partly from her unsophisticated understanding of male domination and class privilege gives *The Street* a very different angle from that taken in the 1940s novels by black male writers who adhered to the school of naturalism. In their work, race reigned supreme in a conflict between black and white men, and black women were the helpless victims of both. Petry's novels search out more complicated truths.

Without suggesting that biography determines artistic choice, Petry's background may account for the angle of her creative vision. Among writers of her generation, few had as great an opportunity to experience, at close range, the extremes of Afro-American life. The members of her family, the only Afro-Americans in the conservative New England town of Old Saybrook, enjoyed a healthy measure of privilege and success. Her grandfather had been a chemist; her father, a pharmacist. The family owned drugstores in Old Saybrook and Old Lyme; one aunt and an uncle were also pharmacists; and her mother was a chiropodist. Thus, in her early years, Petry was sheltered from the low economic status that most blacks of her time experienced, and which she later observed.

When Petry moved to New York following her marriage in 1938, her work on the *Amsterdam News* and the *People's Voice* — two Harlem newspapers — gave her the opportunity to see some of the worst aspects of black ghetto life. During this period, roughly from 1938 to 1944, Petry began to seriously pursue her early creative writing ambitions. Between 1943 and 1944, she sharpened her skills in courses at Columbia University. Throughout the 1940s her stories appeared in *The Crisis, Phylon, Holiday,* and *Opportunity*, among other literary magazines. On the strength of several early chapters of *The Street*, she won the Houghton Mifflin Literary Fellowship in 1945. The following year, not only did the novel appear, but she won national acclaim for "Like a Winding Sheet," a story that appeared in *Best American Stories of 1946. Country Place*, her second novel, followed in 1947, and Petry returned to Connecticut the next year and continued to write while she raised a family.

In *Country Place*, commonly called her "raceless novel" because of its lack of focus on black characters, Petry turned away from the detailed documentation of ghetto life that helped to make *The Street* so successful. The second novel is set in a small New England town of people "trapped by time, prejudice, and their own illusions," to borrow from Bernard Bell.[4] Here small-minded prejudice and bigotry beneath the surface serenity of the town are not directed only at black people, but equally toward Jews, the Irish, and the Portuguese. The novel is Petry's comment on the hypocrisy of the region she knew best. But more importantly, it shows her refusal to allow the boundaries of race alone to define her creative vision. Reviews of *Country Place* were mixed, but Petry received praise for the integrity of her dialogue, the delineation of many of her characters, and her insights into small-town life. She sharpens these insights in *The Narrows*, her most ambitious, and by far her most complex, novel.

The structures of *The Street* and *The Narrows* differ in significant ways. In many respects, the later work resembles a Jamesian novel. In *The Street*, action moves swiftly, propelled by events; in *The Narrows*, the narrative meanders as time shifts backward and forward, through multiple points of view, and subplots and secondary characters fill in a dense and complex network of interrelations between the characters and their world. Another notable difference between the two novels is in their familial support systems. Early in *The Street*, Lutie Johnson's family relationships break down and leave her cut off from a sympathetic community, a situation further aggravated by her inadequate financial resources. In *The Narrows*, however, Petry creates not an alienated protagonist, but one who is so well integrated into his community that he feels as "safe as a church" in his "end of town." Ironically, his sense of security does not preclude either his own personal tragedy or the community's.

The Narrows is set in Monmouth, Connecticut, a small New England town where class, as much as race, defines the terms of most people's lives.[5] The New England setting should not be overlooked in any study of the novel. In an early review of it, Arna Bontemps recognized its wide scope and wrote that while it is ultimately a book "about Negroes by a Negro novelist and concerned . . . with racial conflict," in a larger sense, it transcends such narrow classification, for it is more a New England novel.[6]

The action, which takes place during the late forties or early fifties, occurs mainly on Dumble and Dock streets, along the River Wye — a beautiful river: "the blue of bachelor buttons, of delphinium; [its] small frothy waves, edged with white" (p. 4). The river is a backdrop for the area of town where black people live, where the ugly red-colored neon sign of the Last Chance, a local bar, and a sign advertising "Rooms For Rent" diminish the beauty of the natural landscape. Previously occupied by the Irish, Italians, and Poles in turn, the area has a number of names that indicate this human passage: The Narrows, The Eye of the Needle, The Bottom, Little Harlem, Dark Town, and Niggertown.

The main characters in the novel are Lincoln (Link) Williams, a twenty-six-year-old built-like-a-Greek-statue Dartmouth-educated young black man who loves black history, a good poker game, and beautiful women; and Camilo, a beautiful woman. She is the young, white, idle heiress to the Treadway Munitions Company fortune, and married to an ex-captain of the Air Corps turned businessman, from an old New York family. The central plot turns on the historically forbidden relationships between black men and white women.

Link and Camilo are attracted to each other when they meet by chance, although at first they are unaware of each other's race. Then she, bored with the superficiality of her life, and fascinated by the brown-skinned Apollo with a "voice like the low notes of an organ," initiates a romantic relationship with him, without disclosing her wealth or family name. They fall in love and have a secret affair. When Link accidentally discovers Camilo's true identity, he is stunned and enraged by her flagrant deception, but even more so at her wealth and status, which permit her to believe that she can buy whatever she wants, including him. As a student of Afro-American history, Link sees his relationship with Camilo as one example of how young black men (and all black people) have been used and abused, sexually and otherwise, by white economic power in all its guises. Although he believes that he loves Camilo, he decides to end their liaison, against her wishes. In retaliation for her loss of control over him, she chooses the most powerful weapon at her disposal: she publicly accuses him of rape. Predictably, the novel ends in catastrophe — the cold-blooded murder of another innocent black man. But Petry gives an unfamiliar twist to the traditional tale. Like a mighty Samson pulling down the pillars of the Philistine's temple with him, Link's death is symbolically avenged in the collapse of the Sheffield empire: Camilo's mother and husband are exposed as Link's murderers as they attempt to dispose of the body as "old clothes for the Salvation Army."

From a plot outline that appears to be no more than a sensational story of interracial love — a melodrama of the stereotypes and clichés of race and conflict in the American imagination — Petry has woven a complex novel.[7] She exploits the most predictable and well known American racial/sexual bugaboo to explore more subtly insidious areas of American life. Her focus is on the physical and psychological havoc that lies at the intersection of capitalism and patriarchy, where the most vulnerable are black people (people of color) and all women. The characters and action of the novel illustrate how these become hapless victims.

Though orphaned as a young child, Link Williams knows poverty and deprivation only as he observes them in the lives of those less fortunate than himself. Only once, at the age of eight, did he feel bereft of family love and warmth, when grief and guilt over her husband's sudden death so enveloped the mind of his adopted mother, Abbie Crunch (Aunt Abbie), that she forgot about him for three months. Even then his trauma was tempered by his discovery that black children belong to the community in general, and loving care was his for the asking. He found Bill Hod, the black hustler-opportunist who runs the Last Chance saloon, and Weak Knees, Hod's cook. Both teach Link about his black heritage, offering a perspective different from Aunt Abbie's. While she speaks disapprovingly of much of black behavior, Hod and Weak Knees "re-educate [Link] on the subject of race" (p. 144), teaching him that "black" could be other things and that he need "no longer be ashamed of the color of his skin" (p. 145). This multiple parenting (which further integrates Link into his community) also implies an interesting critique of nontraditional versus traditional child-rearing practices in most Western societies. While Link's various surrogate parents often function at cross-purposes, the conflicts their disagreements generate are valuable elements in the young man's education.

Link, then, is no outsider, no alienated Bigger Thomas for whom naturalism dictates a tragic end. Everything about him denies that formula. Admiring a newspaper photograph of Link on the dock, a black woman remarks that he looks "like he owned [the river], and would throw anybody in . . . who said he didn't. . . . [Looks] like he owns everything in sight" (p. 380). The powerful masculinity in this picture (so attractive to women) creates acrimony in the heart of the white owner-editor of Monmouth's local newspaper, who is upset by the perfection of Link's sculpture-like appearance, and the "controlled carelessness" of his posture. He sees the photograph as one that women, black and white alike, will "clip . . . tear . . . [and] drool over . . . [and over which] every white man . . . [will] do a slow burn." (p. 365).

Using some conventions of naturalism, Petry provides copious environmental details, foreshadowing, past reflections, heightened emotional feelings, and symbolism of nature and naming. Time, place, and chance are intimately related to the outcome of the plot. But unlike the purely naturalistic novel, her characters do not automatically perceive these factors as agents of their doom. Rather, they envision options, choices, and some control of their destiny. And while racism triggers the major conflict in this novel, it neither explains nor determines their fates.

In *The Narrows* Petry focuses on black life both within and without the black community and shows it to be complicated, colorful, painful, joyous, and full of contradictions. She captures this complexity especially in the older black women in the novel — Abigail Crunch and Frances K. Jackson. The widowed Abbie is seventy years old, a poor, genteel, brown-skinned would-be New England aristocrat who owns her own house on Dumble Street, renting a part of it to other families to supplement her meager income. "Erect and full of pride and untouchable because of morals and religion and impossible standards of . . . righteousness" (pp. 72–73), Abbie's rigidity enables her to absorb shocking experiences — even the murder of her adopted son — and to maintain control of her life with dignity. But beneath her deep piety, she is as "superstitious as an Irish peasant" (p. 318). In a moment of tenderness toward her, Link observes to himself: "we might have been friends if you had had a slightly lower set of standards, if your judgements of people had been less unkind less critical; if that outer layer of pride had not been so prickly, so impenetrable" (p. 123).

Abbie shares these qualities with Frances Jackson, her friend of many years. Link sees Frances as "too astute and alert, too logical and too masculine" (p. 73), and too wrong, for being "right at least ninety-nine point nine times out of a hundred" (p. 14). Although her Wellesley education has helped to make her a formidably independent woman in many ways, Frances is emotionally vulnerable. Resigned to the painful realization that her education has denied her "fulfillment" through sexual love and motherhood, she decided to become a doctor. But loyalty to her widowed father forced her to abandon that goal as well and to assume the role of the son he never had. She continues his undertaking business and handles her personal pain with aggressiveness and strength.

In Abbie and Frances, Petry portrays two middle-class black women whose lives have been affected differently by issues of gender, race, and economics. As foils, they represent the options and possibilities that Northern black women saw and exploited in the 1930s and 1940s. Although their incomes are limited (and in Abbie's case, almost inadequate for her needs), both women are self-employed and thus escape many of the daily humiliations Southern black women could not avoid.

While the novel affirms these women's achievements against restrictions of race and class, Petry does not dismiss or diguise their less admirable qualities. Abbie's meticulous preoccupations with personal appearance indicates her acceptance of the class-based female socialization of her time. Looking back over the years, she sees her life as a series of "jumps," but in none of them has she given up her sense of hard-earned propriety. Initially, she was a schoolteacher, one of the few professions open to women of her class and color in her day. Her first "jump" was to become a coachman's wife — for while marriage is always preferable to remaining single, it is accepted that it seldom improves the social status of black women. As a widow, facing pecuniary straits, she is a needlewoman-landlady, occupying a financially precarious but respectable place on the social ladder. Throughout her life, within her financial limits, Abbie has indulged a white-defined patriarchal, aristocratic taste, with its genteel manners for women and accumulated possessions mark her for membership among the aspiring black middle class.

In short, Abbie, with her consciously held upright posture, her hurried short steps, her simple unadorned clothes, neat gloves, polished shoes, and delicate handkerchiefs, considers herself a "lady." Frances remarks that she looks like a duchess — the Duchess of Kent. She likes the comparison. And if her race and economic means compel her to live with poor uncouth black people rather than with white royalty (she feels equally superior to poor uncouth whites), she does not display the crudeness of speech or action that she associates with *black* sharecroppers. Still, for all of her character's pretentions, Petry draws a sympathetic portrait of Abbie Crunch, so that in spite of her misplaced judgments, her rigid moral and spiritual standards, her ambivalence toward race, her embarrassing arrogance, and her lack of social consciousness, she is never vengeful or mean-spirited. Her flaws do not come from evil within her, but instead from her uncritical acceptance of certain white patriarchial values that demean black people and black culture, and keep all women enslaved to oppressive ideas of the meaning of womanhood.

On the other hand, in spite of her strengths, Frances is not haughty like Abbie, or preoccupied with her appearance in the world. Professionally, she is a success, an independent woman who elects to live by her own choices. In her private life, she adopts Abbie and Link as substitutes for the family she never had, and caring for them becomes the fulcrum in their lives. Although what she eventually creates for herself may have fallen short of her original goal, Frances belongs to that stalwart band of black women of all classes: feminists before the word was even known to their generations. Throughout Afro-American history they have made a way for themselves and others where none existed before. The struggles of Abbie and Frances to maintain dignity as black women in a world that values neither blacks nor women, necessarily shape Link's character. Their lives offer him examples of the complex interweavings of the history he has loved and studied.

And if Abbie and Frances represent "proper" middle-class black women, Petry is not unaware of another dimension in the lives of black women who do not fit that model. Although only a minor character in the novel, the young, voluptuous, blues-singing Mamie Powther is signficant for her uninhibited sexuality. This is particularly important in light of the negative stereotypes of this aspect of black women's lives, and the reticence of early black women writers to explore sexuality as a "natural" part of black women's lives. Neither an earth mother nor wanton, Mamie lovingly accepts and takes control of her body, offering us an assertion that sexuality is an important element in the life-force of black womanhood.[8] In her, as in Abbie and Frances, we see Petry's determination to avoid uncomplicated characters, and to emphasize the humanity, contradictions, flaws, and strengths of the men and women who people her imaginative vision.

Issues of class, affecting the entire town, are also an important aspect of that vision in *The Narrows*. Monmouth depends almost entirely on the Treadway Munitions plant for its economic base, an operation owned and controlled by what remains of the town's white American rags-to-riches family, the Treadways. The fortune grew from John Edward Treadway's machine shop in an old barn, where he perfected and patented the Treadway Gun just before the First World War.[9] So strict is the social division between this family and the community, that few people know that the seemingly indomitable widow Treadway, who single-handedly manages the business, has a daughter. For most, the scandal of Camilo's love affair with Link is their first awareness of the younger woman's existence. On one side of the social scale of the town, there is capitalistic power which, even in the hands of a woman, is exclusive, paternalistic, controlling, and inflexible. On the other, there is almost complete economic dependence and deference to the corrupt power of the system.

In the course of events, readers observe the destructive effect of the Treadway dynastic rule on blacks and whites who accede to its dominance. We see it in such characters as Malcolm Powther, the neat, mild-mannered black butler at the Treadway mansion (located on the outskirts of Monmouth), who becomes a Judas figure and unwittingly sends Link to his death. We also see it in Peter Bullock, editor, owner, and publisher of the daily paper, *The Monmouth Chronicle*. Originally, a nineteenth-century abolitionist newspaper, launched by Bullock's great-grandfather, a "highly moral" man, in Peter's hands it loses that tradition. Peter abdicates his ethical responsibilities and turns the newspaper into a public voice for the widow Treadway's social control.

But Petry's rich and socially ensconced characters are vulnerable to time, chance, and retribution in much the same way as her economically deprived groups. Throughout the novel the imminent demise of the Treadway clan is foreshadowed: the male head of the family is dead; there is no son to carry the name forward; the lone daughter has no children, and no interest in connecting herself to the toil and sweat of her inheritance. Her perception of the uselessness of her life propels her into the disastrous affair with Link Williams; and his murder, a desperate attempt by a rich, desperate old woman who thinks she can buy whatever it takes to save the already ruined Treadway social reputation, completes the family destruction.

The Narrows shows Petry at her best. This is a remarkable novel for its time, contemporary in the intricacies of its literary, philosophical, and social implications. In 1953 — in the pre-contemporary feminist days of the 1940s and 1950s, when deliberate black feminist fiction and black feminist interpretations of fiction were ideas whose time had not yet come — it was revolutionary. Petry held a unique black female vision.[10] This is a novel of inclusion, of complex and entangled relationships with demonstrable implications for contemporary feminist criticism. It explores the relationship of race, gender, and class to the lives of all Americans, not just blacks, and exposes the roles that white economic power and sociocultural conventions play in creating racial antagonisms and class distinctions. But despite the "inclusiveness" of The Narrows, Petry's vision of the complicated dynamics of black women's lives is especially compelling. Although Ann Petry never read the novels of Harlem Renaissance writers like Nella Larsen and Jessie Fauset before her own books were published, her portraits of Abbie Crunch, Frances Jackson, and Mamie Powther are studies in the liberation of the black female character in fiction. She features women who, even in a racist and sexist society, seek individual autonomy as their human right. As Toni Morrison aptly notes, black women writers from the nineteenth century to the present have written out of a sense of a "world as perceived by . . . [themselves] at certain times . . . however they treat it, and whatever they select out of it to record."[11] Petry has played a significant role in the development of the strong female characters in the works of contemporary black women writers like Morrison, Paule Marshall, Gloria Naylor, and Alice Walker.

NOTES

1. John O'Brien, "Ann Petry," in *Interviews with Black Writers* (New York: Liveright, 1973), 153.

2. Robert Bone, Alain Locke, and others have compared Petry with Wright and Himes, and concluded that her depictions of "man" versus nature were less effective as representations of that literary tradition. See O'Brien, "Ann Petry," for Petry's disclaimer to complete identification with any specific tradition in writing.

3. Among others, Bernard Bell, Marjorie Pryse, and Sybil Weir argue that Lutie's downfall is closely allied to her identification with Benjamin Franklin's American success myth. The subtitle of Weir's essay on *The Narrows* is "A Black New England Novel" ("*The Narrows*: A Black New England Novel," *Studies in American Fiction* 15, no. 1 [Spring 1987]:80).

4. "Ann Petry's Demythologizing of American Culture and Afro-American Character," in *Conjuring: Black Women, Fiction and Literary Tradition*, ed. Marjorie Pryse and Hortense J. Spillers (Bloomington: Indiana University Press, 1985), 110.

5. Sybil Weir notes the universality of Petry's vision in her choice of the names "Monmouth" and the "River Wye," which are taken from Shakespeare's *King Henry V* 4.7. See Weir, "*The Narrows*," 82.

6. Review of *The Narrows* in *The Saturday Review of Literature* 36 (22 August 1953), 11.

7. Good examples of sensational responses to the novel may be found in excerpts from the promotional blurbs on the jacket of the 1971 Pyramid edition: "Black man, white woman — the scandal of their love inflamed a peaceful town with savage violence." "He didn't know . . . that she was white . . . she was beautiful, rich, oddly innocent, and she meant to have him . . . the whole town was maddened by hate, fear and revenge."

8. See Mary Helen Washington, "Infidelity Becomes Her: The Ambivalent Woman in the Fiction of Ann Petry and Dorothy West," in *Invented Lives: Narrative of Black Women, 1860–1960* (New York Doubleday, 1987.) Washington's excellent new reading of Mamie Powther shows her resisting popular perceptions of the sensual black

woman through defiance, assertiveness, and arrogance — qualities seldom associated with such characters.

9. The phallic symbolism of patriarchal power, with its basis in capitalism, is unmistakable in the image of the munitions factory and the Treadway Gun.

10. This is not to suggest that black women in fiction were not charting courses outside the male tradition before Petry. As new work demonstrates, particularly that by black feminist critics such as Hazel Carby, Barbara Christian, Deborah McDowell, Marilyn Richardson, Barbara Smith, Hortense Spillers, and Mary Helen Washington, black women writers with a unique black female literary vision predate Petry from the early nineteenth century through the years of the Harlem Renaissance and beyond.

11. Gloria Naylor and Toni Morrison, "A Conversation," *The Southern Review* 21 (July 1985):567.

SELECT BIBLIOGRAPHY

Works by Ann Petry

"The Common Ground." *The Horn Book* 41 (April 1965):141–51.
Country Place. Boston: Houghton Mifflin, 1947.
The Drugstore Cat. New York: Thomas Y. Crowell, 1949.
"Harlem." *Holiday* 5 (April 1949):110–16, 163–66, 168.
Harriet Tubman: Conductor on the Underground Railroad. 1955. Reprint. New York: Archway Paperbacks, 1971. [Published in England as *A Girl Called Moses: The Story of Harriet Tubman.* London: Methuen, 1960.]
Legends of the Saints. New York: Thomas Y. Crowell, 1970.
Miss Muriel and Other Stories. Boston: Houghton Mifflin, 1971.
The Narrows. 1953. Reprint. Boston: Beacon Press, 1988.
"The Novel of Social Criticism." In *The Writer's Book,* edited by Helen Hull. New York: Barnes and Noble, 1950.
The Street. 1946. Reprint. Boston: Beacon Press, 1985.
Tituba of Salem Village. New York: Thomas Y. Crowell, 1964.

Secondary Sources

Bell, Bernard. "Ann Petry's Demythologizing of American Culture and Afro-American Character." In *Conjuring: Black Women, Fiction, and*

Literary Tradition, edited by Marjorie Pryse and Hortense J. Spillers, 105–15. Bloomington, Ind.: Indiana University Press, 1985.

Bone, Robert H. *The Negro Novel in America*. New Haven: Yale University Press, 1958.

Christian, Barbara. *Black Women Novelists: The Development of a Tradition 1892–1976*. Connecticut: Greenwood Press, 1980.

Davis, Arthur P. *From the Dark Tower*. Washington, D.C.: Howard University Press, 1974.

Dempsey, David. "Uncle Tom's Ghost and the Literary Abolitionists." *Antioch Review* 6 (September 1946):442–48.

Gayle, Addison. *The Way of the New World*. New York: Anchor/ Doubleday, 1975.

Greene, Marjorie. "Ann Petry Planned to Write." *Opportunity* 24 (April–June 1946):78–79.

Hughes, Carl Milton. *The Negro Novelist 1940–1950*. New York: Citadel Press, 1970.

Ivy, James W. "Ann Petry Talks about First Novel." *The Crisis* 53 (January 1946):48–49. Reprint. Roseann P. Bell, Bettye J. Parker, and Beverly Guy-Sheftall, eds. *Sturdy Black Bridges: Visions of Black Women in Literature*. New York: Anchor Press/Doubleday, 1979.

Lee, Robert A., ed. *Black Fiction: New Studies in the Afro-American Novel Since 1945*. New York: Barnes and Noble, 1980.

Littlejohn, David. *Black on White: A Critical Survey of Writing by American Negroes*. New York: Grossman Publishers, 1966.

Maund, Alfred. "The Negro Novelist and the Contemporary Scene." *Chicago Jewish Forum* 12 (1954):28–34.

McDowell, Margaret. "The Narrows: A Fuller View of Ann Petry." *BALF* 14 (1980):135–41.

Naylor, Gloria, and Toni Morrison. "A Conversation." *The Southern Review* 21 (July 1985):567–93.

O'Brien, John, ed. "Ann Petry." In *Interviews with Black Writers*, 153– 63. New York: Liveright, 1973.

Pryse, Marjorie. " 'Pattern Against the Sky': Deism and Motherhood in Ann Petry's *The Street*." In *Conjuring: Black Women in Fiction and Tradition*, edited by Marjorie Pryse and Hortense Spillers, 116–31. Bloomington: Indiana University Press, 1985.

Shinn, Thelma J. "Women in the Novels of Ann Petry." *Critique: Studies in Modern Fiction* 16, no. 1 (1974):110–20.

Washington, Mary Helen. *Invented Lives: Narratives of Black Women, 1860–1960*, 297–306. New York: Doubleday, 1987.

Weir, Sybil. "The Narrows: A Black New England Novel." *Studies in American Fiction* 15, no. 1 (Spring 1987):80–93.

The Narrows

● . . . I tell you, captain, if you look in the maps of the 'orld, I warrant you sall find, in the comparisons between Macedon and Monmouth, that the situations, look you, is both alike. There is a river in Macedon; and there is also moreover a river at Monmouth: it is called Wye at Monmouth; but it is out of my prains what is the name of the other river; but 'tis all one, 'tis alike as my fingers is to my fingers, and there is salmons in both.

FLUELLEN,
King Henry V, Act IV, vii.

1

● ABBIE CRUNCH began to walk slowly as she turned into Dumble Street, market basket over her arm, trying not to look at the river; because she knew that once she saw it with the sun shining on it she would begin to think about Link, to worry about Link, to remember Link as a little boy. A little boy? Yes, a little boy. Eight years old. Diving from the dock. Swimming in the river.

She could hear the lapping of the water against the piling close at hand; and faint, far off, borne inshore on the wind, the crying of the gulls, the hoot of a tugboat; and she could smell the old familiar dampness from the river. And so, as usual on a sunny morning, she could see herself and Frances Jackson standing on Dock Street, a pushcart at the curb half concealing them, so they were peering over mounds of potatoes and kale and bunches of carrots and countless round heads of cabbage. She was short and fat, no, plump. Frances was tall and thin and bony.

Frances was saying, "Look! Look over there!" and pointing, forcing her to look.

She remembered how she had resented that dark brown fore-finger, long, supple, seemingly jointless, which directed her glance, commanding her to look, and she not wanting to look, but her eyes following the stretched-out arm and the commanding fore-finger.

She saw Bill Hod standing on the dock, wearing dark trunks, short dark swimming trunks and nothing else. His chest, shoulders, arms, white by contrast with the trunks, shockingly naked because of the trunks. His straight black hair was wet, and he was running his hands through it, flattening it, making it smooth, sleek. She remembered too how she had thought, I have lost my mind, lost it, no control over it any more. Because she was genuinely surprised that his hair should lie so flat — she had somehow convinced herself that there would be horns on his head — something, anyway, that would show, would indicate — She closed her eyes. The sunlight was unbearable. She was accustomed to darkness, window shades always pulled down in the house, draperies drawn, no lights turned on at night because she preferred darkness.

Frances Jackson seemed all elbow that morning, tall, elbows everywhere. She poked at her, "Open your eyes. Abbie, Abbie, Abbie — "

Sunlight on the river, sunlight on Bill Hod, sunlight on her own face, or so she thought, hurting her eyes, hurting her face, so she kept her eyes closed. She heard Link's voice, a child's voice, light, high in pitch, excitement in his voice and something else — affection.

She opened her eyes and saw Link dive from the dock, dive down into the river. She wanted to stop him. It wasn't safe. He didn't know how to swim. She couldn't stand any more sudden shocks. He was so little. The river was so wide and so deep, so treacherous. Then he was swimming, going farther and farther away, his head like the head of a small dog, head held up out of the water, moving farther and farther away. She said, "No!"

Bill Hod yelled, "Hey — you — come on back — " Bass voice, arrogant, domineering voice, the tone of his voice, just the tone, was an insult, voice that she could never forget, could hear, even in her sleep —

The head, the small head kept moving away, always moving away, farther and farther out toward the middle of the river, growing smaller, like the head of a newborn puppy now. Then out of sight. No, still there, but still moving away.

Bill Hod shouted, wind carrying the voice back toward the pushcart, back toward Frances Jackson and Abigail Crunch, rage in the voice, "If I — have to — haul you — out of there — come back — "

Was that small head still there? Yes, coming back now, but so slowly. She thought he'd never — why didn't that man —

Then, finally, Bill Hod reached down and pulled Link up on the dock. Bill Hod slapped him across the face. She could hear the sound of the blow, slapped him again, again, said, "If you ever" — slap — "do that again" — slap — "I'll fix you" — slap — "for keeps" — slap.

No one had ever struck Link. Neither she nor the Major. She started to cross the street, thinking, By what right, that man, face of a hangman. Frances Jackson's hand held her back, strength in the bony thin hand, determination in the hand holding her there behind the pushcart, behind the potatoes and the cabbages and the kale.

Frances said, "Abbie — don't. You've lost the right to interfere. Link's been living in that saloon for three months — for three months. Abbie, listen to me — "

That afternoon when they went in The Last Chance to get Link, he ran and hid under the bar, crying, "I won't go back there. I won't go back there."

She could see herself and Frances Jackson down on their hands and knees, pleading with Link, trying to pull him out from under the bar in The Last Chance. And Bill Hod stood watching them, saying nothing, watching, his hands on his hips. His face? She couldn't look at his face. How then did she know that he was laughing inside, why was she so certain that he was thinking, The old maid undertaker and the widow are here in my saloon. She supposed it was the way he leaned against the bar watching them. He made her conscious of the ridiculous picture they must have made: a short plump woman and a tall thin one trying to pull an eight-year-old boy out from under a bar when they couldn't reach any part of him; down on their hands and knees, reaching, reaching, trying to grab anything — pants, legs, sneakers, shirt; and he kept scrambling back away from them.

It was Frances who gave the whole thing up as impossible. She stood up, brushed off her hands, said, "Mr. Hod, I want to talk to you."

Frances was in the habit of giving orders, in the habit of dealing with the bereaved and the sorrowful, with the hysterical and the frightened; and so she knew better than Abbie when to retreat and when to advance and could do either with dignity. But when Frances stood up she looked down at her skirt, surprised. Abbie knew why. There was no dirt, no dust on the dark skirt. The floor behind the bar in The Last Chance was dustfree, dirtfree.

Link was eight years old then. He was twenty-six now and he worked in The Last Chance. Behind the bar. Bill Hod had won — effortlessly, easily.

Whenever she turned into Dumble Street, she always asked herself the same question, If Link had been her own child instead of an adopted child, would she, could she, have forgotten about him for three months, three whole months?

Sometimes she tried to blame this street which, now, in the mellowness of an October morning, looked to be all sunlight and shadow — intricately patterned shadow from the young elm trees, denser shadow and a simpler pattern where the old maple stood near the end of the block; shadow softening the harsh outlines of the brick buildings, concealing the bleakness of the two-story frame houses; sunlight intensifying the yellowgreen of the elms, the redorange of the maple, adding a sheen to the soft gray of the dock. No, she thought, not this street. It was the fault of Abbie Crunch. If she hadn't said to herself, Murderer, murderer; if she hadn't been chief witness against herself, condemning herself to death, willing her own death, so that she forgot Link, forgot about him as though he had never existed, she wouldn't have lost him.

She hadn't meant to look at the river but she had glanced at the dock and so her eyes moved on to the river. She stood still looking at it. In the sunlight, the River Wye was the blue of bachelor buttons, of delphinium; small frothy waves, edged with white, kept appearing and disappearing on the blue surface — a sparkling blue river just at the foot of the street, a beautiful river.

Even the street was beautiful. It sloped gently down toward the river. But the signs on the buildings dispelled the illusion of beauty. The red neon sign in front of The Last Chance was a horrible color in the sunlight — Link already there at work. Then there were all the other signs: Room For Rent, Lady Tenant Wanted, Poro Method Used, Get Your Kool-Aid Free, Tenant Provide Own Heat, Rooms Dollar and Half A Night. Rooms. Rooms.

She could remember when Mrs. Sweeney changed the sign in her window from Room To Let to Rooms For White, explaining, apologetically, that so many of the colored stopped to ask about rooms that she couldn't get her work done for answering the bell. "It's just to save time," she had said, "my time and theirs."

Mrs. Sweeney's sign had long since been replaced by a much

larger and very different sign: "Masters University — Church of Metaphysics and Spiritual Sciences — Revealing the Strange Secrets of the Unseen Forces of Life Time and Nature. Divine Blessings — Healings of Mind and Body. I Am the Way, the Truth, and the Life; no man cometh unto the Father, but by Me. Hear the Voice of the Master: Dr. H. H. Franklin Longworth, F.M.B. Minister, Psychologist, Metaphysician. Everyone Is Welcome."

Yes, she thought, Dumble Street has changed. The signs tell the story of the change. It was now, despite its spurious early-morning beauty, a street so famous, or so infamous, that the people who lived in Monmouth rarely ever referred to it, or the streets near it, by name; it had become an area, a section, known variously as The Narrows, Eye of the Needle, The Bottom, Little Harlem, Dark Town, Niggertown — because Negroes had replaced those other earlier immigrants, the Irish, the Italians and the Poles.

Fortunately, the river hadn't changed. Nor had the big maple tree. But she, Abbie Crunch, had changed because for the last few years she had been calling the tree The Hangman just like everyone else who lived in The Narrows. It was, she supposed, inevitable. People talked about the tree as though it were a person: "The Hangman's losin' his leaves, winter's goin' to set in early"; "Spring's here, The Hangman's full of buds." When it was cold, bone-biting cold, wind blowing straight from the river, the sidewalks grown narrower, reduced almost to cowpaths because of the snow piled up at the sides, a coating of ice making walking hazardous, the great branches of the tree swayed back and forth, making a cracking sound. Then passers-by said: "Lissen. The Hangman's creakin'. Hear him?" or "The Hangman's talkin'. Hangman's groanin' in his sleep," and shivered as they moved away.

She had tried, years ago, to find out why the tree was called The Hangman and couldn't. There would always be something of the schoolteacher's tiresome insistence on accuracy left in her, so she had searched through all the books on horticulture in the Monmouth Library but she could not find any mention of a hangman's maple. She decided that some one may once have said that the big maple was the kind of tree a hangman would choose to swing his victim from — tall, straight, with mighty branches; that whoever heard this statement changed it when he repeated it and called the tree a hangman's maple; that, finally, some imaginative Negro, probably from South Carolina, gave the tree its name. These days she, too, called the maple The Hangman, as easily, and as inaccurately, as the rest of The Narrows.

This morning The Hangman was like a picture of a tree — a picture on a calendar, the orange-red of the leaves not really believable. Sometimes she wished she had not insisted on buying that old brick house which was Number Six Dumble Street. But not now. Who could regret the purchase of a fine old house when the tree that stood in its dooryard was like a great hymn sung by a choir of matched voices?

The Hangman had, of course, been the source of many small annoyances, and, possibly, the cause, though indirectly, of one major disaster. The neighborhood dogs were always in the yard, sniffing around the tree, lifting a leg, digging up the lawn with vigor afterwards. During the day lean cats napped in the dense shade made by its branches and at midnight carried on a yowling courtship. On warm summer nights, drunks sprawled under the tree, in a sleep that was more torpor than sleep. She kept a bucket filled with water on the back steps, and, early in the morning, fear making her heart beat faster, fear urging her back toward the house, she would approach the sleeping man, dump the pail of water over him, recoiling from the smell of him, the awful loosejointed look of him, even as she said, "Get out of here. Get out of here or I'll call a policeman — " There was always the shudder, the stumbling gait, the muttered curses in the thickened speech that came to mean drunkenness, and only drunkenness, as the man lurched to his feet. They always went toward The Last Chance, the saloon across the street, as though by instinct.

Yes, she thought, everything changes, and not always for the best, her mind moving away from the subject of intoxication as she had trained it to do. But her house had changed for the best. Number Six Dumble Street had a very definite air about it — an air of aristocracy. The brass knocker on the front door gleamed, the white paint on the sash of the smallpaned windows, and on the front door, was very white. In this early morning light, the brick of the house was not red but rose colored — the soft pinkish red found in old Persian carpets. The wrought iron railing on each side of the front steps was so intricately and delicately worked that it resembled filet crochet, incredible that a heavy metal like iron could be twisted and turned and bent until it looked like lace.

She gave a little jump, startled, because she heard footsteps close behind her. She turned to see who it was and a man passed her, walking briskly. A colored man. His skin was just a shade darker than her own. Yet he was dressed with a meticulousness one rarely ever saw these days — creased trousers, highly polished shoes, because the back of the shoes gleamed, a dark gray felt hat on his head, the shape perfect.

What could he have thought when he saw her standing still in the middle of the sidewalk? From the back, seen from the back, glanced at quickly from the side, how had she looked to him? Shabby? Old? Like the toothless old women who sat hunched over, mumbling to themselves, in the doorways, on the doorsteps of the houses in The Narrows? The curve of their backs, the dark wrinkled skins, the black glitter of their eyes, the long frowsy skirts always made her think of crones and witches, of necromancy.

Feeling embarrassed, she moved on, walking fast, feeling impelled to take a mental inventory of her appearance. The market basket? It was made by hand by Willow Smith, the old basket-maker. A lost art. Women these days carried brown paper shopping bags, impermanent, flimsy, often replaced. The string handles cut their fingers. She'd had this basket almost forty years. It was sturdy but light in weight; and it was as much a part of her Saturday morning shopping costume as the polished oxfords on her feet, and the lisle stockings on her legs. The shoes had been resoled many times, but the uppers were as good as new. She glanced at her hands — the beige-colored gloves were immaculate; true, they'd been darned, but she doubted that anyone would know it, certainly not a casual passer-by.

She wasn't bent over, she knew that. She had always prided herself on the erectness of her figure; and now, watching the brisk progress of the man walking ahead of her, she straightened up even more. She couldn't have looked too queer to him. The plain black wool coat had been brushed before she left the house as had the plain black felt hat — a hat chosen because it would never really go out of style and yet it would never attract attention. She wore it straight on her head, pulled down, but not so far down that it covered her hair — white silky hair. Proud of her hair. Two or three tendrils always managed to escape from the hairpins, and, shifting the market basket to the other arm, she reached up and patted the back of her head, still neat, as far as she could tell with gloves on.

What made me do that, she thought. I know how I look. But

all my life I've been saying to myself, What will people think? And at seventy I wouldn't be apt to stop doing it. So a short briskwalking man passes me on the street at a moment when I am standing still and I immediately start checking my appearance. Possibly he didn't wonder about me. But he looked at me, sideways, quickly, and then away. He isn't much taller than I am, she thought, still watching him. But he weighs less. Not that I'm fat but I've got flesh on my bones — small bones — so I look plump.

To her very great surprise, this man, this welldressed little man, turned in at Number Six, walked up the steps, and lifted the brass knocker, letting it fall gently against the door, repeating the motion so that she heard a rat-tat-tat-tat, gentle, but insistent. That surprised her, too, for very few people knew how a knocker resounded through a house and thus she was always being startled by salesmen or itinerant peddlers who set up a great banging at her front door, enough to wake the dead.

Now that she was so close to him she saw that his dark suit fitted him as though it had been made for him. His posture was superb, head up, shoulders back. He turned toward her just as she started up the steps and she noticed that he wore black shoes — highly polished. Link always wore brown shoes, most of the young men seemed to these days though she didn't know why. A brown shoe never looked as dressy as a black shoe.

Then the stranger standing on her front steps took off his gray felt hat and bowed and said, "Good morning."

It was done with an elegance that she hadn't seen in years. It reminded her of the Governor, of the Major, both of whom managed, just by lifting their hats and bowing, to make her feel as though they had said: Madam — Queen of England — Empress of India.

"Mrs. Crunch?"

"Yes," she said.

"My name is Malcolm Powther. I've taken the liberty of coming to inquire about the apartment that you have for rent."

"Oh," she said, startled. The Allens hadn't even moved yet.

"I am the butler at Treadway Hall. I have been with Mrs. Treadway for nine years," he said. "I thought I should tell you this so you would know that I can give you references. And also so that you would understand why I came so early in the morning."

Treadway Hall, she thought. Why that's the mansion that belongs to the Treadway Gun people. It sat on the outskirts of Monmouth. You could see the red tile roof from far off. The tile had been imported from Holland and installed by foreign workmen, some of whom still lived in the city. Every Fourth of July, Mrs. Treadway invited all the workers from the plant to a picnic. It was written up in the *Chronicle*. There was always a whole page of pictures of the house, of the park, and the deer in the park, of the lake and the swans on the lake. The driveway that led to the house was said to be a mile long.

She looked at Mr. Powther with something like awe. No wonder he had such an air of dignity. No wonder he was so carefully dressed. Everything about him suggested that his entire life had been spent in close association with the very wealthy. His skin was medium brown, not that she had any prejudice against very dark colored people, but she had never had any tenants who looked as though they were descended in a straight line from old Aunt Grinny Granny. He had a nose as straight as her own. But how had he known that the apartment would soon be vacant? The Allens had lived upstairs for six years and they were moving but not until next week. How had word about this expected vacancy on Dumble Street seeped through the stone walls of that great mansion where he worked?

"How did you know that the apartment would be for rent?" she asked.

His appearance changed in the most peculiar way. At one moment he was a little man with tremendous dignity, his back straight, his shoulders squared, his chin in, head up. And at the next moment all of him seemed to bend and sag and sway, even his expression changed. He flinched as though from an expected blow.

Why whatever is the matter with him, she thought. Perhaps he has gas in his stomach or he's trying not to sneeze or holding back a cough. Then almost immediately he was all right, he had controlled whatever tremor had passed through him.

"My wife's cousin told me," he said, and then after a barely perceptible pause, he went on, "We have to move right away. The city is tearing down a whole block of buildings to make way for one of those new housing projects. We're living right at the corner of the first block to be condemned."

"The Allens haven't moved yet," Mrs. Crunch said. "But I

don't suppose Mrs. Allen would mind if you looked at the apartment. She's home this morning. Won't you come in and I'll go and ask her."

She ushered Mr. Powther into the sitting room and indicated a chair near the bay window. Again she thought how very polished he looked, shoes gleaming, the crease in his trousers so perfect. He didn't sit down until she had turned to leave the room, but out of the corner of her eyes she saw him hike up his trousers with a gesture that was barely noticeable.

He said, "Oh, Mrs. Crunch," and stood up. "It's only fair to tell you that we have three children. It's not easy to find a place to live at best and with three youngsters — well, it's almost hopeless. Do you — perhaps you object to children?"

"Oh, no," she said. "I'm very fond of them." She paused, and then said quickly, "Of course I would have to get ten dollars more a month for rent. That's a rather large family — five people. And there'd be more wear and tear on the house. I'd have to get seventy dollars a month."

There was a flicker of something like amusement that showed briefly in his eyes. She felt she ought to justify the extra ten dollars. "I've always had middle-aged childless couples living upstairs. With five in the family instead of two I'd have to paint oftener, allow more for repairs to the walls and floors."

"You're quite right," he said.

"I'll go up now and see if Mrs. Allen will let you look around."

She went up the front stairs, slowly — she had to because of what she called her "bad" knees, and cool weather always made the ache in them worse — trying to find a word to rhyme with Powther, not wanting to, but not being able to help herself. She had the kind of mind that liked jingles, so she was forever matching words as she called it, lip-sip, tap-nap, cat-mat, long-song, tea-me, love-dove. Powther? Powther? She gave up and made up a word, then made up a line, Malcolm Powther Sat on a Sowther.

Powther was as difficult a word to rhyme with as Major. After she and the Major were married she spent months trying to find a proper rhyme and never got any farther than:

> Along came the Major
> He said he would page her.

Even now, eighteen years after his death, there were times when the memory of him assailed her with such force that she could almost see him, hear him — a big man with a big booming laugh that made echoes even in a room filled with furniture and hung with draperies. A man so brimming with life, so full of energy that it would be easy to believe that he'd be coming in the kitchen pretty soon, humming, that she'd hear him shouting, "Hey, Abbie, you got some food for a starving Abyssinian?"

She stopped halfway up the stairs, wondering why she had been so suddenly overwhelmed by this vivid picture of the Major. It was because of that polite, precisely dressed, little man, waiting downstairs in her sitting room. A matter of sheer contrast. The Major had been such a big Teddy bear of a man that even in the last years of his life, when they could afford to have his suits made for him, he always had a rumpled slept-in-his-clothes look. If he sat down for as much as two minutes his trousers wrinkled at the knees, at the crotch, his coat developed creases across the middle of the back, and a fold of material popped up from somewhere around the collar region to give him a hunched-up look. Little Mr. Powther could sit indefinitely and when he stood up his suit would still look as though it had just been pressed.

Once she got after the tailor about the Major's suits. The tailor, a Mr. Quagliamatti, said, "Mrs. Crunch, it's not the fault of my suit. It's the Major. It's the way he sits, all to pieces, in a chair. I can't make an elastic suit and that's what he'd have to have. He sits in heaps and mounds. You make him sit up, make him lift his trousers. He sits every which way and the material is only goods, yard goods, not elastic — "

She was still thinking about the Major when she told Mrs. Allen that some one wanted to look at the apartment. The Major always had a slightly rumpled look but somehow men never looked as — well, as unattractive as women, especially the first thing in the morning. She tried not to stare at the white cloth wound around Mrs. Allen's head, at the faded house dress with some important buttons missing in the middle so that the dress gaped open over her fat little stomach; couldn't help glancing down, quickly, of course, to see what she had on her feet. She was wearing sneakers, the laces not tied, and she didn't have any stockings on. Her bare legs were a grayish brown.

Mrs. Allen said, voice pitched high, "Let somebody see the apartment? At this hour in the morning? Really, Mrs. Crunch —"

"It's Mr. Malcolm Powther who wants to see the apartment. He's the Treadway butler."

"I'm not going to — " Mrs. Allen's voice went up, way up, high. "The Treadway butler!" she said, her eyes widening. She took a deep breath. "I can't — wait — you give me ten minutes, Mrs. Crunch. Just ten minutes and I'll be ready for him. You bring him right up in ten minutes."

In the sitting room, she kept thinking that Mrs. Allen had the most unpleasant way of squealing when she got excited. She'd be glad when Mrs. Allen moved. It would be a pleasure to have this quiet little man and his family occupying the top floor. She told Mr. Powther that they would go upstairs in a few minutes, meantime she wanted him to notice how very well her white geraniums were doing, all of them in bloom; told him that Pretty Boy, the battle-scarred tomcat dozing in the Boston rocker, was getting old and he wasn't as lively as he once was; spoke briefly of the way Dumble Street had changed, adding almost immediately that it was a convenient place to live because Franklin Avenue where the trolleys ran was just one block away.

"I think we can go up now," she said.

This time when Mrs. Allen opened the door of her apartment she almost curtsied. She had fixed her hair and bangs now formed a curly frieze across her forehead. She was wearing a print dress, and highheeled patent leather pumps. There was rouge on her round brown cheeks.

Rather too much rouge, Abbie thought as she introduced Mr. Powther and then stood just inside Mrs. Allen's living room, listening to the bill and coo of Mrs. Allen's voice which now sounded as though all her life she had been perfecting the sounds of the dove. She was smiling and nodding and saying, "Don't you think so, Mr. Powther? You know what I mean, Mr. Powther."

"I'll wait for you downstairs, Mr. Powther," Abbie said. This would give Mrs. Allen a chance to display all her middle-aged coyness, to titter behind her hand, to arch her thin bosom, without the inhibiting presence of one Abigail Crunch.

In the sitting room downstairs, she tried again to find a word to rhyme with Powther, and ended just where she started:

> Little Mister Powther
> Sat on a sowther.

Whenever she was at peace with the world, and sometimes when she wasn't, she made up jingling little rhymes, not wanting to, but she couldn't seem to help it. She jotted them down on the backs of envelopes, on the brown paper bags that came from the grocery store, on the pads of Dexter Linen that she used for letter paper. Having written them down, she couldn't bear to throw them away; and so she hid them, in bureau drawers, behind the sheets in the linen closet.

She heard Mr. Powther coming down the front stairs, his step light and quick. Little Mister Powther — Sat on a Sowther — she thought.

Mr. Powther said, "It's a pleasant apartment, Mrs. Crunch. I'll leave a deposit on it, subject, of course, to Mrs. Powther's approving the place. Though I am certain she will like it."

"A deposit isn't necessary," Abbie said.

"Thank you so much," he said. "I wonder if we can move in as soon as Mrs. Allen goes. That is, if Mrs. Powther likes the rooms. We're in rather of a hurry because the six months' notice we received expires this coming week."

It doesn't need much of anything done to it, Abbie thought. Mrs. Allen was one of those fussbudget housekeepers, who always had a scrub brush or a vacuum cleaner or a dustcloth in her hand. Poor Mr. Allen was kept busy, too. He was always painting or waxing floors or washing windows.

She said, "The Allens move out a week from today. We will need at least three days in which to freshen up the kitchen and bathroom. Will the thirtieth be all right?"

"Thank you so much," he said. At the door he bowed again.

She watched him go down the steps. He paused for a moment on the sidewalk and looked up at the branches of The Hangman, and then he was gone.

She supposed the young colored men of Link's generation couldn't have manners like Mr. Powther's, though she didn't know why. Wars and atom bombs and the fact that there was so much hate in the world might have something to do with it. There were times when she had thought that rudeness was a characteristic of Link's; that other young men had a natural courtesy he would never have. Then she would see or hear something in The Narrows that suggested all these young men were alike — something had brutalized them. But what?

In Link's case — well, if they hadn't lived on Dumble Street, if the Major had lived longer, if Link had been their own child instead of an adopted child, if she hadn't forgotten about him when he was eight, simply forgotten his existence, if she hadn't had to figure so closely with the little money that she had — rent from the apartment, pension from the Governor (the Major's pension) — and eke it out with the small sums she earned by sewing, embroidering, making jelly. If. But she had managed to keep the house, to feed and clothe herself and Link. It meant that she didn't have much time to devote to him. There was The Last Chance across the street, there was Bill Hod who owned it. He had plenty of money. Sometimes she had believed he was playing cat-and-mouse with her deliberately, cruelly, no — brutally. And she was helpless, unable to compete with him for Link's devotion.

At supper that night when she told Link about the new tenant, she carefully avoided any mention of Mr. Powther's beautiful manners; but she couldn't conceal the pleasure she felt about having him in the house; and she kept talking about the neatness of his appearance.

Link grinned. "You mean you're taking him in just like that? Without having seen his wife and his kids?"

"After all, he's the Treadway butler," she said. "If you had seen what a polishedlooking person he was you wouldn't need to see his family either."

"Miss Abbie, a man hasn't got a corner on virtue just because his shoes are shined. You'd better get a look at his family in spite of the pretty creases in his pants."

"You sound just like Frances," she said, annoyed because he had called her Miss Abbie.

"Well, of course, honey. A man can't have two women in his hair practically from birth without ending up sounding like one or both of them."

"Frances didn't live here with us," she said.

"She might just as well have. She might just as well have. She was here so often that I used to think she was my father and you were my mother."

"She's been awfully good to me," Abbie said, remembering.

"Yeah. I don't doubt that. But F. K. Jackson is right at least ninety-nine point nine times out of a hundred. It's very difficult for us average humans to love a female with a batting average like that. If she'd been a gambler she could have made a fortune."

"A gambler? She doesn't play cards — "

"No," he said, and he half closed his eyes, as though he were looking at a picture that pleased him, half closed his eyes and threw his head back. Abbie looked at the line of his throat, at the slight forward thrust of his chin, at the smoothness of his skin, the perfection of his nose and mouth, the straightness of his hair, and thought, Sometimes, just sometimes, I wish he wasn't so very goodlooking; or rather, I wish that the rest of him matched his good looks. He simply does not care about the right things. How can he go on working behind that bar? What was the point of his going to college if he was going to end up working in a bar?

Was it my fault? Yes. I forgot about him when he was eight. When he was sixteen I had the chance to win him back and somehow muffed it. And now it's too late. Now I do not dare say what I think about his working in that saloon for fear he will leave me and never come back.

"No," Link said, voice dreamy now. "But I wish she did. I wish she played poker. I'd like to see her in a game with Bill Hod. I would pay out folding money to get F. K. Jackson and Mr. B. Hod in a poker game."

Abbie made no comment on this statement. When Link finished college he had said he was going to write history books. Shortly after that he went into the Navy and was gone four years, and when he came home it was to work in a bar on Dumble Street. On Saturdays he played poker until four and five o'clock in the morning, played with his friends: a white man, a photographer, who had the unlikely name of Jubine and the unkempt look of a Bolshevist; a colored man named Weak Knees, who walked as though he were drunk, and did the cooking in The Last Chance; and Bill Hod, who owned The Last Chance and controlled or operated every illegal, immoral, illicit enterprise in The Narrows — though nobody could prove it — and who had the face of a hangman, face of a murderer. Colored, too.

Now Link was imitating Frances, clipping his words off the way she did, pursing his lips, lifting his eyebrows, pretending to remove a pair of pince-nez glasses.

He was saying, "Do you remember the time that F. K. Jackson said: 'Abbie, never never rent out any part of the premises without first seeing all the members of the family. Males have been known to marry females who bear a strong resemblance to the female fruit fly; and females have been known to marry males that are first cousin to the tomato worm. On the other hand, perfectly respectable couples have been known to produce children who have all the unpleasant qualities of the Japanese beetle!' "

Abbie listened to him, thinking, His voice doesn't match the rest of him either. It is a deep, resonant, musical voice. A perfect speaking voice. And — somebody has to go through that apartment upstairs to find out what needs to be done to it before the Powthers move in. If Link went up there now, Mrs. Allen wouldn't care if it was suppertime. She'd look at the breadth of his shoulders, listen to the music in his voice, and immediately start making the sounds of the dove and even show him the inside of the closets.

"Link," she said, "will you go upstairs and ask Mrs. Allen to let you go through the apartment so you can see if anything needs to be done to it before the Powthers move in?"

"Right now?"

"Of course not. After you finish your supper."

"Sure, Miss Abbie, sure. I didn't know. I thought you meant with knife and fork in hand and napkin tied tight under chin. I am, after all, only mortal man and mortal man is so conditioned to attack from immortal female that he — well, he never really knows."

The week slipped by. The Allens moved out. Abbie began to worry about Mrs. Powther. Why hadn't she been to see the place?

On Thursday, toward dusk, Mr. Powther stopped at the door. He wouldn't come in. He was in a hurry. He paid a month's rent in advance, seventy dollars in crisp new bills.

He said, "Mrs. Powther is busy with the packing and the children. She's perfectly willing to take the apartment on my say-so."

After he left, Abbie fingered the bills, wondering for the first time why he and his wife and the children didn't live at Treadway Hall, thinking almost at the same time that one never saw crisp new money like this in The Narrows. These bills looked as though they had gone straight from the mint into Treadway Hall, where they had been handed to Mr. Powther, who in turn handed them to Abbie Crunch. She hoped he was right about his wife's willingness to live on Dumble Street.

She was still thinking about Mrs. Powther, the next afternoon, when the knocker sounded. There was a repeated banging, a thundering on the door, that echoed and re-echoed through the house from cellar to attic, startling her so that she dropped the handle of the carpet sweeper she was using on the stairs. Who on earth would bang on a door like that? She kicked the carpet sweeper out of the way, thinking, I ought to pick it up and take it to the door with me and use it on his head. Anyone would think that he, whoever he is, was summoning a charwoman, and a deaf charwoman at that.

Usually she stood back from the smallpaned windows at the side of the door so that she could not be seen when she looked out. But this time she wanted to be seen, she glared out of the little windows and then frowned. There was a woman standing on the steps. A stranger. Or at least her face was unfamiliar. She'd seen the type before though: young, but too much fat around the waist, a soft, fleshy, quite prominent bosom, too much lipstick, a pink beflowered hat, set on top of straightened hair; the hair worn in what they called a pageboy bob, hanging loose, almost to the shoulders. She had on a light tan coat, very full, very long. Under one arm she carried a big loosely wrapped package which was held together by red and green string, carelessly tied. The package looked as though one good jounce would make the whole thing open up all at once.

The woman lifted her hand and banged the knocker against the door again, a peremptory, commanding knock. Abbie wouldn't have opened the door, but the woman had a little boy by the hand — a bulletheaded, bigheaded little boy. Bulletheaded. Bigheaded. The Major's expressions. They were always cropping up in her thoughts. He loved to describe children in that fashion; he took a special delight in pointing out small dark specimens that she had to agree, reluctantly, really fitted the words. And this child standing on her doorstep was both bulletheaded and bigheaded.

Because of the child she decided the woman might well be someone who had come to see the Allens and didn't know they'd moved. She was certain she'd seen the little boy somewhere. She opened the door, not too wide, just wide enough to be able to shut it quickly if she had to. After all, she was alone in the house. "How do you do?" she said. She made it sound like a question.

"Afternoon. Are you Missus Crunch?"

Abbie nodded, staring, now.

The woman smiled, the thick coating of dark red lipstick on her mouth made her teeth look very white. They were good teeth, even, strong.

"I'm Mamie," she said.

Abbie said, "Yes?" There was music in the woman's voice, a careless, easy kind of music.

"I'm Mamie Powther."

"Mamie Powther? Mamie Powther? Oh — I — oh, of course. Come in, Mrs. Powther."

There was an awkward moment during which they stood in the hall looking at each other, Mrs. Powther smiling and showing her strong white teeth and Abbie trying to maintain an expression of cordiality and welcome. She didn't know when she'd ever felt quite so at a disadvantage. What had she expected Mrs. Powther to look like? She didn't know exactly. Certainly not like this woman. She supposed she had expected a sort of female edition of Mr. Powther, small, neat, precise of speech, businesslike in manner. She remembered Mr. Powther's highly polished shoes and without really meaning to, glanced down at Mrs. Powther's feet. She had on black suede shoes, scuffed at the toe, a kind of ballet-type shoe that bore a most unfortunate resemblance to a house slipper, and there was a bulge on each shoe, a kind of little hump, that only came from bunions.

"This here is J.C." Mrs. Powther said, still smiling.

At the mention of his name, the bulletheaded little boy retreated behind Mrs. Powther's tan coat, clutching at the folds.

"You stop that, you J.C.," Mrs. Powther said sharply. "Come out here where Missus Crunch can see you."

J.C.'s response to this command was to wrap the long full skirt of the coat more tightly around him, disappearing from view entirely except for one scuffed brown shoe and a dirty blue sock.

"He's shy," Mrs. Powther said benevolently.

"What is his name?" Abbie asked.

"J.C."

"But — " Abbie tried again. "What do the initials stand for?"

"Oh, they don't stand for nothing. It's just initials. I thought it was kind of a nice thing to do for him. When he gets old enough he can pick a name for himself, to match up with the initials. This way he won't be worried with no name he don't like for the rest of his life."

"Why I never heard of such a thing."

"No'm. Most folks haven't."

"Aw, Mamie," J.C. said suddenly, his voice muffled. "Come on and look at the place."

"He don't really want to move here," Mamie Powther said. She made no effort to disentangle J.C. from her coat. "He's got a lot of friends over where we been livin'. All 'bout his own age. And he's head man, ain't you, honey?"

Abbie wanted to end the conversation. She needed to think, to sit down alone and think, she'd heard of all kinds of names for children, but initials — what about the other children?

"Mr. Powther said there were three children. Are they — do the others have initials, too, instead of names?"

"No, ma'am. I didn't think of it until J.C. come along," she paused, as though in recollection, smiled. "There's just the twins. They're seven. Named Kelly and Shapiro. It'll take you awhile to tell 'em apart, but Kelly is the quiet one and Shapiro is the loud-mouthed one."

"I see," Mrs. Crunch said. Then she added hastily, because Mamie Powther had opened her mouth as though to continue and she looked like the kind of woman who enjoyed giving all the details of her last confinement, "You go right up and look at the rooms. My knees aren't what they used to be so if you don't mind, I'll stay down here."

She had planned to escort Mrs. Powther through the rooms, answering questions, explaining about the position of the sun in the afternoon, showing off the view of the river that one got from the living room windows. But this Mrs. Powther wasn't the one she had expected. She didn't want to watch this Mrs. Powther's bosom quiver as she walked through the bedroom that she, Abbie, had once shared with the Major.

"You can go right up. The doors are all open. You don't need a key."

"That's fine," Mrs. Powther's voice was cordial. "Come on, J.C."

Abbie sat down heavily in the Boston rocker in the dining room — she still referred to it like that when she got upset, though it had long since been converted into a sitting room. Twins, she thought. Kelly and Shapiro. Why it was fantastic. Incredible. She couldn't very well not rent the apartment to the Powthers. She'd taken Mr. Powther's money, promised it to him, and she'd always been a woman of her word. Perhaps Mrs. Powther wouldn't like the place. Nonsense. Mamie Powther would love Dumble Street. Besides there weren't any places for rent in Monmouth. Or perhaps that horrible little boy, J.C., whoever heard of such nonsense, initials for a name, perhaps he wouldn't like it, because it wouldn't offer sufficient opportunity for him to be head man. Oh, they'd take it. J.C. and Mamie. He didn't even call her Mother. How on earth had that polished little Mr. Powther managed to acquire a bigbosomed creature like this one, painted fingernails, some of the paint peeling off, jingly earrings in her ears, smelling of bergamot or something equally as sickeningly sweet, and the little boy with a distinct smell of urine about him.

Hearing Mrs. Powther's footsteps, soft, heavy, on the front stairs, muted by the carpet, she got up and met her in the hall.

"Well?" she said.

Mamie Powther started drawing a pair of soiled white gloves over her hands, covering the scarlet fingernails. "It's a lovely place, Missus Crunch," she beamed. "A lovely place. Actually I wouldn't have come to look at it, I would have moved right in on the strength of Powther's say-so. He knows an awful lot about houses. But J.C. he wouldn't let me be until I brought him over. Just kept on sayin', Mamie I'm not a-goin' to move until I see where I'm goin'."

"And did you like the apartment, J.C.?" Abbie asked, being deliberately sarcastic.

J.C. disappeared in the folds of Mrs. Powther's coat again.

"He liked it fine. He liked it so much he already moved in, Missus Crunch. His things is up there now."

What in the world is she talking about? Abbie wondered.

"He left his comic books up there. That's what was in that big bundle. He said, 'Mamie if I like it I'm a-goin' to be the first to move in.' It suits us as though we thought it up ourselves, don't it, J.C.?" She paused but J.C. did not answer. "And it's so nice that there's a back stairs, a outside back stairs."

Abbie Crunch thought there was a kind of anticipatory gleam in Mamie Powther's eyes that the existence of an outside back stairs hardly seemed to justify. Certainly there was an extra gaiety in her manner.

"Back stairs do save so much wear and tear on a front stair carpet," Mamie Powther explained. "Children is always runnin' up and down and in and out you know."

Abbie watched them cross the street. Mamie Powther was moving swiftly and J.C. was trotting to keep up with her. Wind from the river rippled the pages of the comic book he held in his hand, toyed with the full skirt of Mrs. Powther's coat.

Bill Hod was standing in front of The Last Chance. He lifted his hat as they passed. Mrs. Powther nodded, lifting one gloved hand in a gesture that was part salute, part wave. Abbie wondered if he knew her or if he was merely paying tribute to her quivery bosom. The ballet slippers gave her a flatfooted appearance. As they disappeared from sight, Abbie decided they looked like figures out of the old Mother Goose books, the proportions all wrong, highly exaggerated. And almost immediately she was rhyming again:

> Mister Powther Sat on a sowther
> Eating his curds and whey.
> Along came a Mamie
> And said, You must pay me.
> And so he did pay, did pay.

How old was Mamie Powther? In her early thirties? Mr. Powther was a lot older, closer to fifty, at least. Link would laugh. Female fruit fly? Japanese beetle? Tomato worm? Not Mamie Powther. Mamie Powther was Dumble Street.

The Major had been dead set against this street. "Fine old brick house, yes. But Dumble Street — Dumble Street — that's not a good place to live." Then he had startled her by saying, "It ought to be called Fumble Street. That's what it is."

She had glanced at him sharply, wondering if he, too, was a victim of rhyming, and that she'd never known it. No. Because he snorted his contempt, his disgust, for the street, unconscious of the endless possibilities for rhymes: dumble, fumble, stumble, tumble, mumble. It had proved itself to be all of those things. The people who lived here near the waterfront fumbled and they mumbled and they stumbled and they tumbled, ah, yes, make up a word — dumbled.

2

Got no roof over my head
Slats keep fallin' out of my bed
And I'm lonesome — lonesome.

Rent money's so long overdue
Landlord says he's goin' to sue
And I'm lonesome — lonesome.

● The words were clear but the voice seemed far away. It came
nearer, slowly, slowly, increasing in volume, until it seemed to
be right there in the kitchen. "And I'm lonesome." A big warm
voice with a lilt in it, and something else, some extra, indefinable
quality which made Abbie listen, made her want to hear more, and
more; as though the singer leaned over, close, to say, I'm talking
to you, listen to me, I made up this song for you and I've got
wonderful things to tell you and to show you, listen to me.

Abbie looked across the breakfast table at Link. The people
next door played records morning, noon, and night. He might
think this was a record. He was buttering a piece of toast and he
didn't seem to hear that big clear attention-getting voice that was
filling the kitchen with song. It isn't a soprano, she thought, it
goes down too far, too easily for a soprano, lonesome was sung
way down, almost down to a tenor's middle range, but head and
bed, sue and due were way up high.

Link looked toward the screen door. "Is that a record?"

Abbie hesitated, wishing she could bring herself to say, Yes, it's a record, a blues or a boogiewoogie or a jazz record or whatever they called the bleating that issued from all the gramophones and radios these days, all of it sounding alike, too loud, too harsh, no sweetness, no tune, simply a reiterated bleating about rent money and men who had gone off with other women, and numbers that didn't come out. It was perfectly ridiculous, she knew it, admitted it, but she did not want Link to see Mamie Powther. Sooner or later he was bound to. The Powthers had been living upstairs for two days now but it was usually noon before her voice came drifting down from an upstairs window.

"No," she said reluctantly. "That's not a record. That's Mrs. Powther, the new tenant."

He went to the back door and stood there so long, motionless, watching something, that Abbie got up from the table to look, too.

Mamie Powther was hanging up clothes in the backyard. Abbie frowned. She'll have to get her own line or I won't have any place to hang my things. She must have got up very early to turn out such a tremendous wash. Very clean clothes they were, too. A big clothes basket heaped to the top stood on the grass under the line. There was an almost hypnotic rhythm about her movements, Abbie found that she, too, couldn't look away. Bend over and pick up shirt, straighten up, and shake it out, reach for clothespins, straighten up, pin shirt on line, bend over.

> Big John's got a brandnew gal
> High yaller wench name of Sal
> And I'm lonesome — lonesome.

She keeps changing the words, Abbie thought, listening, and watching. Wind whipped the clothes back and forth, lifting the hem of Mamie Powther's short cotton dress as though it peered underneath and liked what it saw and so returned again and again for another look. What a vulgar idea. I never think things like that. It's that getup she has on. A sleeveless dress, printed material, white background with big red poppies all over it. A bright red scarf wound around her head. And there among the sheets, the pillowcases, the towels, the children's socks and underwear and overalls, her figure stood out — a gaudy, bigbosomed young woman with sturdy arms, dimpled at the elbows. When she bent over you could see that she had no stockings on, you could see the back of her thighs, more than halfway up, just as though she were leaning over in a bathing suit. The bending over effortless, the straightening up, all in one smooth unbroken motion, the wind whipping the clothes, lifting them, returning them to her, and she singing in time to all this movement:

> Trouble sits at my front door
> Can't shut him out any more
> And I'm lonesome — lonesome.

Watching her, you could almost believe it was a dance of some kind, the dance of the clothes, the wetwash dance. I don't dance. I never could, Abbie thought. I haven't any sense of rhythm and yet she hangs clothes and I think about dancing. I don't believe she's got a thing on under that dress.

When Link turned away from the door, Abbie waited for him to say something funny about the red poppies on the dress, or about the soft brown flesh so very exposed to view.

But all he said was, "My! my! my! So that's Mrs. Powther."

He drank the rest of his coffee standing up, then he leaned down, patted Abbie's cheek and kissed her, straightened up, said softly, "The female fruit fly," and laughed.

For a barely perceptible second there was a break in the rhythm of Mamie Powther's song and Abbie knew that she'd heard that powerful male laughter coming from the first floor. Heard it and probably made a note of it for future reference.

Then he was gone. Whistling. Whistling the tailend of the same tune: I'm lonesome — lonesome.

Somehow she would have to get rid of that big young woman, still hanging up clothes, pausing now and then to look straight up at the sky. Blowzy. No. Gaudy. Well, yes. She simply did not belong in that neat backyard with its carefully tended lawn and its white fences. The brilliant red of the poppies on her dress made the red of the dogwood leaves look faded, washed out. She did not match the yard or the kind of morning that it was. Sunny. Fairly warm. Winter still far away but coming, the potential there, in the east wind, but the grass still green. She dominated the morning so that you saw nothing but Mamie, heard nothing but Mamie, and with a little concentration, it was possible to believe that you could smell nothing but Mamie — that sweet heavy perfume was definitely in the air. Brassy. That was the word. Mamie Powther was like a trumpet call sent out over the delicate nuances and shadings of stringed instruments played softly, making you jump, startled, because it didn't belong there.

"I'm lonesome — lonesome — "

Mamie Powther. Why not Mrs. Powther. Somehow natural to eliminate Mrs. Not a man's wife, permanently attached, but an unattached unwifely female. She didn't belong in the backyard any more than her furniture belonged in Number Six Dumble Street. Such furniture! Lamps with pink rayon shades, and a bed with the headboard and footboard covered with cupids and grapes and grape leaves, a big chest of drawers almost like a highboy, with the same appalling cupids on the handles of the drawers. The packing hadn't been done properly, or rather, Mamie Powther hadn't made any effort to pack at all. There were a thousand-and-one loose items that had to be carried upstairs in piles. Clothing and pots and pans and nursing bottles. There was a battered highchair with food particles stuck on it and a child's pot made of pink plastic. That, too, somehow characteristic of the woman. And toys, she hadn't even tried to get hold of any cartons — legless dolls and broken fire engines and trucks without wheels, and scooters without steering gear were carried up in piles — and she wasn't certain but there seemed to be a great wudge of what looked like soiled diapers, but surely none of those children could be still wearing diapers.

There were two moving-men on the truck — one was big and one was little but their voices were the same size. It took both of them to get some of the furniture up the stairs. The house was filled with their shouts, "On me!" "On you!" Only they made it sound like "Awn me!" "Awn you!" To see what they were doing Abbie had gone to the front of the house. The little one stepped back bracing his body for the weight of a tremendous sofa upholstered in pale blue brocade, shouting "Awn me!" Though the other man was not two feet away from him, he shouted back, "Awn you!" Then when they reached the landing, the big man braced himself shouting "Awn me!" "Awn me!" "Awn you!" and then the children took it up, loving the sound of it, and she could detect no difference in the loudness of Shapiro's voice or Kelly's voice.

As soon as she finished doing the breakfast dishes she would tell Mrs. Powther about the clothesline. She heard a soft drumming sound that came from the front of the house. She listened. What could that be? A muffled drumming, not a banging but a drumming sound.

As she went toward the hall, walking briskly, she thought, I've been afraid of everything, ever since the Major died. No one has ever known how afraid I've been. Any unexpected sound makes my heart beat faster, makes me catch my breath.

J.C. was sitting on the stairs, two steps up, drumming his heels against the riser of the lower step. The sound of his heels striking against the stair carpet made a soft, regular rhythmic sound. Inherited sense of rhythm, she thought. Inherited from Mamie. It didn't seem possible but he was drinking from a nursing bottle. As she approached he took his hands away from the bottle, holding it in his mouth with his teeth, so that it swung back and forth, and he began to rock his body back and forth too. He was staring at the Major's silk hat and at the goldheaded cane — the hat still on the coatrack in the hall, the cane hanging there beside it.

He looked at Abbie briefly, and then his gaze returned to the hat. Again she got the feeling that she'd seen him somewhere before.

He transferred his hands to the bottle, drank from it, gave a little wiggle of pleasure, then, twisting one arm through the balustrades, he half lay down on the stairs. He placed the bottle on the step beside him.

"Crunch," he said, "what's that?" He lisped and it sounded as though he said, "Crunth — whathethat?"

It was perfectly obvious that he was talking about the Major's hat and the cane, because he kept his unwinking gaze focused on them.

"You call me Mrs. Crunch, young man."

"Missus Crunch," he said, giving her a look so adult and so malevolent that she wanted to shake him. "What's that?"

"A silk hat and a goldheaded cane."

"What's a goldheaded cane?"

This could go on forever. If she answered him or tried to, he'd think up a hundred other questions on the basis of her reply.

"You ask your mother and she'll tell you."

"What's a goldheaded cane?" he repeated.

"You ask your mother and she'll tell you," she said again as imperturbably as though he had asked the question for the first time. Then she said abruptly, "What's a big boy like you doing drinking out of a bottle?"

"Drinking milk."

She glanced at him sharply. He hardly seemed old enough for such expert evasion. Four-year-olds didn't usually — Or was he?

"How old are you?"

"Three and a half." He didn't look at her, he was staring up at the hat, at the cane.

"Well, you're old enough to be drinking milk from a glass."

"Me don't like it that way."

"Say I don't like it that way. Not 'me.'"

"I don't like it that way," he said obediently, still not looking at her.

That was fairly simple, she thought. It's just a matter of being firm with them. He had a comic book thrust in the front of his shirt and she started to ask him about it, he certainly couldn't read and she didn't see why he should be so fond of comic books, some one must have spoiled his taste already, and perhaps — But she never got around to the comic book because she heard a faint hissing noise, a kind of h-stt. J.C. was looking at her very gravely and she turned away. Something must have gone wrong with the radiator in Link's room. As she turned she glanced down at the floor, at the polished parquet floor. Those beautiful floors were partly responsible for her insistence on buying this house even though the Major disapproved. There was a little puddle of water there and as she looked it grew larger. She stared at the little boy sprawled there on the stairs, dismayed. Why he isn't trained yet, three and a half years old and he isn't trained. My stair carpet, my floor, and there will be a smell of urine in the front hall just like in the tenements —

"You listen to me," she said angrily. "There are some things I simply will not put up with. And this is one of them. You can tell that mother of yours that I said so."

He didn't reply, just looked at her with that same grave air. "Did you hear what I said?" She laid her hand on his arm.

He flung the hand away, got up, and scuttled up the stairs. When he reached the landing he stopped, peered down at her, shouted, "Jaybird, jaybird, sittin' in the grath, draw back, draw back, shoot him in the — YAH! Crunth — Crunth — Crunth!"

She made a motion as though she were going to pursue him and he stuck his tongue out and then scrambled up the stairs, moving fast, his feet thumping on the steps.

Mopping up the puddle he'd made, she kept thinking, Maybe

he isn't quite bright, three and a half years old and he was still using a nursing bottle, still wetting himself, but his eyes were highly intelligent, almost too much so, and he was inquisitive, always asking questions, just as any normal child should. He'd left the bottle of milk on the stairs. Well, she'd put it in the garbage can and then she'd tell Mamie Powther about the clothesline and tell her, also, to keep J.C. off the front stairs.

Outside in the backyard she walked toward Mamie Powther's bentover figure, thinking, I'll start off by saying, "About the clothesline — "

But she didn't say anything because she heard a man's voice saying, "Hi, Mamie, what's the pitch?"

There, on the other side of the clothesline stood Bill Hod.

Mamie Powther said, "Lord, babe, you sure gave me a turn. I didn't hear you come in the yard. How are you anyway?" She laughed. It was a warm joyous sound. "Come on up and see the place. It's a mess but I can give you a cup of coffee."

I won't have it, Abbie thought. I won't have him in my yard.

Mamie turned toward the house, "Oh! Good mornin', Missus Crunch. I didn't see you," she said, smiling, showing her white, strong teeth. "Meet my cousin, Mr. Bill Hod."

In the kitchen, Abbie sat down heavily on the nearest chair, sat there shaking as though she'd had a chill, thinking, The house, the Major, Dumble Street. In that order. He had disapproved of her choice of a house, not so much the house, though it was big, neglected, had been vacant for years and so repairs would be expensive, not the house, but its location. Near the river. Near the dock. He said rivers and waterfronts were not good places to live. But it was a brick house and Abbie had always wanted a brick house and the price was very low so they bought it.

It was almost twenty years ago that it happened. All of that. Yet the sight of Bill Hod in my yard makes me keep shivering as though it were yesterday. It was on a Saturday afternoon in August. The Hangman was in full leaf. She had gone out to select a handful of especially beautiful leaves to show to her Sunday School class in the morning. She happened to look down the street, down toward Franklin Avenue, and she saw the Major, lurching along, leaning on Bill Hod. Sometimes he stopped and waved both arms in the air, and then gestured vaguely, using the goldheaded cane to accent his gestures, sometimes he dragged it along the sidewalk, then held it straight up in the air.

Inside the house, she waited for them, watching from the window. As they approached the steps, she opened the front door.

"He's sick," Bill Hod said.

She'd seen them before, these "sick" men, pushed and pulled toward home by loyal embarrassed friends. Mrs. O'Leary's husband was always "sick" on Saturday nights and all day Sunday — or so the children said.

"I can see that," she said coldly. She'd seen the stumbling, uncertain gait, the unfocused bleary eyes of the drunken bums who slept in doorways, lurched across the dock, stumbled out from under the sheltering branches of The Hangman, too often not to recognize this type of sickness. The Major smelt of whiskey, not just smelt of it, it was all about him, as though he had taken a bath in it.

"Put him in a chair — " She pointed toward the door of the parlor, hurriedly spread newspapers all around the chair, thinking, My carpet, my beautiful new carpet —

"He should be in bed — "

The Major said something or tried to. It was only a blurred muttering in his throat, a horrible drunken sound, suggesting that even the muscles of his throat were drunk.

She turned on Bill Hod. Oh, she knew him. She had tried to prevent his getting a liquor license for that place he ran right across the street.

"Get out of my house — "

Bill Hod said, "He's a sick man. You better get a doctor."

The Major made that horrible drunken muttering in his throat again and the smell of what she always called cheap whiskey seemed to be everywhere in the room. She thought, I can't stand that smell; if I don't get out of here quickly, I will be sick. Bill Hod hadn't moved; he was looking at her, staring at her, defying her.

She picked up a poker from the fireplace, a very old handwrought poker, black, crudelooking, handed down in her family from one generation to the next, and even as she picked it up, felt the coldness of the metal, the roughness of it, the weight of it, she thought, Has it ever been used as a weapon before?

She said, "*Will* you *get* out of here or will I have to call a policeman?"

The poker slid out of her hand, clattered on the hearth. She thought Bill Hod was going to strike her, no, not strike her, his eyes, his voice, she'd never heard such fury in a human voice, she thought he was going to kill her. Strangle her with his hands. He took a step forward, and his eyes were cold, absolutely inhuman. The eyes of a hangman. Face of a hangman.

He said, "You fool — you goddamn fool — get a doctor — " And he was gone.

She went into the kitchen, sat down at the table. She couldn't seem to think straight. She would have Hod arrested. She kept hearing the Major's breathing, labored, stentorian, like a snore. Drunk. Drunk as a lord. What could have come over him? People would laugh at her. President of the local WCTU and her husband so drunk he couldn't stand up. Ha-ha, ha-ha, ha-ha. The colored president of the white WCTU. A drunken husband. Well, he's colored. Ha-ha, ha-ha, ha-ha.

Six o'clock. Suppertime. And he still sounded exactly the same. Link kept tiptoeing in to look at him, coming back to the kitchen, face frightened, eyes frightened, but too fascinated to pay any attention to her repeated warnings to stay out of the parlor.

She had forgotten that she had invited Frances to have supper with them. Link must have been waiting in the hall, waiting for the sound of the knocker, so that he could get to the door first and let Frances in. Frances came straight back to the kitchen and before she could get her hat off, Link said, "Uncle Theodore's sick. He's in the parlor and he's got newspapers all around him on the floor."

So, of course, Frances went into the parlor to find out how he was, and Abbie went, too. Frances listened to his breathing, stopped just inside the door to listen, and then crossed the room quickly, bent over him, frowning, feeling his pulse, forcing his eyelids open, and the newspapers made a rustling sound under her feet as she moved around him.

When Frances spoke her voice was brusquer than Abbie had ever heard it, and her eyeglasses seemed to have an added glitter. She said, "He's seriously ill, Abbie. Mortally ill. I think he's had a stroke. I'll get a doctor — "

She still didn't believe that he was sick. He was a big man, six feet tall, weighing two hundred pounds, and he looked even bigger than usual, mountainous. Perhaps it was the way his body sagged in the chair. His head lolled on his shoulder, as though it had no connection with his neck, his spine. His mouth was open and a little trickle of saliva was running out of his mouth, down the side of his cheek. His arms were hanging down, dangling, the hands open, limp, dangling too. The drunks who slept under The Hangman in the summer looked just like this, smelt just like this, sounded just like this, the same queer snoring issued from their throats. The only thing — his hands — . She touched both of them. They were cold. His hands were always warm, great big warm hands.

Then Frances was bringing the new doctor into the parlor. Dr. Easter. A black man, young, she supposed, but with a manner so pompous, so dignified, that he might have been seventy-odd. He didn't even open his bag, he felt for the Major's pulse, he leaned over and apparently listened to his breathing, just with his ear, and then straightened up and said, "We must get him in bed. At once."

Why he's a West Indian, Abbie thought. She said, "Is he — "

He interrupted her, "I do not know, madam. He is very ill. I cannot discuss the case now. There is no time. Miss Jackson, I will need help. We must get him in bed. At once."

He made her feel in the way. So did Frances. Frances was at the telephone again. And almost immediately, there were two men at the front door, and then they were in the parlor. Perhaps it wasn't that fast. But it seemed so. When, finally, she went upstairs into the bedroom, they had undressed the Major, put him to bed. The smell of whiskey was gone. She could see now that they were right, he was terribly, terribly sick. It was incredible. He had never been sick in all the years they had been married. The color of his skin had changed. It was gray. Skin gray. He lay motionless under the sheets, under the soft rose-colored blanket, the magnificent head perfectly still on the pillows, the bigboned hands still too, the hands open, fingers straight out, all of them, on the rose-colored blanket.

He never lay still when he was in bed. He turned and twisted in his sleep as though sleep were an enemy and he determined to destroy it, to fight the sheets and the blankets and the pillows which were the enemy's first line of defense. In the morning, in the winter, he was always lying on his side, the covers pulled over his big shoulders, so that when she first woke up she always thought she had been sleeping in a tent, the covers were tent-like, lifted up by the Major's shoulders, and drafts played around her neck and back, down the tunnel that the covers formed.

When the Major got out of a bed it looked like a battleground, all furrowed and riddled, the sheets rumpled, the blankets on the floor. She used to wonder if this bed-mauling was a family trait, just as some families run to cleft palates and buck teeth and rheumatism, so perhaps the Crunches for generations back had been bed-maulers, unable to lie still in a bed, congenitally forced to twist and turn, and pull the sheets and push the blankets and punch the pillows, warring against sleep. She would cast one last disgusted look at him, and then go quietly down the stairs to make the morning coffee.

About seven o'clock she would hear his footsteps on the stairs, heavy and yet quick. He came down the stairs singing in that sweet pure tenor voice, a voice utterly incongruous in so big a man, "You must wake and call me early, call me early, Mother dear," and she supposed he timed it because when he reached the kitchen door he let his voice out, "For I'm to be Queen o' the May, Mother, I'm to be Queen o' the May." Then he kissed her and patted her hand, saying, "Well, Abbie, another day — more dough — as the baker said to the bread mixer," and let out a roar of laughter, so loud and with so much lung power behind it, or perhaps it was the pitch, anyway his laughter made the plates, the cups, and saucers on the table rattle.

She sat there by his bedside all night. There had been something else that would have told her how dreadfully sick he was, something more than his lying so still. When she first came into the room Frances and Dr. Easter had been leaning over him, and when they saw her, they straightened up and stood aside, drawing back, away from the bed, no expression on their faces. It was that standing aside that told her he might not survive. People stood aside like that, not saying anything, when the chief mourner came into the room to view the body for the first time.

Sometimes she held his hand, that big powerful hand — a hand that was all compassion and tenderness, and that might somewhere else and under a different set of circumstances have been the hand of a surgeon because the fingers were enormously sensitive, controlled, skilful. Sometimes she prayed, kneeling by the side of the bed, burying her face in her hands, aware that the sheets smelt ever so faintly of lavender. Pride once in the fine sheets, in the box springs, the hair mattress, the soft blankets, pride in anything now worthless, meaningless. Don't let him die. Her fault. She should have known that he wasn't drunk. He was sick. Dear God, don't let him die. I can't live without him. I wouldn't want to.

At intervals during the night Dr. Easter came into the room. She knew he was doing everything he could for the Major. But his breathing didn't change, except that the sound, and maybe it was her imagination, perhaps she had grown accustomed to it, but it wasn't as loud. Frances was, she thought, always somewhere in the room.

Toward morning Frances said, "Go downstairs, Abbie. Go outside and get some air. I'll be right here. I'll call you if I need you."

She went reluctantly. If he died it would be her fault. It would be murder really. She should have known. She should have called the doctor the moment the Major came in the house. She let him sit there. "He's got newspapers all around him." Link's young voice. Reproach, wasn't it? The new carpet. Newspapers. The *Monmouth Chronicle*. Yesterday's. Spread out on the floor.

She stood outside on the front steps. It was beginning to get light. There were a few stars still in the sky. Or was that just the tears in her eyes? Tears. Not stars. It was daylight. The Hangman bulked large and dark off to the right. Dear God, don't let him die. She looked down at the sidewalk. There was something written there. Right in front of the house. She went down the steps, not wanting to read whatever it was, afraid not to, remembering the stories about the prophetic power of Cesar the Writing Man who went all over Monmouth writing verses from the Bible on the sidewalks. Always writing on Dumble Street.

At first she couldn't make it out. There were so many scrolls and flourishes and curlicues and small adorning parts, in pink, red, blue, and yellow chalk, that it seemed to be just a pattern, intricate in design, drawn on the sidewalk. Her eyes kept filling up with tears, they welled up, again and again, so that she could not see clearly. She kept wiping them away with the back of her hand. Don't cry. Don't cry. Dear God, don't let him die. Don't let him die. I mustn't cry. I mustn't cry.

She made herself stop crying so that she could see what Cesar had written on the sidewalk in front of her house. Having read it, she was assailed by fear, by horror, so that she trembled and cried out, in refutation, "NO! NO! NO!" And the morning was suddenly unbearable, the sun coming out, the air filled with the smell of the river, fog blowing in from the river, damp and cold on her face. She leaned over and read it again: "At her feet he bowed, he fell, he lay down: at her feet he bowed, he fell: where he bowed, there he fell down dead."

She turned and went back in the house, aware of a dreadful giddiness that made her want to pitch forward on her face, fall forward and never get up, went up the stairs, swiftly, listening, listening, listening now for the same sound that had made her so angry when she first heard it, wanting to hear it now, praying that she would still hear it. She stopped in the doorway of the bedroom and heard the peculiar snorelike breathing of the Major, definitely not as loud, not even as loud as when she left the room.

His hands were still cold but they responded to her touch. He knew her. Apparently he could only convey his recognition of her by a slight sustained pressure of his hand.

That night he died. Just before he died he tried to sit up, seemed to bow, and he said, "The house — Abbie — the house — " She couldn't understand the rest of it, the rest of it was just a muttering in his throat, and then he pitched forward and she caught him in her arms.

Blank space. Just weeping. And then the funeral. I will not cry. Where did all these people come from? I will not cry. I will not make a sound. And all the flowers. So many flowers. The whole front of the colored Congregational Church covered with flowers. When they were first married she had suggested that they attend the white Congregational Church and he had said, "I'd never get to be a deacon in the white church. And that's all right. I want to be a deacon so I'm going to belong to the colored church." I will not make a sound. So many people. So many flowers. Old men with bleary eyes. He bought snuff for them, and chewing tobacco. Colored ones and white ones. The Governor was crying. So was his wife. Right across the aisle. And children. How strange. But he always had lollipops in his pocket. Young men, too. Colored ones and white ones. He always had a good story to tell. Born storyteller.

I will not cry. So many people. All those women from Dumble Street who went to work in the morning with little paper bags under their arms. All here. And the tailor and the man from the bakery, and the man who had the grocery. Rich people. Poor people. Young people. Old people. I will not cry. Even the Dumble Street sporting women. Legs and bosoms, always on the verge of complete exposure, all laughter or all tears, all singing or all cursing. He lifted his hat to them as though he were bowing to the Queen of England. Empress of India. The Governor, whitehaired, leaning on a cane, a goldheaded cane exactly like the one he gave the Major. I will not cry. The Governor with tears running down his cheeks. His wife, too.

Look straight ahead. Look at the flowers. Hold everything still inside of you. Frances keeps her hand on mine. Don't let it go. Keep it there. All right so far. Past the prayers. Past the reading from the Scriptures. Past "Lead, Kindly Light." I am the resurrection and the life: he that believeth in me. How will I walk down this aisle. Not cry.

She was not prepared for — oh, who could have. Who planned this? Not that woman. She was standing up. So she was going to sing. Now the organ. The Governor she supposed. A white organist she had never seen. The Major used to sing in the choir. Sing solos. Only three times a year. He said, "You play the organ there, Abbie. If I were to sing solos every Sunday it wouldn't look right. People would think we'd taken over the church." Christmas. Easter. Children's Sunday. He sang solos then. He is risen. Hallelujah. Silent night, Holy night. Voice sweet. Sweet tenor voice. Always humming and whistling and singing.

The strange organist was playing "Goin' Home." That woman was going to sing it. A big woman. Light brown. Freckles on her face. A soprano. From the Baptist Church. She had a voice like a cry from the grave. Sadness. Sorrow. Regret. Reproach — no other voice like it. The high notes a little off pitch, deliberately off pitch, so that it was no longer singing, it was a wail, echoing in the blood, in the bones.

At the first sound of that voice, lifted now, unearthly, terrible in its sorrow, she told herself, Think of something about him that you did not like. If you don't you'll faint. There is a moaning in your throat and it will come out. Think fast.

There were the stories. The stories about his family. She'd never liked those stories. He told them with gusto. He said his people were swamp niggers and laughed. There was Uncle Zeke, his great-great-uncle, who had red eyes and carried toads and roots in his pockets and could conjure. "Don't say goodbye to me." Told them that at a railroad station. Were the stories true? Did they have railroad stations in those days? When they got off the train, Uncle Zeke was standing on the station platform waiting for them. Uncle Zeke could rise up off his bed, in a prone position, and go around in circles, three feet up from the bed, in a prone position, around and around, bony legs thrust out straight from a white nightshirt, lids closed over the red eyes, and he always said the same thing, as he floated around circling over his bed, "Watch that straight coattail, Sam, watch that straight coattail." Nobody had ever known what he meant by it.

Had the Major made them up? Made up all the stories about those other long since dead members of the Crunch family. But the details were so vivid. The stories obviously handed down, handed down, always told the same way, so that they sounded true. She even knew what Uncle Zeke looked like, a small dark man who walked with a limp and his hands were unpleasant to the touch, damp and cold. Whenever anybody got sick they sent for Uncle Zeke. She even knew how his voice had sounded, a highpitched cackling, almost feminine, voice, "Zeke'll ponder it. Zeke'll squat down by the fire. And Zeke'll ponder it. Hush, hush, hush. Zeke is ponderin' it." And wind howled down the chimney.

Shut out the sound of that wail. Keep remembering. You didn't like the stories. He made those people live again. They were an emotional primitive people, whose existence even in the past seemed somehow to be an affront to the things you believed in, and stood for. His great-grandfather, Theodore Crunch, bit an Irishman's ear off in a fight in the dooryard of an inn. And another one of the male Crunches, after the Emancipation, used to glance around his dooryard and then gather up all the little pickaninnies, as he called them, and sell them off for ten dollars apiece, to anyone who would buy them, saying that he was tired of looking at them. Then the rest of the family would have to go scurrying aound the countryside to get the children back.

There was Aunt Hal, who wore men's shoes, and who could conjure, and who had her conjure books buried with her, and the story was that a white man offered a thousand dollars for the conjure books but the surviving Crunches did not dare sell them, because Aunt Hal had warned them, on her deathbed, "Them books goes in the casket with me. Anybody takes 'em out, I'll be back. If I has to come back, I'll take every one of you niggers over Jordan with me."

Aunt Hal stood six foot in her stocking feet, Aunt Hal wore long black skirts, Aunt Hal had a deep voice, bass, like a man's voice. Her eyes were the black unfathomable eyes of a witch, a gypsy. When one of the early Crunches died, Aunt Hal wasn't invited to the funeral. But when the funeral procession got under way, there was Aunt Hal perched on the back of the hearse, riding in the procession, leading the way, holding on with one hand, and with the other hand thumbing her nose at the mourners in the carriages following the hearse. Somebody shouted, "Whip up them horses! Whip 'em up!" And the hearse started going faster and faster, Aunt Hal, holding on, jouncing up and down, faster, faster, and the dead Crunch in the casket completely forgotten. The living Crunches thrust their heads out of the windows of the carriages following the hearse, shouting, "Whip 'em up! Whip them horses! When Hal falls off ride her down! Ride Hal down!" An ungodly crew. None of the stories were ever about goodness and mercy, always death and cruelty. People stopped and stared and wondered at the sight, horses stretched out straight, hoofbeats, fast, furious, the carriages swaying, Hal clutching the sides of the hearse, refusing to be jolted off, and finally, at the cemetery, as the casket was being lowered into the grave, she spat at them, spat at all those darkskinned Crunches who stood glaring at her across the open grave, and said, "Well! I come to the funeralizin' anyway. Didn' I?" Deep bass voice. Man's voice.

The story about Hal, the remembered story, took her down the aisle of the church, following behind the body of the last of the Crunches, the last Theodore Crunch. Home to his fathers. Gone to his long home. Crunches waiting for him. This one, the last of them, never had the son he wanted. Never had any children. A man who loved boys and gardens and horses. Loved boys. So they adopted Link. At the Major's insistence. Where was Link? He wasn't at the service. She thought about him that one time, coming out of the church. Then not again. Forgetting him as though he had never existed. Because she believed that it was her fault that the Major died.

All those years ago, and she remembered it as though it had happened yesterday. Had never really gotten over it. Because there was always the feeling that it was her fault that the Major died. But there had been the smell of whiskey and because of it she hadn't really looked at him, wouldn't look at him. Bill hod brought him home and there was the smell of whiskey.

As she sat there in the kitchen she heard somebody whistling. Then Bill Hod went past the back door. Why, he's been up there all this time. She hadn't heard his footsteps coming down the stairs. He had made no sound at all. There was just the whistled tune, seemingly descending the outside back stairs, coming down, by itself, nearer and nearer. A tune she'd heard before. Where? Of course. The tune that Link had been whistling when he left the house, the tune that Mamie Powther had been singing while she hung clothes on the line: "I'm lonesome — lonesome."

I don't know what to do, she thought. Then she straightened up. She would make some tea and then she would go and ask Frances to help her figure out some way, some polite way, of course, by which she could get rid of the Powthers quickly.

The twelve o'clock whistle sounded at the Treadway Munitions Company. Tea for lunch? No. She heated soup and rolls and fixed a salad. Then set the table as carefully as though she were expecting a guest, thinking, I've always been the Englishman dressing for dinner even in the jungle. Then she sat down at the table and bowed her head as she said the blessing.

"What you doin'?"

She gave a little jump. J.C. was standing in the kitchen, right near the table. His expression was exactly like that she had seen on the faces of a group of people over on Franklin Avenue who were standing in a semicircle looking down at something — a mixture of puzzlement and awe and fear. Ordinarily she avoided crowds that collected on the street, but there was something so extraordinary in the faces of these people that she had stopped to find out why. There on the sidewalk, motionless, oblivious to the crowd standing back at a respectful distance, was a praying mantis. Now she thought, wanting to laugh, I must have looked exactly like that mantis to this dirty little boy; and he was dirty — his face, his hands, his clothes.

"What was you doin'?" he said. Awe still on his face.

"I was saying grace." He moves like a mouse, she thought. I didn't hear him come in here. "I was saying a blessing." No response. "Before people eat," she said slowly, "they bless the food." She thought he would ask why, but he didn't.

"Where to sit?" he demanded. He had moved closer to her, if he came any closer his nose would be in her soup.

Oh, she thought, as she got up from the table, this one time won't do any harm. "Sit there." She pointed to the place where Link always sat. "But wait a minute." She washed his hands and his face. He made no comment. "Now," she said, "you can sit down at the table."

She set a place for him and filled a glass with milk and handed it to him because this was as good a time as any to get him to drink milk from a glass rather than from a nursing bottle. He ate steadily, not talking, but making a rather musical murmuring as he ate, umh, umh, umh, umh. He gulped the milk down, polished off a big bowl of applesauce, grabbed three cookies, said, "Me gotta go now," and went out the back door, fast.

"Well!" she said aloud.

3

● SATURDAY AFTERNOON and Jubine, the photographer, leaned way over the desk, bar, barrier, table, whatever it was that separated the girl behind the switchboard in the office of the *Monmouth Chronicle* from bringers-in of items about weddings and funerals, births and christenings, and complainers about misspelled names.

Jubine leaned way over and whispered in the girl's ear, " 'How beautiful are thy feet with shoes, O prince's daughter — '. "

The girl turned and smiled at him, thus she brought her face quite close to his and did not immediately move it away.

"Jubie!" she said. "I knew that was you before I looked."

"You mean the *Chronicle*'s bright young men no longer speak English? Is it that they speak in unknown tongues? I forgot. They all talk Bullockese — a fiery wrathful blasphemous language. Thus if Jubine even so much as whispers he is immediately recognized." He worked a cigar around in his mouth.

"Where've you been?" the girl asked.

"Oh, around and around and around. In circles. Back and forth and around."

"How come we haven't seen you?"

"We? We? You mean you, don't you? Miss me?"

"Of course."

"Whyn't you call me up?" He didn't wait for an answer. "Too busy? No telephones? No nickels to put in telephones? Or does

40

the telephone company annoy you so you boycott telephones? How about dinner? Tonight?"

"Jubie, I think you're sweet. But I don't want to eat a sandwich at a wake. With or without you. Or on the dock. Or on the back of your motorcycle."

"Breakfast. How about breakfast? Sunday morning. Any place you say."

"Not me. I tried it once. Never again."

He sighed. "Can I help it if I keep believing that one of these days I will come across a small and lovely one with curly black hair, like yours, and dimples in the cheeks, like yours, and a mouth that suggests honey, like yours. But she will not want Simmons mattresses and Toastmaster toasters and Cannon sheets and Gunther coats and De Beers Limited will not rate with her. She will want me. That's all. She will share my pumpernickel and my pail of beer and because she can hold my hand she will not want anything else. And she will look just like you."

"What's De Beers?"

"Little one, you mean you haven't got that far yet? I forgot. You're only twenty-one. But you'll find out. They all do."

"Jubie, you don't want a wife. You don't want a girl. All you need for the rest of your life is a camera. And you know it. You can't kid me."

"I thought perhaps you'd changed your mind."

"Nope." She worked the switchboard, fast, said, Yes, No, Hold on please, ah, shut up you dope, no, fathead, Yes, sir, No, sir. "Did you want something, Jubie? Other than to look at me and practise using words?"

"Is the owner in?" he asked humbly.

"I'll see."

"You don't have to use the technique on me, sweetie. A man that size wearing a camel-hair coat that color could not possibly go out without you seeing him. Besides the Bullock stamps his hoofs as he walks and he exhales smoke and fire through his nostrils. Or does he have a private staircase for emergency use, just in case his past should catch up with him? Besides that five-thousand-dollar-fob Detroit job is right out there at the curb. Dead center in front of the door."

The girl giggled. "If he's in shall I say that you have some pictures for him?"

"I am not here to sell him any pictures unless I feel a sudden wave of pity for him. Which I doubt. You tell the Keeper of the Gate that Jubine is here because Bullock sent for Jubine. Jubine always comes on horseback whenever his friend the editor, owner, and publisher of the *Monmouth Chronicle* gets into trouble and sends for him."

"Trouble? Trouble? What kind of trouble is he in, Jubie?"

"Maybe he's pregnant. That's why I came so fast. I want to know, too."

The girl said, "Mr. Jubine to see Mr. Bullock," into the mouthpiece and waited about five minutes, then she said, "All right."

"You can go right in. But don't bait him, Jubie. He's not feeling so good today."

"Tch! Tch! He should live so. A big strong young man in a camel-hair coat, not feeling so good today. Now remember I had a head, two arms, two legs, and a torso, all intact when last you saw me go through yonder door. Grrrrrrrr!" he growled, and blew her a kiss.

Peter Bullock looked at Jubine and thought, I don't know why I was weak enough to send for him, except that I've had to buy too goddamn many of his pictures lately, sometimes even had to call him up and ask him if he had what I wanted. Just that morning he'd been raving at the halfwits in the photo department, "What's the matter with you? That damn Jubine gets pictures. Why can't you?"

Even while he said it he was thinking, You can't pay a man to do what Jubine does, sleep in snatches, half awake even when asleep, eat where and when he can, ear always cocked to police calls, camera always close by, camera to be woman, children, home, life, sleep, everything. Had thought that and then decided, I'll offer him a job. And so sent for him. And here he was. So he offered him the job — head of the photo department.

Jubine laughed. He took the cigar out of his mouth to laugh, and then put it back in his mouth, lit it. Bullock had never seen him light it before, had figured that the one cigar lasted him a year or so, all he ever did was hold it in his mouth, not even chewing on it, just working it around.

He blew out a great cloud of bluegray smoke. "You know what I make a year, Bullock?"

Bullock shook his head.

"You guess. Sometimes for just one shot, I get more than you could afford to pay me for four months' work."

"I don't believe you. Whyn't you buy some decent clothes and a car? And live in a decent house." Jubine lived in a loft, wore GI pants and shoes, rode on a motorcycle.

"For what? My clothes keep me warm. My loft keeps the rain and the wind away from my person. And I am free. But you, my dear Bullock, you are a slave, to custom, to a house, to a car. You have given yourself little raw places in your stomach, little sore burning places, so that you cannot eat what you want and you cannot sleep at night, because you have turned so many handsprings to pay for that long shiny car, and you've got to keep on turning them so that you can buy expensive tires for it, so that you can buy the expensive gas that goes in its belly. It's a slave ship. Think of it — a slave ship right here in this beautiful little New England city called Monmouth — "

"Oh, for God's sake," he said impatiently. "Go on home and eat roots and herbs from the meadows, go on home and live naked in a cave, I wish to God I'd never — "

"I know, Bullock, I know," voice tender, voice all compassion. "I like you, that's why I enjoy talking to you. You see your newspaper could be so good but you can't afford to fool around with it because it would frighten the readers and they would cancel their subscriptions and the advertisers would get angry and withdraw their advertising and — "

"The advertisers don't run the paper."

"I didn't say they did. But they'd be fools if they didn't let you know when they were displeased, because of a story or an editorial."

"Bosh."

"No advertiser ever tried to keep a story out of the *Chronicle?*"

"You've been reading *Pravda.*"

Jubine shook his head. "You mean to tell me that there is not left in your newspaper or in you even so much as a spark, just the faintest suggestion of a spark of life, that would disturb an advertiser? Not even an editorial that makes an advertiser register a complaint over the telephone?" He paused, eyed Bullock, said, "Do you know what history will record about you and your newspaper?"

Bullock didn't answer.

"Nothing. Absolutely nothing. Neither will history mention the city of Monmouth, as a place of interest. It will be mentioned only as the birthplace of Jubine, the man who spent a lifetime photographing a river, and thus recorded the life of man in the twentieth century. For the first time."

"In that case," Bullock made his voice dry, deliberate, "why do you waste your valuable time talking to me? Why don't you — "

"Because, my dear Bullock, I am trying to save you."

He walked straight into it. "Save me? Save me from what?"

"From ulcers and the fate of ulcer victims, from slavery and the fate of slaves, from whoredom and the fate of whores — "

"Get out," Bullock roared. "Go on, get out, and don't ever come back — "

"Wait. I have brought your Christmas pictures." He opened his shabby briefcase, extracted a large blownup photograph, blew on it, kissed his hand to it. "Look — "

Bullock held the picture a long time. He had seen the church all his life, but never quite like this. Snow on the ground, and in the background the river, the melted snow had increased its size, widening it, or else it was the angle of the camera, the wind must have been blowing because there were little rippling waves in the water, motion in the water, and the church was all slender steeple, going up, up, toward the sky. And a cloud, just one cloud far up. Church, river, sky, cloud, all of it timeless, ageless. Hope in it, in the sun sparkling on the river, on the snow, on that fragilelooking steeple that lifted itself up, and up, up.

"That's beautiful," he said, and sighed.

"Why did you sigh?"

"Don't start talking. Just let me buy the picture and then run along and save somebody else's soul. How much do you want for it?"

"Wait. I have something else to show you. Here. This goes with the picture of the church. You have just seen religion on the River Wye, man's aspiration, his hope, his faith, part of his dreams. But the river reveals many things about men. Here is despair written almost on the face of the river."

He shook his head as he looked at the next photograph. The river was in the background of this one, too, but it must have been taken on a cold night, and the river was black, ugly. It seemed to resent the dock for the dock was in the foreground, snowcovered, and the river had thrown a border of frozen spray along the edge of the dock, as though it had been spitting at it. There were footprints, a man's prints, and off to one side was the body of a man, flat on his belly, snow on him, too. His footprints were black in the white snow, water in the heel prints.

He handed the picture back, said nothing.

Jubine reached in the briefcase again. "I went back in an hour —and this is what I got."

You could see where the man had been lying, the imprint of his body. You could see, in the snow, how he had struggled, clawing at the snow to get on his feet, and then his footprints. He dragged his feet when he walked, the dragging unsteady feet had gone in a zigzag line to the edge of the dock, ended there. There were no footprints coming back.

"You mean — why didn't you stop him?"

"Stop him? I didn't see him do this."

"But when you saw him lying there in the snow, why didn't you find out what he was doing there? You must have known he was heading for the river."

"Me?" Jubine's popeyes widened. He worked his cigar from the right-hand corner of his mouth to dead center, worked it back to its first position. "Me? Am I the hand of God, Bullock? Should I interfere with the inevitable, the foreordained? Interfere with the doomed and the damned?" He made a gesture with his hand, as though he were rejecting the idea, pushing it away. "Not Jubine. Jubine watches. Jubine waits. Jubine records but Jubine never, never interferes — "

"I always knew you set these things up," Bullock said furiously. "Anything for a picture — even a man's life." Jubine reached over, took the picture of the church, and put it back in the briefcase. "Hold on. I want that one."

"All or none. These three pictures belong together. They must be printed together. You cannot use the church by itself. You see, I am interested in the immortal souls of your readers as well as yours. They are poor peons, too. And so on Christmas morning — "

"You couldn't pay me to put those other two pictures in the paper on Christmas Day."

"I was afraid you'd feel like that. Some day I shall become discouraged and I will stop offering you immortality. You are a stupid man, Bullock. These pictures will be reprinted, together, not just one of them, as long as there is any paper left in the world. They will become better known than the Mona Lisa, than a Raphael Madonna, and when I think that they might first have appeared in the *Monmouth Chronicle*, why I weep for you, Bullock. I weep for you."

He supposed it was childish, but as Jubine went out the door he followed him, and when he reached the little anteroom where his secretary sat, he said, loud enough for Jubine to hear, "Don't let him in here again. I don't want any more of his pictures. I don't want to talk to him on the telephone. Tell that cutie on the switchboard the same thing."

The irritation that Jubine had set up in him, hung around him like a cloak; it seemed to increase in size, until when he finally got home even the sight of his own home infuriated him. Lola sensed his mood, the instant he entered the house, and she practically tiptoed around him, and that made him angrier.

We live like millionaires, he thought, got to have a maid and a cook and a cleaning woman and God knows what else. The dinner table set up like it was for a banquet, lighted candles and flowers on the table. Good food, he supposed, and he had mashed potatoes and cream.

"Had a hard day, Pete?"

"Mmmmmm."

That took care of the conversation during dinner. Afterwards they went into the living room, and he thought, Rose-colored curtains drawn across the picture window, glass house, never throw stones when you live in a glass house. Cozy. Almost winter. Stage all set for it. The wife in black velvet, ankle length, fullskirted, gold something or other around the waist, the husband in tweed jacket, pants didn't match, pipe in hand, leaning against the fireplace, fire flickering in the fireplace, fireplace built practically in the middle of the living room, chimney part of the decorative value of the room, according to the pansy who selected the furnishings. Logs of applewood being burned, sold practically by weight, he ought to know, he paid the bill for the goddamn wood and wondered what the hell kind of world this was where you bought wood for a fireplace, when you burned oil to heat the joint with, but then you had a fireplace and you lived in a city so you had to buy wood by the piece from a farmer who insulted you even as he pocketed your money, and then pay a fortune to have it hauled here, and then you burned the stuff not to keep warm but to —
Decorative effect. Hearth. Home. Siamese cat part of it. No children. Siamese cat took their place. Sat in front of the fire warming its behind and sneered. Lola's cat.

Lola was reading a magazine. He thought, I don't hate her. I think I do sometimes. But I don't. I couldn't. It's just the old war between the male and the female. Never resolved and never will be. I couldn't hate her. She's beautiful. A redhead. How the hell did we get here anyway? Why do I get so mad at her, at myself, at the goddamn newspaper, this house, even the wood, burning in the fireplace. It cost a couple of arteries but it burns smoothly, evenly, throws no sparks, stays lighted.

He sighed. Lola looked up, and he thought, she knows me so well that she knows it is now safe to talk to me, that I am now a human being again and not an animal holed up somewhere with a front paw caught in a trap, paw swelling, pain in it, animal crazy with pain, would bite off the hand of a would-be rescuer. Lola. In this light — red hair —

"What're you readin'?"

"Vogue. New issue. It's got the most marvelous photograph. Look."

She came across the room with it, stood beside him, magazine held open. He might have known. One of Jubine's shots. Old colored washerwoman. Taken, he was certain, right here in Monmouth. Looked though as if it had been taken in Charleston. Woman sitting on a stoop. Face like — he didn't believe any such face existed — face like a painting by an old master, master hand, a strong old face, tough, not tough in the modern sense, tough like leather, indestructible, would wear forever, a face that had seen all kinds of things, a face that had survived everything, a face suggesting what — compassion. He had the feeling that if this old woman looked at him, Bullock, she would feel sorry for him. And he thought, That's the thing about Jubine that infuriates me. It's not that rot he talks, it's not that he talks all the time like it was a compulsion, speech cases him, so he has to talk and talk and talk and talk; it's that he actually feels sorry for me. Why did I know instantly that this was a washerwoman, yes, sign right by the door, said Han Launderey, beautifully misspelled, and the old hands were out of shape at the knuckles and joints.

He handed the magazine back to Lola. "He's a goddamn Communist."

"Who?" she said, startled.

"Jubine. The world's greatest photographer. The crackpot who took that picture."

"Why do you say he's a Communist?"

"Because he's against wealth. Every time he gets a chance he takes a potshot at the wealthy."

"Well," she said hesitantly, obviously not wanting to get in an argument with him, and yet determined to show that he was wrong, "I haven't seen all of his pictures. But I can remember two of them that were anything but potshots at the wealthy. Those photomurals of the river in Treadway Hall, in the entrance hall, are just beautiful pictures of a river and that's all. And I remember that shot he took of the Treadway girl's wedding, the wedding party coming out of the church. It was in Vogue four or five years ago. And it was a honey."

"Yeah. He sold the honey to Vogue. Did you see what he brought me? He brought me the one with what he calls the peons flowing into and around the picture. He never says the people and he doesn't use the word peasants, no, he says peons, so you'll get a picture of enslavement, ignorance, racial mixture. And people don't know whether they ought to laugh or get mad. Yeah, he took the honey to Vogue, all light and shadow, the Treadway girl and that man she married, whoever he was, perfect down to the last jewel, the last cufflink, and stretching behind them the aisle of the church, partial view of the altar. I Thee Do Wed, so that even the impure and the dissolute will wipe away a tear when they look at it.

"But he brought me the shot with the peons crowding into the picture, one with no legs practically sitting in the bride's dress, squatting in the folds of the wedding gown, and the damn fool who does the society page fell for that torrent of talk that comes out of his mouth, 'Look at the light, the shadows, the tree branches forming a pattern, look at the contrast, the adoration on the face of the legless man, adoration, same expression on the face of the young groom — but expectancy on the face of the young bride — ' "

"It was true," Lola said thoughtfully. "I remember it now. It was one of the pictures of the year."

"You mean you didn't see what he'd done?" He snorted in disgust. "Where'd the Treadway money come from? Munitions, guns, explosives. How'd the man lose his legs? Shot off in the First World War. Jubine wouldn't miss a bet like that. Contrasts all right but not in light and shadow. He probably paid that legless man to sit outside the church."

She said, softly, "I suppose it's all in the way you look at a thing."

"It is not. It's the way he arranges things, or waits for hours until they arrange themselves, to fit the pattern of his thinking. Why do you think he leaves Monmouth and his precious river every year to attend the opening of the Met? Because he likes music? Hell, no, because he knows he'll get pictures of the rich making fools of themselves, riding horses up the steps, taking their clothes off, or of be-diamonded horriblelooking old women with their skirts lifted, their lean shanks exposed, because they've got their old legs up on tables. He gets quotes, too, like the time that woman lost her tiara, he had her saying, 'I'm cold without it.' You notice none of his poor people, his peons, ever have their mouths open or their tongues stuck out or their behinds bare."

"But he does show them that way. He takes drunks and prostitutes and murderers and you look at the picture and you know what they are —"

"Oh, sure. But he always gives them dignity, even lying in the gutter. That woman who shot her husband, last year, looked like an avenger, a fury, not ridiculous or silly or simpleminded."

"Perhaps the poor have dignity because —"

"That's communism. That's what he's saying in his pictures."

"Wait a minute, Pete. I didn't say the rich were undignified because they were rich."

"No. But you were going to say poor people have dignity because they're poor. Jubine says that all the time in his pictures. And the rich sucker peons eat it up and pay him a fortune for it."

Rich sucker peons. "I always hope that some day you will realize that you are a poor peon like the rest of us. Then you will be a free man." Jubine said that when he brought him the shot of the old governor's funeral cortege. Oh, sure, the *Chronicle's* flashbulb boys had pictures, but not like that one of Jubine's — death in his picture, grandeur in it, and something else that after one hasty glance made you think that you had been an eyewitness to the passing of the last of the aristocrats in government and you were left the poorer because of it.

He said, "I won't buy any more of his goddamn communist pictures."

And then changed the subject because with the female to whom you were legally wed you had to be very careful to avoid an argument, otherwise on a Saturday night you would find yourself sleeping alone in the less comfortable of the two guest rooms.

"What have you been doing all day, beautiful?" He ran his hand through her hair — soft, silky, fragrant. The cat looked up and blinked its eyes and he thought, It's a good house, it's a good room, it's a good fire. The cat? Ah, well, as a cat it is a good cat, as a substitute for male and female children it is a hell of a lousy thing. But as a cat it belongs in this room, like the fireplace, and Lola's hair.

"Love me?" she said.

"I love you. All my life I've loved you. And always will." He put his arm around her waist. "Leave us talk about you." He thought, Jubine's face suggests laughter, yet he doesn't laugh often. Why then? Because it is basically the face of a clown, with a few added touches it would be a clown's face; the potential was there, the mouth a little too large, the nose too prominent, the eyes bulged, the ears stood out, too big. Clown's face.

"Let's go up early," he said, putting his cheek down close to hers. "Gosh, you smell good."

When he turned out the light in their bedroom, he thought, Well, at least that pansy who picked out the furniture knew what he was doing when he put a kingsize bed in here, or maybe it was Lola's idea. And asked her, and she giggled, leaned close to him, then whispered, her mouth in the hollow of his neck, her mouth tickling him as it moved, soft, warm against the hollow of his neck, "Stalin thought it up — part of the Communist plot to hasten the downfall of the capitalist class."

4

● AT MIDNIGHT, on the same Saturday night, Link Williams stood on the dock, leaning against the railing, waiting for Jubine. Fog was blowing in from the river, soft, wet, clinging, all-enveloping fog. He listened to the water lap against the piling. There was a southwest wind and it lifted the fog now and then, blew it back, lifted it, so that he caught an occasional glimpse of the river, of light reflected in it, could see stretches of the dock itself, then the fog would blow in again, thicker than before, billowing in from the river. When he turned and looked in the direction of Dumble Street, it was as though a cloud, a cumulus, was moving in on Dumble Street.

Fog over the river, fog over Dock Street, the street that ran alongside the river. He heard the chug-chug of Jubine's motorcycle, way down on Franklin Avenue, going slowly, visualized him, head bent forward, peering, trying to see both sides of the street at once for fear he'd miss something, miss the chance to photograph someone coming into the world, or just leaving it.

As he stood there waiting for Jubine he grinned, thinking about Abbie. She had been all upset at supper because she had found out that Mamie Powther, Mrs. Mamie Powther, was Bill Hod's cousin. Mr. B. Hod's cousin. He had been kind of jolted himself. But for different reasons. Cousin, he thought. Yah!

Abbie had been so upset he had felt a little sorry for her. But being upset did not prevent her from reciting her regular

51

Saturday night lines. He knew his by heart too. So the whole thing went off smoothly. They'd been doing it for about two years now, ever since he had come back from the Navy, so that it was never necessary for one to prompt the other. His lines, her lines, unchanged, unchanging. The only variation occurred in the comments on the weather. In the summer Abbie said, "This heat" in winter she said, "This cold"; fall and spring, "This wind"; and, of course, rain, snow, fog, hail, whatever form of precipitation fell from the heavens above:

"Those poker games — that man — you get in so late — "

"It's the shank of the evening — "

"Alone in the house — every Saturday night — hear noises — "

"Noises from the street — "

"Someone walks through the backyard — "

"Probably a dog — "

"Knocks over the ashcan — "

"Probably a dog — "

"You ought to wear a coat — this dampness — "

"Don't need one" — whistle, hum, sing "I got my love to keep me warm."

"Those poker games — that man — Saturday night — Dumble Street — the fog — "

He always let that one go without answering it.

"Dumble Street — not safe — people knifed — held up — robbed — this fog — "

"Unlikely — know everybody — for blocks around — safe in Dumble Street — safe as a church — my end of town — "

Why as a church? Why did he always say, safe as a church? Who was safe in a church? Safe from what?

"You don't go to church any more — you ought to go to church — I don't understand why — that man — "

He'd gone plenty when he was a kid, enough to last him the rest of his life. He could remember how church ate the heart, the life out of Sundays. He could see himself, washed and scrubbed and carrying a Bible, walking always within hand's reach of the white gloves Abbie wore. She carried a Bible too. They walked side by side, the straightbacked, smallboned woman and the reluctant boy, the carriers of Bibles. And down at the other end of Dumble Street, in the opposite direction, was the river. Every kid he knew was on the dock, near the dock, around the dock, drying off, sunning himself, diving in, swimming, loafing.

And he, in Sunday School, and then in church, and the new minister's prayers were so long, so long, he closed his eyes and tried not to think, to go to sleep, and the voice went on and on, "Look down on us poor sinners, help us, oh, Lord — "

He opened his eyes and counted the panes in the nearest of the stained-glass windows. He stared up at the ceiling and counted the light blubs in the chandelier, wishing that he could sit in some other part of the church besides the choir loft. Abbie sat in the choir loft because she played the organ so he had to sit there, too, so he wouldn't "get into mischief." He dropped the hymnbook just for the exquisite pleasure of hearing the explosive sound it made, pulled his ear, wriggled in his chair, and then slid way down in it until he was half reclining, then, remembering that Abbie could see him in the little mirror with the oak frame that was right above the organ, he would straighten up.

Sometimes he amused himself by wondering what would happen if he stood up quickly and dropped a hymnbook squarely on top of old Mrs. Brown's head; she wore a squashed-down black felt hat and it would be fun to flatten it a little more. But he never did. It was fidget and twist and turn, put his feet squarely in front of him, turn his ankles in, then out, crack his knuckles, while he contemplated the long expanse of time, limitless, never ending, and he in the middle of it, forced to sit still, when he wanted to run and jump and whoop and holler and land in the river, yelling, "Last one in is a horse's tail."

He tried to figure out ways of waging warfare, open warfare, jungle warfare, leap from ambush, gorilla warfare. He would declare war with a shout, declare war on Abbie, the minister, the old ladies dozing in the front pews, the old men who sat in the back pews leaning on their canes, the choir. He would shoot the soprano just at dawn, she had a quaver in her voice and buck teeth, and was always poking at him with her foot. Then he was God and all the angels, he was Gabriel blowing on a horn, blowing for the Judgment, and he was Ezekiel and he saw a wheel and a wheel and wheels, he was Moses leading his people to the Promised Land, booting his people to the Promised Land.

He was never ten-year-old Link Williams trapped in the choir loft on a morning when there was no school, when the sun was shining and the air was hot and the river ran practically in his front yard. So he lifted the hymnbook and sighted down the length of it, then put it to his lips, getting ready to blow that great big final blast for the Judgment, and then would drop it, bang, just to break the monotony.

Every Sunday, after church, Abbie said, "For heaven's sake, Link, why do you keep dropping your hymnbook? Sometimes I think you do it on purpose."

The afternoons weren't much better. He was caged under The Hangman, still within arm's reach of Abbie. She read the Sunday edition of the *Chronicle*, all afternoon, and he mostly sat around, restless, at a loss, until six o'clock. Right after supper he was on his own for an hour or so and as he took off his Sunday clothes, exchanging them for an old pair of pants and a jersey, he began to feel free. He went straight across the street, around to the back door of The Last Chance and into the big kitchen, knowing that he was just in time to eat with Weak Knees and Bill. Bill said, "Your aunt must have Jew blood. Sundown and the religion is put away for the night."

Weak Knees said, "Pull up a chair, Sonny, and start layin' your lip over this here fried chicken. I know you ain't had a goddamn thing to eat all day."

The putt-putt of Jubine's motorcycle had stopped, he hadn't heard it for quite a while. He must have found his picture though, because it began again, a staccato sound, immediately recognizable, despite the sound of busses starting and stopping, the clang-clang of the Franklin Avenue trolley.

The fog kept lifting and closing in, and he thought that the bleat of the foghorn kept changing with the rolling in of the fog, perhaps it was a change in pitch or in volume due to the shifting of the wind, first it was like a groan, on one note, and then it had two notes, now up, now down, Groan-sigh, groan-sigh, groan-sigh.

He could tell from the sounds that Dumble Street was all set now for Saturday night. It had passed the yawning, stretching stage, was now out of the house, wearing its best pants, razor-edge crease in the pants, clean shirt on its back, had long since patted its hip pocket to make sure the wallet was there, had adjusted its hat brim on its wellgreased hair, run its fingers over its just-shaved jowls, fingertips smelling of carnation talc and lilac aftershave for a good half-hour after contact with the jowls. It had long since taken stock of the potentialities, the possibilities, offered by this stretch of time, payday time, no-work-in-the-morning time, money-and-plenty-of-places-to-spend-it-in time, stay-up-all-night time and lie in bed half the next day, luxuriating in the memory of the conquests of the night before. Dance in the Dance Hall. Yes. Those that didn't want to dance were standing hipdeep in The Last Chance, just drinking and talking. He'd have to duck back in there pretty soon and check the cash register again. The Moonbeam would be packed right straight back to the door. There was, if you listened for it, a kind of hum and buzz in Dumble Street, later there would be fights and holdups and violence — largely unpremeditated.

Whenever the fog lifted he caught glimpses of the street, the harsh redorange neon sign of The Last Chance, the frame houses, the no longer used trolley track, could even see where the sidewalks were broken, broken by coal trucks and moving vans. He turned his back on the river, fog over it, so thick you couldn't see anything, wouldn't know it was there.

He heard the roar, the staccato beat, the putt-putt of a motorcycle. Jubine was getting near the dock; recording angel on a motorcycle, on the prowl, at night, hunting for death, the ones dead by their own hands, the ones dead by knife or gun in some one else's hand. Then motor cut off. Headlight cut off. Silence. He heard him walk across the dock, knew that he was standing still, trying to see the river.

"You're late, Jubie," he said.

"Link?"

"Yeah."

"Jesus, you must be wearing sneakers. You practising cops and robbers or somep'n?"

"The fog deadens sound. But it's a good night for it."

"A lovely night. Night for murder. Night for rape. Night for sabotage. Night for all the poor peons to cry, to wail, to gnash their teeth. The poor peons. It's the nights that get them." His voice soft, compassionate.

Fog all around them, lifting, swirling, now concealing, now revealing, drifting, intangible, wet, there, not there, touching their faces, touching their hands, cold and wet, warm and wet, soft and wet.

Jubine lit his cigar and the sudden spurt splash flare of light, brief, gone suddenly, illumined his face, revealed the popeyes which seemed to be staring at the match, cataloguing it, prying into it. Link thought, It's the face of a born snoop — got to know, want to know, got to see, want to see, ears that are big and out of shape, the mouth, well, the lips full, got to talk, see all hear all, talk about himself, the nose, a flare at the nostrils, as though the nose must smell all, too, and the hands big, capable, black hair on the backs, hands feel all. But the eyes were what held you, embarrassed you, bold bulging eyes that made no pretense of not looking, that couldn't get enough of looking. It was not the childlike concentrated gaze that stared without comprehension; it was the child's unwinking gaze with a lively intelligence added. His voice always came as a shock, it should have been a hoarse tough voice, instead it was soft cajoling — voice of a mother comforting a child, You're all right, I'll put cold water on your knee, and a bandage. See? It's all right now. Tender, compassionate voice, and so people turned toward him and he got his picture.

The fog lifted and Link saw him look toward Dumble Street, turn that inquisitive roving gaze of his down the length of the street.

"Don't you ever stop hunting angles, judging distances, measuring light?"

He shook his head. "You wait, you watch, you listen, and on a Saturday night in Dumble Street, you can catch 'em coming into the world, Sonny, and you can catch 'em going out."

They both heard the whine of a siren at the same time. Jubine said, "Ambulance. Franklin Avenue. See you later."

And was gone again. Link was fairly certain that the poker game was shot to hell and back but he'd wait a half-hour, and if Jubine didn't show up he'd go chew the fat with Weak Knees in the kitchen.

Standing there, leaning against the piling, fog all around him, river lapping under the piling, he could have sworn that the fog touched his face, his hands. He thought about Mamie Powther, hanging up clothes, reaching, bending, a younger shapelier browner edition of China — within hand's reach. Except, this time, too, except for Bill Hod. He was sixteen when he went in China's place for the first time. China. Yellow flesh, warm yellow flesh. "You wait," and he, believing, waited in the hallway.

China had been pale yellow and fat; her face, and he could see it again, clearly, would never forget it, the mouth and the nose pushed in, somehow flattened, even the eyes flat against the face and the whole face not wrinkled or lined yet giving the impression of great age, an old face, due to the thick quality of the skin itself, a tiredness in the eyes that made the face old. Mamie Powther's face had a kind of energy about it, due to the firmness of the flesh, a decisiveness that touched all the features, the nose, the mouth, the eyes, the mouth was really lovely, the lips — well, you knew there were lip muscles there, it was a singer's mouth. The fog lifted, closed in, lifted, closed in. Fog. China and Bill Hod. China said, "You wait right here in the hall." And he waited there in the hallway, and he, believing, waited there in the hallway. Why did he remember it now? It was the fog, he was enclosed by it, and in that hallway he had suddenly got the same feeling of being enclosed.

The fog lifted, closed in, lifted, closed in, so thick now it was like smoke from a fire that had had water poured on it, clouds of it, white, thick, visibility zero, ceiling zero.

He turned and listened. Someone was coming down the dock, running down the dock, running at a headlong reckless pace. There was another sound too, a sound he could not identify, it seemed to accompany, to follow after, the running feet. The footsteps came nearer and nearer, a woman's footsteps, light, fast on her feet. And then the fog lifted a little and he saw a girl running toward him, a girl in a long full coat, running with a kind of frenzy that suggested she was literally running for her life.

He still could not identify the other sound, and he could not see what she was running from. She was visible and then invisible. He caught glimpses of her at intervals but he still could not see what was pursuing her.

As she drew nearer, he could hear the sound of wheels, small wheels moving along the planking of the dock. It meant only one thing. Cat Jimmie — that obscene remnant of a man was chasing a woman under cover of the fog. He wondered how he could follow the girl so closely, guide that flat board on its little wheels with such uncanny accuracy that he never once lost her; true, he knew the dock, he was always hanging around it, but there was always the chance he'd go straight into the road, because he used his arms, the stumps that were left, as though they were oars to propel the wagon. Nobody could see anything in this fog.

Now that he knew he was to look down, he caught a glimpse of him, the worn leather jacket, the stumps of legs, even the fierce gleam of his eyes. The girl still running, running, apparently so frightened that she could not scream. She was so close that he could hear her breathing, a quick gasping, painful to listen to, obviously too frightened, too exhausted to scream. How long had the damn fool been chasing her? He could hear the grunting sound Cat Jimmie made when he was excited.

"Hey!" Link shouted. "This way. This way!" The girl could not see him because of the fog but she headed straight toward the sound of his voice, reaching for him, close now, grabbing at him, holding on to him, clutching at his hand, his arm, her hand with a tremor in it, tremor all over her.

Cat Jimmie stopped right in front of them.

Link leaned down, said, "Get off the dock before I kick your face in," and thought, Even now, not seeing him, I'd know he was there, know exactly where he was, because of that grunting sound, fierce, excited, like his eyes, and because of the stink he gives off.

Cat Jimmie made a threatening sound in his throat.

Link said, "You goddamn bastard," and kicked at the wagon, aiming low, but not too low, thinking, I hope it's his face, and heard the wheels move away, perhaps a foot away, along the dock, and then stop.

"It's Link, ain't it?" voice hoarse, deep in his throat, then without waiting for an answer, he said, "It's Link. Thought it was."

There was the wheeling sound of the flat little cart crossing the street, and then it was gone. Link thought, Probably the only emotion that Abbie and I share, have ever shared, is complete and absolute revulsion at the sight of Cat Jimmie. I should have kicked his face in.

The girl was still gasping for breath. He turned toward the sound, impossible to see what she looked like, she could have been a wraith, a figure created by the fog and the river, insubstantial. He was fairly certain she was one of the clinker tops from China's Place. It's a strange thing, he thought, but that fat woman with the yellow skin managed to leave such a mark on her profession that all the houses run by all her successors, no matter what their names or what they call themselves, are known as China's Place, and the girls as China's girls.

He said irritably, "For Christ's sake, haven't you any sense at all? The dock isn't any place to be looking for business at this hour in the morning."

"I — " she said. "I — "

"I'm not buying any tonight."

She didn't answer, didn't move, stood there leaning against the

railing, gasping. Her hand still clutched at his arm. The fog
lifted and he got a none-too-good look at her, saw that her hair
was either bleached or dyed a pale yellow, that it curled about
her face. She must be new at China's. What the hell was a piece
of crow bait like this one doing hustling on the dock on a Saturday night.

"Go on, honey," he said and moved his arm, not gently, pulling
it away from her hand. "Beat it."

"I — " she said. "I'm afraid to."

"Ah — go on. Beat it!"

He edged away from her, moving quietly, thinking, This little
lonesome gasping female can spread her loneliness around for
some other son of a bitch to appraise and decide whether he'd buy
and at what price. The girl followed him, not really followed
him, followed the edging movement, her hand found his arm,
stayed on his arm, clutched at his arm. And he stood still.

"Look, honey," he said. "Don't follow me. There's nothing
that irritates a man faster than to be followed around by a little
lonesome female wagging her tail, especially when said tail has a
price tag affixed to it." She didn't move. "This dock belongs to
me," he went on, "I laid down a claim to it, staked it out, and
nailed it down a long time ago. You get off the reservation,
honey." Maybe she didn't understand English. "There'll be no
strike today." He took her by the arm and gave her a none-too-
gentle push toward Dumble Street. "Back to the mines, honey.
Back to those bottomless mines that China owns. When you get
there you tell China I said I can still make up my own mind as
to when I want it. I'm a big boy now. I can walk right in there
all by myself. I don't need a convoy or a note from teacher."

"Don't — " she said. "Please. I'm afraid. I left my car two
blocks away."

She was still gasping for breath, and he thought, Oh, what the
hell. I can always get her under an electric light, get a good look
at her, and then take her by the nape of the neck and drop her
in the river. "Okay, okay. Where'd you leave this car?"

They walked in the direction in which she pointed. He walked
fast, purposely. Her footsteps, light, quick, kept pace with his
though she almost ran to keep up with him, and she was still
breathing too fast. She kept looking over her shoulder, peering
into the fog. They walked about a block and a half and she said,
"Here it is."

There actually was a car, parked under the street light on the corner. A long red convertible with New York markers. She quickened her pace as they approached it, and then fumbled with the handle of the door until he opened it for her. He felt the smooth coldness of the upholstery on the inside of the door, and thought, Ha, leather, and a special job, a newer model than the one Bill used to drive. I damn near wrecked his car one night when I was very young. That was the night he used his belt on me while he delivered the Irish cop lecture. Mr. B. Hod on Irish cops. It ought to be on a record.

She fished the keys out of her pocket, and then couldn't find the ignition switch, and kept fumbling for it. So he opened the door on the other side, got in, took the keys away from her, shoved the key in place.

"Can you start it now?"

"I guess so."

"Suppose you wait a minute. Here — smoke a cigarette." Let's know the worst before we get down to first names. He struck a match and held it after he'd lighted her cigarette, and kept on holding it, staring, thinking, What the hell kind of game is this, what is a younger fairerskinned thinner more beautifully put together edition of Mamie Powther doing on the loose on Dumble Street, at this hour. Her hair was pale yellow, soft, silky, curling about her face. Mother of God, he thought, what a lovely lovely face, a lovely frightened face.

"What brought you to this end of town at this hour?"

"I was driving past and I thought I'd see what it was like down here. I'd been reading about it."

"Well, you did," he said dryly.

"Not really. Nothing happened until — "

"Until you started running for your life."

"I thought I was. It was horrible. I couldn't see because of the fog but I kept hearing something moving behind me. It kept getting closer and I started to run, and the fog lifted and I looked back and I saw that cart, and it looked like an animal and I could hear it breathing and grunting and — "

"You need a drink," he said. "Come on." And got out of the car. Any woman who thought about Cat Jimmie long enough would end up with hysterics, and this girl was much too pretty to slap. Even Abbie, who usually managed to retain her composure, lost it completely when she saw Cat Jimmie wheeling himself along the street. He knew better than Abbie what probably went on inside Cat Jimmie's mind, could realize more fully the horror of being a fullgrown male, with all the instincts and urges of the male left, and no way in the world of satisfying them. Besides, he saw him oftener than Abbie did, saw him days and nights too, lurking on the sidewalk, near the bottom of the high-stooped houses, near doorways, at curbs and street crossings, had seen him lie flat on his homemade cart and moan like an animal as he looked up under a woman's skirts, had seen women turn away and cross over on the other side of the street when they saw him sitting on the cart, his back against the wall of a build-ing. Everything about him was repulsive — the flesh on the stumps that once had been arms was red, angry, covered with scar tissue, purposely revealed, because he covered them with leather pads when he propelled himself along on his homemade cart; his shoulders were tremendous, overdeveloped. He was legless from the thighs down, and the same rawlooking angrylooking flesh was exposed to view on the stumps that were his legs. This red rawlooking flesh of the arms and legs formed a shocking contrast to the dark brown skin of his face and neck. His eyes were straight out of a nightmare — there was a red glare in them, there was excitement in them, and hate. Women who caught him in the act of looking under their skirts, moved away from him, horror on their faces, as though they had been violated, just by his eyes.

He could understand why this girl, walking beside him, through Dumble Street, past The Last Chance, still had a catch in her breath. The redorange neon sign was still on. It would be a couple of hours before Weak Knees put it out. He seemed to get a special satisfaction from turning out that sign, as though in doing it he extinguished the public side of the building and turned it into a home, private, comfortable, completely his.

They passed Abbie's house. He turned and looked back through The Hangman's branches, peering through the fog, and thought, No lights. Yes, there was. A pinkish light, dim, upstairs, in the back. He wondered if Mr. B. Hod was paying a cousinly visit on Mamie Powther, wondered how Bill and Mamie placated Pow-ther, that neat precise little man. Maybe they didn't bother. Perhaps Bill stalked into Number Six, jerking the door of Pow-ther's apartment open with that explosive suddenness that sug-gested a physical attack on the door, tied Powther in a chair, and then paid his respects to Mamie. He grinned at the thought of Powther in his neat black clothes, so decent and so proper, being forced to witness a scene that would be indecent and improper. Something about the size or the shape or the maliciousness of the grin must have reached through to the girl, disturbing her, because she said, "Did you say something?"

"No. I was thinking about a friend of mine who has a macabre sense of humor." A macabre sense of humor and no moral scruples. No scruples, moral or otherwise. No scruples and a strong right arm.

"What had you been reading about the dock that made you want to see it?"

"It wasn't just the dock. It was this whole section."

"The Narrows. The Bottom. Little Harlem. The Hollow. Eye of the Needle. Sometimes they just say Dumble Street. It all means the same thing. Where were you reading about it?"

"In the *Chronicle*. They've been running a series of articles on the relationship between bad housing and crime in this section. They used some wonderful pictures — "

Jubine's pictures. Cesar the Writing Man. Old Man John the Barber. The river. Franklin Avenue. Ah, well, he thought, it was nice to have known you and your yellow hair and your light sweet-sounding voice for these few minutes. But a female who talks about the relationship between bad housing and crime ain't for me. Abigail Crunch and F. K. Jackson have, for the last two years, been trying to tie me in the same room with one of those Vassar-Wellesley housing-crime experts. Most of them were put together all right but they talked and talked and talked about housing and crime, about Stalin and Churchill and Roosevelt and housing and crime and Churchill and Roosevelt and Stalin. And they all had names like Betty and Karen.

He had at various times lolled in F. K. Jackson's living room, upstairs over the funeral chapel, and said, Ah, yes, politely, or You don't say, No, I didn't know that, and he could tell by the expression on F. K. Jackson's face that she would like to kick him in the behind and couldn't and therefore her face kept freezing up and she kept thrusting out her jaw, and kept trying to lead the conversation around to dancing or Canasta and the little item from Vassar-Wellesley would keep right on talking about housing and crime.

There had been one who went to Bennington, too. The one from Bennington was a doctor's daughter from Washington, D.C., who most mysteriously and most illogically came to spend the weekend with F. K. Jackson. The doctor's daughter was one of those young brown editions of Marlene, the brown making for a little more voluptuousness, brown skin, smooth skin, lovely skin, and the doctor's daughter had long lovely legs, they undoubtedly started feeding her orange juice and Vitamin D at the proper age of six weeks, long lovely legs and a sweet little behind and we went swimming in the river, diving off the dock, and she could swim and dive and dance and sing and had a face like an angel. She was going to be a dancer, so she talked about the Czar and the Russian Ballet, about Stalin and the Russian Ballet and the Sadler's Wells and Bach and Beethoven. Dedicated. All of them were dedicated. They were so goddam grim about it he could only sit back and try to kid their pants off. The ballet one, when he kissed her, merely shook her head, and said, "I haven't got time for that sort of thing, Link," and she sounded just like a schoolteacher, gentle reprobation in her voice.

The most beautiful one of all was going to be an engineer. Why would the good God take the time and the trouble to put together a female in such a careful beautiful lovely way and then give her the idea of being an engineer? This one walking through Dumble Street with him, this one walking beside him, the one with the silky hair, was probably going to be a doctor or a dentist, maybe a veterinarian. A dentist with that hair would be something extra, "Hey, Doc, move your head, your hair's fallin' in my face."

This one was probably a doctor's daughter, too. The new aristocracy, the new black aristocracy, had been spawned by medical schools. "My father is a doctor," they loved to say it. Ha! Some day he would stare at one of the prideful little females who said that, and ask if her daddy made his pile peddling dope or peddling abortions.

"Do you go there very often? Down on the dock?" the girl asked.

"Yeah."

Silence again. Then she said, "It's foggy, isn't it?"

"It is foggy," he said solemnly. And now I will pay you back, you littlelonesome female stranger, I will pay you back for being interested in bad housing and crime — what was it you said — the relationship between bad housing and crime. Good God. "Yeah, it's foggy. It's a night for murder, a night for rape, or any other dark midnight deed that needs concealment."

Then he said politely, "Do you live around here?"

"No, I don't. I live at the other end of the city. I came down here to look at the river."

Down? he thought. This is up from the other end of town. Don't you know that uptown means us dark folks? That's the second time you've said that. And you don't belong around here, honey, or you'd know that simple fact, that difference. Furthermore, if you really lived in Monmouth you wouldn't be looking at the Dumble Street end of the river at two o'clock in the morning. You'd know better. If your daddy was a doctor, as I suspect he was, he would have taught you better. To the tune of the hickory stick. That's how they always teach the very young. Besides you lie in your teeth. You don't live in Connecticut. You've got New York markers on your car. Maybe you stole it.

They turned into Franklin Avenue. He said, "We can get a drink in here," and guided her toward the door of The Moonbeam.

5

● THE MOONBEAM was crowded all the way back to the door.
Standing in the doorway, he kept his hand on the girl's arm, as
he looked around to see if there was even so much as an inch of
unoccupied space. Yes, he thought, filled with people, filled with
noise, blast from the jukebox, rattle of dishes, clink of silver, roar
of voices; filled with smells, too, beer, cigarette smoke, cheap perfume, and smells from the kitchen, greasy dish water, unwashed
icebox, strong yellow soap. Quite a mixture. Not too much light
in the place, bluish pinkish light from the wall lamps, so dim it
barely illuminated the big room, gave it the effect of a cave.
Waiters hurried through the cave, bumping into the chairs, the
tables, the customers, beer slopping over on the trays, the tables.
They all drank beer because it was cheap and if you drank enough
of it, you could get a slight jag on and if you got a slight jag on,
the little floosey you'd picked up over on Franklin began to look
like Marlene, and the thin straight legs began to look like Marlene's legs, and the toobig stuckout can began to look like
Marlene's. Roar of voices again. People had to talk too loud, to
shout, to make themselves heard over the racket made by the
fans. They kept the fans going all the time, winter and summer,
had to or the customers would suffocate from the smell, smells
they brought in with them, smells indigenous to the place. Noisy
fans. Noisy exhaust in the dirty kitchen.

It was a little too early for a fight to start, the boys really hadn't got enough beer under their belts. After you drank enough beer you would get a jag on and if you got a jag on you could convince yourself you packed a punch like Old Man Louis had when he was young and you said Joe and people knew who you were talking about. But Old One-One ran The Moonbeam and he could stop a fight before it really got started. He had been a wrestler and a stevedore and a weightlifter, or so people said, anyway he looked like Gargantua and he got his name from the fact that he had never been seen anywhere, any time, any place, with a woman. One of the Geechie boys from South Carolina named him Old One-One explaining that where he came from that's what they called the red-wing blackbird — the males and females gathered in separate flocks in the fall and winter, so that the male was always found without a female, only he was strictly obscene about it.

Old One-One was a dirty fighter so that even with a jag on, even having convinced yourself that you were Old Man Louis, but young and fast, a part of your mind would tick off a warning, reminding you of the stories about Old One-One, how he'd grab a bottle and smash it on the bar and go for you with the jagged end, or get out his blackjack, or trip you and once you were down, do his damndest to kick your teeth down your throat, so that even though you were fogged up with beer, once you saw Old One-One plowing toward you through the crowded noisy Moonbeam, you quit believing you were Old Man Louis and left by a side door, because part of your mind remembered all the business about smashed skulls and ruptured kidneys and ruined testicles.

The Moonbeam Café. It belonged to Bill Hod, like a lot of other places, though Link hadn't known it in the days when he was what the law calls a minor, and had sneaked in for a glass of beer, thinking Bill would never know about it. Old One-One belonged to Mr. B. Hod, too, like a lot of other people.

Link suddenly thrust out an arm, stopping one of the hurrying waiters, "Hey, Bug Eyes," he said. "Where can I find a place to sit?"

"In the back, Sonny. Go all the way in the back. All the way in the back. I'll squush some of 'em out of the way with a table."

Bug Eyes moved off, having barely looked up, balancing his tray, high up, arm bent stiff, hurrying toward the back of the Moonbeam, toward the bar. By the time Link and the girl squeezed through the crowd, avoiding tables, stepping over legs, Bug Eyes had a table in place, and two chairs, close to each other. "What'll you have, Sonny? What'll you have?"

"Well?" Link looked at the girl.

"Rye. With soda."

"Okay, Bug. Two. Double rye. Soda."

"Gotcha, gotcha." Bug Eyes was already hurrying away as he said it.

"What's your name?" the girl asked. She had been looking around, at the people sitting close by, now she looked at Link and her expression changed.

"Link Williams." What's the matter with her now? She looks scared out of her wits. If she's got the nerve to wander around on the dock at two in the morning what the hell is there in The Moonbeam to scare her. All good sociologists study the critters at first hand, and true the place is noisy, and true the stink in here is terrific — but these are The People.

"Link?" she said it with an obvious effort. "Is that a nickname?"

"Yeah. A contraction of Lincoln." The Emancipator with the big toobig bony hands, the sad deepset eyes, the big bony hands almost always resting on the outsize knees, an outsize man with outsize ideas. Man of the people. Something wrong with his glands. Overdeveloped? Underdeveloped? All men free and equal pursuit of happiness — words on paper and he believed them. Emancipation Proclamation Williams. Named after him. Why? The women name the children, reward for services rendered, award for valor, for the act of birth, the act of creation. So the creator names the child. What did my mother mean? What was it? Act of gratitude? A way of saying thankyou? Or perhaps some of the males in her own family had been named Lincoln and so she, without thought, without real purpose, simply gave the name to her male child. Lincoln Williams. The name handed on without the trace of a recollection of who or what or how or why, no special meaning, forgotten, long since. Perhaps never known?

He was about to ask her what her name was, though he would have been quite willing to go on calling her Honey, but sometimes the female preferred, or at least pretended to prefer, to retain some trace of the amenities by saying I'm so-and-so, who are you, though what the hell difference it made, only a female would know. But Bug Eyes came toward them just then, moving slowly.

He always ran. Link forgot all about the girl's name, wondering what had slowed Bug Eyes down.

It was the girl, the girl with the silky pale yellow hair. Bug was looking at her, looking at her in the most curious fashion, a covert, all-embracing, analytical stare that transferred itself elsewhere so quickly that Link would have been unaware of this swift appraisal if he hadn't been watching him. Almost immediately his eyes went blank, curtained, but something very like hostility showed in his face.

Link looked at the girl too, critically, analytically, and saw then what Bug had seen and wondered why Bug had seen it so quickly and he hadn't. He had talked to her, walked at least two blocks with her, entered The Moonbeam with her, consulted her about her choice of drinks, without seeing what Bug had seen in one swift glance. He studied her face. If it hadn't been for that wary immediate knowledge in Bug's eyes, there one minute and blanked out the next, would he, Link, have known that she was white? No. Why did the knowledge come to Bug at first glance and to him only now at second hand? Bug hadn't looked at the girl when they came in the place, or when they sat down. Bug was older, more experienced. Nuts. Because? Well, Bug had been born in the South, had lived in the South where his wellbeing, yea, verily, his life would depend on his ability to recognize a white woman when he saw one.

But how could he or Bug or anybody else be certain? He'd seen colored girls with hair as blond and silky, with eyes as blue and skin as white, as this girl's. The colored ones, the Vassar-Wellesley-Bennington colored ones talked just as glibly about crime and bad housing as this little female he had taken in tow.

Take Mamaluke Hill's mother, that is if you wanted to take something for some reason, she was just as blond and blue-eyed as the girl sitting beside him in The Moonbeam. She was the wife of the Franklin Avenue Baptist minister. When the Hills first came to Monmouth, first took over the Franklin Avenue Baptist Church, there was enough energy used up in head shaking and eyebrow raising to run a Diesel motor as people asked: Is she or isn't she? Mamaluke was a skinny brown boy and when Mamaluke's blue-eyed mother showed up at the grammar school on Parents' Visiting Day, the entire school was thrown into shock, because it didn't seem possible or reasonable or logical that she could be the mother of Matthew Mark Luke John Acts-of-the-

Apostles Son-of-Zebedel Garden-of-Gethsemane Hill, known as
Mamaluke Hill. For short. Mamaluke's pappy was a big black
man who sweated easily, and shouted easily, too, you could hear
him all up and down Franklin Avenue, every Sunday morning,
shouting in a voice like thunder, about hell fire and damnation
and the Blood of the Lamb, getting louder and louder as he
worked up to a climax, and just before he got there, he took his
coat off, stopping right in the middle of the preaching to take his
coat off, telling the sisters and the brothers that he had just
broken out all over in a good Baptist sweat. Hallelujah!

Mrs. Ananias Hill was colored but her skin was as white as the
skin of this little frightened one staring at the glass of whiskey on
the table in front of her. He thought, What in hell does she see
in here that makes her look as though she were drowned in fear?
She was staring at the people who were packed in around the
bar and he looked too. Nothing to see but a lot of young men and
young women draining beer glasses.

"What's the matter?" he asked. Because she was now staring
at him in the same way. If she'd been under water for a long
time, a month or so, and then slowly floated to the surface, she
couldn't look more drowned than she does at this moment. "Are
you all right?"

She nodded, apparently unable to speak, and he frowned. What
the hell will I do with her if she passes out in here? Where can
I take her? How explain her? And then — Is she or isn't she?
How can I decide? How know? Mrs. Hill? Dumble Street said
that Old Hell and Damnation Hill didn't know himself whether
his wife was white or colored and snickered, playing endless varia-
tions on a theme — she was white as the Lamb and the Reverend
Ananias was black as the pit itself. Abbie made up her mind
about Mrs. Hill when Mamaluke was christened. F. K. Jackson
went to the christening and came back and told Abbie about it.

F. K. Jackson: They christened him Matthew Mark Luke John
Acts-of-the-Apostles Son-of-Zebedel Garden-of-Gethsemane Hill.

Abbie (long silence): No question about it. She's colored. (another long silence) What will they call him for — well, for everyday use?

F. K. Jackson: His basket name is Mamaluke.

Abbie (absolute outrage in voice): Basket name? What's that?

F. K. Jackson: A kind of pet name that they give an infant until
such time as he's baptized and his christened name is officially

fastened to him. They use the pet name lest an evil spirit learn his real name and turn him into a changeling.

He studied the girl again. White? Colored? Her hair had a wonderful shimmer but — so did Abbie's. He wondered what that pale yellow hair would feel like to touch. Was she or wasn't she? She had slipped off her coat and the dress she wore was made of some kind of dark velvetylooking stuff. She had a long thin senseless scarf about her shoulders, pale green in color, shot through with metal threads that glinted in the dim light. He wondered whom she belonged to and where she had been going in the longskirted coat, with that thin flimsy scarf around her shoulders. So he asked her.

"I was going to a dinner party and I changed my mind. I drove all the way to New York and then I changed my mind."

"Oh." Her voice, on the dock, had been frightened, her breathing a kind of gasping, but now, she was panic-stricken, there was a frantic hurried note in her voice, she kept repeating words and phrases, didn't seem to be able to stop talking.

"When I got in Monmouth I kept driving thinking I would find some place — where I could see the river — and then the fog kept getting thicker — the fog — thicker and thicker — I got out of the car at the dock and walked through some of the streets — and I read the street signs and I decided to look around — look around — but I didn't see anything much — the streets looked like the streets in any other city — then I came back to the dock and the fog was so thick I couldn't see — but I kept hearing — kept hearing — that funny noise — and it kept getting closer and closer — and — " Her voice broke, as though she were about to cry.

"Cut it out. Here, finish your drink and let's get out of here."

She picked up the whiskey and soda and her hand was trembling, and she tried to steady it and spilled part of the drink on the table, and then drank quickly, obviously not liking it, because she made an involuntary face, as though her throat rejected the taste of the stuff. And he, watching her, wondering about her, said, "Shall we go now?"

Outside, on the sidewalk, she said, "Oh! — the fog. It's still foggy," and the gasp was back in her voice. "Which way — I can't even tell which way we came — "

"I could walk it blindfold. Put your hand on my arm." He guided her through the fog, and he thought, She could be purple

or blue in this fog, in this can't-see-your-hand-before-your-face fog.
All cats are gray in the dark. B. Franklin. The cat would eate
fish but would not wet her feete. When all candles bee out, all
cats bee gray. John Heywood. White women is all froze up.
Weak Knees. Quote from L. Williams? No comment. No
quotes. L. Williams shared J. Heywood's opinion: When all
candles bee out —

He said, "We turn here. This is Dumble Street."

"I thought it would lift, that the fog would lift, while we were
inside. It's even thicker — what's that?" She jumped and looked
back over her shoulder.

"Nothing but the foghorn. Car on Franklin Avenue."

She kept looking back as though she expected to see Cat Jimmie behind her, not see him but hear him. How the hell was she
going to drive, drive through this damn fog, shivering and shaking? I can't go off and leave her sitting in that car on Dock
Street, she'd be dead of hysterics by morning.

She said, "The fog — " And stopped.

He thought, the fog, the fog, the fog. She sounds like a record
that's stuck. "Listen," he said. "It's even more upsetting when
the weather or the degree of light changes while you're inside a
place." That's fine, my boy, keep talking, talk fast, before she
starts screaming her lovely little head off. "I remember going to
a movie when I was a kid. I'd never been to one before. When I
went inside the theater it was daylight and when I came out it
was dark. It seemed all wrong. I thought time should have
stopped while I watched the movie. But it hadn't. It got dark
just as it always does."

When he opened the door of her car, she made no effort to get
in. She said, "Would you — would you — like to go for a ride?"

"Not especially."

"I can't drive through this horrible fog — alone. I keep seeing
that thing on the little cart, keep hearing its breathing, keep
wondering if I'll be able to run any more — "

"All right." She started to get in the car, behind the steering
wheel and he put his hand on her arm, thrusting her aside, suddenly bored with the whole thing, the girl, the car, the fog, the
hysterics, Cat Jimmie, Dumble Street. "I'll drive."

He let her get in by herself, let her close the door on the
other side by herself. Then he turned the car around, went
through Dumble Street, past The Last Chance, dark now, turned

into Franklin Avenue, went past The Moonbeam, still lighted. "You've driven one of these before."

"Yeah." One of these, nice way to put it. Oh, you've held a tennis racket before, oh, you've worn shoes before, oh, you've used a toothbrush before. Bug Eyes is a weisenheimer but he was right. The lady is white. That surprised condescension in the voice is an unmistakable characteristic of the Caucasian, a special characteristic of the female Caucasian. The funny thing is they don't even know they do it.

Yeah, he'd driven one of these before and damn near smashed it up. When he was sixteen. That one belonged to Mr. B. Hod. Then when he finished college, Abbie gave him the Major's solid gold watch and the Major's diamond stickpin, reward for finishing, reward for the Phi Beta Kappa key that he had never worn; and Mr. B. Hod presented him with a brandnew shiny Cadillac convertible. Special Job. Bill said, "I didn't think you'd make it. Mark of respect, Sonny."

Abbie stood on the front steps and frowned at the car when she saw it, obviously not liking its size, its shape, its color, its make. Sun shining on the car, making the dark red finish glisten. "It looks like a gambler's car," she said.

"It is," F. K. Jackson said and sniffed, snorted, and the thick-lensed glasses glinted in the sunlight.

And now here with him, beside him, in the same make car, a female smelling of something exquisite. Flowers. Which flowers? The nightblooming stock that Abbie grew in her garden. At dusk the backyard was — well, not filled with the scent because there was always the smell of the river, but if you walked close to the flower border on a hot night in August the smell arrested you, challenged you, made you stand motionless, sniffing the air in disbelief. Your heart beat a little faster. Your breath came a little faster. Because you evoked images in your mind, of women, not short, not plump, not tall, not bony, but the height just right, the bone structure perfect, the amount of flesh covering the bones absolutely right, absolutely perfect. And for a moment, only for a moment, and it was, of course, an illusion, an illusion wrought of the moonlight, the white light, curious, unreal, mysterious light of the moon and the sweet thick incredible smell of the stock, you believed that if you reached out your hand you would touch a woman, not short and plump and erect and full of pride and un-touchable because of morals and religion and impossible standards of cleanliness and righteousness and not tall and bony and nervous and too astute and alert, too logical and too masculine, but a just right, soft to the touch, sweetsmelling, beautifully put together female, with all the parts in the right place, never the look as though if touched, the bone that lay just beneath the skin would reject the hand because of the unyielding quality of the bone or that the flesh would reject the hand because of the righteousness, the pridefulness of the flesh.

The girl sitting beside him was silent. He glanced at her and her eyes were on the road, or what could be seen of the road, the fog so thick the headlights of the car couldn't cut through the white vapor. She was sitting with her legs crossed and he could see the sheer sheer stockings over the lovely ankles, the skirt flaring over the calves of the lovely legs. And he thought he had never seen one quite so beautifully put together — like a swimmer or a racehorse or an airplane, all the essential parts in the exact right place. Lovely.

The car had veered to the right, even in that brief moment in which he took his eyes off the road to look at her. It was a damn fool business to be driving on a night like this anyway, watching or trying to watch what he could see of the black line that was the center of the road, maintaining a thirty mile an hour pace; he stepped it up to thirty-five. Not safe. Slowed down to thirty, slow steady pace. He became aware of the sound of the motor, hum, hum, hum, on and on, eyes on the black line dividing the road. Occasionally he glanced off to the right, toward the shoulder of the road, and when he looked that way the car went off to the right, seemingly of its own volition. Hum of motor, slow steady motion, slow steady pace, slow steady motion, slow, steady, thin black line in the center of the road, graywhite of the concrete barely visible, headlights not strong enough to cut through the fog, fog swallowing the lights. He shifted the wheel sharply to the left because for a fraction of a second he had gone to sleep, dozed off, watching that black line.

I've got to change this pace, he thought, go faster or go slower, sing or whistle or talk, or I'll go to sleep, hypnotized watching that black line. Go to sleep and drive smack into the side of somebody's house, drive right into the front porch, the sunporch, over the straw-matting rug they put on sunporches, right into the glider they put on sunporches, knock over the plants, crashbang as the plants go over, always have plants on sunporches. It's a little early for breakfast though. Wonder what the farmer in the dell would say if a gentleman of color accompanied by a lady not of color should arrive suddenly on the sunporch, driving right up into the sunporch.

Good morning. We came for breakfast.

Ah, but your colors don't match. We will not serve breakfast to a lady and a gentleman who are of a color, who have colors, one of whom is colored, and one of whom is not. Don't match.

They may all look alike in the fog, brother, but not under electric light.

Besides it wouldn't be the farmer in the dell who would give expression to his outrage at the sight of the unmatched colors of the male and the female encased in the red convertible. The farmer takes a wife. It would be the farmer's wife who would shriek and scream at the sight of them.

Scarlet woman! Whore of Babylon!

Say not so, farmer's wife, wife of the farmer in the dell. I found her on the dock. She was a lost and lonely one, a little running lonely little lost one on the loose on the dock in Niggertown. I am here by her invitation. It was not of my making nor of hers, farmer's wife. It was the hand of Fate. It was an Act of God.

I have not laid even so much as the finger of my left hand upon the finger of her left hand. It was, in fact, the other way around. It was she who held on to me, who clutched me to her bosom. She has a lovely lovely bosom. Has she not, farmer's wife? She would not let me go. It was not of my doing at all at all. I was merely the instrument, the vessel, the clay in the potter's hand and the potter turned the wheel, the little wheel run by Fate and the big wheel run by the grace of God. I saved her from a fate worse than death. Actually he only wanted to look. He could not walk, has not walked for years. But she did not know that.

You see? You see how it was, wife of the farmer in the dell? You ask the farmer. He knows about such matters. He will tell you. The old Adam left in him will immediately recognize the situation and he will nod his head and he will tell you, It was the woman.

He dozed off again, and the car went imperceptibly toward the right, way over toward the right-hand side of the road. He jerked himself awake. Jesus, he thought, I've got to talk or I'll be in a firstclass position to find out whether Old Hell and Damnation Hill was right about the blackness of the Pit. He glanced at the

girl again, and then back at the black line in the center of the
road. She had the concentrated look of someone contemplating
the past or the future. It won't make any difference what I talk
about. She won't hear me. She's looking into her own personal
crystal ball. Well, honey, I'll take mine out, too.

He said, "I started to tell you about the time I saw my first
movie." He paused. She didn't even turn her head, and that was
okay, because he wouldn't have to worry about making sense. He
could just talk. "I never quite got over it." Weak Knees was
shocked when he found out Link had never been to a movie,
"Name-a-God, Sonny, here's a buck, you go this afternoon, down
to the Emporium. And buy yourself some chocolit to eat. Name-
a-God, Sonny, a kid your age ain't never seen a movie."

He went to the matinee. Saturday afternoon. He couldn't remember much about the picture but there had lingered in him
down through the years a faint echo of the excitement, the amaze-
ment that had grown in him as he stared at the screen.

"It was broad daylight when I went into the Emporium. I was
only a kid. And I remember that I stopped and looked at the
sunlight on the pillars in front of the place."

He had paused to look at the flickering, moving sunlight on the
big white pillars. It filtered through the leaves and branches of
the elm trees and because the leaves kept moving, the sunlight
moved or seemed to. If he stared hard enough and long enough
he could convince himself that it wasn't the sunlight or the leaves
that moved but the pillars themselves, moving in small irregular
places.

It had occurred to him that the pillars might actually be disintegrating, breaking up into leaf-shaped bits, branch-shaped sections. He thought about Samson pulling down the pillars to
which he'd been chained. He touched one of the big columns
with his hands to reassure himself. When those other pillars
came down, the ones Samson had been so tightly chained to,
they probably broke up into bits and separate parts like these sun-
lit, moving pillars seemed to be doing.

"I touched one of the pillars. Because the sun made them look
as though they were moving. It was made of wood. The pillar.
It was an awful shock. I almost forgot that I was going to my
first movie. I thought those pillars were marble, stone, that they
would be cold to the touch. Instead they were wood. Warm,
almost yielding when compared to the feel of stone."

He had stared up at the column in utter disbelief. It mounted straight up to the roof of the building. There were nine others, spaced along the front at intervals. He couldn't help himself, he had to touch each one of them. They were all made of wood. He felt cheated, defrauded, and angry, too.

"I began to wonder if there were other things I hadn't known about, other things that weren't what they seemed to be. People kept going past me, in through the big doors while I stood staring up at those columns, trying to figure out what other things there were that were something else. It made me furious to find out that a thing could look like something else, not be the thing I had always believed it to be."

Freckled Willie Pratt came bursting out through the door and grabbed him by the arm and said, "Hey, Link, come on in. The pitcher's goin' to start. Mis' Bushnell just set down to the organ with her music and me and Johnnie been spreadin' across three seats in the front row tryin' to save one for you. Come on because he can't keep spreadin' over three seats by himself and somebody's goin' to grab one of them front seats sure. Come on."

When he got inside the music was loud and strong, and everybody got quiet, and he began to get a prickly feeling all over down his back. Then he forgot about the music. Because the picture started and he was gazing into a new and wonderful world, looking straight into it, and as he looked he became a part of it. It was the kind of world that he had suspected must exist somewhere, but here was the proof. The sight of it pulled him forward until he was sitting on the very edge of the hard wooden chair. He held tight to the sides of the chair because he was afraid that if he didn't he would float off around the ceiling, he had grown so light and buoyant. He had left everything solid and commonplace and ordinary that composed his everyday world far behind him.

When the picture ended, the lights came on in the hall. Mrs. Bushnell played some fast, lively march music on the organ, so fast and so lively that the kids got out of their seats, fast, like the music. There was a stir around him, feet scraping on the floor, giggles, talk, scrambling for position, and then the kids were plunging into the aisles. He was pushed out of his seat, caught up, carried along, by the general movement toward the door. He wasn't aware that he was walking or moving his feet and legs, he did it automatically, without thought, really not of his own volition at all. It was like sleepwalking, a trance.

"I went in the Emporium and it was daylight when I went in. When I came out it was dark. It confused me because I thought time should have come to a stop while the movie was being shown. I kept thinking that somehow I had been leading a double life, my own life as the boy Link Williams, and another far more exciting life. The fact that it got dark while I was in the world that was the movie made the whole thing very strange."

Afterwards he stood on the steps of the Emporium, shaking with excitement.

He heard a woman say, "Good picture, wasn't it?"

A man said, "Sure was. The feller who climbed up to the top of the ship was okay."

That was all they said about the picture. Someone else said, "Think it's goin' to rain?"

They all looked up at the sky. Even the kids. He realized then that for them the picture was over and done with. No part of its glory lingered in their minds. But because all of them were looking up, he did too. Far off at the edge of the sky, but faintly, because of the big bright lights outside the Emporium, he could see the evening star.

It looked very small and faint and faraway in the dark sky. Yet the sight of it reassured him. That star could be seen in distant places. Someday, he didn't know when it would be, but someday he would see those places, those big cities with their easily found adventures. As he waited his turn to go down the steps, he tried to find appropriate words to express the feeling that had enveloped him while he was looking at the picture.

The only words that seemed to fit, that were fine words with a special high sound to them were "the power and the glory." He was shocked when he remembered that these words came from the Lord's Prayer. He couldn't quite place them at first and when he did he debated with himself as to whether it was proper to use them ordinary like that in reference to something that had nothing to do with God or the church or Sunday School.

He never did decide about the right or wrong of it. He had to use those words because they summed up how he felt about the new, fabulous, exciting world he'd just looked at, been a part of, could almost touch. A world of buildings, high up, with thousands of people moving around, of traffic so heavy it snarled up constantly, shifting, moving, getting hopelessly entangled and then moving on again. Ships pulled into a dock the like of which he hadn't dreamed existed and the city itself stretched out behind the dock for miles, with its buildings pushing up against the very sky itself.

"I never quite got over it," he said. "I made up my mind then that someday I would conquer the world — don't ask me what world. I believed that the only thing that would ever stop me would be the fact that some other guys got there first. I didn't believe that was possible. I didn't believe there was anybody as smart and as tough as I was anywhere, any time, any place. Or ever would be. So I would get there first. I would conquer the world."

"Don't you believe it any more?"

Her voice startled him. Oh, he thought, so you were listening all the time. I thought I was talking to myself. "Honey," he said, "I'm the day man behind the bar in The Last Chance. And I'm perfectly content to be just that and nothing more. Any itch I ever had in my soul, any run-around I ever had in my heel, I lost when I grew up. You only get those world-conqueror ideas when you're eight years old. After that — uh-uh."

"Why did you feel as though you could conquer the world?"

"I don't know exactly. That was a long time ago and I was just a kid. All I remember is that I had seen a new world, found a new world, a new continent, and like all discoverers I decided to conquer it, make it mine. That's all. Kind of feeble. But that's the way it was."

"What was the name of the movie?"

The fog had begun to lift, he could see both sides of the road and he increased the speed of the car.

"That's gone, too, vanished down the long corridor of time. Like a lot of other things."

He stopped talking, aware that she was looking at him, straight at him, staring, really. Probably trying to make sense out of what he'd said.

She said, "I'm all right now. This is far enough. Turn around and go back."

He went on driving as though he hadn't heard her, driving faster and faster, thinking, She sounded exactly as though she were talking to a chauffeur. Home, James. Well, James had taken off his uniform and cap, James was now wearing flannel pants and a striped T-shirt and James was all set to drive to hell and back and had every intention of taking the madam with him because he wasn't working there any more. He had quit and the madam was

— well — when all candles bee out all cats bee gray. Under electric light? No. Strong hot light of the sun? No. But in the dark, in the dark —

She said, sharpness in her voice, arrogance in her voice, something else he couldn't quite give a name to, not as uncontrolled as rage, but controlled rage, rage because the chauffeur was late, the chauffeur talked back, was impudent, impertinent, had to be put in his place, "I want to go back. Stop and turn the car around."

"This ride wasn't my idea, honey," he said softly. "But I'm beginning to enjoy it. So I plan to ride a long while yet. I'm afraid there isn't a damn thing you can do about it except go along, too."

It was so late that there were no other cars on the highway. On the straight stretches he shoved the speedometer up to eighty. He waited for her to protest but she didn't. Her hands were clenched into fists, and her body was braced, stiffened, against the seat as though against an expected attack. He kept following the river. He would drive forty more miles before he turned back. The girl still said nothing.

She's scared, he thought. She's scared deaf, dumb, and blind. She thinks I'm going to rape her. I'm due to rape her, or try to, because I'm colored and it's written in the cards that colored men live for the sole purpose of raping white women, especially young beautiful white women who are on the loose. How do I know she's on the loose? Well, what the hell was she doing at the dock? She'd scream for help if there was anybody to hear her, and there isn't, so she's braced herself, waiting.

He turned down a side road, parked the car, cut the motor off. The soft hum of the motor had been like a not-listened-to conversation, like a radio tuned low, you didn't pay attention to it until it stopped, and then you wanted to turn it on again, wanted the conversation you hadn't been listening to to continue because the stillness was disturbing. He heard the girl sigh, well, not sigh, but as she exhaled she made a small sound, anxious, afraid.

They sat in the car, silent, both of them, for perhaps five minutes. He was grinning, though the girl could not see the grin. She had moved so far away from him, must have moved away, slowly, imperceptibly, for he had been unaware of any movement, that she was jammed up against the door, had one hand on the door.

Then he stopped grinning because for one moment, one long incredible moment he wanted to, he wanted to — Heat behind his eyes, thick hot feeling in his throat, blood pounding in his ears. He leaned toward the girl, the perfume that was like the smell of stock drawing him toward her, the impulse absolutely uncontrollable now, like standing waiting, years ago, in the hallway at China's Place, waiting, and not thinking, not able to think. He watched her fumble with the handle of the door. Ah, the hell with it, he thought, and started the car — viciously.

He did not speak again until they were back in Monmouth, back at the corner of Franklin Avenue and Dumble Street. He said, "I wouldn't go sightseeing on the Dumble Street dock any more if I were you."

Then he got out of the car, slammed the door, hard, as though he hoped the hinges would tear loose, said, in a matter-of-fact voice, "Thanks for the buggy ride."

6

● LINK WILLIAMS was standing on the dock again, his coat collar turned up, leaning against the piling. He had turned the collar of his coat up about an hour before, and even as he did it thought that no cloth had ever been woven that could deflect the icy wind blowing in from the river. Jubine, the photographer, stood beside him, facing the river, waiting for something extraordinary to happen, just as he did every night.

Link was waiting for something extraordinary to happen, too. He was waiting for the girl to come back, had been waiting, night after night, for two weeks, in spite of fog and rain and cold winds. He kept telling himself that it was illogical, it was against all reason, because no one would return to a place like this, a place where the night spewed forth creatures like Cat Jimmie.

Jubine knew that he was waiting for someone, looking for someone, because each night after he got on his motorcycle and adjusted his goggles, he always said the same thing: "Not tonight, eh, hombre? Ah, well, perhaps another night." And then was gone, putt-putting down Dock Street, going faster and faster, the motor making a sound like a series of gun shots.

At the end of two weeks, having stared at the river, having been stared at by Jubine, having listened to the foghorn and the hoarse hoot of the barges, having listened to the sound of the river like a mouth sucking against the wood of the pilings, having watched the big door of The Last Chance swing open, swing shut, having been wet, having been cold, he gave it up. On a Saturday night. Late.

He crossed Dock Street, heading toward the poker game at The Last Chance. At the door he turned, why he did not know, perhaps just habit, perhaps he turned and looked toward the dock whenever he was on Dumble Street, perhaps some sixth sense told him he would see what he had been waiting to see. Her car was parked near the dock. He looked once, made certain that it was the same car, and shoved the door open and went inside.

Mr. B. Hod and Mr. Weak Knees were getting ready to close up for the night. Jubine was standing at the bar, studying Old Man John the Barber. Bill had evidently booted everybody else home. Old Man John the Barber was nursing a beer, and watching Bill's every move, his lower lip thrust out, his eyes fierce under the shaggy eyebrows, one foot rested on the polished brass rail, the shoes discolored, worn, dusty. His suit coat, once black, was now gray in color, the back hiked up, the sleeves the exact shape of his arms, especially at the elbows.

Link said, "Is it safe to come in here?"

Bill ignored him, ignored Jubine's delighted grin.

Jubine said, "Sure. Safe as a convent. The boss threw a big peon out on his can about an hour ago and damn near broke his neck. A big Swede peon. And his neck made a lovely grinding sound as it very nearly separated in two straight clean pieces. So everything's fine now. Cozy. Homelike."

When Bill opened the door, opening it the way he always opened doors, as though he were attacking it, the clock over the bar said ten minutes to two.

"What you closin' up so early for, Bill? It ain't closin' time," Old Man John the Barber protested. "I ain't got a God's place else to go but here." He hunched over a little farther, blinking his eyes as he looked out at the dark cold windswept street.

Bill kept turning out lights. "Okay, Barber," he said. "You can stay in any of those Saturday night jump joints over on Franklin until three or four o'clock. By that time your wife'll be asleep and you'll have some place to go. You can go home. Okay, Barber, out you go."

In the kitchen, they waited for Weak Knees to brew the coffee. Bill Hod sat down at the kitchen table, shuffling a deck of cards, brandnew deck. Link and Jubine stayed near the stove, watching

Weak Knees. He moved quickly despite his shambling gait. Link thought, They're all at their favorite occupations. Jubine is measuring the light in here, measuring it with his eyes, eyes half closed as he studies Weak Knees. Mr. W. Knees has the dedicated look of a high priest, performing his rites, stove serves as altar, big copper hood over the stove, gives it the gleam and the apartness of an altar. Mr. B. Hod is listening to the music of the cards, swishslish, swish-slish, fast motion, too fast, eye cannot follow but ear can hear.

Kitchen now filled with the fragrance of fresh-brewed coffee. Funny thing, both gentlemen tried hard, did their damndest, to hand their heart's true love on to me — but I wasn't built for it. I still can't make a deck of cards swish-slish like that. And I can't cook. They worked at it though. I used to polish that copper hood when I was a kid, stand on top of the stove, fire out, pink outside sheets of a tabloid newspaper on the stove for me to stand on, so that I always had pictures of bigbosomed cuties under my feet as I rubbed and rubbed the copper. Had to put a chair on top of the stove to reach the top of the hood. L. Williams, the acrobat-acolyte. Liked the job, too, liked the glow and the gleam of the copper, stood on the chair, way up high, and turned to look down at the pots and pans hanging on the wall, liked the glow of them, too, the glow and the gleam. Acrobat-acolyte standing on a chair polishing the copper hood. But Mr. W. Knees said I'd never make a chef-cook. And I didn't. Heart not in it. Swishslish of the new deck. Heart not in that either. Girl with pale blond hair looking for the acolyte at the dock. He grinned. Heart in that though.

Jubine said, "Now what canary have you just eaten, Sonny?"

He grinned again because he couldn't help it. "I haven't yet. But I will, Bud. I have only just got the lovely creature within gunsight."

"Come on, let's get the game started," Bill said. "You guys mess around too much. We haven't had a decent game for two weeks. Sonny's got to watch the river, hunting canaries. Jubine's got to run to a fire or a wake or a suicide."

"I'm always right here, Boss. Ready, willin' and able," Weak Knees said. "I ain't never cut the heart outta the game by not showin' up."

Bill said, "Yeah, you're here when you're not cuttin' the heart out of the game by trying out a new kind of spaghetti."

"That last one was good," Weak Knees' voice, normally high-pitched, dropped a whole register, it had a note of reverence in it. "Best spaghetti I ever laid my lip over. Had salt pork and mushrooms in it. I never done it like that before. And about a peck of parsley. Some American white lady brought that receipt over from Brussels. She got it from a Eyetalian chef-cook. Say, where is Brussels?"

"In Belgium," Jubine said. "When you going to make it again?"

"If I'da been that Eyetalian chef-cook I never woulda give that receipt away. Never tasted nothing like it before. Make it again? Let's see. I'll be makin' that Belgium Eyetalian spaghetti again on Saturday. This Saturday comin' up. I'll make it for after the poker game. Sonny, you goin' to be here for the game or are you goin' to be chasin' canaries around on the dock?"

Link said, "I'll let you know."

Weak Knees frowned. "I never knew they had no canaries around the dock. I ain't never seen none."

Jubine laughed. "You're too old to see 'em. You got to be about twenty-six, like Link. You got to have a build straight from the Greek, like Link. And you got to have one of those Pied Piper speaking voices, like Link. Even at that he only sees 'em when there's one of those London fogs blowing in from the river." He laid his hand on Weak Knees' arm. "Listen, Weak Knees," he said, "make the spaghetti this coming Saturday. Game or no game. And save some for me. I'll stop by for it."

"Okay, Jubie. I'll save half the pot for you. I don't know how that Eyetalian could have give that receipt away."

"If he hadn't given it away you wouldn't know about it," Jubine said.

"Yah-yah — yah. I know that. But he coulda made himself a multonmillionaire just with that one receipt."

Jubine made a sound of derision, "Then he'd of had to come to the United States, that is if he was going to be a spaghetti millionaire. And he'd of spent so much time worrying about his income tax, and his labor problems, and the shortage of salt pork and the shortage of mushrooms and the high cost of everything that he wouldn't be able to sleep at night for worrying. And all that worry would give him little sore places in his stomach and he wouldn't even be able to eat his own spaghetti any more. But he passes the receipt along and a lot of people eat his good spaghetti and they're grateful to him and he can eat anything he wants to, and he gets in his big soft bed every night and goes straight to sleep, because there's nothing in his life to give him nightmares — no CIO, no shortages — "

Weak Knees said stubbornly, "There ain't no shortage of salt pork. There never is because most chef-cooks don't know nothin' about usin' it."

Jubine said, "Sure, sure. But if some scientist should find out it's got some big important vitamin in it like in liver then everybody in America would start using it and then there'd be a shortage. Besides if everybody in this country started buyin' this new spaghetti dish made with salt pork in it why then there'd surely be a shortage — "

Bill said, "For the love of God, will you guys stop that yak-yak and cut for the deal?"

He waited on the dock again Monday night. The air was crisp, cool, clear. He could see the whole length of Dumble Street, and he looked at it and found it good, thinking of it as the street in which he grew up, the street in which he had gone through the seesaw process of reaching manhood, let go of something, hold on to something else, learning, growing, until finally he grew all the way up. Or had he? Or did anybody? Ever?

It was midnight when he saw her car, coming slowly along Dock Street. He watched her as she got out of the car and crossed the road. She walked as though she had always owned the world, and always would own it and knew it. This time she was wearing a suit, a gray flannel suit. She had a striped scarf, vivid green stripes, knotted around her throat. Her footsteps were quick, light. Brown shoes on her feet. And the legs — legs like Dietrich, only better. Actually.

"Hello," she said. There was a sparkle in her eyes, animation in her face, in her voice, a smile kept coming and going around her mouth.

Well, he thought, this is what you wanted to know. This is what she looks like when she's not been frightened half to death.

"Hello, yourself," he said.

"I've been looking for you."

She was standing quite close to him now. He thought, again, the perfume she uses smells like stock on a hot night in August, when there's a full moon — only not as direct and uncomplicated as stock, sweet, yes, but more elusive so that you want to get closer and closer, so that you can keep on smelling it.

"Yeah, I know. I saw you."

"You saw me? You — well — why didn't you let me know that you saw me?"

"Because every night for the last two weeks I waited for you. Right here. On the dock. And some nights it rained, and some nights there was fog, and some nights it was cold enough to freeze the tail off a brass monkey. So — " he patted her arm, "I decided it was your turn to wait."

"Oh."

She was almost pouting, the way a spoiled and arrogant child pouts when you tell him he can't have the fifteenth lollipop. He wondered how she would express her displeasure.

To his surprise she said, "Would you like to go for a ride?"

"No." Pause. "Thank you."

"Well, is there some place where we can go and talk? Perhaps that place where we went before?"

"The Moonbeam?"

"Is that what it's called? It doesn't exactly suit it, does it?"

He let that one go. The Moonbeam Café . Where else would he take a white girl, in Monmouth, at midnight? They would not be stared at, but looked over, carefully, covertly, in The Moonbeam. He took her there before. But he had taken it for granted that she was a high yaller. He couldn't half see in the fog, couldn't half see in The Moonbeam. It wouldn't have occurred to him that the girl was white, not then, anyway, if it hadn't been for the way Bug Eyes looked at her. If he had known she was white, would he have taken her there, anyway? Where else? What kind of race discrimination was he practising here in his thinking? Why was he reluctant to take her there now? He would be reluctant to take any girl there, white or colored, if he wanted to talk to her, to listen to her talk, wanted to go dancing with her, to — He simply did not want to sit in the smoky cave-like interior of The Moonbeam, to try to talk over or under the noise, to be surrounded by a lot of people, all talking, all looking at them, all conjecturing about them, while the jukebox bleated out a song about old lost loves and undying hates and my man gone.

"All right," he said. "We'll go to The Moonbeam and drink beer. If we drink enough of it we'll begin to believe we're somewhere else."

"Wait," she said. "I want to tell you something."

"Well?" She didn't say anything, and he said, "Go on. What is it?"

"That night," she started and then stopped, began again. "That night when I was on the dock, well, I couldn't see anything because of the fog. But once, when it lifted, I caught a glimpse of that creature propelling himself along on that little wagon. I thought I'd never get my breath back. I ran and ran and ran and the thing on the wagon kept getting nearer and there was a smell, an odor, like in the zoo. Or at the circus. And I knew it came from that thing chasing me — on the cart — "

"Wait a minute. What're you going all over this for?"

"I have to. I have to explain something to you."

"You sound as though you were getting ready to explain yourself into a fancy case of hysterics. Or do you enjoy scaring yourself?"

"I'm not scared any more. I have to tell you this. Keep quiet and listen until I've finished."

He lifted an eyebrow and whistled. Then he said, softly, in a singsong voice:

> Come when you're called
> Do as you're bid
> Close the door gently
> Never be chid.

"I'm sorry," she said quickly. "I didn't mean that the way it sounded. But if you keep interrupting, I'll never finish. And I have to tell it this way or you won't understand."

"All right. Go ahead."

"I — I couldn't see where I was going. Not in the fog. It was like a nightmare, trying to run away from something horrible, having to run, knowing that unless I ran and kept running that evilsmelling thing would finally overtake me. It was like running blindfolded, run and run, and not be able to see where you're going — "

"So you ran," he said dryly.

"Yes!" she said, anger in her voice. "I ran. You don't know what it was like so you can stand there safe and superior because you've never been afraid of anything in your life."

"Afraid of anything? Never been afraid of anything? But of course I have. Go on. I won't say anything until you've finished." She was silent and he prompted her. "You ran and then what?"

"Then you said, 'Hey!' I ran toward you, head on at you, not you, but your voice. I knew if I could reach the spot where your voice came from I'd be safe. The fog lifted a little and I could see that you were big enough and strong enough and young enough to fight off that thing, whatever it was, on the cart.'

Then she said, her voice slowing, "I couldn't see very well because I was so frightened and because of the fog. I wanted to keep holding on to your hand and your arm, stay within hearing of your voice, and there was a clean good smell about you. I knew that you were trying to make me go away from you. I don't know what you said. It didn't make sense. But I knew, no matter what you said to me, that I wasn't going to walk through that fog, alone, to reach my car. The foghorn kept blowing, blowing. For all I knew that thing on the cart might be waiting for me, waiting in the fog. The foghorn said so, the river said so, over and over, 'Get you, get you, get you.' It wasn't until I sat down in that place, in The Moonbeam — " She stopped, started again. "You see, I didn't know you were colored. When we got inside The Moonbeam, when we sat down and I looked around and saw all those colored people I was — I began to get frightened, all over again. Then I saw that you were colored too. I couldn't get the confusion out of my mind. I don't know what I thought — "

"But you came back here, anyway?"

"Wait," she said. "You asked me again, there in that place, how I came to be on the dock, and it was the same voice. The voice that I had refused to leave, couldn't have been pried loose from there on the dock. And I kept telling myself, You didn't know he was a Negro and you clung to him, clung to him, because his voice said, You're safe with me, safe, safe, safe, safe. Not in words. You didn't put it in words. I couldn't understand what you were talking about, something about China, but I could understand the clean clear enunciation, the resonance, the timbre — It was a perfectly beautiful speaking voice and it belonged to a colored man. I had to try to match that voice that meant safety with your being colored and I couldn't. In the fog, when I couldn't see, I clutched at you, because all I had to go on was the sound of your voice and the feel of your arm, the long smooth muscle in the forearm, a man's arm, hardfleshed, a man's hand, strong, warm, the skin smooth. Yet the hand and arm belonged to a colored man.

"Then the waiter, the one you called Bug Eyes, stared at me, a long hard stare. His face had been friendly, laughing, a simple peasant face, when you spoke to him about finding us a place to sit. I thought he looked like a South European peasant except that his skin was so dark. When we were sitting at that little table he looked at me and his face changed right before my eyes. It became a closed hostile face, complex and dangerous. I looked around and all of them were staring at me, all their faces were like the waiter's face, closed, hostile.

"I tried to get up, to get out of there, and I couldn't move. My knees wouldn't work, my legs wouldn't function. I knew that even had I been able to stand up I couldn't have walked through that noisy smoke-filled room. And your face had changed, too. It wasn't hostile, but there was something there, something that hadn't been there before, a kind of disdain and a puzzlement.

"When we left there was the fog outside, waiting. It was worse than before. I knew I couldn't drive alone through that fog because I would imagine that wagon was just behind me, always getting a little nearer. I thought that if you got in the car with me, rode around with me for half an hour or so I'd be able to get myself back together. Yes, you were colored but you were the only normal, clean, known creature anywhere in that fog — and you see — you cling to, hang on to, whatever represents safety — security — and — "

She seemed to be waiting for him to say something but he couldn't. He felt a curious kind of anger. He wanted to say, Well, what did you come back for? Do you know what you have just said, what you really said —

The girl said, "When I told you to turn around and you kept on driving I thought, What'll I do, what'll I do. When you finally stopped and parked the car, I thought the same thing, What'll I do, what'll I do? I can't run any more. I can't scream, there's nothing left in me to scream with, there's nothing left to fight him off with. I thought, No, impossible, a man with a voice like that couldn't — Then when you drove the car back to Monmouth and got out, I felt relieved.

"Afterwards I began to be ashamed of myself, ashamed that I had thought, Yes, he's a Negro but there isn't anyone else to protect you and therefore he is good enough for that, ashamed of the whole thing. So I came back."

"Because?"

"Because I wanted to thank you and I felt I owed you an explanation, an apology. And I wanted to know you better."

"Know me better?"

"I thought we could be friends," she said timidly.

"You came back here, to the dock, where you had been so badly frightened?"

"Of course I came back. I planned to keep on coming back until I found you here again. It was the fog that terrified me. I couldn't see anything, couldn't see where I was going. There's nothing here to frighten anyone on a clear night like this."

You're wrong there, honey, he thought, and this is a damn queer way to start a friendship. Friends. Ha!

"Friends, it is," he said. "Shall we go drink beer in The Moonbeam to celebrate the Emancipation? Even though the sight of all those colored people left you limp?"

She looked so completely bewildered that he laughed and said, "Don't try to figure it out. You're much too beautiful to think. Leave us go wet our whistles."

So once again they walked through Dumble Street, quiet now, Monday night quiet, wind from the river, smell of the river, clang-clang of trolley car in the distance, whine of siren somewhere, far off, faint, in the heart of the city, rumble of a truck on Franklin Avenue, lights still on in The Last Chance, the harsh redorange of the neon sign turning a patch of the sidewalk a paler redorange. He looked back at Number Six and saw a pink light upstairs where the Powthers lived, dimly, through the branches of The Hangman. No light downstairs where he and Abbie lived and had their being.

They turned into Franklin Avenue. "Say," he said. "What's your name?"

"Camilo Williams."

"Williams?" he said startled.

"Williams."

That, he thought, I don't believe. Camilo? Yes. Because it's somehow right. Williams? No. You had it all made up, ready to hand, no, you didn't, you handed it out quickly because you weren't ready for that particular question at that particular moment, but you had to have a last name, at least folks do in most circles, so you grabbed at that one. You've probably forgotten that it's my last name, too. For some reason your own last name, your real name, whatever it is, won't do.

They were in front of The Moonbeam when she said, "Oh, look!" and pointed at a man who was kneeling on the sidewalk.

If the girl had not stopped to watch Cesar the Writing Man, Link would have walked past him, because he had seen him so many times, watched him so many times, that he knew his every motion, every change of expression. Cesar always bowed toward the East, making an obeisance that should have been ridiculous and wasn't, then opened the cigar box, put on his glasses, and began writing on the sidewalk. He wrote with a kind of fury, pausing now and then to select a piece of colored chalk from the cigar box, adding the curlicues, the decorations, the little adornments to the capital letters as he went along.

And now Cesar glanced at them, glanced away, made his obeisance, and started writing on the sidewalk. Link wondered how he managed to look so clean when he always wore the same clothes — a heavy brown sweater, gray tweed knickers, dark gray golf hose. The bulk of the sweater, the blouse of the knickers suited his lean wiry build.

The girl stood back a little, as though she were watching an artist at work in oil or watercolor, and was respecting his right to the privacy necessary for the act of creation. She made no effort to read what he was writing until he had finished.

After Cesar removed his glasses, he arranged the blue and red and green chalk in the cigar box, closed the cover. He made another obeisance toward the East and somehow managed to look like a Mohammedan bowing toward Mecca. Then he was gone, walking down Franklin Avenue, with his lithe quick gait, the cigar box under his arm.

The girl leaned over and read what he had written on the sidewalk, reading it aloud: "Is there anything whereof it may be said, See, this is new? It hath been already of old time, which was before us. Ecclesiastes I:10." She leaned over a little farther, studying the curlicues, the flourishes, and decorative lines that adorned the writing.

"What does it mean?" she asked. "Why did he write it?"

"Mean?" Link repeated. "Why I suppose it's a kind of admonishment, a small sermon written on the sidewalk, for the benefit of anyone who stops to read it. He could have been describing The Moonbeam, saying that there have always been places like it and that there always will be. Or he may have been telling you or anyone else that no matter what your troubles or your worries or your pleasures or your delights may be, other people have experienced the same thing before and will again.

As to why he wrote it — who knows? He's been writing verses on the streets and sidewalks of Monmouth for years — Eastside, Westside, Uptown, Downtown. He calls himself Cesar the Writing Man."

She said, softly, as though to herself. "It hath been already of old time, which was before us."

Then they were standing inside the door of The Moonbeam. It was filled, even now, on a Monday night, with a goodsized crowd, filled as usual, every night, with the oversize bleat of the jukebox. In all these places, Link thought, they play the same song, a different record, and a different singer, and perhaps a different tune, but the same song about lost loves and old hates, violent love, blue violent love, the man gone, gone, gone, sung in a blurred fuzzy voice, not sung but moaned, pain in it, regret in it, a wail in it. The young men and the young women sitting at the tables, leaning against the long bar, looked as though they had been thinking about the man gone, the woman lost, remembering the old loves, the old hates, for the last hundred years.

While he stood there looking down the length of the big dimly lit room, he began to think about China and the smell of incense, about Bill Hod and China, about Bill Hod and Mamie Powther.

Bug Eyes approached them, hurrying, tray balanced on the palm of his hand, tray held high. He smiled at them, said, spontaneously, "I gotcha a nice table, this time, 'bout midway. Gotcha a nice table."

It was, Link supposed, a nice table. The nearest arms and legs and ears were about three feet away. So they could talk, if they wanted to, without including six or seven others in the conversation. Whenever he looked at the girl, at the passionate lovely mouth, the deepset blue eyes, the arched eyebrows, the pale yellow hair that had a silky shimmer even in the dimly lit interior of The Moonbeam Café on Franklin Avenue, he was aware of a thickness in his throat that would have interfered with any words he might have said. What, he thought, does one say to a white female who has expressed horror at the thought of having laid her hand on the arm of a Negro? Her reaction to him, Link Williams, and "to all those colored people" had been exactly the same as her reaction to the repulsive creature who had chased her through the fog. Cat Jimmie on a cart equals terror, equals drowned-in-fear. All those colored people in a beer garden equals terror, equals drowned-in-fear. Link Williams, once one knows he is colored, also equals terror, equals drowned-in-fear. Equals friendship? Highly implausible. Come to think of it, what in hell had she expected to find on the Dumble Street Dock, in a beer garden on Franklin Avenue? Polar bears, maybe? You see some of Jubine's pictures somewhere, so you think you'll find Old Man John the Barber and he will not look like a Negro, he will look like an etching by Rembrandt, and therefore all the colored people who live in this area will look like etchings by Rembrandt, only they don't, they look like a whole mess of colored people, and they talk with their mouths, and they pour beer down their throats, and they move around, and their clothes look all wrong to you, and their voices sound all wrong to you and my voice was okay until you saw the color of the skin on my face, color of the skin on the outside of the throat from which the voice issued. Ha!

He ordered beer. She didn't drink it. She looked at the glass that Bug Eyes placed in front of her, and then sat forward, leaning her elbows on the table.

She said, "Tell me what you do, where you've lived, and how. I want to know everything about you. Were you in the war?"

"In the Navy. Censor. Navy installation. Hawaii. I read all the guys' letters. Read I love you, misspelled in all the known ways and some new and unknown ways, read I love you, figuratively blotted with tears, figuratively sticky with heart's blood, literally stained with sweat. I read I can't live without you, written the same way, and then — I love you, over and over again."

She took her elbows off the table and sat up very straight.

"Did you like it?" she asked, voice even, voice a little constrained.

"You mean the Navy? Or the reading of another guy's sweat and blood and tears spelled out in one-syllable words?"

"I mean the Navy."

"Not especially. Good? Bad? It isn't that simple. I know that for four years I sat on that damn island reading I love you, I love only you, I love you only, I will always love you. I don't know whether I felt any way about it at all except that I hoped to hell we wouldn't get blown to kingdom come early some morning. Sometimes I hoped that we'd get blown up just a little bit, to change the pace." He grinned at her because each time he had said I love you, her back had got straighter until now she was sitting up just like Abbie or Queen Victoria.

"Do you like living in Monmouth?" she asked.

"Sure. I grew up here. I doubt that it would be possible to really and truly hate the place where you grew up unless something happened to you that destroyed your belief in yourself. And nothing much happened to me — I just grew up — pretty much like anybody else. With a couple of exceptions that may or may not have been average."

He thought, All life goes in a circle, around and around, you started at one place, and then came right back to it again. "It hath been already of old time, which was before us." In a way, his life had really started inside The Last Chance. So he was back there again, working as day man behind the bar, ten in the morning until six at night, right back where he started. And the girl? This girl, who at the sound of the words "I love you" repeated, and he had been repeating them purposely, had withdrawn, moved away, is she someone you have known before? No. He had never known anyone with quite so easy and natural a manner. There was something gay about her and something quite imperious. When he had wrung changes on all those different ways of saying I love you, her back had stiffened. Did he still believe that all cats bee gray? Well, yes. Well, no. This little one with her head lifted, chin up in the air, revealing the flawless throat, the long neck, ballerina's neck, small hollow place at the base made for kissing, had revolt, refusal to submit, written in every line of her tautly held body. She was like a thoroughbred racehorse balking at the barrier. All cats bee gray? No.

"What do you do?" he asked.

"Do?"

"Do for a living."

"Oh. I write about fashions. I go to all the openings and look at the new clothes. And write about them. I fly to Dallas and Chicago, to Paris and to London, and back to New York to look at all the new glitter that the fashion designers dream up."

"Where do you live?"

"In New York most of the time. Sometimes in Chicago, sometimes in Montreal. Sometimes in London and in Paris and in Monmouth."

New International Set, he thought. Pictures in *Life* magazine. French Riviera, Eden Roc, Hôtel du Cap, Ali Khan, Shah of Persia, Argentina millionaires. Maybe she's an international tramp. He studied her face, No, impossible, even in this dim inadequate light, the eyes are too beautiful, too honest, the whole face too young, too pure, an absolutely vulnerable face, an expectant face. There's something she isn't telling and it's making her uncomfortable but international tramps, no matter how beautiful they are, do not have this look of wonder, of expectancy, this eagerness in the eyes, in the mouth.

"Where were you born?"

"In Monmouth."

"But you — did you grow up here?" Do you mean, he thought, that we've walked the same streets? You and I? Impossible. I would have seen you somewhere. If I had seen you only once, watched you cross a street only once, and never seen you again, I would have remembered it.

"Off and on — mostly off — "

He tried to picture her living in Monmouth, going to high school here, growing up in this small bustling city, and couldn't. Perhaps Monmouth turned them out like this, but he didn't believe it. Now as he looked at her, he thought that she might have been sitting in a drawing room, drinking tea, visiting over the teacups, she seemed so unaware of the noise, the blare of the jukebox, the smoke, the dim light, the people. He supposed it was the way she sat, her back so very straight, her head lifted, that made him think of Abbie. He had seen Abbie sitting midway in a crowded trolley car, talking to F. K. Jackson, and Abbie, too, gave the impression that she was in her own living room serving tea. Up until now he had thought this air of quiet elegance was an attribute of a handful of aristocratic old colored women and a handful of aristocratic old white women, thought too that it came only with age. Yet here was this girl with the same quality. It suprised him and puzzled him. And strangely enough, he found it delightful.

"Did you go to college?" he asked.

"Of course. I went to Barnard and loved it. I was good at it. So good at it that I was offered an instructorship in English once I got an M.A., preferably at Columbia."

"Professor Williams," he said and laughed. "That I can't picture. I'm trying to picture the rest of it — but that — that's funny."

"No it isn't," she said sharply. "It was something that I did by myself with my own brain. Don't laugh at me. I would have been good at it. I would have been somebody in my own right and instead — instead — "

"Instead?" he prompted.

She pushed the beer glass away from her as though she were

not only rejecting beer but a whole way of life. "Well, I traipse around Paris twice a year thinking up new ways of saying that the skirts are longer or the skirts are shorter. The waistline is up or the waistline is down." Then she stood up, and said. "I'm driving to New York tonight so I'll have to get started."

When he held the door of the car open for her he was still wondering what really came after the "instead" — Instead what? Obviously something more than fashion reporting had interfered with her being somebody in her own right.

He said, "When will I see you again?"

"Saturday? Here? Is that all right?"

"Not Saturday. Sunday. Late in the afternoon."

"Fine," she said.

"About five-thirty?"

"Fine, again." She shook hands with him before she got in the car, and said, "I enjoyed myself." And smiled. Then, for no reason at all that he could determine, she laughed — a bubbling joyous sound.

He watched her drive off, and frowned, thinking, She drives too fast. She zooms past those side streets as though she had a police escort in front of her, clearing the way. Then he stopped frowning, remembering what her face was like when she laughed, the mouth curving with laughter, the eyes lighted, head thrown back, showing the long line of the throat. It's not possible, not possible, but inevitable, he thought. There is nothing I can do to stop the process. I am falling in love with her. Not falling in love with her. I am in love with her. I have already, at the sight of that beautiful laughing face, once again, placed my trust, my belief, placed it irrevocably, in the hands of another human being. Hopelessly, inextricably involved. Again. For the third time. First there had been Abbie Crunch, and then Bill Hod, and now — a girl.

This time? This time? Would this girl with the laughing beautiful face, the long neck, the deepset eyes, would she, too, play some fantastic trick on him? "Such fantastic tricks as make the angels weep."

He went in The Last Chance. Bill Hod was behind the bar. Alone.

"Friend," Link said, "let us drink to the night."

Bill stared at him, face expressionless, black obsidian eyes expressionless. He said slowly, "Sometimes I think you smoke reefers."

"Even so, Comrade. Even so. Have a drink with me, anyway."

"Okay. What'll it be?"

"Whiskey and soda."

Bill mixed the drinks quickly. Link watched his hands, deft hands, clean hands, hands with the nails carefully filed, hands that could hold a gun or a knife or a blackjack, hold anything, use anything, quickly, deftly. I bet when he's a hundred and two he'll look exactly the same, sound exactly the same, use his hands exactly the same. Indestructible.

Bill said, "What're we supposed to be drinking to?"

Link said, "We will drink first to Bill Hod, then to Bill Shakespeare. The immortals." He leaned against the bar. Bill obviously thought he was high as a Georgia pine, there was no reason why he should hesitate to present him with further evidence of the advanced state of intoxication he was supposed to be enjoying. He said, " 'How many goodly creatures are there here! How beauteous mankind is! O brave new world, That has such people in't.' Bill Hod, who stands behind the bar and Bill Shakespeare who forever sits on my shoulder." He paused, eyed Bill, repeated, " 'O brave new world, That has such people in't!' " Then he drained the glass, quickly. "Bill," he said, "just between friends, and confidentially, of course, absolutely confidentially, have you ever been in love?"

"Whyn't you go across the street and get in bed before you reach the cryin' stage?"

"What kind of answer is that? Here, Mr. Boss, give me another one of these."

"No," Bill said flatly. "You're drunk now."

"Be damned if I am. One whiskey and soda. That's all I've had. Right here before your eyes. No reefers. I have never smoked a reefer in my whole life long, chum. They stink too bad. Friend of mine took me in one of those joints once. In Harlem. Dark blue lights inside, hellish light. And the cullud folks were all mixed up with the white folks, all groaning and moaning, legs and arms and torsos all mixed up on sofas and on rugs, too. I got one whiff of the interior and I said to my friend: My dearly beloved friend, I promised my dear old whitehaired mother, when I was in knee pants, that if I ever hit a joint that had a stink in it like this one, a stench, a stank, an offense to the nostrils of this kind and nature, I would leave at once and get some clean fresh air. I said: I have a bottle of clean fresh air in my pocket, and I am now leaving, and when I get outside I will take said bottle out of my pants pocket, and breathe that clean fresh air until my nose begins to forget the offense, the insult, that has damned near made it stop functioning. I must go immediately for if I linger in this — er, odor, this — er, smell, this — er pollution and corruption one moment longer, I will — er regurgitate — " He smiled sweetly at Bill. "I have not been smoking reefers, old man."

"What in hell's the matter with you then?"

"If you will be kind enough to refill this tall tall glass, I will tell you. Come, come, señor. No drinkee. No tellee."

Bill filled the glass. "Here," he said. "If this is the only way to get you out of here, for Christ's sake drink it up fast and get out."

Link drank it slowly, sipping it delicately. "Stuff tastes like hell. Not fit for human consumption. Oh, it's good liquor, Boss Man, but this one followed the first one too fast. I have a delicate stomach, a nervous stomach, Father Hod. My stomach does not like the way this stuff tastes. Neither does my throat. Say," he said, using the conversational tone that a man uses when he plans to talk a long time, "did you know that F. K. Jackson has a nervous stomach? Imagine an undertaker with a nervous stomach. Partner, can you picture how her stomach must jump when she lays the boys out on the cooling board? Come to think of it, they call themselves morticians, don't they?" He paused just a little too long, he gave Bill a chance to say something.

Bill said, "Well?"

"Well, what?"

"If you're not drunk, what's the matter with you?"

Link grinned at him. "That's right, we made a pact, didn't we?" He started walking toward the door, turned, said "Shhh! Don't tell anybody, friend, but — I'm in love." He opened the door wide, stepped over the threshold, leaned inside, and let out a rebel yell — long, high in pitch, wild, repeated it until the wild highpitched yelling made the glasses tinkle on the shelves.

The sound brought Weak Knees running from the kitchen, falling over his feet. Link heard him shout, "Whassamatter, Boss? Who did that in here? Who did that in here? I'll kill the bastard — "

Link let the door swing shut, stood outside, on the street, looking up at the sign. The Last Chance. Redorange, harsh redorange, see-it-for-a-block neon sign. And laughed. Because once again he felt as though he could conquer the world. The Last Chance. The Last Chance.

7

● LINK HAD FINISHED EATING his breakfast.

Abbie Crunch said, "I wish you'd — " stopped, said, "I — " and never finished what she was going to say.

They both heard the screams that came from upstairs. Link knew by the volume, by the pitch, that these hair-stand-on-end screams, these curdle-the-blood screams could only have issued from the throat of Mrs. Mamie Powther; thinking how aware of her he had become, how familiar with the sound of her voice, that he should recognize it even when lifted in distress.

Abbie said, "Why — what — " shuddered, took a deep breath and said, "Link — go and see what — "

He ran up the outside back stairs, ran up them, thinking, Well, perhaps Powther had come hurrying home, in his dark suit, razor crease in the pants, in his black shoes with the mirror shine, had come home, and found Mr. B. Hod in his bed, and had murdered Mr. Hod, and was now murdering Mrs. Powther.

In the kitchen, upstairs, Mamie Powther was standing on a chair, skirts wrapped around her, held high, wrapped tight around her, so that knees, leg, thighs were exposed. She had red sandals on her feet. No stockings. One hand over her eyes, the other hand holding up the skirts. He thought of a girl wading, a girl with her skirts wrapped around her, skirts lifted, wading. Not good enough, what then? Venus. Why Venus? Goddess. It was the shape of the calf, the swelling of the thigh. Only the Greeks

99

reproduced it like that. Goddess. Hardly. Well, a profane goddess then. Lead us not into temptation. But who would not follow where Mrs. M. Powther's softfleshed thighs —

He glanced around the kitchen, looking for an intruder, a robber, an outraged husband. Nothing. Nobody. Dishes piled in the sink. Coffee cup on table.

He said, "What — "

"That way — " she didn't point, she just said, "That way. Oh, get him, get him, get him — " One hand clutched at the skirts, the other covered her eyes.

He went all through the apartment. Nothing. He stayed longest in the Powthers' bedroom, recognizing it immediately because of the cupids that adorned the bed. He grinned at the cupids, saluted them, thinking, Friends, Fellow Travelers, Eyewitnesses, Comrades-in-Arms. Hail, Cupids!

He returned to the kitchen. "What was it?" he asked.

She took her hand away from her eyes. "Oh, it's you — "

"Yeah," he said. "Who went — er — that way?"

"Mouse."

He looked at her for a long moment, skirts still held up, wadded up, had she forgotten them or —

"You mean a small four-legged gray creature, relative of the rat?" Sometimes Dumble Streeters gave choice, highly appropriate names to friends and enemies. "Mouse" could be a second-story man.

"A mouse," she said, dropping the skirts.

So she really did forget about them. I wish you hadn't though, Mamie Powther, after all a man can dream, he thought, and said, "Well — uh — no mouse — anywhere. He was probably as scared as you were."

He held out his hand, intending to help her down from the chair. She got down by herself, gave her skirts a shake, patted them in place.

She smiled at him, a great big flashing heartwarming smile, and said, "Thanks. I'm all right now. Only thing I'm scared of is mice. I been tellin' Powther to set a trap — "

The instant he re-entered Abbie's kitchen she said, "What — "

"Mice," he said. "A mouse ran across the kitchen floor. She's afraid of 'em." Not men. Mice. Not afraid of men because if he had stayed up there another five minutes, he and the cupids on the headboard of the bed would have been better acquainted. He would have been able to study the cupids, just lift his eyes and study them — wings, behinds, grapes, et al. Invitation in Mrs. M. Powther's eyes, in the curve of her mouth, invitation cordially, consciously, graciously extended.

Abbie said, "You mean to tell me that that woman, a big woman like that, is afraid of mice?"

"Yeah. She was standing on a kitchen chair, her hand over her eyes, screaming her head off. Because she's afraid of mice."

"How perfectly ridiculous," Abbie said, anger in her voice.

"One man's meat, Miss Abbie," he said lightly and went on across the street to open up the bar for the day, thinking that Abbie's voice when she said "that woman" had the same tone as when she referred to Bill Hod as "that man."

He wedged the door so that it would stay open. It would be two hours before Old Man John the Barber stalked in for his morning beer. By that time the place would be aired out, cleaned up, slicked up.

While he worked, opening cases of liquor, cleaning out the beer pumps, polishing the bar, he thought, not about the girl, the girl who called herself Camilo Williams, not about Mamie Powther, not about China, but about The Last Chance.

When he was eight years old, and he always went back in his thoughts to the time when he was eight, The Last Chance fascinated him, with the special fascination of something evil, forbidden, mysterious. He tried to imagine what it looked like inside and couldn't. Would there be vats of beer and strong drink? When men drowned in the strong drink and the beer, did they wade in by themselves, or did other men put them in the vats and hold them there until they drowned? He couldn't picture it in his mind, though Abbie was always talking about the place, using the phrase "drowned in drink."

Eight years old. And when he and Abbie set out for church on Sunday mornings, Bill Hod, who owned this mysterious place, was always standing across the street, sleeves of his white shirt rolled up, a white bulldog lolling on the sidewalk beside him. The kids on the block said the dog had a gold tooth. Link didn't quite believe this. He wanted to. But it sounded like the kind of stuff kids told you just to see if you were fool enough to fall for it. He didn't ask Hod about the dog's gold tooth because he knew that Abbie wouldn't like it if he talked to Hod. Though as far as Link could see, there was nothing about Hod's appearance that suggested he drowned his customers as part of the day's work.

The other man who lived at The Last Chance was quite extraordinary. He was a short darkbrownskinned man and he walked with a shambling, shuffling, unsteady gait, like the off-balance walk of a drunk. He wore white cotton pants and a dark brown sweater buttoned all the way up to the neck, and a dusty out-of-shape felt hat jammed on his head, not tilted, but set square on his head and pulled down. The only change he made in this outfit was in winter when he added an overcoat to it; and he didn't button the coat so when the wind blew, as it often did, straight from the river, the coat ballooned away from his body, and Link could see the brown sweater buttoned up to the neck just as it was on a hot day in August.

He saw the man with the funny walk every Saturday when he went to market with Abbie. Those trips to the stores, especially to Davioli's fruit and vegetable store, were deeply satisfying. He was in love with Abbie in those days, he wanted to be with her all the time, and though he called her Aunt Abbie when he spoke to her, he called her Abbie in his mind because he thought it a beautiful name and liked to say it. Eight years old. So he was going to marry her when he grew up, though he did not know exactly how this would be accomplished, in view of the fact that she was already married. Anyway he was always going to live with her.

When they went shopping, he carried the market basket, swinging it back and forth, delighting in the quietness of the street, in the quick brisk way Abbie walked, in the sound of her voice, in the fact that she called Mr. Davioli "Davioli," leaving off the Mister, clearly establishing the social difference between them. She referred to Davioli's store as the greengrocer's, putting together two words that didn't belong together, that no one else used, and yet when he thought about it, the words belonged together even though they sounded strange.

They always saw the same people, saw them almost always in the same places, on those Saturday morning trips. Abbie said that even though they didn't know each other, the fact that they were all of them dressed, heads combed, teeth brushed, had had breakfast, and were out on the street, at eight o'clock when the rest of Dumble Street still lay abed, faces sticky with sleep, heads tousled, there was always the possibility of their becoming acquainted, because this business of early rising was something they all had in common.

Sometimes they met the man with the funny walk when he was coming away from Davioli's, carrying two big brown paper bags, celery always sticking out of the top of one of them. He carried the bags in front of him, close to his chest, his arms around them, and the dark green leaves of the celery came right under his nose. By half closing one eye Link could almost convince himself that this was a horse or a cow coming down the street, head deep in meadow grass, and not a man. It was the kind of celery that Abbie didn't like and whenever Davioli tried to sell it to her, she shook her head, saying, "It's too coarse, Davioli."

One morning he and Abbie reached Davioli's store earlier than usual or else the dark brown man was late. Anyway, Abbie was selecting oranges and Link was wandering around enjoying the fruity smell, thinking what a pleasant place this store was. There was a small stove in the middle of the floor that gave off just enough heat to keep the vegetables from freezing and made for comfort on a cold windy morning. There were chairs where you could sit down and look out on Franklin Avenue and the radio was always playing good and loud and there was the smell of Davioli's coffee — all of which made the store like the inside of a house. Davioli kept a big white enamel coffee pot on the stove, and while he waited for the customers to make up their minds, he drank coffee from a thick brown mug and took big bites out of a doughnut.

Davioli handed him the bag of doughnuts every Saturday and said, "It's okay, Mis' Crunch. Boys is always hungry. I know everything about the young fellers. The old woman and me made four boys. Now you just eat up, young feller."

Link was munching on a doughnut, hoping that this morning Davioli's nephew, the one he called the Idiot, would come in the store before he and Abbie left. Abbie said he really wasn't an idiot, just a trifle slow mentally, and that Davioli was such a quick-moving, fast-talking little man that the slow speech, the slow movement, of his big fourteen-year-old nephew irritated him. Link had never seen the Idiot close to but he always hoped that he would. Sometimes they met him peddling his bike slow, slow, up Franklin Avenue, his mouth open, looking as though he were asleep on the bike.

He was thinking about the Idiot when he heard Davioli say,

"Excuse me a minute, Mis' Crunch. I gotta get some vegetables outta the back for Weak Knees."

He turned and saw Davioli and the man with the shambling funny walk go toward the back room of the store. He thought, Weak Knees, Weak Knees, that's his name and it suits him; it matches the way he walks. Weak Knees.

Davioli said, "Here's your mushrooms and I got ye some pink grapefruit and a basket of them Cortlands. I'll send them apples over by the Idiot if he ever gets his big can outta bed and here's a coupla bunches of pasqualey and there's kale and some of them oranges ye wanted, and the mother finocchio."

Weak Knees said, "Check," and came out of the back room carrying two big bags. He put the bags down on a chair. "I forgot the garlic. Davie, you got fresh garlic?" fingered through the garlic on the stand, said, "These are as dried up as my — " stopped abruptly and tipped the shapeless dusty felt hat, saying, "Good morning, ma'am, didn't see you," to Abbie. Then, "How're they runnin' this morning', young feller? How're they runnin'? Yours out in front?" to Link.

He had a funny highpitched voice but Link found the tone of it pleasing. He had sounded exactly as though he were talking to someone his own age. He said, "Fine, sir," and wondered what Weak Knees was talking about. He noticed that Abbie didn't say good morning, she looked away, and nodded, well, half nodded, half bowed, in the general direction of a big mound of potatoes, and started picking out some small ones though they had enough potatoes at home to last at least another week.

When they left the store, Weak Knees was just ahead of them. Link remembered thinking, The trouble is his legs are crooked and they're getting more and more crooked as he goes along. One leg suddenly gave way. It just doubled up and Weak Knees almost fell. He was way off balance and as he strove desperately to straighten up, he seemed to have fifty legs, all of them completely out of control, his weight first on one and then the other, the leg he tried to stand on buckling and as that leg straightened itself out, the other leg went under. It was like a dance, a crazy kind of dance. Link stood still, watching him. Weak Knees made a final dreadful effort to stand erect and both bags went out of his arms, fell on the sidewalk, split, broke open, oranges, grapefruit, kale, celery, mushrooms, lettuce rolled in every direction.

Weak Knees said, "Oh, God damn that crocus sack anyway. God damn — " He looked back over his shoulder, brushed at something that Link couldn't see, muttering, "Get away! Get away, Eddie!"

He turned and looked, too, saw no one. Looked for a wasp, a bee, a mosquito, decided that it must be a person, because there weren't any insects anywhere nearby, besides no one would try to nudge a mosquito away, and Weak Knees was now making a nudging motion with his elbow, saying, "God damn it, Eddie, get away. Get away."

Abbie said, "Come along, Link."

He didn't move. He said, "Let go my hand, Aunt Abbie. I want to help him pick his stuff up."

Abbie tightened her grip on his hand and because he loved her, though it often meant leaving something exciting and new and very puzzling, like this man — this Weak Knees who was still muttering, talking to some unseen person, poking at the person with his elbow — he followed the tug and pull of her hand, even matched his gait to hers, so that they moved away from Weak Knees and the scattered fruit and vegetables, quickly.

When they got home, he said, "Aunt Abbie, who was Mr. Weak Knees talking to?"

"I don't know."

"Well, what did he mean when he said, 'Get away Eddie'?"

"I don't know. I don't know anything about him. He's not the kind of person I'd be apt to know."

That night, at supper (Saturday night — so it was baked beans and brown bread, homemade pickles and coleslaw, gingerbread and applesauce, hearty, and filling, and cheap, according to Abbie) he patiently waited for a moment when Abbie and the Major weren't talking, so that his question wouldn't be lost by Abbie's saying, "You mustn't interrupt, dear."

The Major took the cover off the big earthenware bean pot, leaned over and sniffed the fragrant steam that issued from it. He served all the plates and while he sliced the brown bread with a string, Abbie put coleslaw on the plates, both of them talking because they hadn't seen each other all day. He thought they'd never be done with talking, then the Major said the blessing, and there was a little pause.

Link said, "Uncle Theodore, what's it mean when somebody asks you how they're runnin'?"

The Major said, "Well, now let me see. Who asked you that and just how did they say it?"

"It was Mr. Weak Knees, the man with the funny walk. I saw

him at the greengrocer's and he said, 'How they runnin' this mornin', young feller? Is yours out in front' What's that mean?"

"He wanted to know if everything was all right with you," the Major said, and let out a great roar of laughter, laid his knife and fork down, leaned back in his chair, held on to the edge of the table, and seemed to laugh all over. Abbie smiled and then laughed. So did Link.

"That's what he meant," the Major said. "He must be a race-track man. Probably loves horses. About the best thing that can happen to a man that's got a passion for racehorses is to have the pony he put his money on start running way out in front. The Governor's a great man for horses. That is," he said, glancing quickly at Abbie, and then away, "he was in his younger days. When his horse was so far out in front there was no question but what it would come in first, he'd jump up and down, hollering and shouting, just like a crazy man. There's something about a horse when he's running out in front, in a race, that — "

Link liked the Major's stories but he had to get back to Weak Knees. He said, "Is he crippled? I mean, Mr. Weak Knees."

"I suppose you could say he is. He's got something wrong with his legs."

"Well, who was he talking to when he said — "

"Why are you asking so many questions about him?" Aunt Abbie said.

"Let the boy talk, Abbie. He's got the right to an honest answer to an honest question. Go on, Link."

"Well, he dropped his groceries, I mean his vegetables, and the bag broke and he nearly fell down. He was all off balance and when he finally got his legs sort of straightened out he kept saying, 'Get away, Eddie, get away,' and he kept brushing at something, pushing something away from him. Who was he talking to? There wasn't anybody around but me and Aunt Abbie." He paused, remembering the early morning quiet of the street, and the small man in the dusty hat with the fruit and vegetables scattered all around him, saying, "Oh, God damn that crocus sack anyway." Then he said quickly, lest Abbie interrupt again, "I'd probably of found out if she'd let me pick his stuff up for him. I didn't see how he was going to get it up off the sidewalk with his legs going all to pieces like that. And after I picked the stuff up I was going to ask him who he was talking to but she didn't give me a chance to. Who was he talking to, Uncle Theodore?"

Abbie said, "I'm sure if he couldn't pick the fruit up himself the other one would have seen to it that it was picked up."

"The other one?" Link said.

"The other man. That Mr. Hod who owns the saloon."

Link knew that if Abbie ever got started on The Last Chance and the vats of beer and the men who drowned in them, he would never find out what he wanted to know. He said, "Oh," to Abbie and then without pausing, said again, "Uncle Theodore, who was Mr. Weak Knees talking to?"

"Whenever he's upset he seems to think that an old friend of his is standing near him. So he nudges him and says, 'Get away, Eddie, get away.' Weak Knees believes he killed his friend. It happened years ago in Washington. They were wrestling with each other, just for the fun of it, and Eddie, who was Weak Knees' best friend, fell and struck his head, and died."

"Who told you that?" Abbie asked.

"Bill Hod. Sometimes he's standing across the street when I come home at night and I stop and pass the time of day with him. One night we got to talking about good cooking and good food. Hod told me that Weak Knees is probably the finest chef in this country but he's never had really firstclass jobs because of his legs. People always thought he was a drunk and wouldn't hire him. Right after that Hod told me the story about Eddie."

Abbie gave the Major a long level look, "Really, Dory," she said, "I should think it would be possible to find a — well, a better type of person to talk to."

Even now, almost twenty years afterwards, Link could remember the sound of the Major's voice when he answered Abbie. The Major loved to eat, eating steadily until he had finished, talking, but never really pausing in his eating. He stopped eating, put his fork down on his plate, voice heavy, the same heaviness in his face, voice slow, face somehow slow, too, though Link did not know why his face should look slow but it did, as he said, "Abbie, if you believe that the Lord watches over and cares about a sparrow, then you must also believe that He watches over and cares about Bill Hod."

Silence in the dining room. Link stared at the white place mats on the polished table, at the brown teapot, at the tea cozy that covered it, watched Abbie's hands, small plump hands, busy with the cups and saucers, with the teapot and sugar bowl and creamer, hands busy pouring tea, looked at the Major's hands, flat on the table, big dark brown hands flat on the table, not holding a fork or a spoon, not holding anything, just flat on the table. Then the Major picked up his fork and he and Abbie were talking and laughing again as they always did at supper.

That was on a Saturday. A week later, the Major was sick, taken suddenly sick, in the afternoon. The Major had a Saturday afternoon to himself every other week, he always spent it working in the yard or in the house, and Link came in the house looking for him and there was the Major sitting in what Abbie called the gentleman's chair, in the front parlor, head lolled over on his shoulder, head somehow loose, no longer connected to the rest of him, mouth open, and a little trickle of saliva coming out of the side of his mouth. He was snoring. He smelt of whiskey. There were newspapers spread on the floor under the chair, in front of the chair, under the Major's feet. Link stared at the newspapers, trying to figure out why they were there. Newspapers on the floor. Abbie put newspapers on the floor under the cat's box. Why under the Major? What did she expect the Major to do?

Despite Abbie's objections, he kept going in the parlor to look at the Major. Then F. K. Jackson came to have supper with them. F. K. Jackson sent for Dr. Easter. And Dr. Easter came and stayed and stayed and stayed.

He knew that Abbie was worried about the Major and he could understand why, yet he couldn't quite understand why she should forget about one Link Williams, forget to tell him to go to bed, forget to fix anything for him to eat, Saturday night and all day Sunday, and Sunday night, too.

She forgot all about him. Then the Major was dead.

Early Monday morning, F. K. Jackson came down the front stairs, quickly, quietly, and meeting Link in the hall said, not looking at him, not really talking to him, but talking apparently to the striped wallpaper, because she kept looking at it, "You must be very quiet. You must be very good. The Major is dead. You will have to look after your Aunt Abbie. You will have to take care of her now." She patted his shoulder with one of her thin, bony hands, and he drew away from her, drew away from the hand. Abbie's hands were soft, plump hands, small hands, quieting hands, and F. K. Jackson's hands were big, and bony, and nervous, and the touch of them made him tremble.

He sat in the kitchen, waiting for Abbie to come downstairs and tell him about the Major. He had seen a dead person close to, last summer. The Hangman was full of leaves. People were sitting on the front steps and in the small backyards. Only the children were running about, shouting. He was out on the sidewalk in front of Number Six, running and shouting, too. It was close to bedtime and so the shouting was louder and longer, wilder, more fun than usual, for all of them knew that in a few more minutes they would be herded into bathtubs, would be listening to all the threats, and the orders to hurry up, wash behind your ears, scrub your feet, hurry up, that accompanied the business of going to bed.

Suddenly they all ran toward the dock for no reason at all, one of the boys headed that way so they followed him. Once on the dock, they stood still because there was a woman there, lying flat on her back.

Link said. "It's Pearly Gates. Come on, we'll have some fun with her. Let's poke at her till she wakes up."

One of them leaned over and touched her hand, poked at her hand, and then straightened up, scared, strangeness in his voice, fear, puzzlement, "She's kind of cold. Here, Link, you feel her — "

He touched the hand and was revolted, absolutely revolted, by the coldness of it.

The other boy looked at him, frowned, said, "I think she's died — I think — she's so cold — she's died — I think — "

They turned tail and ran home, each one of them ran into his own house, up the front steps, hurrying to get inside a house. Because just that morning, Pearly Gates had been alive, they had all seen her in the morning, staggering down Dumble Street, mumbling to herself, black felt hat crooked on her head, black clothes all a which way, long black skirt trailing on the sidewalk, the edges graybrown from dirt and dust, smelling all over of whiskey. They had all seen her and run after her, yelled at her, and if this thing whatever it was could happen to her, it could happen to them, too.

Link went inside Number Six, and was sick, violently sick at his stomach, and Abbie said, "Link, what on earth have you been eating?"

He could only shake his head, he would never be able to tell her that he had touched death with his own hand, he would never be able to tell anyone and he would never be able to forget it.

Now this same thing had happened to the Major.

While he was sitting in the kitchen, he heard someone coming down the stairs, he thought it might be Abbie, and he went into the hall to meet her. Thus he saw three men bringing a heavy bag down the stairs. He did not want to believe that the Major was inside that canvas bag but he knew that he was — he could tell by the way the men looked at him, frowning, and flicking their eyes, and shaking their heads.

He went outside and sat down on the back steps, shivering, tasting the sour acid taste of the saliva that poured from the inside of his cheeks, feeling his stomach contract as though it were being squeezed by a big hand. Sparrows scratched in the loose dirt under the hedge, the high privet hedge that Abbie said was cheaper to keep up than a fence, fences had to be painted, and the posts replaced, but with a hedge you just kept it clipped; and the hedge cut off the view of the depraved goings-on of the Finns next door in summer, and served as a screen in winter, when it didn't really matter what the Finns did because with the doors and windows all closed you couldn't hear the Finns fall out of the windows, cursing each other in English, though when they were sober they spoke in Finnish. Every winter a drunken Finn fell out of the window. A bluejay was screaming like crazy in the pear tree, he watched it fly away, with a sudden upswoop, making a flash of blue, its harsh cry was like the sound of the Finns' cursing. The Finns cursed as they died.

Why had they dumped the Major in a sack like that? Why hadn't they had a funeral for him, like they did for other people. For the Finns?

Late in the afternnon, he went in the house to ask Abbie about it. F. K. Jackson was in Abbie's room, and came and stood in the doorway, barring the way, whispering, "You mustn't bother her now. She's gone to sleep. You run along now, and get yourself something to eat. She'll be all right. You run along now."

He couldn't eat anything. He went to bed. When he finally went to sleep, he kept waking up, remembering.

The next day they brought the Major back. He didn't know when they brought him back. He was tiptoeing down the front stairs, and when he reached the hall, he stopped and took a cautious look into the parlor, stood on the threshold looking in and saw that they had brought the Major back. He was lying in an open coffin. The coffin was in front of the fireplace.

The parlor looked queer. Someone had taken down all the

pictures, taken down the long goldleaf mirror that the Governor's wife had given to Abbie, taken out the plants, taken away the books and the magazines that stood on the marbletopped table near the fireplace, pulled down the window shades. There were white candles in a pair of three-branched candlesticks that he had never seen before. The candles were lighted and they kept flickering, as though a draft was blowing through the room. And there were flowers, all around the coffin, flowers, red, and white, and yellow flowers, he had never seen so many at one time, in one place.

He walked over to the coffin. The Major was dead, and he was wearing his best black broadcloth suit, and a striped necktie; and he did not look like anyone Link had ever known, bore absolutely no resemblance to the Major, lids closed down over his eyes, lids shut tight over his eyes; his face lopsided, thinner, even his hands, thinner, bonier; hands crossed, no, folded, and a Bible, with a worn leather binding, black but mottled with brown, in one hand, held loosely in one hand, not held, the hand placed over the small Bible, and a carnation, a white carnation in his buttonhole. All of him thinner, smaller. Link bent over the coffin and there was a queer, sweetish, sickening smell that made him gasp. He made himself touch the Major's hand, his face. The Major was dead. Dead meant cold. Dead meant not moving. Dead meant to feel like a stone. A cold stone picked up in the winter, fingers withdrawing from its coldness, its hardness. Pearly Gates. And now the Major. He stayed there by the coffin, too frightened to move away.

He turned around because he heard F. K. Jackson talking to someone in a soft voice. F. K. Jackson was leading Abbie into the parlor. Abbie didn't seem to see where she was going and she was saying, "Oh, Dory, Dory," over and over again.

"It's all right, Abbie. It's all right," F. K. Jackson said.

Abbie didn't answer. She walked straight to the coffin, and went down on her knees, weeping, saying, "Our Father — Our Father — Dory, Dory — "

F. K. Jackson said, "Link! I didn't know you were in here. You run along and play. Go outdoors and play, dear."

"I don't want to. I can't — "

"Run along now. I'll look after Aunt Abbie."

He sat on the dock and looked at the river, hunched over, his arms folded, sitting like an old man. He felt like crying, and didn't, couldn't. He stayed there until eight o'clock at night and then went home. No lights anywhere in the house. Total darkness. House cold. He turned the hall light on. Abbie was in the parlor, by the coffin, not kneeling, sitting in a chair, weeping. The sound of her weeping hurt him deep inside.

He said, "Aunt Abbie — "

She didn't even turn her head toward him, just sat there, weeping, weeping, weeping, not seeing him, not hearing him. He tiptoed out of the room, wondering if perhaps she thought he was, somehow, though he did not know how, somehow responsible for the cold stonelike unmoving condition of the Major.

He felt guilty and ashamed and afraid and so alone that he did not dare go to sleep. Finally, in that upstairs bedroom, across the hall from Abbie's and the Major's room, he collapsed into sleep, with all his clothes on, lying on top of the clean white bedspread.

Some time during the night, he made up his mind that he could not, would not, go to the Major's funeral. He wandered about the dock all day and toward dusk, hungry, cold, lonely, he went home. Abbie would be angry and scold him but he was glad because then he could explain everything to her, about the sack, about Pearly Gates, about being afraid.

He left the house almost as quickly as he had entered it. Abbie was in bed, flat on her back in the big mahogany four-poster bed, and the lamp by the bed had a tan-colored cloth draped over the shade, so that the light in the room was very dim. F. K. Jackson sat beside the bed, holding Abbie's hand, murmuring to her in a soothing voice that made him think of the cooing of pigeons. F. K. Jackson had a shawl around her shoulders, big, bulky, dark in color. It made her look fat and humped over and so different that he stared at her, not speaking, thinking that everything was changing, even Miss Jackson, referring to her like that in his mind, not as old Frances Jackson, or F. K. Jackson, but as Miss Jackson. She was sitting right near the bed, and the dimmed light from the lamp threw a shadow on the wall, Miss Jackson's shadow, huge, doubled up; and the shadow was the exact shape of the bag they had carried the Major away in.

He said, "No! No!"

Miss Jackson turned around, saw him, said, "Did you want something, Link?"

He wanted to talk to Abbie but he didn't say so. He walked

over to the bed, and Miss Jackson moved closer to Abbie, as though she were using the dark bulk of the shawl to screen Abbie, block his view of her. He had to peer around Miss Jackson.

Abbie's eyes were closed. She looked smaller in bed. As he looked at the two women, the one lying flat on her back in bed, and the other biglooking, humped over, wrapped in a shawl, sitting by the bed, he began to shiver as though he had a chill. They hadn't even missed him. They didn't know he hadn't been at the Major's funeral. They had shut him out of their lives, cut him off from them. He didn't care about Miss Jackson and what she did or didn't do. But Abbie had been his whole existence, she had watched over him, listened to everything he said, told him what to wear, what to eat, when he should go to bed, had loved him. Now she had forgotten all about him. It was like being nowhere. Lost. Nowhere at all.

He made himself look at the ugly shadow on the wall, at Miss Jackson who was holding Abbie's hand, and had begun that soft lowpitched pigeon cooing in which he could not make out the words, could only hear sounds that must have been words, repeated, over and over again, as though she were saying, There, there, there, Yes, yes, yes, I know, I know, I know, I'm here, I'm here, I'm here.

He thought, Yes, the two of them together — but what about me?

Abbie sat up, reaching for Miss Jackson and Miss Jackson put her arms around Abbie, enveloping her in the big dark shawl. Abbie had on the gray bathrobe, dark gray, the one she called a fright and a horror because it was so big and shapeless, because of the color, a muddy gray; but it was warm and it was perfectly good, not a brack or a break in it, so she couldn't throw it away though it did make her look exactly like Aunt Mehalie.

The first time he had heard her say this, he had asked her who Aunt Mehalie was and Abbie had laughed, saying, "Nobody, really. It's just a very old and rather funny way of describing all slovenly black women. When a colored woman looks old and fat and rumpled and not too clean we say she looks like Aunt Mehalie. That's the way this bathrobe makes me look."

He thought, she sounds like Aunt Mehalie too — old and rumpled. She was saying, "Oh, Dory, Dory — " She wasn't crying but it sounded like crying and her voice was muffled by the shawl. They were both under the shawl now, wrapped up in it.

He wanted to push Miss Jackson away, push her out of the house. He blamed her for the way Abbie looked, the way she sounded, the way she acted, the dreadful way she had changed.

He left the house quickly. He was cold. He was hungry. He was alone. He was afraid. Worst of all, he now distrusted Abbie. Though he did not know it, he was already seeking for something, or someone, to put in the place that Abbie had held in his heart.

Bill Hod was standing across the street in front of The Last Chance. It no longer mattered that Abbie had always referred to him as that other one, that Mr. Hod, that man, the tone of her voice saying, the horned one, the one with hoofs, the evil one, it didn't matter at all, because he was the only person in sight on Dumble Street. So he went and stood beside Bill Hod, not saying anything, just standing beside him, in the hope that being near a grownup would help some of the misery, some of the lonesomeness to leak out of him. This man would not say, "Oh, Dory, Dory"; neither would he say, "Run along and play."

Bill Hod said, "Hi, Sonny. How're they runnin'?" and put his hand on Link's shoulder.

It was a warm firm hand. Link said, in response to the touch of the hand, to its warmth, its firmness, hand that could grip, could move, you could feel life in it, not meaning to say it, "Mister, have you got anything I could eat?"

"Eat? Eat? Oh — sure. Come on in the kitchen."

So for the first time he went inside The Last Chance. He followed Bill Hod through the big swinging door, almost stepping on his heels, he walked so close to him. The strange yeasty smell, not unpleasant, that he caught a whiff of now and then in summer when he walked past the open door, was stronger inside. He cast a swift side glance at the dark polished wood of the bar, at the brass rail, at the bottles, row on row of them, on shelves on each side of the biggest mirror he had ever seen, looked longest at the man who stood behind the bar, wiping a glass, a man in a white coat. Except for the mirror and the bottles it seemed to Link a barelooking place, disappointing in its bareness. Abbie was wrong. There were no vats anywhere. On the other side of the room, across from the bar, there were chairs and tables. And not very many of them. That was all.

Then they were in the kitchen, a kitchen almost as big as the barroom, and filled with such delicious smells of food that he was afraid for a moment he would cry, smells like on Franklin Avenue over near the bakery on Saturday morning when they were baking bread, and just the smell of it made him hungry, and baking cakes, and he thought they smelt as though they ought to be a mile high, and covered thick with chocolate frosting; smells like on Sunday on Dumble Street, and he coming home from church with Abbie, getting hungrier and hungrier, one o'clock and he hadn't had anything to eat since seven-thirty, and his stomach sucking in on itself, and Dumble Street filled with the smell of fried chicken and baked yams, and kale cooked with ham fat, and Abbie going slower and slower, and he trying to hurry her along so he could get something to eat before he died of starvation, starving to death in a street filled with heavenly smells, that came at him out of every doorway and every window.

It was warm in this big kitchen. There was a lot of light. Weak Knees was standing by a tremendous stove, copper hood over the stove, tasting something, stirring something in a pot and tasting it, and he didn't turn around until Bill Hod said, "The kid's hungry."

Weak Knees looked at Link and his mouth opened slightly, as though he were surprised. He said, "Hiya, Sonny. Yours out in front?" and turned back to the stove. "Park it anywhere. Just park it anywhere. It'll be on the table by the time you get it parked."

And it was. Weak Knees filled the plates right at the stove. There wasn't any waiting to pass your plate, he filled them up and put them on the table, a round table, the wood white and smooth. There weren't any doilies or place mats or tablecloth. No napkins either. Link tried to eat slowly because both of them seemed to be watching him, but he was so hungry, so empty, his stomach felt as though it were empty all the way down to his heels, that he gulped down a plate of fried chicken and rice and gravy and kale and four biscuits and swallowed a glass of milk before the other two had really got started good. And even then didn't feel quite full.

Weak Knees said, "You want more cow, Sonny?"

"Cow, sir?"

"He means milk," said Bill Hod.

"Yes, sir."

Now that he was beginning to feel better, he looked around the kitchen. The wall nearest to the stove was almost covered with all sizes and shapes of pots and pans and frying pans, colanders and strainers, longhandled spoons and cake turners, all hung on the wall. Some of them were made of aluminum, some of copper, some were black iron, and they were arranged so that they looked like a design on the wall, a kind of decoration. Abbie kept all her pots and pans stuck away in cupboards and drawers where you couldn't see them, and he thought this was a much better way, handier, and betterlooking too.

He heard a sound that startled him, a kind of snoring that came from under the table. He looked a question at Bill Hod.

"That's Frankie," Hod said. "He's still young but he snores just like Yellow Man Johnson."

The white bulldog was on the floor, under the table, asleep. He lifted his head, probably because he heard his name mentioned, got up, sniffed at Link's legs, wagged his tail, and settled back into sleep. Link drew his legs tight together, remembering Abbie's stories about strange dogs and how they might bite you, with no warning. The big white bulldog ignored him, went on snoring, and he relaxed a little. He wondered who Yellow Man Johnson was, and why he snored so loudly, and didn't ask because Abbie was always saying you mustn't ask questions when you were a guest in someone else's house.

Weak Knees put a piled-up plate down in front of him. He said, "There was just this one little lonely piece of chicken settin' there in the pan, a piece of leg meat, best part of the bird, breast meat's dry, leg meat's moist and sweet, breast meat's only good for samwiches and salat where you can wet it down. And there was this little forkful of rice that was setting there waitin' for a spoonful of gravy and the gravy was right there in the skillet waitin' to lay itself over the rice. So there you are, Sonny, there you are. Start layin' your lip over it." He said it all on one breath.

"How they comin' now?" Weak Knees asked.

"Fine, sir."

"I ain't no sir. You can just call me Weak Knees."

"He's just a plain man from plain people," Bill Hod said. "Call him Weak Knees and call me Bill."

Link nodded. It would be easy to say Weak Knees. Not so easy to say Bill. There was something about Mr. Hod that — well, he was quieter than anyone he'd ever been around. He didn't say much. He seemed to see everything, he had known Link was scared of the dog. Looking at him, close to, he couldn't understand why Abbie called him "that man," or "the other one," just as though she were saying that outcast, the leprous one. Bill Hod's hair was straight, absolutely straight, and Abbie thought it was wonderful when a colored person had straight hair. His skin was light, and Abbie thought that was good, too, in a colored person, even though she herself wasn't exactly light, and neither was the Major. Then he remembered that what Abbie thought, or said, no longer counted with him. He could no longer depend on her. So he would form his own opinion about Bill Hod.

Weak Knees said, "You got room for a small piece of cake? A man ain't really full till he's put a sweet taste in his mouth — that's the finish line — and you ain't got there till you had some sweet — "

He had room for two pieces of chocolate cake. He was finishing the second piece when Bill Hod asked him if he liked to swim. He said that he didn't know how, that he'd never been swimming.

Bill said, "You come on down to the dock with me, next Sunday, and I'll teach you."

Link thanked him though he knew that it wasn't possible because he had to go to Sunday School, and to church, with Abbie because Abbie was superintendent of the Sunday School, and they had to set an example for the other colored people, so even if it rained or snowed, they went just the same.

But he wasn't going to live with her any more, he wasn't going back to that cold house across the street, house of weeping, house of darkness, in which for the last four days he had lived with fear, moving through the rooms as though he were a ghost, not even a ghost, for Abbie would have sensed the presence of a ghost, reacted to it in some way, at least turned the lights on. She walked slowly through the house, she who had always been so erect was now bent over like an old woman, she held one hand in front of her as she walked, feeling her way, like she was blind, didn't comb her hair, wore a nightgown and that Aunt Mehalie bathrobe all day, and either went barefooted or wore felt slippers. He couldn't go back to that house.

He had finished eating. So had Weak Knees. And Bill Hod. He had better tell them now. Tell them? Ask them. Explain.

It was warm in the kitchen, and there was so much light that there weren't any ugly shadows on the walls, there was no sound of weeping. The big teakettle boiling on the stove was making a hissing-bubbling sound, and the dog kept up his snorting-snoring, sometimes so loud that it sounded like coughing, sometimes he seemed to clear his throat, and grunt.

Bill Hod said, "Yellow Man Johnson is a lightweight compared with Frankie when it comes to snorin'. Hey, Frankie, cut out the racket, you'll put us all to sleep."

Weak Knees laughed. The highpitched cackling sound he made was so very different from the bass rumbling, the great roaring, that had been the Major's laughter, that Link stared at him, verifying the fact that this nervous cackling was really laughter. He decided he liked the sound.

"Could I live here?" he asked.

They both looked at him: Weak Knees with gravity, concern in his face, a frown wrinkling his forehead; Bill Hod with no change of expression at all. Neither of them said anything. Weak Knees moved his feet, shuffled them under the table. The dog stopped snoring.

"He died," Link explained. "And she cries all the time."

They still didn't say anything and he thought, If he could make them know what it was like, the dark cold house, the being afraid, the not being looked at, or listened to, or talked to, and ended up saying, "She don't see me and she don't even hear me when I talk. She don't seem to know it when I'm there."

Bill Hod shrugged, said, "So?" and then to Weak Knees, "He can sleep in the room in the back. Fix it up for him."

"Okay, Boss."

Weak Knees fixed the room for him by making the bed. Link went to sleep almost immediately. He didn't know how long he had been asleep, but he woke up, covered with sweat, sobbing, "I didn't do it. I didn't do it." At least that's what he was trying to say, though he didn't know why, but the words wouldn't come out, instead there issued from his throat a dreadful groaning, a sound so horrid that it terrified him. He had no control over it, couldn't stop it, and yet he knew that it was he who made it, and as he lay there groaning, aware of the darkness, aware that he was alone in a strange room in a strange bed, he told himself all over again that the Major was dead, remembered how he looked in the casket, remembered touching his hand, his face, and he began to cry.

Bill Hod's hand, firm, warm, patted his shoulder, touched his face, lightly, offering warmth, comfort. He recognized the feel of his hand in the dark.

"There, there, Sonny," he said. Then, his voice a little more insistent, "You're all right," the pressure of the hand stronger as he said, again, "You're all right."

He kept on shivering and sobbing. It wasn't just the Major. He had lost Abbie too, and so was lost himself.

Bill Hod said, "Come on. Get out of this." He pushed him into a sitting position, helped him walk across the bare unfamiliar room, across a hall, into Bill's room, into Bill's bed, where he fell asleep.

When he woke up the next morning, warm and relaxed, the room was full of sunlight. No curtains at the windows, no pictures on the walls, walls painted white, and so there was sunlight or reflected light everywhere. As he looked around, Bill Hod came into the room, naked, nothing on his feet. He stared at him, surprised, a little shocked, because he had never seen a grownup without any clothes on.

Once he'd seen the Major soaking his feet in a big foot tub in the kitchen. Abbie hadn't liked it because Link had squatted down, nose practically in the tub, staring, pointing at the bunions and the corns, asking the Major what they were, and how they got on his feet. Abbie had said, "Dory, I told you not to do that here in the kitchen. It's the kind of thing sharecroppers do."

He supposed he ought not to look at this man who was walking about the room barefooted. But he couldn't help it. He had no corns on his feet, no bunions. His stomach didn't stick out, it was flat, absolutely flat; his waist was narrow and his shoulders were wide. The skin on his body was almost white, the forearms, and his face, tan by contrast. He made no sound as he walked, and Link thought, He's air-borne, light as air.

The windows were wide open so that the room was not only full of sunlight but full of air — cold air; and he could see the branches of the trees outside. As long as he lived that picture of Bill Hod, naked, moving about as though he enjoyed having no clothes on, lingered in his memory, inextricably mixed up with sunlight, and fresh, cool air.

Bill Hod stopped collecting his clothes, and lit a cigarette. He glanced at the bed, saw that Link was looking at him, said, "Hungry?"

He said, "Yes — Bill."

It would have been impossible for him to describe the way he felt about Bill Hod at that moment. He had been living in dark, heavily curtained rooms, always within hearing of Abbie's weeping, and it had been like living alone, trying to live alone, deep down in the earth where no light could enter, with the sound of mourning always in his ears; this man, Bill Hod, had taken him out of the dark and put him in the sun. He had loved Abbie but in a different way, a quieter, less violent way. There was something of worship as well as passion in his feeling for Bill Hod.

That time he lived at The Last Chance for three months. For three solid months Abbie Crunch forgot that he existed.

He learned to swim, to cook, to hit a target with a rifle, to love a dog, a dog who really and truly had a gold tooth. He took showers instead of baths. He answered to the name of Sonny instead of Link.

And, on Saturdays they didn't have baked beans.

Early, on a Saturday afternoon, he went in the kitchen, and found Weak Knees stirring something in a tremendous frying pan, on the back of the stove. It smelled so good that he could have eaten some of it right then, even though he wasn't really hungry. He asked Weak Knees what he was making.

"Meat sauce for the spaghetti."

"Is it for tonight?" he asked.

"Sure thing."

"We always had baked beans on Saturday nights," he said, surprised. Eight years old, and he thought everybody ate baked beans on Saturdays.

"Baked beans? Saturday nights?" Weak Knees stopped stirring the sauce, turned away from the stove, and looked at him with something very like horror. "Name-a-God, Sonny, what kind of eatin' is that? Make a man fart all night."

When Old Man John the Barber stalked in through the open door, Link was putting on one of the starched white monkey jackets that the bartenders wore in The Last Chance; thinking, My idea, it pleases me that Mr. Hod's bar keep boys should be done up all proper and elegant.

Barber smacked a dollar bill down on the bar, said, "Beer," and glared at Link, glared at the monkey jacket, as usual.

Link drew a glass of beer, placed it on the bar in front of the old man, then put a copy of the *Chronicle* right beside the glass. "There," he said, "that should take care of you almost indefinitely. Now — if any gentlemen with unquenchable thirsts should enter through yonder door and should inquire as to the whereabouts of the bartender, will you be so kind as to tell them that he is in the kitchen laying his lip over a cup of honest-to-God coffee while he talks with his friend and mentor, Mr. Weak Knees. Kindly call me, Mr. Barber, if any customers should arrive."

Barber grunted by way of reply.

8

● He lay flat on his back, eyes half closed; half awake, half asleep; he was aware of a sense of expectancy that was quickening the beat of his heart, causing a slow increase in the pressure of his blood; he deliberately prolonged this moment in which his conscious mind had not yet analyzed, explained, whatever it was that had not yet happened, but was about to happen. Wonderful whatever the thing was. Indefinably wonderful.

Then he remembered. This was Sunday. He had a date with Camilo Williams.

He took a shower in the expensive bathroom that Bill Hod had paid to have installed, in what had once been a big closet, in the front parlor, in Abbie's house. Same front parlor where the Major's coffin had stood all those years ago. After Abbie and F. K. Jackson got him out of The Last Chance, they turned the parlor into a bedroom for him; and it continued to look like a front parlor until Bill Hod paid an interior decorator to do the room over. It was still a good room. Though Abbie would never think so.

He had almost finished dressing when he heard a peculiar scrambling sound. It came from his bedroom. He frowned, listening. Oh, damn that cat, he thought. Anyone would think Abbie was an old maid all of whose latent passion, emotion, affection, suppressed sexual desires were hung around the neck of a tomcat — even to the name, Pretty Boy.

Taking his shoes in his hand, he opened the door that led into

121

the bedroom. I'll brain him, he thought, flatten him out. He's having a wrestling match with the stuff I left strewn around on the top of the desk.

It wasn't the cat. It was J. C. Powther. He was not scrambling around in the stuff on top of the desk, he was going through the top drawer, methodically, and yet quickly, his round head almost inside the drawer, his small behind bobbing up and down in the most tempting fashion as he reached farther and farther inside the drawer.

Link said, "Hey! Get the hell out of there."

J.C. turned, looked at him doubtfully, obviously estimating the degree and the strength of Link's wrath but one hand stayed inside the drawer, feeling, clutching, and discarding, continuing the investigation, while the rest of his body drew itself together in preparation for flight or counterattack.

J.C. said, "You got a penny?"

Link handed him a nickel. "Here. Go buy yourself an ice cream cone. And choke on it while you're eating it."

J.C. gave him a black and venomous stare. He did not move away from the desk, simply reached for the nickel and knotted his fist around it, saying, "They costs six cents now." Having dismissed Link as a source of danger, he turned his attention back to the drawer.

"Here's a dime. It's blackmail but like all other victims of blackmailers I hope it's insurance. Anyway, you stay out of my room. If I catch you in here again I'll cut you up in little pieces and boil each piece separately in oil."

J.C. grabbed the dime and started backing toward the door. "I'm goin' get me some Kool-Aid."

Link glared at him. "You get yourself some arsenic, old man. You trot down to the candy store right now, six-fifteen in the ayem and you kick on the door until Mintz opens it at six-thirty and you say, 'Mintz, I want me a half-pound of arsenic.'"

"Mintz don't run the candy store."

"No?"

"Miss Dollie has the candy store. She don't open until near nine o'clock."

"Well, well, well. Is Miss Dollie colored or does she belong to the same race as the Great White Father?"

"She's cullud."

"Ah! That accounts for the late opening. In my day the candy store on the corner of Franklin and Dumble belonged to a gentleman named Mintz and a man could refresh himself with a soda pop or an ice cream cone at six-forty-five in the ayem if he were so minded. Mintz opened up early and closed up late. Your Miss Dollie'll never get to be a millionaire opening up at nine. Anyway when she does get the joint opened, you go right down there and order up a half pound of arsenic from her and you eat some every morning at this hour and — "

"Yah!" J.C. paused in the doorway. "You don't know your ass from your elbow," he shouted and ran up the front stairs, his feet making a soft thud on the carpeted stairs.

Link yelled after him, "I catch you in here again, you little bastard, and I'll guarantee you'll know yours because it'll be the part you can't sit on for a month."

Abbie came out in the hall. "What in the world — "

"Good morning," he said. "I was just telling my little friend to batten down his hatches. I trust I did not unduly disturb you with my bellowing. I hope I did not rudely thrust you forth from the arms of Morpheus — "

"Arms of — arms of — whose arms?" she asked. "Was he in your room? Link you confuse me so. You do it on purpose. Why don't you talk like other people? Was J.C. in your room?"

"Yes, ma'am. I ejected him. Verbally. Not forcibly. It was the threat of force that you heard."

"Arms of — whose arms — what were you talking about?"

"I meant that I hoped I didn't get you out of bed, Miss Abbie. But you were up, weren't you? Come on, I'll help you get breakfast. Sunday morning. Special breakfast."

He could tell by her eyes that she was surprised by this unexpected offer. Whatever she thought or felt was instantly revealed in her eyes — fine eyes; the expression, on the whole, one of valor. Yet she wasn't valorous. Or was she? She was afraid of everything under the sun, storms, strange dogs, tramps, drunks, any unexpected sound. Too much imagination, that was all. She could visualize disaster, see it, feel it; and had never liked it because he refused to share her fears. But she had survived a personal disaster, a big one; and that accounted for the valor in her eyes. He thought, as he looked down at her, smiling, We might have been friends, if you had had a slightly lower set of standards, if your judgments of people had been less unkind, less critical; if that outer layer of pride had not been so prickly, so impenetrable.

Abbie said, "Help me? Why, I suppose you could. But you —
somehow you're different this morning. What's happened to
you?"

"It's the time of year," he said solemnly. "I always act like this
in the fall. I shed my hair and get a brandnew crop of hair, and
it — well — it stimulates me. Preparation for winter. You know,
like a cat or a dog or a woodchuck or a squirrel. Makes me brisk.
Ho! Leave me make the coffee."

"Link! You're barefooted. Go put your shoes and your socks
on."

"Not me, honey. That's due to the change in the seasons, too.
My feet cry out for freedom at this time of year. That's the native
African in me. Come on. Leave us brew up the coffe and fry up
the bacon and scramble up the eggbeggs."

They had just started to eat, he and Abbie, when he heard
Mamie Powther's voice, voice lifted in song, voice ascending and
descending the outside back stairs, voice increasing in volume,
voice diminishing, almost disappearing, so that he found himself
listening, straining to hear as though something important depended on his not losing the sound. Then it slowly increased
again, increasing, increasing, as she came down the stairs until
finally it seemed to be right beside him, not just the voice but the
woman, too. Sometimes at night he'd heard her singing, the voice
sounding faint, faraway.

Abbie had opened the kitchen windows. No matter how cold
the morning, she always aired the kitchen out, always said the
same thing as she flung the windows up, "Colored people's houses
always smell of food, ham and fried chicken and greasy greens.
Sometimes I think they're all stomach and no mind." He was
always tempted to say, "But Miss Abbie, that's not possible.
Aren't you colored, too?" and never did.

With the windows open Mamie Powther might just as well
have been standing right beside him, as she sang:

> Same train carry my mother;
> Same train be back tomorrer;
> Same train, same train.
> Same train blowin' at the station,
> Same train be back tomorrer;
> Same train, same train.

He supposed that it was a song about death and it might have been a spiritual originally though he'd never heard it before, but that smooth warm voice singing it now turned it into a song about life, about man and his first fall, about Eve and all the wonders of her flesh, about all the Eves for generations back and generations yet to come. She may have been singing about a female who rode on a train, a train that would come back again tomorrow, but the texture of the voice, the ripeness of it told you that there must have been a male aboard that train.

Abbie said, "She never remembers to bring down all the things she'll need. She keeps going up and down the stairs, to get clothespins, to bring down clothes that she's forgotten, and then goes back again after a clothesline. She always washes on Sunday just as though it were any other day in the week and then hangs the wash out. I asked her not to. There's something about clothes hanging on lines on Sundays that — well, it's slovenly and it's outrageous. But then she has children and I suppose — "

She got up and looked out the window. "I should think she'd be cold. Nothing on her head. Her arms practically bare — "

Link got up to pour himself another cup of coffee and glanced out of the window on his way back to the table, and stood, coffee cup in hand, watching Mamie Powther. A cold morning, early, so that the sunlight was thin, pale, and Mamie Powther wore a cotton dress, and a red sweater, the sweater accentuating the big breasts, the sleeves rolled up, revealing the forearms, dimples in the elbows. All of her vigorous, elemental — the arms, the breasts. Softfleshed. Smoothskinned. Brown.

Mamie Powther leaned way over, back toward the house, no stockings on, bare leg exposed, part of thigh exposed. Highheeled red shoes on her feet.

Abbie said again, "I should think she'd be cold. Her arms are practically bare."

"She's probably got her love to keep her warm," he said. Arms practically bare — ha — well, everything else was practically bare, too. Abbie could look smack at the woman's behind, and either not see it, refuse to see it, or see it, and something, some part of her mind, would not admit having seen it, so she spoke of the arms.

That's what's the matter with me, he thought, it's that woman out there bending over a clothes basket. Who the hell could live under the same roof with Venus Powther and not make a pass at the lady, especially when the lady practically waves it in your face, when the lady is built for it, when the lady knows, and I would take an oath on it, I would swear on the Book that the lady knows that at this early morning hour I am always about to lay my lip over a cup of coffee.

That's what's the matter with me. I'm not in love. It's Mamie-PowtherChinaCamiloWilliams that has me by the throat. She is what all men chase and never capture, some one man finally touches her with the tips of his fingers and then spends the rest of his life with his hand outstretched, reaching for the warm soft flesh, and all the other women that he chases and finally captures are not what he really wants, he only pursues them because of some real or fancied resemblance to MamiePowtherChinaCamilo-Williams: tone of voice or turn of head, line of throat or — It's MamiePowtherChinaCamiloWilliams that has turned me into a mooncalf, aware of sunrises and sunsets, staring at the bare branches of The Hangman grayblack against the morning sky, staring in the same astonished fashion at the brass knocker on the front door of this house just last night before I put the key in the door, standing, arrested, looking at a knocker I have seen a thousand-and-one times, admiring its size and shape, thinking that it looked like pure gold gleaming in the light from the street lamp; looking back at Dumble Street, Dumble Street at night, lights in the houses, voices, sound of laughter, the tempo of the street increasing, night concealing the broken pavement, shadows softening the stark upanddown shape of the buildings, shadows lengthening the street, widening it, transforming it, no longer bleak, downattheheels, overcrowded, but all light and shadow, all murmur of voices and ripple of laughter.

By four o'clock he was at the dock. There was a pink-and-red-orange glow across the western sky. The river was redgold along the edges, the windows of the buildings on Dock Street, and what could be seen, at an angle, of Dumble Street were redgold, too. He walked up and down, up and down, impatient, restless, thinking, All I need is a tight little bouquet of flowers, field flowers, daisies and buttercups, wudged together in my hot little hand, and a volume of poetry, limp leather binding, and inside the small book all the monologues and soliloquies about love: My dust would hear you and beat; come live with me and be my love; make me immortal with a kiss; it was the lark; her lips suck forth my soul; I will make thee beds of roses and a thousand fragrant posies. Frankie and Johnnie. He was dressed for the part too; he had shaved again; he had bathed again; he had changed all of his clothes again — clean from top to toe, head to foot. Did he believe that business — my dust, my soul, my love. No. And never would. Was absolutely incapable of the kind of total and complete immersion in another human being that was necessary before one could think in phrases like that. Yet he would never be able to quite forget this girl, this Camilo Williams, not the face, not the figure, but the impression she gave of absolute innocence, of laughing innocence.

He had been looking at the river, and he turned because he heard footsteps on the dock, the girl was walking toward him, smiling. He thought of Mamie Powther singing Same Train, of China, leaning in the doorway of the hall in that house on Franklin Avenue, incredibly fat, no longer young, treacherous as a snake. Why did this girl in a black suit, white gloves on her hands, dark brown fur around her shoulders, fur reaching to the knees, girl with a walk like a ballerina's, with the straight back and the long neck of a ballerina, girl with a look of elegance, air of innocent gaity, girl smelling of nightblooming stock under an August moon, why should she make him think of China, of Mamie Powther? There was absolutely no resemblance. They might have come, all three of them, from different planets, and yet — there must be something, an emanation, an aura, something that made him bunch them together. He decided it was the facial expression: part challenge, part expectancy, part invitation.

Camillo said, "Link! How wonderful. You came early, too," smiling, standing close to him.

He nodded. "The early bird — "

"Do I look like a worm?"

"You look — " he said, and couldn't finish the sentence. She was standing too close to him — all of her too close to him: eyes, mouth, hair.

"I look like what?"

"Like an angel."

"Have you ever seen one?"

"No," he said. "But when Gabriel lets loose that great big final blast on his horn and Peter checks the record and then opens the gate for me, he will be surrounded by lovely winged creatures all of whom will take one look at me and say, 'Link, how wonderful,' and sound as though they meant it. That is the Williams version of heaven."

"Golly! That's what you were supposed to say but I didn't know it could sound like that."

"Good?"

"Like a poet."

"That's because I was thinking 'come live with me and be my love.' It was in the back of my mind. There's something contagious about the stuff." She stiffened as though from an electric shock and he wanted to grin, and didn't; instead he said, slowly, carefully, so that she could not be certain whether he was issuing an invitation or whether he was idly quoting, "Make me immortal with a kiss."

He thought, Honey, your back can't get any straighter, if it does it'll break. You'll have to duck out of this some other way, indicate your displeasure by boxing my ears, or by saying, Sir, how dare you. If you didn't expect me to give some indication of interest in you, why did you come back here?

She said, coolly, "Now that we've got that out of the way, I want to make a suggestion."

He said, " 'Her lips suck forth my soul.' " Voice soft, voice caressing.

She skipped that one. "I thought — "

"Is it the necktie? I spent two hours selecting this tie. I thought it was a pretty good job. Sort of enhances the beard. Gray tie. Gray beard."

"They're both beautiful. That's not the suggestion. I came early because I thought it might be fun to drive to New York, see a movie, and then go somewhere and eat."

"To New York?" He thought, Lady, you go so fast. You should have been an executive. The female doesn't usually direct the movement of the troops, at least not right out in the open. The female normally deploys her forces from ambush in order that the beginning of the attack shall be concealed.

"Why not? Two hours going. Two hours coming back. Why should we waste our Sunday afternoon costumes, your tie, your beard, my wings, and my halo, on The Moonbeam — "

"Okay."

When they reached the car, he said, "I'll drive."

"Why? Don't you trust my driving?"

He waited until he had started the car before he answered her.

Then he said, "To be truthful, no. You drive too fast. You ignore the intersections. You act as though you were driving a royal coach, with outriders clearing the way. The peasants, taking the air on the Merritt Parkway, heading for New York, in their Fords and Chevrolets, might not recognize the royal coach, might not know they were blocking the royal route. Therefore, I will drive."

"Why did you say that?" she said sharply, frowning.

"I have watched you drive off in this crate. Twice. Both times you made my hair stand on end. I do not like to have my hair stand on end and my hair does not like to stand on end because it knows that human hair is not supposed to do that. My scalp is outraged by the unnatural action of my hair and cries, Halt, Stop, Cut it out."

"You're laughing at me," voice muffled, angry.

She was silent as they left Monmouth. Dear me, he thought, this is a temperamental little one and I have no liking for the silent treatment. I do not respond to it properly. My hackles rise. I will have to practice walking on eggshells. I have no experience, no previous experience, in eggshell-walking and therefore I will not be able to give a good performance. They skirted New Haven, entered the Parkway and she still hadn't said anything.

He increased the speed of the car, then he said, softly, "Did you ever hear a very old saying to the effect that where there was no offense intended, no offense should be taken?"

"No. But it sounds reasonable."

He let it go at that, said, and he'd been wanting to say it, "Whenever I see a sky like this one, brassy color rioting all over it, I always wish I could paint. Show the sun going down incredibly hotlooking, and show, too, that the air is cold, make the whole thing look as though the sun were throwing down a gauntlet to winter, shoving it down the throat of the long cold nights."

"You could write it," she said.

"Writing's inadequate. It's not fast enough. A gaudy winter sunset done up in color straight out of the tropics, the whole thing set down in the brutal cold of New England, calls for paint. You see you've got to get it across in the first glance, show the impossible, incredible contrast, bare branches of trees, gaunt, gray-black, silhouetted against that smashing color — all across the horizon — " He took his hands off the wheel, made a wide all-encompassing gesture, using both hands, and the car swerved to the right. He pulled it back on the road quickly.

Camilo said, politely, "Quote. I do not like to have my hair stand on end. My hair does not like to stand on end because it knows that human hair is not supposed to do that. End quote." She laughed. "I'm sorry, but I really couldn't help it."

"Just for future reference, what was wrong with what I said about your driving?"

"I can't bear to be laughed at."

"I was teasing you. I wasn't laughing at you. Even if I had been — why can't you bear to be laughed at?"

"It makes me feel as though I were fourteen again, and back in boarding school, and so fat that I have to wear size forty-two clothes, and a girl named Emmaline is holding up one of my nightgowns, laughing, laughing, laughing, and saying, 'It's like a tent. I bet three of us could get inside it and there'd be room left over. Look! It's like a tent.'"

He said, "In one way or another, it happens to everybody." He thought, I was ten, and they called me Sambo, and I died a little, each time. Well, we have a little more information. You went to boarding school. I didn't think they turned 'em out of Monmouth High School with your stance.

"It's a funny thing," she said. "But when you're that young, people think you haven't any feelings. We were weighed every month, and every month part of me shriveled up and died because I weighed so much it was a joke. Everybody laughed, the nurse, the doctor, the other girls. I wanted to look like GarboCleopatra and I looked like Dickens' fat boy but with pigtails, and wearing a size forty-two tent, not a dress, but a tent. So at night I escaped from the ridicule and the fatness by reading poetry; then after the lights were turned out I would stay awake a long time, making up a dream lover, a dark, handsome man who would recognize the beauty of my soul and fall in love with me, not with any of the pretty, emptyheaded, thin ones.

"In every boarding school, there's a girl with the face of a Botticelli angel and the tongue of an asp, to let you know exactly how awful you look. The one at the school where I went was Emmaline Rosa May Carruthers. In my dream world, Emmaline always died of jealousy, because the dark, handsome lover jilted her and ran off with me."

He thought, listening, how wonderfully complicated the female is, even at fourteen. Fourteen, fourteen, fourteen. What was I like at fourteen? I was damn near being a professional football player, baseball player, basketball player; and I was hellbent on swimming the English Channel. Somebody must have conquered the Channel about then, otherwise I wouldn't have been practically living in The River Wye, covered with grease. Weak Knees and Bill Hod, on the dock, egging me on. Nobody could have paid me to go near a girl. I thought they were dumb, none of 'em could dive.

Camilo said, "I hated those girls, all those pretty curlyheaded girls. But I bought them candy and cake and silk stockings, hoping that if they were in my debt they wouldn't laugh at me. They ate the candy and the cake, and wore the stockings and laughed at me just the same. It was a brandnew, unpleasant experience. Even now, I get angry if I'm laughed at."

"I can't somehow picture you as a fat little girl. But you must have been beautiful." Certainly the hair, the eyes, the mouth, must have been exactly the same.

"I wasn't though. No child can be dreadfully fat and still be beautiful."

"How long have you been looking the way you do now?"

"Ever since I was eighteen."

"What happened then?"

"I was in college by then. In my second year at Barnard. Nobody laughed at me there. But all the girls had boyfriends I did, too, but mine were the toofat ones who wore thicklensed glasses, or the toothin ones, whose backs were hunched over from studying. So I went on a diet and for the first time in my life I learned what it was like to be hungry, all the time. When I'd got thin enough to wear size fourteen clothes I had my hair cut off. In June, one of the fat boys peered at me, then his eyes opened, wide, and he said, 'Why, you're beautiful!' I felt like the Count of Monte Cristo because I'd dug my way out of what amounted to a tomb of fat, and done it alone, unaided."

She was silent and then she turned toward him and said, "You know, when you told me about going to your first movie and how you believed that the world was yours, I was startled. Because the same thing had happened to me. When that boy said, 'You're beautiful,' I believed the world was mine, all I had to do was reach out and take it."

He asked her the same question she had asked him. "Do you still believe it?"

"Of course not. I was awfully young at eighteen, terribly young."

"You still are."

"Not in the same way. It's all right to believe that the world is yours when you're eight. If you're eighteen you're liable to run into trouble."

In New York, he paid a buck and a half to park the car in a midtown parking lot. The attendant looked at Camilo, looked at Link, blandly, incuriously. Link thought, In New York all the black boys who go in for what they like to call Caddies also go in for white girls. So this is old hat to him. He figures that if I'm rich enough — numbers or women or rackets of one kind or another — to drive one of these crates, then almost any goodlooking white girl is going to find me acceptable. Money transforms the black male. Makes him beautiful in the eyes of the white female. Black and comely. No. It was black but comely. Black and comely, take it for granted that blackness and comeliness were not only possible but went hand in hand. A taken-for-granted condition. The other was an explanation and an apology. He thought, That far back. They started that far back. Ah, well.

"Which movie, honey? It was your idea."

"I've got reservations for Radio City," she said.

"How much?"

"Oh, these are Annie Oakleys. I'm always getting tickets to this or that because I write about fashions."

He made no comment but he didn't quite like the idea. He sat beside her in the brilliantly lighted vastness, the elaborateness, of the Music Hall at Radio City, thinking, Well, it's a new experience. I've never been took to the movies before. I must say she's a rather highhanded little female.

The lights went down, and his resentment vanished, because there was always a moment, in any theatre, just before the curtains opened, when he could convince himself that he would, once again, experience that disembodied feeling he had known, at his first movie, when he was eight years old. He never did. Yet, even here, where he knew in advance pretty much what he was going to see, he leaned forward, watching the curtains part, half convinced that this time the magic would work, and he would behold a new and wonderful world.

He saw a stage full of dancing girls, wearing fabulous costumes, and he sat back in his seat. He glanced at Camilo. She was watching the stage, completely absorbed, leaning forward, as though she were alone here, as though this particular show had been staged for her, for no one else. She had removed the white gloves. The soft brown fur that she'd worn around her shoulders was in her lap, mounded in her lap. His hand brushed against it. He resisted an impulse to touch her hand, to say something, anything, that would turn her attention from the dancing girls on the stage to the man sitting beside her.

Finally, the dancing girls moved off the stage, kicking high. They were so exactly alike, the legs, ankles, thighs, breasts, so exactly alike, that they might have been turned out of a mold. Even the high kicks, high kick and turn the head, high kick and turn the head. Maybe they had some kind of meter machine in the rehearsal hall that measured the height of the kicks. It could be simpler than that, maybe they'd worked out something like the automat, put in a nickel, in a giant machine, located on Forty-Second Street, and out would come a girl, or girls, who would meet the requirements as to size and shape, and would be kicking up her legs, just so far, and thus they could not her right up to this theatre, without any further effort on the part of the dance director.

The dancing girls were followed by a pair of dancing colored comedians. He thought, Why, this is the minstrel show again. I'm right back in the Arsenal School on Franklin Avenue and Miss — pause — Dwight is saying, "We won't have to use any burnt cork on — pause —Link."

On the way down, Camilo had said, "It's a funny thing but when you're that young, people think you haven't any feelings." She was fourteen then. Well, he was ten when Miss pause Dwight, who was his teacher, must have come to the conclusion that he didn't have any feelings.

It wasn't just Miss Dwight either. As Dumble Street changed, and more and more colored kids began to go to the Arsenal School, he learned about a new and different kind of insecurity. He was never certain whether the white kids would let him play with them. Sometimes, after school, they played baseball and the kids shouted, "Throw it to old Link, throw it to old Link, Link's good!" Then again the white kids would band together in a tight invulnerable group, welded together by their whiteness, and he, the outcast, the separate one, would be turned on suddenly, ostracized by a gesture, a look, a word.

He kept his fears to himself. They were varied, peculiar. He was afraid of pigeons, afraid of those fat, outrageously breasted birds, that fed on the school lawn, waddling across the grass, in groups, murmuring to themselves, Look at the coon, Look at the coon, Look at the coon, until finally it sounded like one long word, Lookatthecoon.

At least that's what the white kids told him the pigeons were saying. They laughed when they told him. If he grew sullen, furious, and showed it, they said, "Lookit old Link. We ain't talkin' about you. That's what them pigeons say," and then the pigeons and the kids would say, Lookitthecoon, Lookitthecoon, Lookitthecoon, over and over.

He hated crows and grackles and starlings — all the black birds. Because the kids giggled, their eyes sliding around to him when they saw these big black birds, "Blackbird!" they said, and meant him. He hated storms too, thunderstorms, rain clouds, wind clouds, any big black cloud that piled its darkness in the sky. "Storm comin' up," the white kids said. They said it easily, with laughter, innocent-eyed as they looked at him, "A big black cloud's around so a storm's comin' up." "Link's here. A storm's comin' up."

Then, just as suddenly, they welcomed him, accepted him. But he was wary of their acceptance. He never knew at what moment he would be betrayed, thrust out, because of the presence of some other dark creature like himself, perhaps a starling or a crow or another colored boy; betrayed by the gross redlegged pigeons, calling, Lookitthecoon, Lookitthecoon.

Even his name betrayed him. His teacher, Miss Dwight, managed to make it a peculiar name; she hesitated before she said it, made it laughable, and her eyes rejected him, "Speak up — pause — Link." The pause before the name turned it into something to be ashamed of.

It was Miss Dwight, Miss Eleanora Dwight, who decided that his class would give a minstrel show, to raise money, to help raise money for the Parent Teachers' Association. She gave him a part in the show. When the other kids heard her read the lines that would be his, they laughed until they almost cried. He was the butt of all the jokes, he was to say all of the yessuhs and the nosuhs, he was to explain what he was doing in the chicken house, Ain't nobody in here, boss, but us chickens; he was to be caught stealing watermelons; he was to dance something that Miss Dwight called the buck and wing; he was to act sleepy and be late for everything. His name in the minstrel was Sambo.

He could dance better than the other kids. But Miss Dwight

and her pause — Link made him ashamed of his ability to dance. "You know the buck and wing, don't you, pause, Link?"

"No, ma'am," he said politely and let his answer lie there unadorned, no explanation, just the denial.

Miss Dwight said, "Oh, well, any of the dances you know will do," and waited.

Link said nothing.

"What other dances do you know?"

"I don't know any dances, Miss Dwight, except the ones they teach us here in school."

"I thought — " Miss Dwight said and frowned. "Well, we'll make up something. Perhaps your father could teach you the buck and wing or some dance like it." When he didn't reply she said, "Answer me. Can your father teach you the buck and wing?"

He said, "Miss —" then he had a sudden inspiration. He paused before he said "Dwight" just the way she paused before she said "Link." He gave his voice the same intonation as though the name were very strange, very foreign, very funny, and the other kids giggled. Miss Dwight's face turned red, the red seeped into her neck, up to her hairline. "My father's dead," he said; and her face turned even redder. Silence in the room. Stillness.

She went on reading the lines that would be his, and her face stayed red. He felt triumphant. He had beaten her at her own game. But when she finished reading, the kids laughed. It wasn't quite as spontaneous, not quite as hearty as it had been before — but they laughed. She looked around the room, not looking at Link; and he thought, She's going to do something to show I'm different from the rest of the kids.

Miss Dwight said, "Of course this is to be done in black face. You know, like Al Jolson in Mammy." She studied Link's face. She said, "We won't have to use any burnt cork on Link though."

For the first time in his life he was ashamed of the color of his skin. He decided that he would get sick. He would go to all the rehearsals and two days before, no, on the very night of the minstrel show, he would get sick, so sick that he wouldn't be able to be Sambo. None of the kids would be able to take his part on such short notice. So there wouldn't be any minstrel show.

Abbie read the *Chronicle* every night after supper. "I see they're having a minstrel show at school," she said.

Link said, "Uh-huh."

"Are you in it?"

"In a sort of way," he answered and left before she could ask him any more questions. Storm clouds, black birds, gross pigeons strutting on the school lawn, but infinitely worse than any of these — minstrel shows, minstrel shows gotten up by teachers named Miss pause Dwight, teachers who took your name and made it a thing to laugh at, changing it.

At rehearsals he kept getting clumsier and clumsier, bumping into tables and chairs, falling over his own feet.

Miss pause Dwight laughed and choked and coughed and laughed again. "Oh, he's wonderful!" she said. "He makes the show."

The kids began calling him Sambo, during school hours, after school hours, on Saturdays. When they met him on the street, they said, "Hi, Sambo," in chorus, and waited, eying him for some sign of anger. He muttered, "Hi," and walked away.

On the stage, in Radio City Music Hall, one of the dancing colored comedians, slowed his furious pace, lay down, flat on his back, sleeping, sleeping, sleeping. The other dancing colored comedian annoyed him, tormented him, moving about him with the swift darting motion of a mosquito or a fly or a gnat. The sleeping one brushed at the dancing one, slapped at him, moved an arm out of range, moved a leg, shook himself, refusing to wake up. The pantomime was skilful, carefully thought out, comic.

He smiled, as he watched this rhythmic performance, thinking, Well, well, Sambo is still sittin' in the sun. He glanced at the girl. She was laughing, head flung back, revealing the long line of the throat; possibly because she had changed her position he was more than ever aware of her perfume. He thought, I have come a long way. If it hadn't been for Bill Hod and Weak Knees, the color of your skin would disturb me as I watch you laughing at Sambo sittin' in the sun.

9

● HE COULD STILL REMEMBER some of the things that Sambo
was to say: Yessuh, ain't nobody in here but us chickens; nosuh,
watermelon's mah favoritest vegittible; ah'm Sambo, yessuh,
Sambo, just sittin' in the sun, suh; just catchin' up with mah
sleep, suh.

Ten years old. And on the day of the minstrel show, he woke
up feeling hot, suffocated. His head ached. Abbie called and
called for him to come and eat his breakfast. She came in his
room and said, "Why, Link," and put her hand on his forehead.
Her hand felt cool, dry. He was sweating.

Abbie said, "You get right back in bed."

He went to sleep and when he woke up, Dr. Easter was leaning
over him, saying "Hmmm —" Then Dr. Easter was gone but it
couldn't have been as fast a visit as that because he kept remembering the cool hard feel of a thermometer under his tongue.

He went to sleep again. The ringing of the telephone woke him
up. He heard Abbie say, "He's very sick, Miss Dwight." Silence.
"Oh, no!" Her voice was crisp, cold. "Absolutely impossible. He
can't get out of bed."

He stared up at the ceiling. He had forgotten about the minstrel show. Was he really sick or had he made himself sick? Could
you make yourself sick, not really meaning to? Not really meaning to? Then you could make yourself go crazy, too.

He sat up, frowning. He hadn't made himself sick. It had just
happened. Maybe he had the mumps. But he didn't ache any-

where. He felt strong, cool, comfortable. He wanted to get out of bed; he felt like going swimming.

If he wasn't sick any more, he ought to get dressed, and go down to the school auditorium and be Sambo, sittin' in the sun. He'd sold out, hadn't he? Sold what out?

He got dressed. He went out of the front door very quietly so Abbie wouldn't hear him. Miss pause Dwight would be happy. He would be unhappy. But he had to be Sambo, sittin' in the sun. He walked slowly, up Dumble Street, over to Franklin, down Franklin to the school.

He stood still. People were going up the long walk, in through the front door. Cars were parked on both sides of the school driveway. He couldn't be Sambo sittin' in the sun in front of all those people. Ain't nobody in here but us chickens.

If Abbie knew about this, she'd say that he'd let The Race down. She said colored people (sometimes she just said The Race) had to be cleaner, smarter, thriftier, more ambitious than white people, so that white people would like colored people. The way she explained it made him feel as though he were carrying The Race around with him all the time. It kept him confused, a little frightened, too. At that moment The Race sat astride his shoulders, a weight so great that his back bent under it. When he turned away from the school, he was walking fast.

In school, the next morning, Miss pause Dwight said, "I thought you were sick, pause, Link."

"I was," he said.

"You know you ruined the minstrel show. We couldn't have it. On account of you. I should have known that you'd fail me at the last minute."

He knew what she meant about failing her at the last minute. There wasn't much about The Race that he didn't know. Abbie kept telling him all the things he could, and could not, do because of The Race. You had to be polite; you had to be punctual; you couldn't wear bright-colored clothes, or loud-colored socks; and even certain food was forbidden. Abbie said that she loved watermelons, but she would just as soon cut off her right arm as go in a store and buy one, because colored people loved watermelons. She wouldn't buy porgies because colored people loved all the coarsefleshed fish and were particularly fond of porgies. She wouldn't fry fish, she wouldn't fry chicken, because everybody knew that colored people liked fried food. She was always on **time,** in fact, way ahead of time, because colored people were always late, you could never count on them, they had no sense of responsibility. The funny thing about it was that when Abbie talked about The Race she sounded as though she weren't colored, and yet she obviously was.

All of this was why Miss pause Dwight had known that he'd fail her at the last minute. But she couldn't have known. He had been sick, really and truly sick. Then he got better. He had got out of bed, and come all the way down to the school, yesterday; but then when he got here he just couldn't be Sambo sittin' in the sun. Not in front of all those people.

All that morning Miss pause Dwight said: "I might have known"; "Sit still"; "Stop wriggling"; "Answer me!" "Are you asleep?" "Stand up!" "Sit down!"

By the time the noon bell rang, he knew he wasn't going back to school. Not ever. He spent the afternoon down on the dock. He found there were three other colored boys, older than he, who were playing hookey too. They figured out that if they showed up for meals, and got home just about the time the other kids came from school, and left their houses in the morning when the other kids were leaving, their families wouldn't know they were playing hookey. The mail was delivered in the morning before they left for school, so if the principal sent a notice home, they could get it first, tear it up and that way — well, they'd stay out for a long long time.

During that long wonderful week, F. K. Jackson and Abbie and The Race and Miss pause Dwight disappeared from his world, dispelled by sun and wind and fog. He forgot there was something wrong, bad, about the color of his skin. When it rained they went, all of them, single file, quietly, quickly, around the back of The Last Chance, and sat inside the old unused chicken house, and played cards and read comic books. Even when it was raining they went swimming in the river.

Abbie found out, finally, by the most unforeseen, the most appallingly unforeseen, of accidents. She went to see the principal, without saying anything to Link, suddenly, on impulse, because she wasn't satisfied with Link's reading. She kept telling him that when she was ten years old she could read and understand poetry, the Bible, Shakespeare; and he said that he could read better than any kid in his grade; and she said, "Well, in that case they must all be morons and idiots because you can barely spell out the

words in a primer, and you can't write so that anybody can read
what you've written." They usually stopped right there — but he
felt so free, the river seemed to have soaked into his bones and
blood, he felt like air and water and sun, and The Race no longer
sat astride his shoulders, Miss pause Dwight no longer prodded
him and The Race, at one and the same time, that he said, "Well,
Aunt Abbie, other people can read my writing. Maybe you need
to get new glasses." And she got mad and went to the principal's
office to find out if something couldn't be done to improve his
reading.

About three-thirty in the afternoon, he came in through the
back door, as usual, so he wouldn't muddy up the front hall floor,
came in through the back door, whistling, not a care in the
world, feeling as though there were a grin inside him that was
spreading, spreading, and he kept telling himself to be careful so
the grin wouldn't show in his face.

Abbie and F. K. Jackson were waiting for him, in the sitting-
dining room, dining-sitting room, both looking as though they
were sitting up with a corpse; he knew instantly that he was the
corpse and that they had been waiting for his arrival. He could
tell by the way Abbie sat in the Boston rocker, her hands folded
in her lap, and she never sat still like that, she was always cro-
cheting or knitting, as though she would not, could not, waste
even so much as a moment of time; and F. K. Jackson was leaning against the marble mantel; one bony elbow on the mantle.
They were both frowning. F. K. Jackson's pince-nez had more
glitter than usual.

Abbie said, "Link — "

F. K. Jackson interrupted her. She said, "Why haven't you
been in school this week?"

He went straight to the point, just like F. K. Jackson, and said,
just as abruptly, "I got tired of it."

That was a mistake. F. K. Jackson said that his staying away
from school was an evasive dishonest action which could lead to
other larger kinds of dishonesty, far more serious than this; that it
already had because he had tampered with the United States
mail; and thus he had taken the first step straight toward the door
of a reform school. She kept walking up and down, and frowning
at him, as she talked. Finally, she shook one of her long, bony,
forefingers, practically under his nose, and said, "You're an ingrate. That's what you are — an ingrate!"

Then Abbie talked and talked and talked. About The Race. She said that there had been a time (she always avoided mention of slavery) when it was a crime in this country to teach a colored person to read and write; and, because of that period in the history of The Race, it behooved all persons of color to take advantage of the free education now available to everybody. (He smiled because he thought about Fishmouth Taylor and Fishmouth's comment on practically everything: free schools, pretty white teachers, and dumb niggers. Abbie must have got mad because he smiled; otherwise she would not have said what she did.)

She said it particularly behooved Link Williams, orphan, adopted out of the goodness of the Major's heart (she wiped away a tear) and her heart, to go to school, every day, and learn, and learn, and learn, so that he would stand at the head of his class, in everything, so that he would be a credit to The Race.

The stage show came to an end in a whirling spectacular finale, composed of dancing girls, and dancing colored comedians, brilliant lighting, and music that sounded as though it had been lifted whole from the swoop of the "William Tell Overture," and the curtains closed. The lights came up, all over the theatre, then went down. The curtains opened again. The movie started.

He watched it for a few minutes. It bored him. He wondered why women liked movies. What had Camilo said, on the trip down? Something about the dark handsome lover. Maybe the female was always hunting for him, maybe in the back of the female mind was the belief that he could be found, even after the female was married and had six children. Hollywood knew this. So the demon lover, the dark, handsome, rapacious lover, showed up in all the movies; and the females could believe he was theirs for about an hour and a half. So right after they finished the supper dishes, they went around to the neighborhood theatre, and sat there, legs apart, mouths open, panting a little, because now they were young again, and there was no fat around their waists, no varicose veins marred the flawless beauty of their legs, and the demon lover took them in his arms. They always looked dazed when the picture ended and the lights came up.

Camilo was watching the screen just as she had watched the stage show, with the same degree of concentration. He wondered how she could identify herself so completely with the action that took place in a movie. When he was eight, a movie could carry him straight into another world but he'd seen a hell of a lot of different worlds since then, and he'd had far more at stake in all of them than he'd ever have in anything they cooked up in Hollywood. Demon lover, he thought. Was Camilo still hunting for one? It seemed doubtful. But if a theory was going to hold water, wouldn't you have to try applying it? Abbie? Had she hunted for one? She found one, in the person of the Major. She lost him when he died, and she was never quite the same afterwards. F. K. Jackson? Impossible to think of her hunting a mate, handsome or otherwise. She was too brusque, too selfsufficient. Perhaps she, in her own person, was the dark handsome lover, and to her Abbie had been the ChinaCamiloWilliams that the male hunts for and rarely ever finds; and even if he finds her, never quite manages to capture her.

Ah, the hell with it, he thought.

Ten years old. And he played hookey. A week later he was back in school, feeling ashamed and resentful. He wasn't an ingrate. Nobody had told Abbie and the Major to adopt him. He would have been better off if they hadn't.

Miss pause Dwight was still mad about his ruining the minstrel show, was furious because he'd played hookey. All day long, or so it seemed, she said: "I might have expected it"; "Link, will you please wake up?" "Are you deaf? I asked you a question."

He stopped trying to learn anything. There wasn't any use. He thought she might forget about him if he acted as though he were deaf, dumb, blind. So she told the principal that he was totally unresponsive. The principal sent for him and urged him to make an effort, "You're a bright boy, Link. You can do anything you want to do."

Miss pause Dwight complained about him again, saying that he could no longer stay in her class. The principal sent for Abbie, and sent for Link too; and told them both that Link would soon have to go in the class for the mentally retarded, the dummies as the kids said, because he was now behaving as though he were halfwitted. He kept right on acting as though he were deaf, dumb, blind.

Abbie cried. F. K. Jackson scolded. They talked about him, discussed him, all the time, even when he was in the same room with them.

Abbie: Maybe he's sick.

F. K. Jackson: I don't believe it. He eats like a horse. If he were sick he wouldn't eat like a horse.

Abbie: I'm going to send for Dr. Easter.

F. K. Jackson: Don't be foolish. Take the boy around to his office. It costs a dollar less. Besides there isn't a thing wrong with him.

Dr. Easter poked at him, pried at him, weighed him, measured him, said: He's as fine a specimen as I've ever seen. Not a thing wrong with him, Mrs. Crunch.

Abbie reported this to F. K. Jackson and said, a quaver in her voice: Maybe there's something wrong with his mind, Frances. Do you think there's something wrong with his mind?

F. K. Jackson snorted: It's just stubbornness. He's just like a mule. Somebody ought to — and didn't finish whatever she was going to say.

He wasn't supposed to go in The Last Chance except on Saturdays, because of some kind of compromise that F. K. Jackson had worked out with Bill Hod. But he went anyway. On a Wednesday. Late in the afternoon.

Weak Knees said, "Hiya, Sonny. You got here just in time. I got red rice in this here pot. In the middle of the afternoon, like now, a man could eat up all this rice and then turn around and start in all over again." He put a plate of red rice on the table. "Come on, Sonny, start layin' your lip over it, just start right in." Then he looked at Link, really looked at him and he said, "Whatsamatter, Sonny? You don't look so good."

The rice cooled on his plate while he told Weak Knees about the pigeons and the black birds, about Miss pause Dwight and the minstrel show and Sambo sittin' in the sun; and Bill came in and scooped up an enormous plateful of rice, pulled up a chair and sat, listening, not saying anything, just eating red rice, as Link told about The Race, and how he was responsible for all other members of The Race even though he did not know them; and how he couldn't do it any more, it sort of paralyzed him because he never knew whether he was doing something because he, Link, wanted to do it; or whether he did something because of the undesirable color of his skin, and that meant he had no control over what he did — it just happened.

All of a sudden Bill started talking. He was talking about the Chicago riots. Link leaned forward, listening, listening. He'd never heard anything like this before.

Bill told about Ma Winters, an old woman who ran a rooming house on the South Side, in Chicago; and how white men broke down the door and surged into the downstairs hall; and how Ma Winters stood at the top of the stairs with a loaded shotgun in her hand, not shouting, not talking loud, just saying, conversationally, "I'm goin' to shoot the first white bastard who puts his foot on that bottom step." And did. And laughed. And aimed again. "Come on," she said, "some of the rest of you sons of bitches put your white feet on my stairs." And they backed out of the door, backed out of the door, kept backing out of the door, and left a white man, a dead white man, there in the hall, lying on his back, a bloody mess where his face had been.

It seemed to be just a story, a good story, an exciting story, yet he was certain it had some other deeper meaning that he couldn't quite grasp. Certainly the old woman who stood at the head of the stairs firing the shotgun, killing a white man, threatening to kill other white men, didn't carry The Race around on her shoulders. The burden of race lifted a little from his own shoulders.

The next day Abbie told him that if he wanted to he could go back to The Last Chance to live. He didn't know why this should be so but he gladly moved back across the street.

Shortly after that, Bill visited the school. Right after that Link noticed that Miss pause Dwight started being nice to him; oddly enough she referred to Bill as his uncle, Mr. Hod.

Weak Knees and Bill re-educated him on the subject of race. After supper Weak Knees sat down at the kitchen table and read the newspaper, a tabloid newspaper. He spread it out flat in front of him, fingering his way down the columns. When he found something that was especially interesting, he picked the paper up. Link could see the pink outer sheets, the big black type, and Weak Knees' dark hands like a pattern on the pink paper. "Name-a-God, Sonny, lissen to this. Here's a bank teller, just a ordinary smart white boy, free of course 'cause he's white so he done stole hisself thirty-five hunnerd dollars. Done fixed himself so he ain't goin' to be able to cuddle any little gals and he's goin' to have to eat that slop they throw at 'em in jailhouses for the rest of his natural — all for thirty-five hunnerd dollars. White folks sure is smart. Tee-hee-hee." The kitchen was filled with his highpitched cackling laugh. Link had never heard white people laughed at before and it made him uncomfortable at first.

Weak Knees bought a bird feeder, and hung it in a tree in the yard in back of The Last Chance, hung suet in the tree, scattered crumbs.

"That's for my black boys," he said. "Watch them black boys, Sonny. They drives all them other birds away. Tee-hee-hee. Bestlookin' birds of any of 'em. Look how them tail feathers and them breas' feathers shine in the sun. Lookithat big one peck that other bird. Lookithat! Lookithat! Tee-hee-hee."

Black was bestlooking. It was a new idea. He mulled over it. Not possible. Black is evil. Satan is black. Abbie said, Black people, and there was disapproval in her voice. Black was undesirable. Black sheep — the bad one. Black cat — bad luck. Black was ugly, evil, dirty, to be avoided. It was worn for funerals. It meant death, too.

They proved to him, Weak Knees and Bill Hod, that black could be other things, too. They did it casually. Ebony was the best wood, the hardest wood; it was black. Virginia ham was the best ham. It was black on the outside. Tuxedos and tail coats were black and they were a man's finest, most expensive clothes. You had to use pepper to make most meats and vegetables fit to eat. The most flavorsome pepper was black. The best caviar was black. The rarest jewels were black: black opals, black pearls.

After a month of living with Bill and Weak Knees he felt fine. He felt safe. He was no longer ashamed of the color of his skin. One morning when he went to school he carried a rock in his hand. When he reached the lawn, he aimed at, and hit, the fattest of the pigeons. Squawks. A fluttering of wings. The rest of the pigeons flew up, were gone. The fattest one lay on its side. It too tried to fly, fluttered its wings and lay still.

He knew then what that story of Bill's meant: If you were attacked you had to fight back. If you didn't you would die.

The long full curtains covered the screen at Radio City Music Hall. The lights went up.

Camilo turned toward him. "You weren't looking at the picture," she said. "Didn't you like it?"

He shrugged. "Sometimes I look at my own movies." He helped her put the long soft brown furpiece around her shoulders, stood up, waiting, while she put on the white gloves. "Where would you like to eat?" he asked.

"I know a place not too far from here. The food is wonderful. Suppose we go there."

They walked up Fifth Avenue. Even at this hour he thought

that the people who passed them seemed, even in walking, to buck their strength against the city, against the concrete sidewalks, against the skyscrapers, and the steam heat inside them; always that suffocating dry heat inside the buildings and outside in the streets the same bone-chilling cold there was in Monmouth — damp, penetrating.

He supposed all these people they passed were hellbent on the same thing, hurrying after the same dream, chasing it up and down Fifth Avenue. He thought of Wormsley, G. Granville Wormsley, who had been his classmate at Dartmouth. Once he and Wormsley had walked along Fifth Avenue, stopping now and then to look in the store windows, just as Camilo was doing now. Only Wormsley was always hunting paintings and books; Camilo was hunting dresses and shoes and jewelry — at least that was what she looked at longest, standing, head cocked on one side, looking.

Link said, "About five years ago I walked along here with a friend of mine, a guy named Wormsley. After he'd looked in some of these store windows he said, 'This is what brought my father here, this is what keeps me here. I look in these windows, go in these stores, and I begin to believe all over again that I can conquer this city. It's the sight of the loot in these windows that keeps people in New York.' About a year after that he came to Monmouth, to say goodbye to me. He said it was hopeless, nobody could win against New York City, and that it wasn't what he wanted so he was going to London. Six months later he was back. He said he didn't know why he had left, that he never intended to leave again, because if he lost, and now he was no longer certain about the outcome, he would rather lose in New York, in the midst of the cold and chill, in the midst of the only other kind of weather the city offered, heat and heat and heat, than to survive, let alone win, anywhere else in the world."

Camilo had stopped to look at a red evening gown, displayed on one of those incredibly thin, very natural-looking figures they use in the windows of department stores. A seated figure, the long thin legs crossed, the trunk bending forward. Link looked too, and thought, Well, Sambo may still be sittin' in the sun, sleepin' in the sun in Radio City, but Mrs. Sambo now sits in the windows of the specialty shops, the exclusive dress shops. Some skilled and skilful hand makes all these store window dummies look like colored women, the hair frizzed, the skin color no longer

pink and white but the offwhite of a high yaller. O wondrous
world.

Camilo said, "What did your friend Wormsley want to win?"

"I asked him that. And he said, 'All of it. All of this city. I
want to control it.' Then he said, 'I want to be a kingmaker, not
a king you understand, but a kingmaker.' Kingmaker Wormsley."

"Why he's a fascist at heart."

"No," Link said slowly. "That doesn't allow for his other
quirks. Fascist in his desire for power — but then aren't we all?
Even you and I? Eventually won't you want to control me? And
I, of course, already want to control you." You've got a terrific
drive, an urge, toward and for power, little one, though you evidently don't know it. "That doesn't make us fascists."

She said, "Is he a kingmaker?"

They turned off Fifth Avenue, started walking east.

Link said, "In a smallish way. If he lives long enough he will
be one in a largish way."

"What does he do?"

"He's a psychiatrist and a damn good one."

He studied the street ahead of them. Let's see, he thought,
where would this little exquisite be likely to think the food was
wonderful? It will be the place where the striped awning extends
over the sidewalk, offering protection to the silk hats and the
poodle cuts emerging from the limousines and taxis, where the
evergreens squat in little red pots, where the doorman in the
plum-colored costume stands like the keeper of the gate, even to
the stance, separating the sheep from the goats before they get
close enough to bang on the gate. Yea, verily, many are called,
but few are chosen.

He was right. She said, "Here we are," and tucked her hand
under his arm, steering him so that they turned in under the
striped awning.

The headwaiter, no, manager, no, owner, well, whatever the hell
he was, stood just inside the door, short, swarthy, dressed in evening clothes, greeting the customers also dressed in evening
clothes. He bowed practically to the floor at the sight of Camilo,
saying, "Mademoiselle! What pleasure! We have missed you!"
He had a French accent, like Old Madame Tay-tay's, who for
years was the only colored Catholic in The Narrows.

Link remembered how he used to watch her sitting on her doorstep, muttering under her breath, as she fingered her beads. She

nodded her head, at frequent intervals, so that the long gold earrings she wore, dangled back and forth, making a tinkling sound. The kids said she was born in New Orleans; and that she was creole, and therefore neither colored nor white. Later, they also told him, that when she was dying, she had said her prayers in French. For a long time afterwards, he had wondered how God, whom he had always assumed to be a Protestant and an American, had been able to understand her; and didn't dare ask Abbie lest his question be dismissed as blasphemous.

Camilo said, "I've been away, Georges. In Dallas."

After a quick shrewd glance at Link, Georges bowed again, though not quite so near the floor, said, "*Monsieur!* What pleasure! This way."

Georges personally escorted them the length of the restaurant, past the tables, flowers on the tables, lighted candles on the tables, past the shaded wall lights and the muted voices and the muted laughter. It was warm inside the restaurant. Link caught whiffs of perfume from the females in evening clothes. They went past a small bar and there was the faint smell of alcoholic beverages, alien smell in this warm perfumed room, old familiar smell of The Last Chance, of The Moonbeam, in this restaurant for the very rich. All cats bee gray —

They went up a flight of stairs into a small room where there was a table set for two.

Georges said, "I hope everything will be of a perfection, *mademoiselle, monsieur.* Your waiter will be here at once. Aha, here he is."

The menu cards were big, elaborately decorated. Link thought, You could mat 'em and have 'em framed and they'd make a splash even on the walls of Grand Central. And this tall thin man, in a tail coat, who is our waiter, makes me understand how Weak Knees feels when he says, "Get away, Eddie. God damn it, get away." If he doesn't stop breathing down my neck I shall say the same thing.

Camilo said, "Roast duck, and a salad, and a vegetable. Broccoli for the vegetable."

Link handed the outsize menu back to the waiter. He said, "Steak and whatever your chef thinks an American ought to eat with steak."

The waiter left and Link said, "Did you reserve this?"

She smiled at him. "Yes, I did. Is it all right?"

He nodded, thinking, It's all right from your point of view and in your world. It's all wrong from where I sit.

The food was good though M. Georges's chef wasn't in the same class with Weak Knees, which was only to be expected. He didn't know as much about vegetables, didn't know anything at all about the possibilities of the humble potato. But he knew a good deal about steaks.

While they ate, he told Camilo about Weak Knees, about the new receipt for spaghetti, and how Jubine had said there'd be a shortage of salt pork if all chefs started using it, not really thinking about what he was saying, just making talk, while he studied her face. In the flickering light of the candles the blue of her eyes was a dark unidentifiable color; the pale yellow hair had an added gleam, it fairly shimmered in the dancing flickering light.

"Jubine?" she said. "The photographer? I know him, too."

Pleasure in the light musical voice, pleasure in her face, because Jubine linked them together, common acquaintance, their worlds came closer because they both knew Jubine. He thought, Motorcycle, GI shoes, cigar in mouth, inquisitive eyes — how did she meet Jubine?

She said, "Sometimes he takes fashion pictures for me. They're absolutely wonderful. But he doesn't care much about photographing models and clothes."

When they finished eating, he said, "I'll ask for the check now so that we can get out of here sometime in the next hour."

She said, "Oh, there isn't any check. It's almost the other way around. If Georges could, he'd pay me to eat here."

"Look!" he said. "If Georges would like to pay you to eat here why that takes care of you. It doesn't take care of me. I'm going to pay for my part of this meal."

"Oh, no, you mustn't."

He rang for the waiter, took his wallet out of his pocket.

"Link," she said, "don't make a scene."

"A scene?" he said. "A scene? What do you mean by that? What kind of a scene do you think I'm likely to make in here?" Sambo was still sittin' in the sun in Radio City Music Hall, maybe he was still sittin' in the sun in Camilo's mind, honing his razor.

"If you insist on paying for something that isn't supposed to be paid for why you'll have to be unpleasant about it. Georges isn't going to take your money. You'd have to force him to take it — and — "

He put the wallet back in his pocket. Georges isn't going to take your money. Why wasn't Georges going to take his money?

The tall thin waiter said, "Yes, sir?" and hovered, again bending down, over Link's shoulder.

Camilo said quickly, "We'd like some hot coffee."

Now that she had got her own way she smiled at Link. She said, "Let's do this again. Next Sunday."

"Go to the movies and then afterwards come here and eat?"

She nodded. "Then you did enjoy it!"

"And when we come here again, next Sunday, I suppose you will already have ordered what you want me to eat."

"Of course not. Why would I?" She stared at him and the laughter, the gaiety, went out of her face. "You mean I'm — "

"The only reason I've put up with this — " he gestured toward the table, the flowers, the candles, the covered silver dishes, the wine glasses, "is — well — I think I'm in love with you. But either we play this my way and ride in whatever hay wagon or tractor or freight car I can provide, or — we quit."

"I think we'd better quit," she said evenly.

As they were leaving, Georges said, "Was everything all right, monsieur?"

Link said, "Oh, quite. Everything was of a perfection," unconsciously imitating the accent of Madame Tay-tay. Two on the aisle provided by the lady. Dinner afterwards. Private dining room reserved by the lady. Meal obviously paid for by the lady. Plantation buck. How many generations back? Oh, possibly four. Jump four generations and he shows up as a kept man. Objective about race? Hell, no. Nobody was. Not in the USA.

Georges glanced at him, sharply. "Monsieur has an excellent memory."

Camilo said, "Everything was perfection, Georges. Thank you very much, and, good night."

"Good night, mademoiselle. Good night, monsieur."

They were silent, both of them, all the way back to Monmouth. He stopped the car on Franklin Avenue, got out, closed the door. He had been trying to figure out something to say ever since they left New York. And ended up saying, simply, inadequately, "Goodbye," though he was certain that he would not see her again.

Four nights later. Midnight. He came out of The Last Chance, turned his coat collar up, frowned, listening to the wind keening

in the branches of The Hangman, thinking, It's too damn cold to
go prowling through these streets again tonight. The Weather
Bureau had been predicting this sudden change in temperature,
attributing it to a cold mass that was moving in from Canada.
Said cold mass had been signaling its arrival for three days, mer-
cury in the thermometers dropping, dropping, wind shifting, shifting; had obviously moved in now and brought all the relatives, including the great grandpappy and the kissin' cousins.

He glanced down Dumble Street. It was as bleak and deserted
as a street in a small town where a curfew has rung. Everything
closed down, shut up, all the lights out. The other streets in The
Narrows would be just as dark, and silent as this one. He knew
because he had been walking through them for the last three
nights, not going anywhere, just walking, in the hope that when
he went to bed he would be so dogtired he would go to sleep instantly and not dream about the girl.

He had walked and walked, listening to the sound of his own
footsteps, echoing behind him on the sidewalk, as though in viola-
tion of the imaginary curfew that had long since sent everyone
else scurrying home. No matter how far he walked, how tired he
became, he never achieved the dreamless sleep that was his objective.

He always had the same dream. It came toward morning. It
was so real that he could have sworn the girl was lying beside him,
that she had her arms around him, and he thought he could feel
the warmth from her body, and so turned on his side, turned toward her. A haunting, beautiful dream. The unpleasant part came
when he woke up. The dream was so vivid, dream and desire and
reality so inextricably mixed up, that as he lay there in the early
morning grayness that was neither daylight nor dark, he extended
his hand, expecting to find her beside him, within hand's reach.

Each morning, when he awakened, and found that she was not
there, he had known a sense of loss, so real that it was painful.
He had tried to assuage, to allay, the pain by re-creating her in
his mind's eye, the shape of her face, the silkiness of her hair, the
arched eyebrows, the deep blue eyes, the absolute perfection of
the mouth and nose, the way her face lighted up when she smiled,
the haunting fragrance of the perfume she used. Then he would
scowl, wanting to forget her. Instead of forgetting her, putting
her out of his mind, he went on remembering her, the way she
walked, the light musical sound of her voice.

He knew he would never forget her. He would go on dreaming

about her at night, thinking about her during the day, forever and
ever. Or stand, motionless, bemused, on a cold windy street, just
as he was doing now, because he was suddenly assailed by the
memory of her.

He heard the creaking of the branches of The Hangman, and
thought, It's too damn cold to stand here and play the mooncalf,
and there's no moon, and you're a big boy now, but your wits are
out, your wits are out, like Hans Kraut, and crossed the street,
moving quickly, going toward Abbie's house, listening to the
sound of his own footsteps, hearing the creak-creak of The Hangman so loud that he looked up, saw the bend and sway of the
great branches high overhead, thought, Heavy heavy hangs over
thy head, what wilt thou do to redeem it, redeem it, never can
redeem it, lost it, not lost it, threw it away, own volition, nobody
made you, you stiffnecked —

He started to go up Abbie's front steps, and put his hand on the
old wrought-iron railing, felt it cold under his hand, and then
turned and glanced in the direction of the river, and saw the girl's
car parked under the street light at the corner, and so walked
toward Dock Street.

The girl got out of the car, and he stood still watching her as
she came toward him. The wind was blowing her hair about her
face. He felt his throat constrict, so that he couldn't swallow,
could not at that moment have spoken if his life had depended on
it. As she came nearer he felt a thickness rising in his throat, filling his throat.

"Hello," she said, her face alight, alive, glowing. "I came
back."

"I've missed you." He put his hands on her arms. He had never
touched her before and she looked up at him, the eyes darker
than he had remembered them, or perhaps it was due to the darkness of this winter's night.

She said, "Link — " and it sounded like a question.

He pulled her close to him, looking at her face, thinking, Win
or lose, all or nothing, Hobson's choice. Then he leaned down
and kissed her, and felt her lips respond to his, felt her mouth
soft, warm, slowly opening.

She said, finally, "Shall we go back to where we started — to
The Moonbeam?"

"All right." He hoped he sounded matter of fact, though he
doubted it. Win or lose. And he had won. He had taken a long

running jump and landed on his feet. He had won Mamie-PowtherChinaCamiloWilliams for keeps. He knew it and he couldn't quite get his breath back.

Inside the door of The Moonbeam, they both stood still, not saying anything, just looking. He saw Old One-One ploughing across the big smoke-filled room, heading toward two young men, two dark young men, who might have been embracing each other, passionately; swaying from the force of the emotion that made them hug each other in a tight, close, hot embrace. Was this a sudden access of love, he wondered. No. It was hate. One of them had a knife and —

"Let's not go in," he said and turned the girl around, shepherding her out of the door, pushing her gently out of the door, controlling an impulse to bury his face in her hair, thinking, That's too long a jump for anyone to have to make, from the private dining room of a French restaurant in the Fifties in New York to Old One-One and The Moonbeam Café on Franklin Avenue in Monmouth.

"Where will we go?" she said. She was looking straight at him, studying his face, just as he had studied hers, in the moment before he kissed her.

He was silent, watching her, because she was deciding something. "Well?" he said.

She took hold of his arm, put her hand in his. They retraced their steps, walking slowly along Franklin Avenue, then down Dumble Street. He could smell the perfume that she used, faint, sweet. He thought, Rooms, Dollar and Half a Night, shabby hotels, dingy rooming houses, rent a room on Franklin Avenue, one-night stand, smell of kerosene, dogs, people.

He said, "This way."

They turned into Number Six Dumble Street, went up the steps. He unlocked the door. There was no sound at all, not even a faint click as the tumblers turned in the lock. Then they were standing in the hall, the only light came from what Abbie called the night lamp, an oldfashioned oil lamp, marble base, wired for electricity. In the dim light you could see the long carpeted staircase, the curve of it, see the polished parquet floor, he turned a little and he could see the gleam of the Major's goldheaded cane in its usual place in the hatrack, gleam of the Major's silk hat which Abbie brushed every morning, gleam of the walnut backs on the pair of Victorian chairs, chairs silhouetted against the striped wallpaper. He remembered how F. K. Jackson appeared to be addressing the wallpaper when she said, "The Major is dead — "

He thought there was a movement, thought his eye caught the tailend of a motion, something moving, some gesture, something, in the deep shadows of the landing, and he looked up quickly. There was nothing. There was no sound at all, anywhere in the whole house. Perhaps it was the stillness that lay over the house, perhaps it was the careful way he had opened the door, but the girl had said nothing, still said nothing, even after he opened the door of his room, turned the lights on.

Then she said, "I love you, I love you, love you."

They were in Harlem on Christmas Eve. It was snowing. They stopped to buy a newspaper and he turned and looked at her, at the snow falling on the soft brown fur coat, on the tip of her nose, on the pale yellow hair, on the scrap of black velvet that was her hat. Right there on 125th Street, corner of Seventh Avenue, he kissed the tip of her nose — because he couldn't help it. The redfaced news vendor, who had been watching them, leaned out of the newsstand and said, "Mister, you got all the Merry Christmas a man could want standin' right there by you."

Camilo smiled at the man and said, "Merry Christmas to you!"

Link thought, We're both at the stage where we love everybody, news vendors, and elevator men, and bus drivers, and charwomen, and beggars — anybody and everybody who doesn't have the hold on ecstasy that we have. We keep wanting to spread it around.

He reached in his pocket just as though he were a millionaire, just as though he plucked five-dollar bills from The Hangman every morning just before breakfast, and handed five bucks to the news vendor and said, "Buy yourself a drink. As a matter of fact, here's another one, Mack. Buy yourself two drinks."

He said, "Christmas present," to Camilo and kissed her again.

She said, "Merry Christmas, darling!" and handed him a small square package, wrapped in dark green paper. It was tied with a silver ribbon, and there was a red poinsettia smack in the middle of the package.

He held it in his hand, lightly, balancing it on the tips of his fingers.

"Camilo, will you marry me?" he asked, voice soft, voice caressing.

He wondered afterwards why he'd asked her. Was it the absolute envy in the eyes of the news vendor, as he leaned forward, watching them, his elbows on a pile of newspapers, his bulky figure silhouetted against the gaudy covers of the pulp magazines, hung all around the inside of the newsstand? Or was it the snow? Snow everywhere, even on the sidewalks, coming down so fast that it obliterated a footprint almost as soon as it was made, snow softening the brilliant redgreen of the stop lights, snow muffling sounds; turning Harlem into a place of enchantment, straight out of Grimm's Fairy Tales, no, Andersen's, because the snow and ice were in Andersen. Few people on the street. No traffic. Everyman is at home with all the lights turned on; all the houses and the apartments are full of something strangely like hope, like delight, like love, and there are children — and Christmas trees — and piles of presents.

He said, again, "Camilo, will you marry me?"

She touched his cheeks with the tips of her fingers, then put both arms around his neck and whispered, in his ear, "One of these days. Come spring. Time of the singing of birds. Yes."

"Why not now?"

"People would swear that I'd married you to keep warm," she giggled, "to keep my feet warm. And they'd be right."

They stood on the corner of 125th Street and Seventh Avenue, laughing; the snow was wet on their faces, the snow was cold on their faces.

In love with love, he thought. Was that it? No. In love with CamiloWilliamsChinaMamiePowther? No. In love with Camilo Williams.

10

● SATURDAY, and Malcolm Powther was off for the evening, off
early, too. He stood in the doorway of a side entrance to Treadway Hall, trying to raise his umbrella. The wind kept shifting,
blowing the umbrella back against him and then swooping under
it so that he very nearly lost his grip on the handle.

He braced himself against the door in preparation for a further
struggle with the umbrella. It was a strong wind. Almost a gale.
The big-leaved ivy on the walls of the house rippled, moving back
and forth in the wind. The electric lights on each side of the
door gave the ivy a strange yellowgreen tinge. The color of the
ivy, and the constant back-and-forth motion of it, suggested that
moths, millions of them, had been pinioned to the walls, and were
fluttering their wings in a desperate effort to free themselves, painful to watch because it was a silent struggle.

Something eerie about the ivy tonight, he thought. First I think
of moths but if I keep watching it with the wind making it quiver
like that I shall begin to believe that it is not the ivy that's moving but the thick stone walls of the house.

He began his struggle with the umbrella again and then stopped
because he saw Al coming up the driveway, heading for this same
entrance. Al had his chauffeur's cap on the back of his head,
which meant the Madam wasn't ready to leave yet.

"You goin' now?" Al asked.

Powther nodded.

"Come on, I'll drive you to the car line, Mal. I'd take you all the way but the Widow's goin' to feed her face in Bridgeport tonight and I gotta have that crate waitin' at the door of the shack the minute the outside air hits that mink."

They walked down the driveway together. The town car was parked in front of the house. Powther hesitated before he got in.

"Do you think — " he said.

Al interrupted. "I ain't goin' to let you walk to the trolley, not in no nasty weather like this. Come on, get in. I got time enough. The Widow'll be gettin' her tiara fixed on her head for a good ten minutes yet."

It was warm inside the car. He leaned back against the soft upholstery, listening to, and enjoying, the faint hum of the motor, the swish-click, swish-click of the windshield wipers. He was glad that Al had insisted on giving him a ride. A cold rainy night. Windy, too. He probably wouldn't have been able to keep his umbrella up.

Al went down the milelong driveway, fast. The big entrance gates were open so that he didn't even have to stop to toot his horn, just slowed a little, and then went straight out onto the highway. A trolley was just coming to a stop. They watched the conductor get out and change the position of the trolley pole.

Powther thought, Well, now this is very nice. Drummond is the conductor tonight. We'll have a chance for a visit.

"That's a job I sure wouldn't want," Al said. "Specially on a night like this."

"Neither would I." Powther started to get out of the car.

Al leaned toward him. "Wait a minute, Mal," he said. "I got somethin' I been wantin' to ask you."

There was something unusual about the tone of his voice, something of relish, of gloating, that made Powther turn and stare at him. He said, "Yes?"

Al lowered his voice. "You noticed anything funny goin' on at the shack lately?"

"Funny?" Powther repeated and frowned. None of the plate was missing, he always counted it himself. The maids? They were all doing their work and doing it very well. None of them was in the family way. "What do you mean?" he said sharply.

"Well," Al said and stopped. "Well, if you ain't noticed nothin' I ain't got time to go into all of it right now." He shoved the chauffeur's cap straight on his head. "I gotta go, Mal. I'll tell you about it the first chance I get. I gotta go pick up the mink cargo."

Powther stood in the rain, watching the red taillights of the town car diminish in size, grow smaller, then disappear, just as though they had been swallowed up by this dark rainy night. What was Al talking about?

He ignored the rain, the wind, while he inventoried the rooms. Gainsboroughs in the dining room, yes, all of them; the Cellini peacocks and the Da Vinci trays, the Bateman tea set and the Paul Revere in the dining room; yes, all there; prayer rugs in the library, yes; Aubusson in the music room, yes. He thought of spots on rugs, irreparable damage to fine wood, moths in upholstery or rugs, snagged draperies. Perhaps someone had marred the photomurals in the entrance hall. No, they were perfectly all right.

I should have gone back with Al and gone over the entire downstairs to see that everything was as it should be. Wine cellar? He was down there in the afternoon, right after lunch, checking the Château d'Yquem, the only wine the Madam really liked. But surely Mrs. Cameron, the housekeeper, would have noticed anything wrong or anything missing. They held a conference every morning. She had said, when was it? yesterday, that the house had never been more beautiful that it was this winter.

Drummond, the conductor, stuck his head out of the trolley.

"Mr. Powther," he said, "is that you?"

Powther said, "Yes." He boarded the car, dropped a nickel in the coinbox.

Drummond said, "It's a sour night, ain't it?" and looked a question at Powther.

Powther said, "Yes. Funny, isn't it? It's pitchdark so all of us talk about the night though it's only five o'clock." He's wondering why I was standing out there in the rain, ruining the crease in my trousers. "Rain in January is always worse than snow. It's so devilish cold. Warm in the trolley though."

He helped Drummond reverse the seats. He could think better when he was doing something, and he liked Drummond, a talkative kind of chap, full of odd bits of information about the people who rode on his trolley.

"How are you, Drummond? I haven't seen you for a couple of weeks."

He only heard part of Drummond's answer. Al had said, "You

noticed anything funny?" Funny. Funny. But Al wouldn't notice a scarred floor or a chipped porcelain vase. Al wasn't interested in anything but cars. Al's domain was the garage. There must be something missing in the garage, something queer in the garage. That was Al's affair. Al was responsible for the garage.

He thought, Isn't it funny how you can get all upset about something that concerns you, but the instant you find out it's the other fellow's misfortune, you can relax, and look at it from a long way off, and think, Now isn't that too bad. He had just used the word funny. Queer. Strange. Unusual.

Drummond said, "When you get past fifty your legs kind of bother you."

"It's good you've got a sitting-down job, on a trolley," Powther said.

Past fifty, he thought. He was past fifty but his legs didn't bother him. He could walk that mile from the Hall to the car line, easily. He enjoyed it. Even in the rain. The driveway was always lighted at night, and it was like walking alone down a broad tree-lined boulevard. It offered beauty, fresh air, exercise, and time in which to think, all at once. In winter, snow clung to the arbor vitae, and the hemlocks, and it was like walking through a forest, a snowcovered forest; and in the spring, when the rhododendron and the French lilacs were in bloom, it was like walking through a florist's dream of heaven. Al would never be able to understand why he liked that long walk. He was always insisting that he ride, would stop his own work to take him in one of the cars, often took him all the way to Dumble Street.

Drummond said peevishly, "Trolleys are all right." He started the car and he had to raise his voice against the clang-clang so that he sounded angry. He almost shouted, "But they sure beat the hell out of your kidneys after a while."

"I suppose so," Powther said. "But I should think a bus would be worse. I hope it'll be a long time before they get around to putting busses on this line."

"Same here. You got room on a trolley. The air's better too. Sometimes I wonder what I'm goin' to do when they get around to puttin' the busses on. You're lucky, Mr. Powther. You don't know how lucky. Here I am gettin' along on the other side a little further every day, and liable to be out of a job any time. But you're set for the rest of your life."

Powther hoped another passenger would get on soon. He didn't like to listen to a man feeling sorry for himself. It was probably the weather, that cold, fine rain, and so much wind. You couldn't see anything out of the window. Pitchdark outside. Trolley rocking and swaying. A sour night. Lucky, he thought. I'm not lucky. I worked and studied and worked and studied to get where I am. Get where I am. Where am I? He frowned. He was about to do the same thing Drummond was doing, about to start feeling sorry for himself.

Drummond brought the trolley to a stop. A big slowmoving man got on. He had a metal lunchbox in his hand. Powther thought, You rarely ever see a workman with a lunchbox any more. When you did you wondered why he had to pinch his pennies, wondered what kind of misfortune forced him to deny himself that small extra sum per week with which to buy his lunch. The big man sat down near the front, right behind Drummond, and they started talking.

Drummond said, "How is she?"

The big man said, "Oh, I don't know. She ain't no worse but she ain't no better either. I don't know what to think, Drummond. Here I am gettin' older every day and I'm spending my old-age money for doctors and sicknesses."

"But if you didn't have it," Drummond said halfheartedly.

"If I didn't have it then I could get her treated free," the big man said.

Powther stopped listening to them. It was this unpleasant weather that had got them down. This sour night. Now that Drummond had someone to talk to, he could go back to thinking about Al and the garage. Perhaps something had happend to the old Rolls. It must be twenty-five or thirty years old, at least; and Al was always working on it, tuning up the motor, polishing it. He even replaced the side curtains every two years.

He'd seen Al start the motor of the old Rolls and then get out, lift the hood, and stand listening to it, head cocked on one side, eyes half closed, just as though he were listening to a concert.

Al had said, "Lissen to her, Mal. Lissen to her sing. They don't make nothin' like this no more. Nobody gives a goddamn what's under a hood no more just so they're ridin' in a shined-up crate that's long as a hearse. This baby will outlast all them Caddies them rich bastards is so crazy about."

Powther had nodded agreement. The car looked unfashionably high to him, though he supposed the lines were still good considering its age. Certainly you wouldn't turn around and stare at it if you saw it being driven along a highway. He knew absolutely nothing about motors so he couldn't agree or disagree as to the quality of what was under the hood.

"You know," Al said, and he put his hands on his hips, still looking at the car, still listening to the motor, "even if I wasn't workin' here no more, I'd come back here for just one thing."

"What would that be?" Powther asked. He knew what he himself would come back to Treadway Hall for, it would be to rub up the Cellini peacocks just for the sheer pleasure of handling them once again. But Al, who did not know one rug from another, one type of silver from another, one flower from another, what would he come back for?

"I'd come back here, Mal, just to watch the Widow drive this crate through the park at the Fourth of July picnic. She sits in it, drivin' it, and she's listenin' to the motor all the time. I've watched her and I know. She's almost as crazy about motors as me. Only woman I ever see that was."

Yes, Powther thought, comfortably, something must have gone wrong with the old Rolls-Royce. But Al was a good mechanic. He would soon have it back in running order again. He liked Al, but there was a coarseness, a vulgarity about his speech that Powther found unpleasant. Al constantly disparaged the Madam, in small ways, without ever giving direct expression to his dislike. Powther felt that if you didn't like the people you worked for, you shouldn't take their money, you ought to find another job. Al referred to the Madam as the Widow; called Treadway Hall, that great stone mansion with its park and formal gardens and its magnificently furnished interior, the shack; and all of the Madam's cars, the limousines and town cars, the station wagons and convertibles, were crates; and the Madam's friends, whether they were gentlemen or ladies, were always rich bastards.

Despite his disapproval of Al's way of talking, they were friends. Al had given him a nickname, the first one he'd ever had, and he liked it. If anyone had told him that he and Al would be friends, he wouldn't have believed it because when he first went to the Hall to work, Al was openly hostile. He was always staring at him. He had pale blue eyes that bulged, and those pale eyes showed they did not like what they saw when they rested on Powther. His hair was blond and cropped close to his head, revealing the roundness of his skull, emphasizing the roundness of his skull. A big man with a big tough face.

He had never been guilty of violent reactions against people, but he found himself referring to Al, mentally, as the Nazi. The Nazi never spoke to him. If Powther had to give him a message from the Madam, the Nazi stared at him with those pale, cold eyes, did not answer, turned his round hardlooking head away.

One morning, the Nazi did not show up when he was supposed to take the Madam to the munitions works. She waited in the hall, tapping her foot, while Powther rang the garage and rang and rang and got no answer.

"Where could Albert be?" the Madam said. "What on earth is the matter with him?"

"I'll go and see what the trouble is, madam," Powther said.

Al lived in quarters over the garage. He ran to the garage, climbed up the inside stairs, quickly, knocked at the door of Al's bedroom, got no answer, and went inside. Al was in bed, eyelids covering the pale blue bulging eyes. He seemed drowsy. He was muttering under his breath.

He touched Al's forehead lightly. It was hot. He was obviously running a temperature. He looked somehow vulnerable, lying there, pajama coat unbuttoned, thick blond hair covering his chest, a big man with broad thicklooking shoulders, formidable when dressed and on his feet, but diminished now, weaklooking.

He said, "Al, Al. Who else drives?" and had to repeat it, "Al, who can drive for you?"

"Jenkins," Al said, with an effort.

In a few minutes the limousine was at the door, Jenkins was at the wheel wearing one of Al's caps. The Madam said, "You managed this so quickly, Powther. Thank you."

He managed more than that. He nursed Al through a four-day illness and looked after his own work as well, running out to the garage to sponge him off, to give him the liquids and the medicine the doctor had ordered. Al was grateful, he was more than grateful, he insisted that Powther had saved his life.

He said, "Mal, I got to explain to you. I never had worked with a colored feller before. And you was the butler and that meant you was over me. And I didn't like it. But you're just like a white man, Mal. That don't sound right." He rubbed his forehead. "I mean you're okay, Mal. You musta knew I didn't like you but you come in there and looked after me like you was my mother. Anybody ever bother you, you let me know. Anything you ever want, you let me know, Mal. I mean that."

Ever since then Al had been driving him to the trolley line or all the way home.

They were getting near the small factories now. Workmen were boarding the car; and every now and then a pretty young woman would get on. He liked to watch these little stenographers and typists and bookkeepers. If a workman in overalls with heavy jacket and cap was sitting in a seat, the girls would move along until they found an empty seat, or one occupied by a fairly well-dressed man or another woman. It amused him that they should maintain some sort of class line on a trolley, a class line based on appearance, because the workmen unquestionably earned twice as much as the stenographers. You didn't see many workmen on the trolleys anyway. Most of them drove their own cars to and from the plants. Al was always suggesting that he buy a car.

"You get yourself a car, Mal, and I'll keep it in firstclass shape for you. You ain't even got to buy a new one. I'll help you pick out a good second. A man oughtta have a car when he lives as far from his work as you do."

He said, "Thanks, Al. But I can't afford one." And maybe for a month or so Al wouldn't say anything about it.

It wasn't that he couldn't afford a car. He could. But if he had one, Mamie would use it, and he would never know where she was, never know. As it was, he often found Kelly and Shapiro and J.C. in the house by themselves. He'd say, "Where's your mother?" The answer was always the same, "Mamie's out."

She liked to go to the movies, and she loved to go shopping but — He sighed, and then frowned, wondering if Mamie was still on a diet. He hoped not.

Once again he reminded himself, as he always did whenever he felt a little low in his mind, that though he was constantly defeated at home, he was a conqueror, a victor, at Treadway Hall. His predecessor at the Hall had been an Englishman, and though he knew he was the equal if not the superior of the Englishman, he also knew that he would have to fight and win a war against the other servants before he was accepted. Mrs. Treadway had never had any colored help, which made it a little difficult at first.

But he had worked for Old Copper, who was just about the richest man in the country. Thus he could, in all truth, look at the Treadway plate, the Treadway porcelain, the Treadway Aubussons and prayer rugs and Persian carpets, the Treadway mahogany with a slightly contemptuous air because he had seen better, handled better, and the other servants knew it. A war of the kind that he was involved in had to be won quickly, and the ammunition consisted largely of a way of looking down one's nose, and a good stock of stories about the tremendously rich, fabulously rich, families one had worked for.

He won hands down. It wasn't really a war. Just a skirmish or two. Except, of course, for Al. The housekeeper, Mrs. Cameron, who was Scotch, made it clear that she liked and admired him. She was always saying, "Now, Mr. Powther, that youngest Copper, whatever became of him and the coal miner's daughter he married. She was Polish, wasn't she?"

Then Powther, sure of his audience, would tell all over again the world's favorite fairy story, how Cinderella (twentieth century so she was the daughter of a coal miner) and the prince (youngest son of the richest man in the United States) were married. The housekeeper and the maids, all the female help, would lean forward, listening, listening.

Fortunately, Old Copper was not only rich, he was eccentric too, so that Powther was never at a loss for a good story about his racehorses, his airplanes, his yachts, his adulteries, his private railroad car, his town houses and country houses. Treadway Hall seemed a thin, anemic sort of place by comparison; just the Madam and the one young lady, Miss Camilo, in the family. Then Miss Camilo got married, so that left just the Madam.

Old Copper had five sons. The five sons married big buxom women; and in an age when most women felt they had made the supreme sacrifice if they had one child, let alone two, the women who married Old Copper's boys had five and six children apiece. So the town house in Baltimore was filled with life, fecund, uproarious life.

The trolley stopped at the corner of Dumble Street. Powther got off. Drummond said, "Good night, Mr. Powther." Powther said, "Good night, Drummond," and hurried down the street. He aways hurried down Dumble Street, hurrying home to Mamie. Uncertainty urged him on. He was afraid that some time, some night, he would open the door of that apartment upstairs in Mrs. Crunch's house, and find that Mamie had gone, leaving no note of explanation, nothing, just darkness, silence, emptiness. He could picture himself blundering around in the rooms, searching for a note that he knew he would never find because Mamie was not the kind who would write a note. Writing didn't come easy to her, and even if it had, she would have preferred the direct contact offered by speech, not the impersonal business of using a pen or a pencil to inscribe an explanation or an apology, or an apologetic explanation, on a piece of paper, thus foregoing the pleasure and the excitement of an explosive violent scene.

And so, hurrying home through this early winter night, darkness already set in, cold in the street, the kind of night when J.C. would be able to "see" his breath, wind blowing straight from the river, blowing the fine rain against his face, cold sting of the rain making him lower his head, he stopped when he got near the house, and looked up toward the windows, to see if they were lighted.

When he saw, through the bare branches of The Hangman, that familiar pinkish light, warm, glowing light, in the windows of that room he shared with Mamie, he knew a sense of delight, of anticipation. He felt as though he could see into the room, see Mamie, laughing, her head thrown back, see all the soft brown flesh waiting for him, see himself laying his head between her breasts, soft, soft, soft, and smell the strong sweet perfume she used.

That strong sweet smell came from a stick, a graywhite stick, wrapped in tinfoil, the whole thing encased in a round glass bottle. He loved to watch her uncork the bottle, carefully unwrap the tinfoil, and then smear the stick perfume on her wrists, her elbows, the lobes of her ears, the back of her neck. Everything smelt of it, her clothes, her body, her hair, the sheets and the pillowcases. He could never separate the smell of that perfume from Mamie, the two inextricably entwined; and all he asked in life, really, was — well, not to keep his job, not long life and good health for himself and his family, not sufficient food, or ample clothing, all he asked was that Mamie would, as long as they both should live, let him sleep with her on those nights when he was not at Treadway Hall, let him sleep with her so that he could go down, down, into sleep with the strong, toosweet perfume all around him, tangible assurance of Mamie's presence.

Now that he had seen the pinkish light in the bedroom windows, he started moving faster and faster, until he was very nearly running when he went up the outside back staircase. In the back entry, he stood still for a moment. He could smell pork chops frying on the stove, thought he could hear the spit-spatter of grease as the chops cooked, could smell kale being cooked.

He opened the kitchen door, stepped inside, and had to shut his eyes for a moment, half blinded by the brilliant light from the hundred-watt bulbs Mamie used in the kitchen; and it was hot, steam came from the open pot where the kale was cooking, bubble, bubble, bubble, smell of kale. Mamie was leaning over, bending over, opening the oven door, yams in the oven, corn muffins in the oven, fragrance issuing from the oven; and over it all the smell of her perfume, strong, heavy, toosweet, overriding the food smells, and he looked at Mamie bent over like that and could hear Old Copper's big voice, roaring, "Get one with a big ass, Powther, get a big wench with a big ass, and by God, you'll be happy for the rest of your life," could see Old Copper slapping his knee, could hear him laughing, and there was Mamie, bent over, and he looked away, because of the desire that rose in him, a sudden emotion, that made him feel as though he were going to choke, and he couldn't think straight, couldn't see, he wanted to be on top of her, and he told himself there was a fresh baked cake on the kitchen table, and he heard J.C. whining, "I want cake. I want cake. I want cake."

Mamie closed the oven door, cuffed J.C. away from the cake.

Shapiro yelled, "Hit him over the head again, Mamie. Give him a good one this time."

"Ah, shut up, Shapiro," Kelly yelled back, "you big mouth, you —"

"Whose a big mouth? Whose a big mouth?"

"You — you — you —"

They rolled over on the floor, over and over, clutching at each other, shouting, faces contorted with anger.

Mamie hummed under her breath, turned the pork chops in the frying pan with a longhandled fork, apparently unaware of the noise, the brilliant light, the sound of food cooking, smell of food cooking. She was impervious to it, Powther thought. No, a part of it, not ignoring, but enjoying, liking, the heat, the light, the confusion, the noise, the boys scuffling on the floor, J.C.'s yelps of rage.

Suddenly they were all looking at him, all silent, J.C., Shapiro, Kelly, Mamie. He supposed that he had brought the cold wet air from the street in with him, the darkness of the street, the silence of the street, brought it straight into the hot, brilliantly lighted, filled-with-food-smell, noisy kitchen; and their eyes questioned him, challenged his right to enter this place that was the heartbeat of the house, heartbeat pulsing with heat, sound, life.

Mamie said, "Powther, you sure gave me a turn. Come on in. Come on in and close that door. Supper'll be ready in a minute."

He went through the kitchen, down the hall, into the bedroom. He always hurried to get here, inside the house, home, and yet he always felt as though he were an alien, a stranger, strangeness, a sense of strangeness, in the kitchen, here in this bedroom. It was always the same room no matter what the address, the room where a pink-shaded lamp shed warm pink light on the bed, on the table by the bed, on the pink taffeta spread, not too clean. Cupids on the bed.

He put his hat on the closet shelf, hung his overcoat on a hanger in the one closet — a closet jammed full of dresses which were paid for by Bill Hod. His coat would smell of Mamie's perfume, just as all these dresses did. He got a clothesbrush out of the one drawer of the chest which was reserved for his use, brushed his hat, his overcoat, then rehung them in the closet, and in a petty unreasoning kind of anger, born of what he could not say, he pushed the newestlooking dress from its hanger and watched it fall, in a heap, on the closet floor.

Tomorrow morning, if he had time, he would rearrange the closet before he went to work. Mamie liked having him fix up her clothes. He pressed her dresses, sewed on buttons, repaired the split seams under the arms. He couldn't leave that dress on the floor of the closet. He reached down, picked it up, shook it out, examined it for split seams, from force of habit. Mamie had put on quite a few pounds lately. Was she still dieting? He hoped not. True she lost weight, but she was so cross, so irritable, when she was dieting, slapping the children, swearing at him, that nobody could stay in the house with her. Two weeks ago, when he was off, he went to the movies and sat there dozing away the hours, those precious hours, of his days off, trying to think of something that would be so good to eat, so appealing, that she'd taste it and then eat it, and would be off the diet. He sat through two shows and then went home, walking warily around the side of the house, going quietly up the back stairs, sniffing the air, thinking that if she was cooking, at so early an hour, in the afternoon, she was still on the diet, still not eating.

When she went on these starvation diets, she seemed impelled to torture herself by handling food, by cooking food that smelled to high heaven. She would sit at the table with a cup of black coffee and a package of cigarettes in front of her, sit there and sip the coffee; and smoke one cigarette after another, and watch them eat, watch forkfuls of the great round crusted roast of beef, and the browned potatoes and the beautiful fresh vegetables and the rich buttery dessert go into their mouths; her eyes followed the course of their forks and spoons from the plate to mouth, mouth to plate, her eyes eating the food with them, her lower lip thrust out, mouth a little open.

He imagined he saw saliva at the corner of her mouth, and would stare, fascinated, knowing that he was imagining it, but knowing, too, that it ought to be there, that the saliva glands were working overtime. Then Mamie would catch him staring and turn her belligerent baleful hungry eyes toward him, and he would look away, eating faster and faster, eating more than his stomach could possibly hold, afraid to stop eating.

It was a horrifying business to come home and find that Mamie was still on a starvation diet that might last anywhere from two days to a month. Once she'd held out for a whole month, a month during which she watched them eat cream puffs, chocolate éclairs, strawberry shortcakes piled up with whipped cream, all the rich sweet fattening food she loved most, while she drank black coffee, and wolfed down some kind of dry hard tasteless crackers.

For a whole month, they tiptoed around her, almost whispering, and she cooked from the time she got out of bed in the morning until she went back to bed at night, using up pounds of butter and quarts of cream and God only knew how much sugar and flour and vanilla. Kelly and Shapiro began to look like small round young pigs being fattened for the kill. J.C. gorged himself to the vomiting stage every night.

Night after night, Powther sneaked out to the corner drugstore for a large dose of sodium bicarb and oil of peppermint, afraid to mix it on the premises, even in the comparative privacy of the bathroom, because Mamie would have smelt the peppermint and known he'd eaten too much and been furious, with that quick unreasoning fury of the starving.

When she was hungry like that she couldn't sleep. He remembered the tenseness of her, lying there motionless beside him, flat on her back, as though she did not have the energy to turn over, not moving, tense, stiff, hungry. And he lay there beside her, afraid to touch her.

He had looked forward to this Saturday night, unexpected time off. A cold, rainy night. The kind of night a man needed a woman's arms around him. And now —

Hot in the house, he thought. Hot in the bedroom. He was sweating. Forehead wet with sweat. He'd get a clean handkerchief, mop his forehead. One of the old handkerchiefs. They were at the bottom of the pile in the top drawer of the chest.

Someone had been in the drawer, had mussed up the handkerchiefs, had put them back every which way. J.C. was getting completely out of hand, he would tell Mamie to get after him. He didn't ask much but he simply could not, would not, stand having anyone paw through his things. He'd rearrange them. He took them all out, turned the pile upside down, started to put them back, one by one. His hand touched something cold and metallic. He stood on tiptoe, looked in the drawer. There was a cigarette case in there. It had been under the handkerchiefs.

Perhaps it was a present, a surprise, from Mamie. He took it out, wondering why she had given it to him, because he didn't smoke. He turned it over. There were initials on it. L.W. picked out in brilliants. Who was L.W.? What was his cigarette case doing in this drawer?

He took the case over to the light. He turned it over, moving it back and forth, and the stones that formed the initials flashed, seemed to wink at him. It said Tiffany & Co. on the inside. A gold cigarette case. The initials were formed by small absolutely perfect diamonds. No question about their being diamonds. He used to see Old Copper's collection. Night after night the old man sat in the library holding a few of the stones in his hand, letting them trickle between his fingers. Old Copper told him about them, told him that finally you got so you could pick out the perfect ones without a glass, but a man ought always to carry a glass with him, just in case, just to verify what his naked eye told him. He went over to the closet, got a jeweler's glass out of his coat pocket, looked at the stones through it. Oh, yes, absolutely perfect, flawless, small stones. A gold cigarette case initialed in diamonds. L.W.

L.W.? Link Williams. Link Williams. Mrs. Crunch's nephew, or whatever he was, the tall arrogant young man who did not look like Bill Hod but resembled him, the way he held his head, the way he talked, even the eyes.

Bill Hod was no threat. At least he told himself that all the time; he told himself over and over again, as he hurried home on his days off, that Bill Hod would never encumber himself by permanently annexing a woman, not even Mamie Powther. And the closer he got to the house, the more convinced he became that Mamie had now, finally, gone off with Hod. But she hadn't. And then he would be certain that she never would, and the knowledge would last about a week or ten days and then he would begin to wonder and to doubt, and hurry home to make certain. But Link Williams, Mamie — .

He shivered. Perhaps she was telling him in this curious, subtle, not really to be understood, business of the cigarette case, had placed it where he would certainly find it, and thus would know that she and Link —

He put the case back in the drawer, piled the handkerchiefs on top of it, slowly, carefully, force of habit making him square them up, line them up, one on top of the other, taking a long time to do it because his hands were trembling. Mamie laughed whenever she saw him carefully arranging the contents of a drawer, "Law, Powther," she said, "you musta spent half your life in the army, must spent half your life puttin' things in piles."

He would pretend the cigarette case was not there. It would be the easiest way for everybody. It meant Mamie would have to figure out some more direct way of telling him whatever it was she was trying to tell him about herself and Link. If he had seen Link Williams before they moved in here, if Mrs. Crunch had said, "I have a very handsome young nephew, if you cherish your wife, your life, if you have a susceptible, loving wife, do not, under any circumstances, do not live under the same roof with my handsome unscrupulous young nephew."

Link Williams belonged to the Copper breed, so did Hod. You could tell by looking at them, by listening to them, that they weren't to be trusted, that no woman was safe around them, not really. Mamie. For instance, it wouldn't have been safe to leave Mamie around Old Copper. What the dickens was he thinking about anyway, mind all in a jumble.

If Mrs. Crunch had only said, well, that day he stood wiping his feet so carefully on the doormat, instead of saying, "How did you know about the apartment?" she should have said, "I have a very handsome, very lawless young nephew."

Even if she had said it, he wouldn't have believed her. Because looking at her he would have said that her nephew — Was Link Williams her nephew? He couldn't be, not with that handsome closed arrogant cruel gambler's face, with those expressionless gambler's eyes, he couldn't be her nephew, couldn't have in his veins any of the same blood that had produced short, plump, hawknosed, kindly faced, kind-but-proud-faced, expressived-eyed Mrs. Abigail Crunch. It was a mobile face, a dead-give-away face, give away of whatever she was thinking, so were the plump, moving, always-in-motion, always gesturing hands. With that white hair piled on top of her head, with the very black eyebrows — well, it was a face and head you couldn't easily forget. She had New England aristocrat written all over her, in the straight back, in the quick but not hurrying short steps she took that meant she covered a lot of ground but was never guilty of striding down the street, in the Yankee twang to her speech. She wore the kind of clothes he liked, simple, unadorned and yet completely feminine, white gloves on Sundays, small black leather pocketbooks, carefully polished shoes, pretty small hats, a feather the only gay note on her best felt hat, and the seams in her stockings always straight.

He had met her, walked along Dumble Street with her, when she went marketing in the morning, tan cotton gloves on her hands, the fingers so neatly, so cleverly darned, the darning so beautiful that only an expert would notice that the gloves had been darned; a market basket over her arm, and her pocketbook in the basket; and he knew just as though he had looked inside it that it contained a clean linen handkerchief that would smell faintly sweet (violet or lilac or lavender), the front doorkey, and a billfold and small pencil with a pad; and on the pad would be a list, the grocery list, containing all the items that she would want that particular day, so that this one trip, early in the morning, would take care of all her needs.

In Mrs. Crunch's house, there would not be, say at five o'clock, that harumscarum running to the store for the thousand-and-one things that had been forgotten as there always were in his house. Mamie never knew what she was going to have for supper until the very last minute. She would start for the store, forget her purse and hurry back to the house to get it, laughing at herself, as she came in. He had seen her change her mind about an entire meal at the sight of a choice cut of meat at the butcher's; she would hurry home with the meat and ten minutes later she'd send Shapiro scurrying to the store for potatoes and before Shapiro could get back in the house, Kelly would be sent out to get butter and bread. The only reason J.C. wasn't employed in this marathon to and from the store was because he couldn't be trusted on an errand with or without money; J.C. just never bothered to come back at all and was usually found hanging over the dock, looking down at the river, with that awful concentration of the very young.

Breakfast was the same way; at least two members of the family had to go to the corner store and back before the Powthers could break their fast in the morning. He should have married a woman like Mrs. Crunch, who never had to diet, who would never under any circumstances have permitted familiarities from a man to whom she was not married, whose every word, every look, every gesture told you that.

Then Mamie was standing in the doorway of the bedroom, tall, all soft flesh and curves, all soft warm flesh, saying, "Pow-ther! Pow-ther! I've called you two times already."

"I was just getting — " he started to say getting a handkerchief, and said, "I was just getting ready to come out to the kitchen."

He watched her walk down the hall toward the kitchen, watched the rhythmic motion of her legs, her arms, and thought, Yes, if I'd married Mrs. Crunch or someone like her I would never have wondered if I'd come home and find that she'd run off with another man; but then neither would I have known the absolute ecstasy and delight of Mamie, in the dark, in bed, the soft flesh yielding, yielding, the feel of those curves, the pressure of her arms around me.

He would never give her up, never, never. He was going to act as though Link Williams did not exist, as though that cigarette case with its sparkling monogram did not exist, as though — Why had she put it under his handkerchiefs? Link Williams. What was he doing with a cigarette case like that? Why not? Hod probably gave it to him. Or a woman. Some rich, dissolute, white woman. Link Williams was the type they fell in love with, it was the way he was built, it was his height, and the breadth of his shoulders, and it was his face, he looked like a brute, and women, white and colored, loved men with faces like that. Let's see, he thought, this is the middle of January. So some rich dissolute white woman probably gave it to him for a Christmas present.

Mamie said, from the kitchen, "Come along now, Powther. Supper's ready."

In the kitchen he blinked, the light was so brilliant. It was hot. Steam came from the plates on the table. Mamie always piled food on plates. J.C.'s plate was just as full of food as Shapiro's or Kelly's or his own. And Mamie was still on a diet because there was nothing at her place but a cup of black coffee.

Shapiro and Kelly ate in silence. J.C. tried to talk with his mouth crammed with food, so that no one understood what he was saying, thus he carried on a monologue, a mumbling mouth-full-of-food monologue, that was also an indication of contentment because he swayed from side to side as he ate and mumbled.

Mamie sat and glared at them as the pork chops and the yams and the kale and the corn bread disappeared from their plates. Occasionally she took a sip of the hot black bitter coffee.

Powther threw small secret appraising glances at the coffee cup, lipstick all around the edges, brown stains on the side where the coffee had dripped and spilled over, the saucer splotched with a whole series of dark brown rings. She used the same cup all day long, picking it up, sipping from it, refilling it with hot coffee when the stuff cooled off.

J.C. said, "Missus Crunch — " and the rest of the sentence was lost because he had crammed his mouth full of corn bread and went on talking and chewing, talking and chewing.

Powther wondered how he could bring the conversation around to Link Williams, how introduce his name, so that he could see how Mamie acted when his name was mentioned.

J.C. pushed his chair away from the table, backed the length of the room, still chewing, eying Mamie as he edged toward the hall door, then he was through it, gone.

Powther said, "I don't think you ought to let J.C. go downstairs to Mrs. Crunch's so much." He heard J.C.'s footsteps, thud, thud, on the inside staircase. It wasn't what he had planned to say, he hadn't really planned to say anything, he was just feeling his way, if he could get a conversation started about Mrs. Crunch then perhaps he could mention Link, easily, naturally.

Mamie glared at him. "Why not?" she said.

"Mrs. Crunch will get tired of him."

No answer. Perhaps she hadn't heard him. "Mrs. Crunch will get tired of him," he repeated. "I don't think you ought to let him go down there so much. It's late. He ought to be in bed."

"Oh, for God's sake, Powther, why don't you shut up?" She pushed the coffee cup away, with a sudden violent jerky motion, and got up from the table.

He watched her as she left the kitchen. She slammed the bedroom door and he listened, and could not tell whether she had turned the key in the lock.

Kelly said, "Mamie been like that all day, Pop. Me and Shapiro been outdoors in the rain the whole afternoon."

"It ain't safe to talk to her," Shapiro said. He stuffed his mouth full of cake, and cut himself another large wedge-shaped piece.

"J.C. left because he knew he'd get in trouble if he stayed around here," Kelly said. "Mamie been awful mean to him." He watched Shapiro gulp down the cake. "Mamie say he's got a tapeworm." He pointed at Shapiro.

Shapiro said, "I have not."

"You have too. Mamie say nobody could stuff their gut like you unless they got a tapeworm."

Shapiro picked up a fork with the evident intention of stabbing Kelly with it. Powther said, "That's enough of that."

He got up from the table, took a key out of his pocket, unlocked a cupboard high over the kitchen sink. "Here," he said, and handed them each a new comic book. He didn't approve of comic books but as he evidently was going to have to contend with the boys until bedtime, he didn't know of anything else that would keep them from killing each other while he did the dishes.

He found an apron, tied it tight around his waist, and set to work, clearing the table, washing the dishes, scouring the pots, then scouring the sink, boiling the dish towels. He swept the kitchen and then mopped it, mopping carefully around Shapiro and Kelly, who were lying flat on their stomachs, totally absorbed in the comic books, thinking that if he'd been Old Copper, he would have taken the mop handle and pushed and prodded them out of the way.

J.C. poked his head in through the door, looked around the kitchen, "Where's Mamie?" he demanded.

"Gone to bed," Powther said. "Come on in and I'll tell you a story."

J.C. loved fairy stories, and Powther, feeling suddenly sorry for him, feeling that J.C. needed a mother and didn't have one, and that he must therefore be both mother and father to him in this storytelling, said, "Here, you sit on my lap and I'll tell you a new story."

Powther cleared his throat, said, slowly, "Once upon a time," and Shapiro and Kelly looked up from the comic books, and he thought, It's got to be extra good to hold their attention.

"Once upon a time," he said again, "there was a princess with golden hair who was kept chained deepdown in a dark cold dungeon. The guardian of the door that led into the dungeon was a wicked giant who was blind in one eye. The princess cried all the time because she was hungry and the giant beat her and the only food he gave her was dry hard bread and water. But he brought her precious jewels to play with, great diamonds and emeralds and rubies and sapphires and pearls; and beautiful clothes to wear. When the giant left to go about his dreadful business of robbing innocent people who passed through the woods, he would leave his dog to guard the princess. The dog was a ferocious white bulldog, also blind in one eye, and if anyone ventured near the castle he would growl; and his growling was so fearful that they went on their way again.

"One day, Gaylord, the valet in the king's palace, a man who was small in stature but quick of movement, and noted for his kindness and the quickness of his thinking, was walking through the wood. As he neared the castle, he thought he heard sobs. He tried to enter, but he could not gain entrance because of the ferocious dog who guarded the entrance. He turned and walked away, puzzled, and he made up his mind to return again and explore the place when he had the golden needle with him. Gaylord was a persistent man, and not to be discouraged by danger or the threat of danger, for he was really a prince in disguise. He had been kidnaped and taken away from his kingdom at the orders of a jealous uncle. He was severely beaten and left for dead but an old peasant woman who lived on the edge of the forest where he had been left, found him, and nursed him back to health. After he recovered his health, he looked after the old woman, took such good care of her, that on her deathbed she gave him a small round silver case, almost like a tube, but heavily and curiously carved.

" 'Open it,' she said. 'Careful, now.' To his surprise he found a very fine golden needle inside the case.

" 'It will sew by itself,' she told him. 'You say, Stitch, Needle, stitch this leather, and it will stitch for you. It will stitch anything, water, wine, soap, wood, stone, fire. Guard it well. It has been in my family for five hundred years. I have no children to pass it on to so I will give it to you. You have been like a son to me. And whoever has this needle will always have whatsoever he wants.'

"A week later, Gaylord returned to the castle. This time he had the needle with him. The dog growled and would not permit him to pass the entrance. Gaylord said, 'Stitch, Needle,' The needle looked like a small flaming sunset flashing about the eyes of the dog, stitching up both eyes, just in case the blind eye was not blind, as so often happens in real life where a blind eye is often a fake, based on an old rumor that nobody knows whether or not it is true and it possibly isn't true, because most rumors are started by someone who has something to gain by it, and to be thought blind in one eye when you weren't would give a person an advantage over other people.

"The dog emitted piercing cries of pain, and ran and ran, put his head down to the ground and rubbed his eyes on the ground and the needle stitched the dog's heavy leather collar to the stone wall.

"Gaylord said, 'Well done, Needle,' and held out the small round silver tube and the needle came flashing through the air and settled inside the tube.

"He then went unmolested into the castle, and followed the sound of the sobs, and went down into the dungeon and found the beautiful goldenhaired princess chained there, with a great golden goblet beside her, half full of water. She said, 'Save me, save me, kind sir!'

"At that moment the giant entered the dungeon and lunged toward Gaylord. Gaylord said, 'Stitch, Needle! Stitch both his eyes, Needle!' and held out the small round silver tube and the needle flashed through the air, and stitched both the giant's eyes. The giant let out a roar of rage and pain; and started blundering around in the dungeon, hands outstretched before him. Gaylord said, 'Stitch, Needle! Stitch hand to stone!' The needle flashed through the air and when the giant blundered near one of the walls of the dungeon, the needle stitched the giant's hand to the stone.

"Gaylord said, 'Well done, Needle!' and the needle came flashing through the air and settled inside the small round silver tube that Gaylord held out.

"Gaylord then took the keys from the giant's girdle and unlocked the padlock, and released the beautiful princess with the long golden hair.

"They left the castle together, their arms clasped around each other's waists. Then they returned to Gaylord's rightful kingdom where they were married and lived happily forever after."

J.C. said, "Tell it again! Tell it again!"

Shapiro and Kelly had long since left the comic books on the kitchen floor. They were leaning against Powther now, and they said, together, "Whew! Tell it again, Pop. Tell it again."

"Not tonight. It's too late," Powther said. He felt a little glow of pride, of accomplishment, it was a good story. But he wouldn't tell it again.

He washed all three of them, helped all three into their night clothes, tucked them under the covers, opened the window, turned out the light. When he closed the door of the bedroom J.C. was saying, "All gold. She was all gold. She came right in the front door — Stitch stone to leather." But because he left the "s" sound off words, he was really saying, "Titch tone to leather."

11

● POWTHER TOOK his shoes off in the living room. He padded quietly down the hall in his stocking feet and tried the door of the bedroom that he shared with Mamie, turning the knob, slowly, cautiously. It was locked.

He had no blanket, nothing to cover himself with. If he should sleep on the sofa in the living room, with his clothes on, his trousers would be wrecked by morning. He undressed down to his underwear and went back to the boys' room and got in bed with J.C.

It was like trying to sleep with a dyamo. J.C.'s feet and knees were in his stomach, his chest, his back. He seemed all bone, all knobby knees and sharp elbows and hard round head, no flesh on him anywhere, though he was a plump child, his body putting a strain on every seam of his clothing.

Powther turned and twisted, trying to get comfortable, thinking of Old Copper, "Get one with a big ass, Powther, makes for happiness." Did it? The boy, the old man's youngest son, Peter, beat his wife, the miner's redheaded daughter, with a horsewhip. Did it? Mamie Powther locked Malcolm Powther out of the bedroom.

He remembered that the newspapers somehow got wind of that story about Peter and his wife and when the reporters came, Old Copper sat in his big leather chair in the library and laughed at them; and ordered whiskey and soda for them, whiskey and soda, whiskey and soda. That afternoon Powther mixed drinks, passed drinks to the thirstiest set of men he'd ever seen.

Old Copper kept bellowing, "True? How in hell do I know if it's true? Hope so, gentlemen. I certainly hope so. Ha, ha, ha. Funniest thing I ever heard. Ha, ha, ha."

The reporters were in a deliciously rosy state when they left, laughing, talking. Powther wondered when they would realize that they didn't have a story, that Old Copper had neither denied nor confirmed the story; and he supposed they would hold long confused discussions as to whether they should print his statement, "How in hell do I know?"

One of them, a short sharp-eyed young chap, who had politely refused the whiskey and soda, cornered Powther in the hall and said, "Look here, old man, what's this all about anyway?"

He had sidestepped out of the corner. He said, "I hope the whiskey was satisfactory, sir," and walked fast down the hall, the great hall lined with those tremendous oils of monstrously outsized, monstrously pinkfleshed females painted by a Dutchman. Old Copper was standing in the doorway of the library. He was grinning, looking up at one of the paintings, grinning at it. At that moment it occurred to Powther that those paintings belonged to Old Copper in a peculiarly intimate sort of way. He was always leering at them, and the big nude women in the paintings seemed to leer back at him.

He shoved J.C.'s knees out of his stomach again, and thought, Makes for happiness, and pursed his lips. The Copper boys fought with their big wives, filled the house in Baltimore with the sound and fury of their quarrels. And yet, because of the paintings, because of the blatant lecherousness of the old man, but especially because of the paintings, he, Powther, fell in love with a woman who might have been painted by the Dutchman.

One of the sons, the oldest one, came home for a visit, accompanied by his wife and his four-month-old son, and the wife's personal maid, and the baby's trained nurse, a lean fortyish looking and acting and sounding woman in a starched white uniform and cap. Old Copper met them in the hall. The nurse was holding the baby. The old man let out a roar, like a maddened bull, "Who's that?"

They stood there, in the hall, all of them, the oldest son, and his wife, and the nurse, and the maid, and Powther, all motionless, all frozen, frightened by the roar. The baby, probably sensing the consternation of the adults, began to wail.

Young Mrs. Copper, the mother of the child, said, bewildered, "Why it's the baby, Jonathan Copper Four."

"Dammit I know that," Old Copper roared. "Who's that lean-shanked witch that's holdin' him?"

"The nurse. His nurse. A trained nurse."

Old Copper bellowed, "Give me that baby." There was a kind of seesaw movement for a moment, the nurse trying to retain hold on the baby and Old Copper pulling at him, and the baby bellowing too, now.

"Powther," Old Copper shouted, "where's Powther?" He held the baby in his arms, glaring, cursing. "God dammit, why don't none of these people have any brains? Powther, go get a nurse for this baby. Go get a big fat colored woman." He turned on the nurse. "Here, you. You're fired. Get out."

The nurse said, "Mr. Copper, you can't, you mustn't. Give me the baby. You haven't washed your hands." She got quite excited and said, "Germs, germs, germs," as though she were talking to an idiot, and had to repeat one word, over and over, in the hope that something would trickle through the idiot's mind. "Germs," she said again.

Young Mrs. Copper said, "Oh, no. You can't do that. You can't do that. You mustn't. She's so wonderful."

"Shut up!" Old Copper shouted. "Powther, stop standin' there with your mouth open. Go get a big fat colored woman to look after this brat, a big fat colored woman that can sing. Don't stand there — "

He walked out the front door, hatless, thinking, A big fat colored woman. He was supposed to pull one out of thin air. Where in the city of Baltimore was he going to find a fat colored woman who was suitable? She had to be suitable.

He went, finally, and logically enough, to an employment agency. He explained to the thinfaced white woman who was in charge of the agency what type of nurse Mr. Jonathan Copper II wanted. She searched through the files and found a Mamie Smith who sounded promising.

The thinfaced woman called the number listed on the filing card and asked to speak to Mamie Smith. There was quite a delay, at least fifteen minutes, during which the employment agency woman grew impatient, threatened to hang up, bit her lip, tapped her foot, muttered under her breath something about colored people being so slow, until apparently Mamie Smith came to the phone; also apparently she explained with suitable apologies that she had a job, but that there was a lady who was highly suitable, who lived in the same rooming house, that said lady, a Mrs. Drewey, was expected back in a half-hour, and was listed at the agency under nursemaid's work. The thinfaced woman conveyed this information to Powther. He said he'd go right out there and interview her himself.

It was a big frame house, in need of paint, in need of repairs, in fact, as he rang the bell, he studied the house, and decided that what it really needed was to be torn down and rebuilt. It even needed a new foundation.

A lean, light-colored female opened the door a cautious crack. He knew instantly that she was the landlady, because of her eyes. She summed him up, all his potentialities and possibilities in one quick shrewd glance. He asked for Mrs. Drewey. Mrs. Drewey was out, and the door started to close. Then he asked for Mamie Smith, and explained hastily and untruthfully that he had come about a job for Mamie Smith, and the door opened and the landlady said, "Step inside, and I'll call her."

He stood in the uncarpeted hall, waiting. He heard footsteps upstairs, somewhere; and then a woman came down the stairs. He stood, not moving, looking up at her. She came down the stairs, slowly, the uncarpeted badly-in-need-of-paint stairs, of a rooming house in the least desirable part of Baltimore, and his heart started beating faster and faster, and he wished he had brought his hat with him, he needed something to hold in his hands. If he had brought his hat, he could have turned it around and around, as though shaping and reshaping the brim, brushing it off, because his hands needed something to do with themselves, desperately needed something to do, because there in front of him coming down the stairs, in the flesh, was a woman exactly like the women in the great oil paintings with the ornately carved frames that hung in the long hall of Old Copper's town house.

This woman was clothed, of course. She had on a dress, sleeveless, and short of skirt. She was wearing shoes, a flimsy kind of sandal, runover at the heel, but no stockings. The dress was a rather awful shade of brown. And her skin was brown, deep reddish brown, skin as smooth and flawless as that of Jonathan Copper IV with the same dewy quality, and it was just as though one of those big women in the paintings was coming down a staircase, the curve of the leg was the same, and the deepbosomed, big-bosomed look of her was the same.

"Yes?" she said. "You wanted to see me?"

Her voice was like music and it confused him even more, excited him even more, so that he swallowed twice and cleared his throat before he could answer her. "I'm Malcolm Powther," he said. "I'm the butler at the Coppers'. We need a nursemaid and the employment agency where I made inquiries phoned here about the job just a little while ago. I came straight here from the agency because a Miss Smith suggested a Mrs. Drewey."

"I'm Mamie," she said. "I was the one who suggested Drewey. She's good. She's about the best in the whole of Maryland. Come on in and sit. She'll be along pretty soon."

He couldn't get over her voice, and he kept asking her questions, just to hear her talk. It was more like listening to singing than listening to someone talk. He knew he shouldn't stare at her, that he ought to look away, and he tried to keep his eyes focused on some part of the room. But who could keep looking at a shabby, cheap rocking chair, at soiled badly fitted slipcovers on horrible overstuffed chairs, at sagging curtains in need of laundering, at a dreadful newlooking machine-made rug, all garish colors, and at dusty beaded lamp shades, when Mamie Smith was sitting on a sofa with her legs crossed, leaning her head back? He thought, I've got to have her. If it takes me the rest of my life, if it costs me my job, if it costs me all my savings, my life savings, I've still got to have her.

He asked her questions, just to keep her talking, just so he could keep hearing that voice that was like music. She lived in one of the upstairs rooms, across the hall from Mrs. Drewey. She had been married and was divorced. She didn't like Baltimore, it was too Southern a city for anybody like her who had been born in the North. She wanted to live North again, and as soon as she could leave, had enough money saved to tide her over the business of finding another job in a new place, she would go live in a small Northern city, any small Northern city.

He thought, Enough money. I'll be back here again. I can spend money, I've saved it all my life but I'm going to spend it now, spend and spend and spend, until I can buy Mamie Smith.

He said, "Miss Smith — "

"Oh," she said, and waved her hand in the air, waving his words away, "don't be so formal. Everybody calls me Mamie."

"Mamie, will you, could you have dinner with me this coming Thursday? Go out to dinner with me?"

"Sure," she said easily. "Any night you say. Thursday's fine."

He was about to set the hour, when the front door opened and Mamie said, "There's Drewey. Come on in, honey. I got a job for you. Powther'll tell you all about it."

Drewey sat down in the parlor with them, on one of the worn, sagging chairs. He thought, Suitable. Highly suitable. She was more than that. She was exactly what Old Copper wanted. She looked clean but not starchy. She was big, with a lap made for sitting on and a feather-pillow bosom made for laying the head on, and arms big enough to enfold and cuddle the young Jonathan Copper in, for five or six years.

"Can you sing, Mrs. Drewey?" Powther asked.

"Sing?" Drewey repeated, frowning, "Course not. Is this a singin' job? I didn't put in for no singin' job at the agency."

Powther explained about the job, about how he felt that she was exactly what was wanted. He carefully avoided using the old man's phrase "big fat colored woman," because after all — Then he said, "I mean, can you, ah, sing enough to say, sing a baby to sleep while rocking him in a rocking chair?"

"Lord, yes. I don't call that singin'. That's just a little hum-a-byin'."

"Would you mind sitting in that rocking chair over there, just, you understand, so I can get an idea, and do a little hum-a-byin'?"

Mrs. Drewey looked as though she were going to refuse and Mamie said, in that voice that was like singing, "Aw, go on, Drewey, hum-a-by for Powther. It could mean a lot to you workin' for them stinkin' rich Coppers."

Mrs. Drewey sat down in the shabby, cheap rocking chair, her hands stiff on the arms, and glared at them. Then she began to rock, back and forth, back and forth, and the chair creaked a little every time she rocked. The glare subsided in her eyes, and she closed them, her hands relaxed in her lap, and she began to hum, and the humming, at some point, Powther didn't know just when, became a soft singing. If there was a tune, it was not one he had ever heard before, if there were actual words they made no sense whatsoever, and he thought it was the most comforting, relaxing, beautiful sound he had ever heard.

His eyelids drooped over his eyes, and for the first time in his life he must have gone sound asleep sitting in a chair because when he opened his eyes, Mrs. Drewey was no longer in the rocking chair, she and Mamie Smith were sitting on the sofa, both of them looking at him, both of them laughing. It was evidently the sound of their laughter that woke him up. He felt like a fool, going to sleep like that in a chair, and he wondered if his mouth had been open, wished that he had teeth like Mamie Smith's, big, strong, evenly spaced teeth, very white in that coppery brown face.

He sat up straight. "I'm sure you'll do, Mrs. Drewey. Can you come for an interview right away?"

When Old Copper saw Mrs. Drewey, he promptly roared an order for a rocking chair, roared another order to the effect that Jonathan Copper IV be placed in Mrs. Drewey's lap. Young Jonathan was still howling his head off, and the instant Drewey tucked his head into the fleshy part of her arm, covered his little feet up with a blanket and started rocking and hum-a-byin', he stopped howling, sighed, and promptly went to sleep.

Mrs. Jonathan Copper III stared, amazed. "Why, he's asleep. He hasn't been asleep for six hours. He's done nothing but cry. I've never seen anything like it."

"Just wanted a big fat colored woman," Old Copper said. "Don't never give no male Coppers to no bony white women to bring up."

Powther told Mamie about Drewey and the baby when he took her to dinner on Thursday night. While he talked he studied her, trying to analyze her weaknesses. He decided that she would never be able to save the money to tide her over until she got a job in a small Northern city, that there would always be something that she wanted to buy. After all, the Northern city was an intangible, and the gaudy costume jewelry or the flimsy shoes were tangible, touchable, seeable, right there in a store window.

He knew, too, just by looking at her, that if she married him, he would always find gentlemen callers in his home. He couldn't foresee Bill Hod, and the general shape and size and viciousness of him, because he had led a life in the houses of the very rich which prevented him from being aware of the existence of the Bill Hods, but he could foresee jealousy and insecurity. Knowing this, he still intended to marry Mamie Smith, and so directed all his resources toward that end.

Whenever he saw her he talked about the disadvantages of living in rented rooms, about the luxury it was possible to enjoy in a small place of one's own.

He bought presents for her. Just before Christmas he sent to New York for three nightgowns, three such nightgowns as he was certain she had never dreamed could possibly exist. There was a gray one, because he knew the color would surprise her; a flaming red one, because she had a passion for red; and a peculiar yellowish one that would bring out the coppery tones of her skin. They were more like expensive evening gowns than like anything to sleep in.

But they were worth the price he paid for them because on Christmas Eve when she opened the box, she stared, and said, "What on earth — "

She took the nightgowns out of the big beautiful box, out of the layers of tissue paper, and sat with them in her lap, holding them, hugging them, spreading them out so that the long full pleated skirts foamed over the floor, covering part of the cheap, garish, machine-made rug.

He thought, If I had my choice I'd ask her to put on the yellowish one.

Mamie said, "Powther, you want me to try one of them on for you?"

He was suddenly overcome by emotion, a kind of shyness, and he nodded, holding his head down because he couldn't look at her.

"Which one?"

He pointed at the yellowish one, the almost mustard-colored yellow one, but not quite mustard, it had more green in it than that, a peculiar color. She swept all the gowns up in her arms, and he heard her going up that long uncarpeted staircase, walking swiftly.

A few minutes later, she said, "Powther!" from somewhere upstairs.

He stumbled on the stairs, striking his knee so that it hurt unbearably, and the pain halted him, halfway up. She called again, "Powther!" and he hurried up the stairs, his knee aching, stiff; and there she was standing in the doorway of a room, and the nightgown was made of a fabric so sheer that he could see through it, see all of her, and yet it was as though there were veiling over the flesh, and the flesh was so beautiful, that his eyes filled with tears; and that moment seemed to sum up all of his future relationship with Mamie, rapture, but pain, too.

After that he set to work to make himself indispensable to her. When he went to see her he brought choice crackers and old cheeses and beautiful fruit, in case she wanted something to eat late at night. He slipped the landlady ten dollars so that Mamie could cook in her room, which was against the rules. He bought a small electric icebox and an extremely efficient small electric stove so that she could bake and fry as much as she wanted to. He used all of his efficiency, all of his knowledge of the luxurious, and most of his bank account, in his courtship of Mamie Smith. He transformed that rundown dismal bedroom into a very comfortable one-room apartment.

Finally, he went to New York and registered with a highclass employment agency, explaining optimistically that he was going to get married, that his fiancée preferred to live in Connecticut. The Treadway job was offered to him and he went to Monmouth for an interview. He explained to Mrs. Treadway that his wife preferred not to live on the premises. Though he was certain Mamie would have gentlemen callers, he did not intend to have the Treadway chauffeur, cook, gardener included in their number. It would make for an impossible situation, all of them being white. Before he went back to Baltimore he rented an apartment for Mamie in the colored section of Monmouth. It wasn't what he wanted but it would do until he could locate something better.

When he told Old Copper that he was leaving, the old man let out one of those roars that made people jump back from him, startled, awed.

"Whatsamatter?" he bellowed. "I'll raise your pay. Is that the trouble? You want more money? You want more money?"

"No, oh, no, sir. It's just that I'm getting married."

"You are? Good God!" Old Copper looked at Powther half questioningly. "Has she got a big — "

Powther said hastily, "My fiancée don't like Baltimore, sir. The only way I can get her to marry me is to offer her the chance to live in Connecticut."

Old Copper snorted, "Connecticut! Of all the godfosaken swampy places to live," he shuddered. "It's got the goddamndest climate, the goddamndest weather in the whole United States. They got drought in August, flood in MarchApril, hurricanes in the fall, winds howlin' down the chimneys all winter long. The goddamndest — I know what I'm talkin' about, Powther. I was born there." He sighed, sank deeper in the leather chair. "When you leavin'?"

"In three weeks."

"I'll give you a weddin' present, Powther. Bring her around

before you leave and I'll give you a weddin' present. And if those goddam farmers you're goin' to work for in Connecticut don't treat you right, you come back here and I'll pay you twice what they been payin' you."

Powther nodded, thinking, I may never go to Monmouth. I may be wrong about Mamie Smith. He stayed away from her until the day before he was to leave, stayed away for three weeks, hoping that she would wonder about him, miss him, become aware of the disorder in which she lived without him.

When he finally went to see her, he carried two big packages of food with him. He walked through that shabby downatthe-heels crooked street where she lived, thinking, Too many people, too many dogs, too many smells. Spring of the year but already hot. Heat waves rising from the sidewalk, nearly naked children toddling down the street, crawling up and down the highstooped steps in front of the houses.

He would tell her about spring in Connecticut, about the dog-wood and the laurel, about the smell of the river, the curve of the river, sunlight on the River Wye, about the grass, and the birds, the pigeons that strutted on every available patch of grass, about the friendliness of the people, about how clean Monmouth looked, how the houses, many of them, were painted white and the blinds were green, so that even though it was a city, it looked like a toy city compared to Baltimore with its dingy streets and its gray old buildings.

He wondered what Mamie had been doing these past three weeks while he had been completing his carefully thought out campaign. Had he made himself indispensable? He soon found out that in one way he had, and in another, perhaps more important, way, he hadn't. The bleak furnished room that he had turned into a colorful, rather luxurious, one-room apartment was in a state of dreadful disorder. He took off his coat, rolled up his shirt sleeves and set to work, washing dishes, making the bed, cleaning the room.

She must have been going to the movies rather often because there were innumerable stubs of tickets from the colored theatre, on the floor, on top of the chest of drawers. She hadn't bothered to fix a decent meal for herself because there wasn't a scrap of food in the icebox. She'd had a caller, or callers, there were six empty beer cans on the floor, and she didn't drink beer; two empty whiskey bottles, and several sticky glasses and innumerable empty ginger ale bottles. He found a man's socks, large size, loud red and green stripes, medium-priced, under the bed. Indispensable? For some things. Not needed for companionship though. He held the socks in his hand, wondering, conjecturing, and then tossed them into the dustpan with the rest of the rubbish.

He had set the table, one of his gifts, a card table, very expensive, actually a folding table, heavy, unshakable, and the steak was just about ready to serve when Mamie came home from the restaurant where she worked.

She had a parcel under her arm, wrapped in brown paper, almost the color of the brown dress she wore. No stockings. No hat. Perspiration on her forehead. She looked hot and tired and so beautiful, so big and beautiful, that he swallowed twice, in an effort to get rid of the lump that rose in his throat. He didn't say anything to her because somehow he couldn't.

"Powther!" she said, pleasure in her voice. "My God! Ain't it hot!"

She looked all around the room, looked longest at the table set for two, at the white tablecloth, the carefully folded napkins, made no comment. He watched her cross the room, sit down in the chair by the front window, slip her feet out of her shoes, and then he turned back to the stove, stuck the French bread in the oven, served the plates, poured wine in the wine glasses.

She ate in silence, ate with a relish that made him wish he hadn't stayed away so long. She must have been hungry. He watched her with a tender, yearning feeling, and thought, surprised, That's the way mothers feel about their children. She ate four of the pastries he'd brought with him, drank coffee, and then nibbled at the white grapes.

"Powther," she said. "I haven't eaten a meal like this since the last time you was here. Where've you been?"

He leaned forward, grasped the edge of the table. "I've been getting a new job. In Monmouth. A small city in Connecticut. I've got an apartment there. And all you've got to do is to say the word, just say the word, and you can go with me. I leave tomorrow." He opened his wallet, took out two railroad tickets. "One's for you and one's for me."

"I couldn't," she said. "It was right sweet of you to get the ticket for me but I haven't got a job in Monmouth. I've tried and tried to save the money so I'd have enough to tide me over but I haven't got ten dollars to my name and that's the God's truth."

"That's just it," he said eagerly. "You won't need any job. I thought, well, will you marry me? I earn enough money to more than take care of both of us."

She threw her head back and laughed. "You're a funny little man," she said. "Here I been thinkin' I'd done something to hurt your feelings and you been away makin' plans." She was silent for a moment. "Suppose I said no?"

"I —" he began, and stopped. What would he do? He'd die. That's what he'd do. He couldn't live without her. "I'd — I'd just turn the unused ticket in when I got to the station tomorrow afternoon."

"You mean you'd go anyway? Without me?"

"I have to," he said. "I have a job there. I have to go."

She looked around the room again. He wished, afterwards, that she had looked at him, appraised him, studied him, but she didn't. She looked at the room, at the stove, at the table, at the chairs he'd bought, at the comfortable bed. He supposed she was weighing the comfort and luxury, the good food, the cleanliness, against the disorder and discomfort of the past three weeks. He knew that people got accustomed to luxury very quickly, accepting it finally as their due, and no matter what strain and struggle, what utter poverty they may have known, they soon forgot it, they soon reached the point where they could not survive whole without comfort, luxury. It softened them up. He knew that. He had used it to win Mamie with, but he couldn't help wishing that he, as a person, had been the one important factor in her decision.

Picking up one of the tickets, she started humming under her breath. "I'll wear that new navy hat," she said. "And that new navy suit because it'll be cool up there and I've got some new navy suedes and I've got a big red pocketbook that'll go good with it. Let's see, what time's this train go anyway?" She frowned at the ticket, examining it.

It was as simple as that, as quick as that. He couldn't quite believe it, even while he packed her things, and made arrangements to have a moving van pick up the furniture.

On their way to the railroad station, the next day, they stopped to see Old Copper. He stared at Mamie a long time and to Powther's great discomfort, Mamie stared right back.

"You done well, Powther," Old Copper said. "If I was younger I'd give you a run for your money." Then he got out of the big leather chair, in the library, sat down at his desk, wrote a note, made out a check, put the note and the check in an envelope, and handed it to Powther. He handed the envelope to Powther, but he kept looking at Mamie, staring at Mamie, and Mamie was staring right back. Powther felt more and more uncomfortable, embarrassed.

Old Copper said, "Well! Good luck!" and shook Powther's hand, and patted his shoulder and said, again, "If them goddamn farmers you're goin' to work for don't treat you right, you come straight back here."

He followed them to the door, and once outside Powther looked back and Old Copper was still staring at Mamie, watching her go down the steps, and he knew a sudden rush of sheer maleness such as he had never felt before, suddenly hated the old man because of his wealth, the whiteness of his skin, wanted to go back and punch him in the jaw. When Old Copper saw Powther looking at him, he closed the door suddenly.

While Mamie was in the ladies' room, on the train, he opened the envelope. Old Copper's check was for a thousand dollars, and the note, written in that bold heavy hand, sounded as though the old man had spoken to him:

> Watch what I tell you. Someday she'll leave you for another man. If you're ever broke, ever need a job, ever need anything, just let me know, because God damn it, Powther, there's nobody else in the world can look after me like you done.

He was tempted to tell Mamie, after all they were married now, that he had to go back to Old Copper, that now that he had left, he knew he couldn't stand a new place, new people. And there was, too, the old man's warning, "She'll leave you for another man." In a new place it was much more likely to happen than in Baltimore.

It was all a dreadful mistake. He had spent money like a millionaire and his bank account had practically vanished. But he had Old Copper's check. That would serve as a stake, a kind of cushion against disaster. He folded the check and put it in his wallet, tore the letter into tiny pieces and thrust the pieces far under the seat.

Mamie came swaying down the aisle, swaying partially because of the motion of the train, but also because it was the way she walked. And he thought, Well, I can't go back to Old Copper's,

not with Mamie. They had looked at each other, stared at each
other, just as though they were testing each other out, as though
they had immediately recognized some quality they had in common and were instantly defiant, instantly jockeying for position
for some final test of strength.

He knew that he would have rivals, knew that he would find
gentlemen callers in his house, but he could not, would not, make
it possible for Old Copper to be included among them.

And now as he lay in this bed, beside J.C., turning and twisting,
in vain, wasted effort to avoid the child's knees, elbows, head, he
asked himself if he regretted that decision he'd made on the train.
Should he have gone back to Old Copper? More important still,
was it a mistake, the whole thing? Wouldn't he have been better
off if he hadn't married Mamie? No. He had never known such
delight as he had experienced with Mamie.

J.C. moved for the millionth time, turning over, and then
inching up in bed. He put his arm around him thinking to re-
strain his movements, and J.C.'s head caught him under the chin,
hard, heavy, the impact was such that Powther thought his jaw
was broken, then that he had cracked his bridge, but he had only
bitten his tongue, viciously, painfully. It felt swollen and he lay
there, pain along the edge of his tongue, moving it back and forth
cautiously, exploratively, expecting to feel a gush of blood at any
moment. J.C. muttered darkly to himself, under his breath.
Kelly and Shapiro echoed his mutterings. They were talking in
their sleep, repeating words, phrases. Then they turned over,
sighed, groaned, kicked the covers off. He could hear their feet
rejecting the covers, getting free of the covers.

I will never get to sleep, he thought. And I have to be at the
Hall early tomorrow morning. He heard the clang-clang of the
last trolley that went up Franklin Avenue. It seemed like a long
time after that that the lights went off in The Last Chance. This
room in the front of the house became suddenly darker, the pink-
orange light from the neon sign went out suddenly; and just before it went out, there was a little eddy, a gust of talk in the street
below, suggesting wind, eddying, gone, as the last of the beer
drinkers, and the seekers after Nirvana, left The Last Chance,
heading reluctantly toward home.

The Last Chance. The Last Chance. Last chance to do what?
Get a drink? Burn in hell? Look at Bill Hod?

He sat up in bed, listening. He thought he heard footsteps in the hall, then the click of a lock. He really couldn't tell, not in this room with its restless sleepers.

Getting out of bed, he covered J.C. carefully, closed the door of the boys' room behind him, and went down the hall, slowly, quietly, in his bare feet, the floor cold to his feet. He stood outside the door of the bedroom, listening, and he thought he heard Bill Hod's voice. But he wasn't certain. He couldn't see anything except a thin thread of pinkish light under the door.

The thread of pinkish light disappeared from under the door and there was silence, no sound at all, nothing, just the darkness and the cold floor under his feet. He stood there waiting for some further sound. There was nothing at all, no sound of voices, no movement. Silence.

He went back down the hall, opened the door of the boys' bedroom, and got in bed with J.C., refusing to think about what he thought he'd heard, thinking instead, I will not sleep on that damn sofa in the living room, I will sleep in a bed, a rightful bed, even if I cannot rest. I am not a refugee. I have a right to a bed. I work all day and half the night, and come home to — Bill Hod? Link Williams? Cigarette case incrusted with diamonds.

At five o'clock the next morning he was dressing in the living room. The boys were good for another two hours at least. While he was putting on his shoes, he thought he heard the thud-thud of the percolator in the kitchen, was certain that he smelt coffee. But he didn't know how to greet Mamie this morning, so he finished dressing and then went down the hall. The bedroom door was open, the room was empty.

Mamie called from the kitchen, "You up already, Powther? Set the table for me, will you? Mebbe we can eat without them starvin' Armenians sittin' in our laps."

He decided that he must have dreamed that business last night, had a nightmare, a night horse, as his father used to say. She was so gay this morning, her eyes sparkled, her lips kept curving into a smile, and she sang as she turned the bacon in the frying pan, cooked the pancakes.

"Soup's on," she said. He thought even her voice was lovelier this morning, there was more music in it than ever. And she was off the diet. She ate everything in sight.

When they finished eating, she leaned back in her chair, sighed and lit a cigarette. "Let's leave the dishes," she said. "And go get back in bed. It's too early for any poor black sinners to be up."

He nearly tripped over his feet getting there, and later, he went to sleep, relaxing into sleep, easily, quickly, contentment seeping all through him, so that he smiled in his sleep, aware just before he slid down into the total darkness, the blackout, the delicious oblivion of sleep that Mamie's soft warm naked body was pressed tight against him, and the strong sweet perfume was all around him, like a cloud.

When he woke up he looked around the room, trying to remember where he was, and how he got there, and then he smiled, remembering. He sat up in bed and saw that Mamie was up, and getting dressed.

She always put her shoes on first, she never wore any stockings in the house, and now she was leaning over, back turned, putting on a pair of green highheeled sandals. He liked to tease her about putting her shoes on first, telling her that she must have been born in the South, must have been a little barefoot pickaninny, and then she finally acquired a pair of shoes, sign of prosperity, mark of distinction, that set her apart from the rest of the black barefoot tribe, so precious a possession that she slept with them under her pillow, her hand resting on them, like an old-time prospector with a small bag of gold dust never out of reach of his hand. When she woke up, she felt under her pillow for her shoes, and then got up, and put them on, just as she was doing now.

He changed the story each time he told it, changing the emphasis, changing the details, embellishing it, sometimes the shoes were scarlet, sometimes they were gold, sometimes she lost them and could not find them, but always on the morning when she first got them, she went around singing, "All God's chillun got shoes."

Mamie straightened up and the new story about the first pair of shoes went out of his mind. She was shaped almost like a violin, like the base of a violin, big beautiful curve, and as she turned toward the bed, he thought, If she were standing inside a frame, naked like that, with that look of expectancy on her face, all the museums in the world would sell their Da Vincis and their Manets and their Rubens in order to own this one woman.

He said, "Mamie."

"Powther!" she said. "You awake? Here I been tippin' around —" She crossed over to the bed, sat down on the side of it, put her arms around him, hugged him close to her, and kissed his cheek.

He thought, I, I, I, cuckolded as I am, worried as I often am, after a night with you, you, you, soft warm flesh, smell of perfume, toosweet, toosweet, toostrong, deep-soft-cushion feel of you, feel of the arms, the legs, the thighs, me incased in your thighs, all joy, all ecstasy, all pleasure, not caring, forgetting, completely forget, not forgetting, not caring, who else does this to you, defying Bill Hod, conquering Bill Hod and you and the world, even I, an old man, sorrowful sometimes, frightened always, living forever afraid that you will leave me, don't ever leave me, even I can, could, walk for miles, could sing, could shout, could believe that I will live forever and ever, that I will never die, I am too alive, too filled with joy to die.

He had to get up, get dressed, get back to the Hall. He left Mamie, sitting on the side of the bed, singing:

> *Tell me what color an' I'll tell you*
> *what road she took,*
> *Tell me what color an' I'll tell you*
> *what road she took.*
> *Why'n'cha tell me what color an' I'll*
> *tell you what road she took.*

12

● SUNDAY. Quarter past twelve. Powther put on his overcoat and his hat.

"I've got to speak to Albert for a few minutes," he said to the second man, who was his assistant.

It would be at least a half-hour before he started to set up the dining room and he had just finished checking the entire downstairs. Everything was in order, everything polished, spotless, gleaming. Flowers everywhere.

Al was not in the garage. He heard the slush-slush of water from somewhere behind the garage, so he walked outside to the area where Al washed the cars. Al was hosing down one of the station wagons, his face was red, and there was something violent in the way he manipulated the hose, as though he were beating the car with it. Powther wondered why he was washing it.

He said, "It's a nice sunny morning, Al." Sunny but cold. Very cold. Too cold to be washing cars outdoors.

Al looked up. "Hi, Mal," he said and turned the hose off. He kicked at one of the tires, scowling at it. "Rogers must carry horse shit around in this crate all day. He's got a stink in it that would choke you to death. It's got my garage stunk up like a stable. So I'm out here, in January, hosin' it down."

Rogers was the head gardener and Powther wasn't the least bit interested in whatever it was he carried in the station wagon.

He said, "I haven't got much time, Al. I've got to get back

195

and set up my dining room. What did you mean last night, when you asked me if I'd noticed anything wrong?"

"Not wrong, Mal. Funny. Funny ha-ha and funny boo-hoo, too." Al lowered his voice. "You know where my room is? Right in the front part of the garage? Upstairs, right over the doors?"

Powther nodded. It wasn't the Rolls-Royce, it couldn't be, though people often began to tell you something by introducing the extraneous, the obvious, but he couldn't somehow connect the location of Al's room with the Rolls-Royce.

Al laid the hose down. He said, "Well, from them front windows I gotta view of the drive, a clear straight view. And I been seein' Camilo's car come up that straight stretch of drive, night after night. For weeks on end now, she's been stayin' out half the night." He hesitated for a minute. Then he said, "She must be doin' eighty when she comes up that drive. Somebody oughtta tell her, Don't drive like that, or she's sure goin' to have a smashup."

"How do you know it isn't the Captain coming in late?" Scandal, Powther thought. Al isn't interested in the rate of speed, it's the scandal.

"How do you know it isn't the Captain?" he repeated. "Are you sure it's Miss Camilo?"

"Am I sure? Listen, Mal, she puts the car up herself. She always puts it up herself. She ain't like some of them rich bastards I've worked for who could drive just as good as me but would leave their cars out in front of their shacks for me to put up because they were scared they wouldn't get their money's worth out of me if they put a car in a garage themselves.

"For two nights straight I thought it was lightnin' flashin' through them Venetian blinds upstairs. It woke me up. Two nights straight. So the third night I decide it ain't lightnin' flashin' in my face, not in December, three nights in a row, so I get out of bed and look down, out of the window. And there's Camilo in the car. She's got to wait for them doors to open up. Them automatic doors ain't hooked up to go up in no split second.

"Ever since then I been lookin' at her, out of the window, three or four nights a week. She comes in later than ever on Saturdays. I seen her, even in bad weather settin' down there at the wheel of her car, the top down, her head lifted watchin' them doors go up. Ain't nobody else looks like her, or got hair like hers. It's Camilo all right. On Saturday nights, she comes in about four or five in the mornin', drivin' like a bat out of hell." He stopped talking and frowned.

Then he said, "She — well, if I was the Captain, I'd, well, she looks like an angel, sittin' down there in that car with her face lifted, watchin' them doors open up."

Powther thought, No wonder the Captain has been looking so discontented. Even when Miss Camilo was away, the Captain had dinner with the Madam on Sundays. Lately the expression on the Captain's face had made Powther wonder what was the matter with him. Now he understood what caused it.

He, too, knew what it was like to lie awake wondering where a woman was, what she was doing, knew what it was like to pretend to be asleep when she came home at some ungodly hour, came home from God knows what, God knows where, and undressed and got in bed and relaxed into sleep almost instantly, knew what it was like to prop himself up on his elbow, cautiously, so as not to disturb the sleeping woman, to examine her face, study her face, try, in a room dimly lighted by the street light outside to figure out from that placid, relaxed, beautiful face where she had been, what she had been doing, because he would never dare ask.

Al said, "Where's she go?"

"I don't know," he said sharply. "I wish I did know. I'll probably never know." Then he remembered that Al was talking about Miss Camilo. "I'm sorry," he said, "I was thinking about something else. I haven't any idea where she goes."

"This town closes up tighter'n a drum after ten o'clock. There ain't no place for nobody to go. What's Camilo doin' out in a closed-up town till all hours of the mornin'? In all kinds of weather. She don't know nobody in Monmouth."

"She probably goes to New York," Powther said. He felt impelled to steer Al away from this affair which was none of his business. "Her friends all live in New York. Or Boston. Young people like to drive a hundred miles or more, to a party or a dance."

"No, she don't," Al said.

"How do you know?"

"Because I measure the gas. I don't question she's in New York on the weekends. But the rest of the time she ain't. She don't use a half-gallon of gas from here to wherever she goes and back here again. She goes somewhere right here in Monmouth. And she don't know nobody in Monmouth."

Powther sighed. "Look, Al," he said, "maybe she plays Canasta or goes to the movies or — "

"There ain't no movies open at three in the morning," Al said stubbornly. "The Treadways ain't never had nothin' to do with the town. I been with them for twenty years and the widow don't even buy her clothes in the town. Camilo don't even know the names of the streets. There ain't nothin' there for her. What's she doin' there, Mal?"

"She's probably got friends in Monmouth," he said firmly. "Well, I've got to set up my dining room now. I'll see you later."

"Come on out when you get through and I'll drive you to the car line, Mal."

"Thank you, Al," he said. When they were driving to the car line he would have to somehow convince Al that whatever Miss Camilo did or did not do was none of Al's business. He wondered why if Al had known this, "for weeks on end," he had kept it to himself up until now.

He liked Miss Camilo. In many ways she was like the Madam, younger, of course, but with the same kindness and kindliness about her. Good people to work for. Thoughtful.

As he moved about the dining room, he forgot about Al and Miss Camilo. He always set his own tables, because he enjoyed doing it. He prided himself on the result. For this intimate family dinner, he placed a small round table in the great bay window. The dining room faced west and by dinnertime, the winter sunlight would lie across the table like a spotlight. In his early days, he had trained under an Armenian, a peculiar man, totally unreliable and unpredictable but an artist at heart. He was always saying, "Now the food it is important, yes. But the dining room is even more so. You must set it up like a stage, Powther, like a stage. You must vary the setting to go with the food, and the hour of eating so that everything fits itself together."

So for these Sunday dinners, in winter, served at the unfashionable hour of three o'clock, he always used the Crown Derby and the old silver goblets, and the Versailles flatware. For the centerpiece he selected an Imari bowl, and filled it with chrysanthemums, because the reds and tawny yellows were like the coloring of the Crown Derby china. By the time he announced dinner there would be sunlight on the table, reaching into the room, shining on the Gainsboroughs, on the mahogany paneling, on the fireplace brasses, so that the entire room would seem to pick up and echo the colors used on the table.

At quarter of three, he lit the fire in the dining room fireplace, and stood watching it, to be sure it was going to burn evenly. He kept thinking about Miss Camilo, found himself shaking his head, saying, Dear me, under his breath. He should have known this would happen eventually.

One morning last summer he was walking past the garage, going toward the house, when he saw her backing that long red Cadillac out of the garage. She turned her head, watching where she was going, and he saw that her face was sharply impatient, set, not smiling.

She waved at him, and said, "Oh, oh, oh. Where've you been, Powther?"

"Home with my wife," he said, and then, "It's going to be a beautiful day, Miss Camilo."

She had looked up at the sky. "I suppose so," she said. "Yes, I guess it will. Though sometimes they seem pretty much alike."

He had thought, Oh, dear me, as he watched her drive off, at your age and looking the way you do, with that shining silky hair and that lovely smile, you ought to be saying, Oh, it's good to be alive on a morning like this, it ought to show in your face, the morning, the joy at being alive. You look as though you were neither dead nor alive, sort of half of each.

It was one of those mornings when he felt like singing, like shouting, because Mamie had held him in her arms, half the night, and he had watched the car go down the driveway too fast, going faster and faster, flash of red disappearing around the curve, top down, silky yellow hair blowing back in the wind, not dyed, people thought she dyed it, but she didn't; thinking, Oh, dear me, why can't that youngest Copper's wife die, so Miss Camilo can find the man she's looking for.

One minute of three. He opened the doors of the dining room, took one quick backward glance, sunlight in the room, fire burning quietly in the fireplace, red damask draperies in even folds at the windows, Gainsboroughs all straight on the walls, Persian rug free of lint. He'd done a good job. Big as the room was, your eyes went straight to the table, even at this distance away. All the sunlight was concentrated on the table, even the wood of the Adam chairs gleamed in the sun.

At exactly three o'clock, he entered the drawing room, and announced dinner. He got the impression that all three of them, the Madam, Miss Camilo, and the Captain, welcomed the announcement, that they had been sitting there together, saying nothing.

As he moved quietly about the dining room, serving them, he thought about the Captain, wondering why he had written the Captain off, that day last summer when he watched Miss Camilo go down the driveway. Written him off, just as though he didn't exist. But then everybody did, all the servants, even the Madam.

The Captain was handsome, a big young man, with a fine looking head and face. He was unquestionably a gentleman. But — Al said he was a tame cat. For once, Al's description of some one really fitted. The Captain was too nice, too gentle, too wellbred. Powther thought, Well, he came from an old New York family, perhaps the blood line ran out, got too thin. Some of his ancestors should have married into lusty peasant families.

But Miss Camilo — He studied her as she sat at the table, talking and laughing. She has become a raving beauty. There is a gleam about her, a gleam that competes with, no, it surpasses the gleam in this room. It's in her flesh, her hair, her eyes. I know what it is, he thought, I saw the same thing happen to Mamie.

He rarely ever followed the trend of a dinner table conversation, unless it was something very unusual; he was more concerned about the smoothness of the service. But today he listened to them.

The Captain (poking at the nearest flower in the centerpiece with a forefinger, not looking at the flowers, but at Miss Camilo): The chrysanthemums are lovely, Mrs. Treadway.

Once again Powther thought how strange it was that the Captain should call his mother-in-law Mrs. Treadway, not Elinor, not Mother, always Mrs. Treadway.

The Madam: Rogers says it's because we've had so much sunlight this winter. Everything in the greenhouse is flourishing.

The Captain (still looking at Miss Camilo): Let's go for a ride after dinner, Cammie.

Miss Camilo: A ride?

The Captain: Yes, let's go as far outside of Boston as we can go and still get back to Monmouth at a decent hour tomorrow morning.

Miss Camilo: You mean spend the night?

The Captain: Of course. At the first likelylooking inn we come across. We'll play hunt-the-inn until we find a place that's absolutely perfect, even to the Windsor chairs and the fireplaces (the tone of his voice changed, grew softer), the way we used to."

The Madam: You'll probably find snow along the way and the countryside is beautiful in the snow.

Miss Camilo: You come too, Mother. You've never been on a trip with us.

Powther watched the Captain's face and he decided that the Captain was holding the muscles of his face in the exact expression it had had when he first spoke, but the eagerness, the young eager look, left it, the glow went out of his eyes.

The Captain: Good idea. You come too, Mrs. Treadway.

The Madam: I really can't. I've got a nine o'clock appointment at the plant. Thank you for inviting me.

Miss Camilo looked at the Captain, and Powther frowned, not meaning to, unable to prevent the frown, because the look Miss Camilo gave the Captain was a caressing, lingering kind of look, and Powther thought, She has a lover and because she is so happy, she is going to let a little of her happiness spill over on the captain, and he will believe that it is he who has made her happy, but some day, some day —

In the butler's pantry, he waited for them to finish the second course. He thought about himself and Mamie.

A year after he and Mamie were married he knew that there was something wrong, but he did not know what it was. He could read the evidence in the droop of her mouth, the infrequent laughter when laughter had been as natural to her as breathing, now there was a languor and an indifference that disturbed him. He had thought, If we had children, and she agreed. After Kelly and Shapiro were born she was like she used to be but by the time they were two years old, she was bored with them, cross with them, impatient with them, and then, about a year after that, she was a Rubens female again, her flesh glowing, the house always filled with the rippling sound of her laughter. She was always singing, and her voice acquired an added depth and richness, a beauty of tone that he explained to himself by saying that childbirth wrought wondrous changes in women.

He would have let it go at that except for the new clothes. He knew the contents of Mamie's closet far better than most husbands do, he was always brushing her dresses, cleaning and pressing them, making minor repairs. He kept finding new dresses, new coats, new suits. The drawers of the chest were filled with new underwear and stockings, stockings by the dozen.

He knew deepdown inside him that she had a lover, that some man had entered her life, came home unexpectedly one afternoon and found a man sitting in the kitchen. In his shirt sleeves. Starched white shirt. No necktie. Collar open at the throat. Sleeves rolled up. He was drinking a glass of milk. When Powther entered the kitchen, the man stood up, getting up quickly, all in one motion.

Mamie said, easily, unselfconsciously, "Powther, meet my cousin, Mr. Bill Hod. Bill, this is Powther."

He saw a man put together like a statue, no fat on him anywhere, tall, broad of shoulder, narrow of waist, a man with a quick graceful body and a face like the face of one of the early popes, in a small dark oil painting that hung in Old Copper's library, a cruel face, with eyes that saw everything and disclosed nothing, with a narrowlipped, cruel mouth, a shark's mouth.

He gave Powther one swift, all-inclusive glance, nodded, sat down again, and finished the glass of milk. He left right afterwards.

Powther made cautious inquiries about Bill Hod and learned very little about him that any discerning person couldn't have guessed just from looking at his face. In the barber shop, they said he was the owner of The Last Chance, that he was a gambler, an operator of houses of ill fame, a numbers king, probably nearer the truth, that nobody really knew what illegal enterprises he directed or controlled but that he was unquestionably a racketeer. He was reported to be blind in one eye but nobody knew which eye, both eyes looked equally blank, and nobody knew how he had lost the sight of the eye, assuming that one of them really was sightless. No one knew how old he was; looking at his face, just his face, you could safely say that he was an evil old man of eighty, but he had the thick black lustrous hair of a young man in his twenties.

He couldn't prove that Mamie had a lover, or that if she had one, it was Bill Hod. For all he knew, Hod might really and truly be her cousin. But he had to find out. So he took to playing that most dangerous, most hazardous, of all the games that husbands and wives play with each other. He had to find out, to make sure, he had to know, could not live without knowing, so he finished his work at the Hall as quickly as he could, arriving home at unexpected hours, entering the house quietly, unannounced.

Sometimes Mamie was alone in the house, sometimes she was not there at all. Once he found Bill Hod sitting in the kitchen, drinking milk, sleeves of the white shirt rolled up, collar of the white shirt open at the throat, and Mamie was seated across the table from him, drinking coffee and eating doughnuts.

Mamie said, "Have one, Powther. Weak Knees made 'em. He's the cook at Bill's place."

Powther ate one of the doughnuts, drank a cup of coffee, moving nervously back and forth, in front of the kitchen sink, thinking, There's something about him, what is it, it's not just the face, it's more than just the face, I don't know what it is, but I'm afraid of him. His hands began to shake so that he put the unfinished cup of coffee down in the sink, afraid he would drop it, and nibbled at the doughnut, not really conscious that he was eating, and yet aware that the doughnut was incredibly good, better than any he had ever eaten, and that on the strength of those doughnuts, Weak Knees, whoever he was, could cook in the White House. Though the best cooks sneered at the White House as a place to work, prestige, yes, but a pinchpenny kind of place, you couldn't really let yourself go there as you could in, say, the kitchen of any millionaire in the country.

He glanced in the dining room to see how near finished they were. And then went all the way inside and started removing plates. The Madam and the Captain were about to start another argument about politics.

The Madam: Oh, Bunny, you talk such nonsense. If all the wealth in this country were divided up, in less than a year's time the same people would be rich and the same ones would be poor.

The Captain: I doubt it. Because —

Miss Camilo (she gave the Captain another one of those long-lingering caressing glances that Powther was certain were not directed at the Captain but inspired by someone else and therefore directed at the other man even though he was not there): Let's drive north for eighty miles and then go east for twenty miles and see what we find.

Miss Camilo had changed the subject, so abruptly, so quickly, Powther didn't see how the Madam and the Captain could possibly bring it up again. He could tell by what the Madam had been saying that she and the Captain were heading straight for one of those long unpleasant arguments about Roosevelt. No matter where they started they always ended up arguing about Roosevelt, and the Madam always managed to call the Captain a fool.

Powther served the dessert, brought in the coffee service. They were talking about the projected ride again.

The Madam: Did you ever find anything wonderful that way?

Miss Camilo: You'd be surprised at the things you find when you're just out riding and don't know where you're going. Even here in Monmouth.

The Captain: You're right. Monmouth's full of surprises. Especially if you follow the river.

The Madam: What kind of surprises?

The Captain: Views of the river. Maybe it's because of the mural in the entrance hall, perhaps the mural made me really see the river. But you can catch the most marvelous glimpses of it, looking down some of the side streets, and then when you actually come to it, and follow its course, you feel as though you had made a personal discovery, come on a secret that no one else has ever found.

Miss Camilo: That's the way I feel about it, too. It's almost as though you had finally found something you'd been hunting for all your life without really knowing that you'd been looking for it. And then you see that it's there, the thing you've been hunting for is there, in the river.

Powther passed the coffee cups as the Madam filled them. He was a little surprised when Miss Camilo again urged the Madam to go for a ride with them.

Miss Camilo: Mother, you come with us. It's such fun to go somewhere, not knowing where you're going or what you'll find when you get there.

The Captain, quickly: We'll all go exploring. Do come and play hunt-the-inn with us, Mrs. Treadway. Each and every-man-Jack of us will be Christopher Columbus. No. You can be Cortez, he was a better man than the rest of them. Cammie will be Ponce de León. I'll be, well, I'll just go along for the ride, and keep the log.

The Madam gave Captain Sheffield a funny sharp look. Powther looked at him, too, and couldn't decide whether the Captain was joking, teasing the Madam and Miss Camilo in some fashion that he, Powther, could not understand or whether he was angry, anger born of fear that the Madam would ignore the fact that three's a crowd and go with them, and so was being sarcastic.

The Madam: Thank you for asking me but I really can't go with you. Besides even if I could, I don't like the idea of hunting for a place to spend the night. I honestly prefer my own bed in my own room, or a bed that's equally as comfortable in a hotel room that's been reserved for me in advance.

Miss Camilo: Well, we tried, didn't we, Bunny?

The Captain: You'll go with us some other time, won't you?

The Madam: Not when you're going to play hunt-the-inn. But some time when you know where you're going, and you let me know beforehand, I'd love to go along.

Miss Camilo: Okay, Bunny, we'll start as soon as I can get a toothbrush in a bag.

Al backed the car out of the garage. He said, "Camilo musta took her Cadillac. I didn't see her get it."

Powther said, "She and the Captain are going away for the weekend."

"Camilo and Bunny?" Al said, and he sounded surprised.

"That's right."

"You mean they went off together some place?"

"That's right."

Al was strangely silent. Powther glanced at him a couple of times. He seemed to be thinking about something, puzzling over something. When they reached the car line, Al slowed down, then said, "Ah, what's the differ? I'll drive you all the way, Mal. I ain't got nothing else to do."

At one point Al got stuck behind a trolley car, and was forced to follow it block after block, going slowly through the streets, unable to pass it, because of all the Sunday traffic. Because of Miss Camilo and the captain, Powther kept thinking about the day he rode on a trolley car from early morning until late at night. It was a hot day, too, it had started off hot, early in the morning, and the Madam suddenly decided to go to Newport to visit friends for a long weekend.

As soon as he had organized the Hall for the day, and conferred with Mrs. Cameron as to who would be off and when, he hurried home. He kept mopping his forehead with a handkerchief, trying to hurry the trolley car along, and the effort he put into it, the hurry, hurry, hurry, made him feel hotter and hotter. He was still going home at unexpected hours because he had to find out whether Bill Hod was Mamie's lover, or whether he was her cousin just as she said.

He entered the apartment house quietly, tiptoeing up the stairs, though he knew that there was no reason to move quietly in the hall, but the moment he entered the street door he began to feel like a spy, a conspirator, and so he walked on tiptoe up the stairs of that old building where they had lived before they moved into Mrs. Crunch's beautifully kept, fine, old brick house on Dumble Street.

He had been in and out of that building hundreds of times, but for some reason, perhaps because he was extra sensitive to everything that day, the heat was dreadful, he was sweating, the hall impressed him as being singularly ugly. He paused on the second floor, just standing there, on the landing, thinking, Why couldn't whoever painted this hall have made it two-thirds green and one-third tan, or three-quarters green and one-quarter tan? His eye kept following the dividing line between the two colors, hunting for some break in the evenness. It was so damn monotonous and he was under some peculiar and inexplicable compulsion to touch the design stamped in the metal of the wall, his fingers kept seeking it out. It was repeated over and over again, at the exact same interval, the metal cool under his hands, his hands hot, too hot. He tried to figure out what the design was. A leaf? A fleur-de-lis? Just a conventionalized pattern, senseless, unrecognizable. But repeated, repeated, repeated.

Ordinarily when he walked up the stairs he chose the side next to the wall, avoiding the banister, for fear he might brush against it, it was always greasy. He had never stopped to study the wall. His heart was beating faster and faster, and he thought, There's something wrong upstairs. Perhaps Mamie isn't there. Perhaps she's left me.

He kept reaching toward the wall, his fingers seeming to find some sort of satisfaction in verifying the distance between the designs stamped in the metal. He drew his hand away, and it would reach out again, apparently of its own volition, as though something in his hand needed to find this senseless pattern always in the same place, the place where it ought to be.

Mrs. Adams owned this building, he thought. She was responsible for this ugly hallway. She must be seventy and yet she had only a few gray hairs, and the effect of the black thick woolly hair above the face with the dark brown skin, deep lines at each side of the mouth, was all wrong. One eye went off at an angle, so that he was never certain whether she was looking at him or something over his head or to his right.

Mrs. Adams had a silly kind of manner. When she wasn't whispering, she talked in a thin whining voice. An arch and silly manner. He was certain the pearl earrings she wore were real ones, and he had thought she would verify this when he admired them. But she didn't. She arched her long neck, and bridled, and said, "They belonged to my Grandmother Williams." And that was all.

Whenever he thought of her, he thought of the pocketbook she carried. She never let it out of her hand, out of her arm, actually, because not only did her hand rest on it, but it was always tucked under her arm as well. She never put it down, no matter what she was doing. She collected the rents herself, counting the money carefully, and then opening the pocketbook just wide enough to push the bills and the coins inside and then snapped it shut, the whole thing done awkwardly, the bony hands clutching and fumbling with the powerful clasp, because she never really let the pocketbook get out from under her arm all the time she was opening and closing it.

She was thin all over, arms, shoulders, legs, feet, long lean feet. But she had a tremendous, pendulous, belly, the sag and sway of it suggested a big tumor inside. She walked with a slow, stiff-legged gait, as though her legs were brittle, and she had to plan each step in advance lest one of them snap.

Right after he and Mamie moved into the apartment, he met Mrs. Adams in the hall, just coming in, pocketbook clutched under her arm, hand resting on the clasp, and he told her that he'd like to have the apartment painted.

"Everything's so high, Mr. Powther," she had said, leaning toward him. Her manner became highly confidential. She began to whisper. "What it costs me to keep this place heated, and a new furnace last year, and now they've just made me buy new garbage cans. The Board of Health made me buy them and the old ones was perfectly good except the covers was gone. Those little niggers runnin' through the street all the time, steals all the covers off the garbage cans. The big niggers steals the handles to use as blackjacks, and the little niggers steal the covers, for what I don't know. And what it cost me to buy those new cans I could have put that money by for a rainy day, and it woulda carried me for a long time to come. And then I bought chains and chained the covers on. I told that man from the Board of Health, 'Listen, I'm just a poor black woman and a widow, and I can't throw money around like that,' " she paused, sighed, moved a little closer to Powther. "Well, it didn't do any good."

The eye that wandered seemed to find something of interest behind him, on the stairway, halfway up, anyway it focused there and the other eye seemed to be studying the top of his head. Dear God, he had thought, why did I ask her anything about paint? Why did I ask her anything at all?

Mrs. Adams moved a little closer, and her great belly brushed against him, soft, huge. She smelt old and musty, and most unpleasantly of some kind of perfume. He moved away, and her belly followed him, pressed against him.

"As for paint. Well, I rent these apartments as is, Mr. Powther. I can't pay out a single penny for paint. Not one penny. You might as well say I'm the janitor for all the good I get out of this place."

So he paid the painters himself, hired them himself, and then right after that had new plumbing fixtures put in the bathroom, though he knew if he and Mamie ever moved, Mrs. Adams would get double the rent for it because of the money he'd spent improving it.

He didn't know why he should have thought about Mrs. Adams, didn't know why he was standing motionless, on the landing, the second floor landing of Mrs. Adams' rundown house. He'd done everything for Mamie, given her everything, let her do exactly as she pleased. He didn't have to live in this colored slum. If it hadn't been for Mamie, he would have lived at the Hall, in his own quarters, as fine a setup as any man ever had. But Mamie wouldn't have fitted in with the life there. It was bad enough to come home and find Bill Hod in his house, it would have been unbearable to have found Rogers, the gardener, Al, the chauffeur, the French chef, the men he worked with every day on intimate terms with Mamie.

Besides, Mamie was always saying, "Powther, there is things about white people that I never will understand. And to tell you the God's honest truth, I don't intend to try. I am a hell of a lot more comfortable, and it gives me a lot more honest-to-God pleasure just to write 'em all down as bastards and leave 'em strictly

alone. Live and let live is what I say. I don't bother them and
they don't bother me, so we get along fine. If they say the same
about me, it's perfectly all right. That means we're even Steven."

Then she'd start to sing, and you couldn't talk, couldn't argue
with her when she was singing, you had to listen. Perhaps that
was why she sang, it meant he couldn't discuss anything with her
that she didn't want to discuss. She began to sing that song he
didn't like. He thought it was a spiritual, but she made it sound
like the kind of song they banned on the radio, banned on records:

> Same train carry my mother;
> Same train be back tomorrer;
> Same train, same train.
> Same train blowin' at the station,
> Same train be back tomorrer;
> Same train, same train.

If it hadn't been for Mamie, his life would have been as tran-
quil and as satisfactory as anybody's life could be. He was doing
the kind of work he loved. He did it superbly and knew it, he was
well paid for it, all the help liked him, respected him. So did the
Madam. She even confided in him. Not even her personal maid
had as much of the Madam's confidence as he had. When he first
went to Treadway Hall he was certain she had qualms about him,
wondered if she hadn't made a mistake, she'd never had colored
help before so he supposed it was understandable. He could tell
by the way she watched him, something skeptical in her gaze. But
by the end of that first year he had turned in such a magnificent
performance, that she forgot all about his being colored. Finally,
she told him that she had never known how beautiful the house
could be, until he took it over.

Yes, everything would have gone smoothly without Mamie.
But he couldn't live without her. He would die. He would shrivel
up and die if she left him. He had felt suddenly old, horribly old,
and so sorry for himself that for a moment he thought he was
going to cry. It's this goddamn hallway, he thought. It's just like
Mrs. Adams, it's enough to depress a saint. He started tiptoeing
up the stairs again, going quickly.

Once inside the apartment, he found out what he had already
known, deep inside him, found out because he saw the evidence
there in the bedroom he shared with Mamie, Mamie, Mamie.

He had furnished the room with simple, unadorned, soundly constructed furniture made of good wood, carefully finished. Mamie had slowly replaced it with overornate imitations of period furniture, horrible, cheap stuff, not cheap in price, they charged enough for it, but it was the kind of furniture that was despised by people who really knew fine things, the sort of stuff sold in poor neighborhoods to Italians and colored people and Puerto Ricans. The bed was a copy of a copy of a Louis Something-or-Other, the wood, God knows what the wood was, stained and varnished and the headboard and footboard covered with cupids and doves and flowers, all turned out by machine and glued on.

Mamie and Bill Hod lay there, side by side, in that fake Louis Something-or-Other bed. Mamie asleep. Bill Hod, lying on his side, back to the door, something in his position suggesting that he was not asleep. Both of them naked. Hod's body bore absolutely no relation to his face, his body was young and beautiful and with no knowledge of evil.

Powther told himself that he was a coward, that he was a fool. He tried to think of more searing descriptions of himself and couldn't, as he went down the stairs, softly, afraid of being heard, afraid of Bill Hod, of Mamie, of himself, half blind with fear, and with rage, and something else, something that made his eyes fill with tears. He couldn't see where he was going, and his throat was filling with mucus, so that he couldn't swallow, thickness in his throat.

He got on a trolley car, more by instinct than because he actually saw the car coming, and decided to board it. Anyway, there he was, standing in the front of the car, dropping money in the coinbox and he did not remember how he got there. He rode to the end of the line, and paid another fare and rode to the center of the city, and got a transfer and boarded another trolley, going in another direction.

All that day and part of the night he rode on trolleys, the clang-clang of the car, the rattling, covering up the sound of the sobs that kept bubbling up in his throat, the sound of the groans that kept forming in his throat, the swaying of the car covering up, concealing, helping to conceal the convulsive heaving of his chest.

At ten o'clock that night, he went home. His only concern was whether he would find Mamie there, because he had reached a point in quiet despair, in which he knew that it did not matter who Mamie slept with, so long as she let him sleep with her, so long as she did not leave him. That was all he asked, all he wanted.

Prideless. Pride gone. Even that last vanishing traditional male right of ownership gone. Even that vestige of it which had been nourished by his final meeting with Old Copper was gone, never to return. He had faced and acknowledged the fact that Mamie was all he wanted in life. If Bill Hod was what she wanted then he would accept Hod, go on day after day pretending that Hod was her cousin.

Mamie was waiting for him when he got home. She had supper ready. She seemed so happy, humming under her breath, laughing, talking, that the sheer music of her overwhelmed him.

It was a wonderful supper, shrimp salad and hot biscuits and a soup so flavorsome that he ate two bowls of it. He hadn't had anything to eat all day. He hadn't stopped to eat breakfast that morning, hurrying, cutting every possible corner, as he had done for weeks, hurrying through his work at the Hall so that he could arrive home unexpectedly, in order to find out, find out, what he had finally and dreadfully found out, and then knew that he had been better off when he didn't know, when he only suspected.

He had said, "This is good. This is wonderful. This is like the salad the Frenchman makes at the Hall."

Mamie said, "Weak Knees fixed it up. You know he's the cook at Bill's place."

He went on eating, chewing carefully, putting measured forkfuls of the shrimp salad in his mouth, avocado and garlic in it, the flavor so perfect, chewing, making himself chew at the same rate, not pausing, not stopping, feeling sick, his throat rebelling against the idea of swallowing.

He laid the fork down and looked at Mamie, the redbrown skin, the big soft breasts, the flimsy elaborate-with-lace pink nightgown, that he had not bought, that Bill Hod had bought, not of course in the sense that he had gone into a store and said, I will have that one, saying in his mind, for the wife of another man into whose bed I sneak, sneak, no, for the wife of another man into whose bed I walk boldly, unafraid, not caring whether he knows it or not.

He said, not meaning to, "I don't like Bill Hod coming here so much."

The expression on her face did not change. She sat in the same position, elbows on the table. She said, in a matter-of-fact voice, "I'm right fond of him. If you don't like his comin' here, Powther, I can always go live somewhere else."

He had said, hastily, panic in his voice, "I didn't mean that. It's all right. As long as you want him here, it's all right. I thought maybe you didn't want him here so much. It's all right."

She must have known that his reply was senseless but she didn't bother to say so. She just sat there, elbows on the table, humming under her breath, "Same train carry my mother, same train be back tomorrer . . ."

He thought sullenly, She speaks of going to live somewhere else just as though she were talking about buying a new pair of shoes. What about Shapiro and Kelly? What about me? She would probably never even think of us again, never mention us, even in casual conversation, just as she had married him, and left Baltimore, never looking back, never questioning the advisability of what she planned to do, just doing it, marrying him, getting on the train, because it was convenient, it suited her plans, fitted in with her desire to live in a small Northern city. If he hadn't packed her clothes she would have left them there in that rooming house in Baltimore, left everything behind her, and never regretted the leaving. She had never mentioned Baltimore since they'd been living in Monmouth.

Al stopped the car at the corner of Dumble Street and Franklin Avenue.

"Say," he said, almost reluctantly, "say, Mal, you live down that street, don't you?" He pointed toward Dumble Street.

"Yes," Powther said. He hoped Al wasn't fishing for an invitation to spend the afternoon. He liked Al, yes, but he didn't think he could bear watching Al's pale blue eyes travel over Mamie's curves. As he waited for Al's next words he tried to think of a plausible excuse for not inviting Al to go home with him. Sickness. Mamie. He would say his wife was sick, and everybody knew that the husband didn't bring his friends home to visit when the wife was sick.

"What's down that way?" Al pointed again.

"Nothing. The street ends at the dock. The river's there. You can see it. That's all."

"I shoulda told you before, Mal. One night last week I followed Camilo's car. You see I kept thinkin' to myself, night after night, I'd pay out good money to know where she goes all the time. So I parked outside the gates, way down, and when she come out on the road drivin' like a bat out of hell, I followed her."

Al stared down toward the river. "She come right in this street. I lost all trace of her right here in this street. I shouldn'a done it, followed her like that, it ain't none of my business where she goes but I had this curiosity about her."

"Here?" Powther said. He shook his head. "You must have been drinking too much beer, Al, and followed the wrong car. I live on this street, my family lives here, but this isn't, well, Miss Camilo might go a lot of places in Monmouth but Dumble Street wouldn't be one of them. It's the toughest, noisiest street imaginable. I don't walk along here myself after ten o'clock. It isn't safe. Anything could happen on Dumble Street, even in the daytime. If I know I'm going to be late getting through at the Hall, I spend the night there."

"Whyn't you and your wife live at the Hall?"

"Mrs. Powther doesn't want to," he said, stiffly. "She prefers her own place."

"She's right," Al said. "When the husband works in service and has a wife and they live in, the Madam is always hellbent on puttin' the wife to work. Last place I worked before I come to the Widow's, the old maid I worked for was always sayin', 'Albert, whyn't your wife do the upstairs? We need another upstairs girl.'

"That's why me and my old woman broke up. She said she wasn't goin' to do no chambermaid work for nobody no matter how rich they was. She said handlin' other people's dirty sheets all day long was her idea of nothin' at all, even if they was so fine they felt like silk between the fingers, they was still dirty sheets. She blamed me, but hell, Mal, I figured like the old maid, there she was settin' round on her can all day, she might as well be doin' somethin' to earn herself her beer money.

"Well, anyway, I was wrong. After two weeks of doin' the upstairs she quit me cold, just walked right out of the house. She got up one mornin' and cooked me my breakfast. Best meal I ever ate. And I said so, and she said, 'Well I'm leavin', now, Al, I can't stand this place no more.' She had called a cab and it was waitin' right outside and she got in it with a coupla suitcases and was gone. I ain't never seen or heard of her from that day to this."

Powther said, "I'm sorry to hear it, Al."

"I don't know what made me start shootin' off at the mouth, but sometimes, on my day off," he shook his head. "Well, see you in church if not before."

Powther waved his thanks to Al and walked down Dumble Street, thinking, If I knew the Captain better, if there was between us something approaching friendship, only there isn't and never will be, I would tell him to let Miss Camilo alone for awhile, let this love affair of hers run its course. Run its course? Bill Hod and Mamie, that love affair had never run its course. It was like an ocean, limitless, unexplored.

But he would still tell the Captain, if he could, to let Miss Camilo alone for awhile. It would be hard, the waiting, the fear, the anxiety, the nights. During the day it wasn't so bad. But at night, the nights, when your mind worked overtime, painting pictures, making up dialogue between yourself and Bill Hod, between Bill Hod and Mamie, the nights are indescribable, Captain, too long, too dark, too full of sounds.

What's the matter with me, he thought. The Captain isn't the one who has to make up conversations with Bill Hod. It's me. Why do I care what happens to them, why should I worry about them, about the Captain, and Miss Camilo and some man who lives in Monmouth. They're rich and they were all three born holding the world by the tail.

He shook his head. "That's not enough," he muttered.

He looked around quickly to see if anyone had heard him because he was horrified to think that he'd been walking along the street, talking to himself. He wished that he had someone to talk to, someone to whom he could explain his very real concern about the Captain and Miss Camilo. The fact that the Captain was white and rich could not in any way diminish the feeling of outrage he would experience when he found out what he must already suspect. If only the Captain wouldn't try to find out whether she had a lover and who he was, wouldn't try to make certain, it was better to just go on suspecting, much, much better.

Nice little man, Al thought, watching Powther hurry down Dumble Street. Runs just like a rabbit, all the time. Just like a rabbit, all day long. I'd pay good money to know what in hell his wife is like, must be some reason why he's never asked me to go in his house, probably just like him, and runs right along side of him, Momma Rabbit and Poppa Rabbit. Never saw a colored feller just like him before, never knew there was any just like him. Now why did I tell him about my ex? Something about his face. And he listens good. I wish I could find me a little whore, a nice little whore, beddy-by with a nice little — My! My!

He honked his horn at a curvey colored wench, who was just turning into Dumble Street, curving into Dumble Street, swaying into Dumble Street. She turned and smiled straight at him, showing all of her white even teeth.

"Hey," Al called out, tooting on the horn again, dum-dee-dah-dah-dah, "come on and get in here with Poppa."

She shook her head but she kept smiling. "My God!" he thought as he watched her, "I'da paid good money for a piece of that."

He could have followed her and argued with her, tried to persuade her, but this was a colored neighborhood and many a white man had been found on a roof with his pants, his shoes gone, and his skull split wide open, in neighborhoods like this. He sighed, and drove off, following Franklin Avenue until he found a good place to turn the crate around in, thinking about that big one who had just gone down Dumble Street, he wasn't sure but what it wouldn'ta been worth getting his skull split open to have a piece of that.

Mrs. Mamie Powther said to herself, as she walked toward Number Six Dumble Street, Wonder where that big one came from. A smile kept appearing around the corners of her mouth, and in her eyes.

13

● ABBIE CRUNCH was ostensibly adjusting her best winter hat, looking in the sitting room mirror as she settled it on her head at what she thought was the most becoming angle; actually, she was admiring the shine of the black coq feathers that adorned the hat, blueblack feathers that were astonishingly effective against her white hair. Sealskin cape, sealskin muff, plain black wool coat, white gloves. It added up to an extremely smart winter outfit, if she did say so herself. If she hadn't been looking in the mirror, she wouldn't have seen J.C. enter the room. He came in through the door, sideways, walking on tiptoe, which was unnecessary because he was wearing sneakers and she wouldn't have heard him come in.

He stood in back of her, touched the sealskin cape, tentatively, gently, and then stroked it.

"Is dat fur, Missus Crunch?" he asked.

"Yes, it is."

"Fur," he repeated. "Her's got one, too."

"J.C., take your thumb out of your mouth. Where will you get a new one when you've got that one all chewed up?" To her surprise, he actually took his thumb out of his mouth.

Is that fur! she thought. It's Alaskan sealskin. Cape made from the Governor's wife's old sealskin coat. The Governor's wife had given it to her in the fall of the year the Major died, saying, "Mrs. Crunch, I brought this to you because I thought you might be able to get collars and cuffs out of it."

216

When Abbie took it to Quagliamatti, the tailor who used to be on Franklin Avenue, and explained that she wanted a cape and a muff made out of it, he held the coat up, turned it around and around, muttering, "Rump sprung. Rump sprung. Have to cut around it." He was such an expert and so inexpensive that she did not reprove him for his unnecessary vulgarity for fear that he might refuse to work on the coat. He had turned out this rippling cape and the fat round muff. By treating them with care, having them stored, and worked over every year, they would last as long as she did. She turned slightly so that she could see the way the cape flared in the back, and thought, as she always did, that the cape would have done credit to a Fifth Avenue furrier.

J.C. said, "You goin' out?"

"That's right." She was going to Deacon Lord's funeral.

"Kin I go wid you?"

"No."

"What'm I goin' do?"

"You're going right back upstairs to your own part of the house and talk to your mother or play with your brothers."

"Mamie's out. Them bastids Kelly and Shapiro is in the movies, 'n they wouldn't let me go. What'm I goin' to do? They told me to stay down here."

"Good heavens!" she said. He was standing close to her, looking at her, his thumb in his mouth, his round hard head on one side, something speculative in his black eyes. I knew it was a mistake to let that woman stay in my house. I've changed. I knew I would. A woman like that always changes things, her mere presence is like water working on stone, slow attrition, finally a groove, stone worn down. I no longer state my objections to the child's language. He uses the word "bastard" and I say nothing, because if I do he'll just repeat it again and again. He's watching me, waiting for me to do something about him. He knows I won't leave him alone in the house.

She'd known Frances for twenty-five years. Or was it thirty years? Anyway, in all that time Frances had never once said, Abbie, will you do something for me? Never asked a favor. Until yesterday morning. The phone rang, and Frances, who was usually quite clear about what she wanted had sounded excited, and what she said didn't make sense.

Frances had said, "Howard's a fool — "

Howard? Abbie had thought. Had something happened to him? He was Frances' assistant, a tall, softlooking man, not young, not old, with reddish hair, and skin almost the same color as his hair.

"Funeral tomorrow afternoon. Deacon Lord's funeral," Frances had said, talking faster and faster.

What does she want me to do? How does that involve me, she had wondered, frowning.

"Go to South Carolina. Bring back the body of the Smith boys' mother," Frances said, and she'd sounded as though she were barking into the mouthpiece.

She remembered having said, "Wait a minute, Frances. Wait a minute."

She had been completely confused. Did Frances want her to go to South Carolina? Pretty Boy had been asleep in the Boston rocker, white paws tucked under him, so mounded up, so curled up, that he looked like a big gray and white cushion.

While she was standing there in the sitting room, holding the receiver, trying to think, J.C. had suddenly appeared in the room, edging in, not there one minute, there the next. He pulled the cat out of the rocker, tried to make him walk on his hind feet. Pretty Boy had clawed at him, and J.C. let him go. Then he tried to sit on Pretty Boy's back, saying, "Dis a horse. Dis a horse."

"J.C., leave that cat alone," she had shouted, right into the mouthpiece of the telephone, "Leave him alone! You go back upstairs. Did you hear what I said, J.C.? I'm trying to talk on the telephone. Now go on upstairs! Go on!"

J.C. had backed out of the room. He was always backing away, perhaps because he was conditioned to sudden violent attack from the rear. She had watched him. Did Frances want her to go to South Carolina? Pretty Boy had jumped back in the rocker, curled up again. The cyclamen were in bloom now. The white geraniums were resting. Dormant. Cyclamen almost too brilliant, too vivid, almost red. When Mr. Powther had stopped in to pay his January rent, he had looked at them and said, "What beautiful plants, Mrs. Crunch!" He noticed everything beautiful, appreciated everything beautiful. How he ever came to marry that careless young woman, she couldn't imagine. Frances gave her the cyclamen at Christmas, every Christmas, plants. How long would she have to stay away? Who would water the plants?

"Yes," she had said firmly into the telephone. Frances had never asked a favor.

"They don't want her buried there. They say they won't even

leave their dead in the South, nothing of theirs will they leave there. They never could get her to come North to live but they hate the South so they won't let her be buried there."

South Carolina, she had thought. Not buried there. Somebody's mother. What difference would it make? South or North, if you were dead, you were dead. Where you were buried didn't matter. She hadn't traveled that far, alone, in years. What did she think would happen to her? But she couldn't go. What would she do with Pretty Boy? And there was J.C. always wandering around, always poking and prying into things. He had the awful curiosity of the very young. She was certain Link hadn't been like that at that age. J.C. looking under Pretty Boy's tail, asking, "Where docs his bowels move?" or standing staring her, "Where does you wee-wee?" And Link — Link out all night —

"Will you come over tomorow afternoon? Funeral at two. If you'll just see that everything goes all right. Howard's a fool," Frances said.

"You mean at your place?"

"Of course."

"Oh. I thought you wanted me to go to South Carolina."

Silence. Then, "South Carolina? And you were going?"

"Certainly."

"Abbie," tenderness in Frances' voice, the voice pitched lower, "why, Abbie — " Laughter. Then, "Abbie, you're wonderful. I wouldn't dream of asking you to go to South Carolina. I wouldn't go myself but they're paying me so much money that I can't very well refuse."

So much money, she thought. "Who are they?"

"The Smith boys. They're numbers bankers. So they can well afford to spend as much as they want to on a funeral or anything else."

Frances had said, "I wouldn't ask you to come over but Howard's such a fool. I'll be back tomorrow afternoon. Not in time for the service. Right afterwards though. And we can have tea over here."

So here she was, dressed in her best clothes, on her way to attend the funeral of a Baptist deacon that she had never known except by sight, because some numbers bankers whom she had never seen did not want their mother buried in South Carolina. That was complicated enough in itself; in addition, here was this child of Mamie Powther's, standing in front of her, sucking his thumb. She thought, Of all the unprepossessing sights — his overalls were torn at the knees and he was standing on one foot, and there was a hole in the toe of one of his faded blue sneakers. They were too short for him. His big toe had made that hole. Hole in his sock, too. At that age their toes were always freeing themselves, in fact, the big toe was like a separate aggressive appendage, an added something on the foot which was impelled to keep working its way toward light, going through fabric, leather.

She said, indignantly, "Well, you'll have to change your clothes."

He ignored the indignation, took his thumb out of his mouth, looked up at her, his eyes sparkling, his lips curving into a smile. She thought, He has a lovely smile, and she patted his shoulder.

"I kin put 'em on, all alone, Missus Crunch. And I be right down de tairs." Voice eager, face eager.

She waited for him in the hall, smoothing her gloves over her fingers, with a nervous impatient motion, because she was certain that she would have to dress him. Then he came clumping down the stairs, wearing new brown shoes, different overalls, dark gray, newlooking, too, and a bright red jacket that was much too big for him, the sleeves so long they covered his hands.

"Are you going to be warm enough?" she asked, fingering the material of the jacket. It seemed to be wool but what a dreadful color for a little boy.

"I be warm enough," he said. He sniffed. "Smell it?" he asked, head cocked on one side.

"Smell what?"

"It's the printhess," he said. "It's her smell."

"Come," she said. "We'll have to hurry or we'll be late." You in your red jacket, and I in my sealskin cape, you looking like a thumbling and I looking like Mother Goose. She wondered why a man as sensible, as businesslike, as efficient as little Mr. Powther told fairy stories to his children. J.C. was always muttering about robbers and giants and a princess who was all gold.

They were halfway down Dumble Street, J.C. trotting along beside her, holding on to her hand, when she stopped, said, "J.C., did you go to the bathroom before you left?"

"Yes, Missus Crunch," he said meekly. Silence. Then he said anxiously, "Ain't they got no wee-wee chairs dere?" He tugged at her hand, "Missus Crunch," he said, "where we goin'?"

"We're going to Washington Street. In the next block. To — uh — " she paused. What was she going to do with him during the funeral service? "We're going to Miss Jackson's house."

"Ain't they got no wee-wee chairs dere?"

"Yes," she said absently.

She looked back, down the street. The Hangman, leafless now, was a darker gray than the sky. In fact the lower end of Dumble Street looked like a steel engraving, dark gray river, and sidewalk and buildings. All the buildings looked gray this afternoon. Except Number Six which was a dark red. She did not look at, but was aware of, the redorange neon sign in front of The Last Chance. She shivered, feeling suddenly cold, remembering Bill Hod's black fathomless eyes, for no reason at all, thinking, Full fathom five thy father lies —

Was the child warm enough? She used to walk along the street with Link, just like this, holding him by the hand. Their hands always felt so hot.

They turned into Franklin Avenue. Smell of kerosene. From the newsstand on the corner. Woman in the newsstand, so wrapped up, so bundled up, dark blue knit cap pulled down over her forehead, bundled up to the eyes, like a Mongolian, layers of clothes, and the little kerosene stove right near her.

Franklin Avenue was filled with people. Curiously enough there were no children in sight. She saw just one woman with a small child by the hand. But there were countless young women wearing red coats and highheeled shoes, and long gold earrings that dangled against their brown cheeks. Voices. Laughter. Most of the older women were milling around in Davioli's market, talking and laughing, too. Street suddenly warm, because of warm air from the Five-and-Ten, revolving door, going around and around, people going in, coming out, blend of frankfurters, coffee, mustard, perfume.

No wonder there were so few children on the street. They were all queued up in front of the Franklin Theatre, in a crooked, constantly in motion line, a line that suggested a caterpillar, inching along. Argument going on —young, determined voices.

"Dat's my place."

"It ain't."

J.C. stood still, studied the line.

"Dat's my place."

"It ain't."

"You git out."

The line that was like a caterpillar swayed, violent motion in the center, broke in two, became two separate parts, and then bent in on itself. Small boys and girls, all looking. Some in coats too long, some in coats too short, some with no coats, shivering, bent over, hands in their pockets. All watching two small boys who were pushing each other.

"Git outta the way."

"Git outta the way yourself."

J.C. said, delight in his voice. "That's them bastids Kelly and Shapiro." Two small boys rolled over and over, on the sidewalk, shouting at each other, their voices muffled.

"Kick him in de ass. Kick him in de ass," J.C. yelled, jumping up and down.

"J.C.!" Abbie said sternly, pulling him along. "How many times have I told you that you simply cannot use that kind of language when you're with me. I simply will not have it."

"Yes'm," he said.

Then she pulled him across the street, crossing Franklin Avenue though they would only have to recross it when they reached the corner of Washington Street. But she had seen Cat Jimmie propelling himself along on his little wooden wagon. She couldn't bear to walk near that creature on the wagon, it wasn't just the smell of him, it was the whole horrible degenerate look of him, his eyes, and the mutilated flesh on the stumps of legs and arms, exposed even now on this cold windy afternoon. Pass by on the other side, she thought. "If you believe the Lord looks after and cares about a sparrow, then you must of necessity also believe that He looks after and cares about Bill Hod." That's what the Major had said. And she supposed that he would feel the same way about Cat Jimmie. The Major had a capacity for including all men in his sympathy, his understanding, that had sometimes annoyed her, sometimes surprised her. But Cat Jimmie — "there came down a certain priest that way: and when he saw him, he passed by on the other side. And likewise a Levite, when he was at the place, came and looked on him, and passed by on the other side. But a certain Samaritan . . . when he saw him, he had compassion on him."

Fall of a sparrow, she thought. Bill Hod? Compassion? For Hod? And that inhuman creature on the wagon? Mouth open, eyes like the eyes of a trapped animal, fierce, crazed. She turned and looked back, and he was lying down on the wagon, looking up under a woman's skirts, and the woman jumped away from him, went running up Franklin Avenue. Oh, no, she thought, he is no longer human, he is an animal, and it does say, "A certain man went down from Jerusalem to Jericho, and fell among thieves —" fall of a sparrow — Bill Hod — compassion — Cat Jimmie.

Once she'd stopped to speak to that creature on the wagon, something in her, pity, compassion, something, made her stop. She saw his eyes, horrible, the whites were red, and she turned away, mounting the steps of her house, and looked back and the pity, the compassion, vanished, replaced by revulsion, because he had propelled himself close to the bottom step and was looking up, trying to look under her skirts, panting, his mouth working, the eyes fierce, vengeful. For a moment she was so overcome by nausea that she couldn't move, and then she ran up the last two steps, hurried inside the house, and slammed the door.

They walked as far as Washington Street and then crossed Franklin Avenue again.

J.C. said, "What we cross over Franklin for, Missus Crunch?"

She hesitated, thinking, Evasion? outright lie? the truth? Truth. She said, "I didn't want to walk near that man on the little cart."

J.C. looked back, down Franklin Avenue. "Aw, him!" he said, contempt in his voice. "Mamie say he don't hurt nobody. She say he can't git it no other way but lookin'. And she say seein's dat's the only way he can pleasure himself, best thing to do is just let him go ahead and look."

I know what I'll do with you, young man, she thought, I'm going to leave you with Miss Doris. Miss Doris was Frances' maid, housekeeper, cook, whathaveyou, and Miss Doris' husband, whom she called Sugar, mowed the lawn, looked after the garden, and made all the repairs. Miss Doris could have a white cloth tied around her head, and have on very worn, very faded, but very clean, slacks, and be down on her hands and knees weeding a flower bed, and when she looked you over, she could make you feel as though your hair were uncombed and there were runs in your stockings.

When they turned in at the F. K. Jackson Funeral Home, J.C. tugged at Abbie's hand, again. "Is we goin' to a funeralizin', Missus Crunch?"

"I am," Abbie said. She looked down at his upturned face. His eyes were sparkling with excitement, pleasure. "But you're not. You're going to stay with Mrs. King until I come back."

Hand in hand, they climbed the front steps. Abbie rang the

bell. The door opened almost immediately.

"Good afternoon, Mrs. Crunch," Miss Doris said. She had a white cloth wrapped tight around her head, a shorthandled dust mop in her hand.

Abbie thought she looked more than ever like a statue, short, wide, not fat, but bulky. Her flesh had the hard look of metal, and her voice was hard, cold, suggesting metal, too.

"I were not told to expect you so soon," Miss Doris said, reproach in the hard metallic voice. "Or I would have been in a state of preparation."

Abbie said, apologetically, "I'm early, Miss Doris. But I wanted to ask a favor of you. Will you look after this little boy for me, until after the funeral?"

Miss Doris and J.C. eyed each other with suspicion. Miss Doris said, "All right, boy. Come in." She frowned. "I see you brought your lollipop with you."

Abbie looked at J.C. He was sucking his thumb again but he didn't have a lollipop.

J.C. took his thumb out of his mouth. "Ain't got no lollipop," he said indignantly. Then put the thumb back in his mouth.

"What's that in your mouth?" Miss Doris said, sharply.

No answer. Scorn in his eyes. He cocked his round, hard head on one side, studying her.

"Come on, boy. I can't stand here all day," Miss Doris prodded J.C. with the shorthandled mop, pushing him inside the door.

Abbie turned away, quickly. She heard J.C. say, "You take dat mop off my clothes," and then the door closed.

The F. K. Jackson funeral parlor occupied the basement floor of the building where Frances lived, a building that reminded Abbie of the brownstone-front houses in New York. She and the Major had spent their honeymoon in a house very much like this one, same long flight of steps leading to the first floor, same type of basement with a separate entrance, at street level.

Howard, Frances' assistant, was standing just inside the door of the office.

Abbie said, "Miss Jackson asked me to see that everything — to — asked me to come over," faltering, remembering Frances' brusque voiced statement, "Howard's a fool."

Looking at him now, as he hovered in the doorway, she thought he was built like a eunuch, or what she thought a eunuch would be built like, very tall, very fat, soft fat, too broad across the hips, and he had a waddling kind of walk. He came waddling toward her, holding out his hand, and he bowed over her hand, then straightened up and looked into her eyes. He said, gravely, "Ah, yes, Mrs. Crunch. So very kind of you. Miss Jackson couldn't have found a more impressive representative."

The skin on his face was like a baby's skin, a kind of bloom on it. Amazing skin. A peculiar color. Almost the exact color of the fuzzy redbrown hair, not much of the hair left, he was getting bald, hairline receding, so that seen close to, without a hat, and she had never seen him hatless before, he appeared to have a high domeshaped forehead, a forehead that just never ended. And he had a moustache, a feather of a moustache, which seemed to have just taken rest, for a moment, over what in a woman would have been an incredibly pretty mouth. Baby's skin. Woman's mouth.

He said, "There are always so many details. I almost forgot your gloves. We'll put them on in Miss Jackson's office." His manner confidential, his eyes widening a little.

Abbie smiled at him, feeling as though he had just shared a delightful secret with her. She leaned toward him, ever so slightly. Then she checked the bend of her body, stiffening, straightening up, no longer smiling, frowning a little, thinking, Why the man's a hypnotist.

The glistening of his eyes told her he was waiting for this leaning response of her body, had known it would come, that he was practised in this business of subtly conveying the idea that here were his strong masculine shoulders, and the whole long smooth-skinned length of him, for widows, for orphans over sixteen, to lean on, to find solace in the leaning.

In the office, he helped her put on a pair of black gloves. He smelt ever so faintly of liquor and she thought of the Major — and that day he died. Frances' hands were long and bony and hers were short and plump. But they got the black gloves on and then he escorted her to a seat midway in the chapel. She sat staring at the ends of the glove fingers, black, empty, wiggled them once, thought they looked like the armless sleeves of a scarecrow, that a child would be frightened by these empty glove fingers, wondered what J.C. and Miss Doris were doing.

But she was here to see that everything was all right, went all right. The chapel was filling up with people, there were flowers in the embrasure where the casket stood in front of the windows, drawn curtains and shaded lights that cast a mournful pinklavender light. An airless room. Too hot. And filled with the heavy toosweet smell of roses.

The family came in. The widow was heavily veiled, there was a uniformed nurse in attendance, pallbearers in gray gloves. Everything seemed in order. Everything in order except the pressure, the feeling of tremendous pressure about her head.

The service started on time. Then the Baptist minister, Reverend Ananias Hill, grown older these last years, gaunter, slower of movement, even his voice had changed, the thunder had gone out of it to be replaced by a quality that was sad, sorrowful, spoke of the late Deacon Lord, and prayed for his immortal soul, and read from the Bible: "Thou shalt love the Lord thy God with all thy heart . . ."

A tremulous old man with an old man's voice. Mamaluke Hill's father. Queer the things you remembered about people. For years The Narrows had conjectured about Reverend Hill's wife, trying to decide whether she was white or whether she was colored. Nobody ever really knew. They said Reverend Hill didn't know himself whether she was white. The child's name, Mamaluke, would suggest that she was colored. She finally died in a rooming house, on Dumble Street. The fact that she left Reverend Hill, no longer lived with him, was a minor scandal.

Abbie heard Reverend Hill say that the late Deacon Lord had loved God, and had loved his neighbor as himself, and then she stopped listening to him. She began thinking about Dumble Street. About Link. About the night the Major died.

The Major had said, "Abbie, the house, the house." And she could smell the morning, the river, see fog blurring the street, feel it wet and cold against her face, drifting in in waves from the river, fog undulating, blurring the sidewalk, and once again she leaned over, blinked her eyes, wiped her eyes, so that she could read what had been written on the sidewalk, in front of her house, "At her feet he bowed, he fell — "

Reverend Hill said, again, "Thou shalt love the Lord thy God with all thy heart." And the pressure, the feeling of pressure increased. All of us, she thought, young and old, all of us here in this funeral chapel were brought up on the King James version of the Bible, all able to quote it, part of our thinking, part of our lives, and we keep moving away from it, forget about it. Even though we go to church. But we attend a funeral and something in us is fascinated, and afraid, and we keep going back into the past, trying to find ourselves or what we believe to be ourselves, a part of us lost somewhere back in the past.

Someone screamed. She thought for a moment that it was she who had screamed. Then she saw that the relatives, the family, were filing past Deacon Lord's coffin. It was the widow who had screamed, not so much screamed as wailed. She was a large woman, dressed in black, wearing a black veil so long, so thick, that it was like a curtain, a drapery over her face. Abbie thought of the Major and his favorite joke, "When I mourns, I mourns all over."

"I won't let him go," Mrs. Lord wailed. "I won't let him go, I won't let him go. Hubborn, come back, come back." The "come back" sounded as though it were being sung, on one high note, sustained, repeated.

Mourn all over, she thought. People do, in one way or another. Then, very quickly, they were all outside on the sidewalk, standing there, and Howard and two other men were shepherding the people into the proper cars, darting in and out, just like sheepdogs, impatiently nosing a group of slowmoving and very stupid sheep over a stile.

Howard turned to Abbie. "Ah, yes, Mrs. Crunch," he said, taking her by the arm. "Miss Jackson always rides in front with me. So if you'll get in here. But first," he opened the back door of the car, "Mrs. Lord, this is Mrs. Crunch. She's Miss Jackson's personal representative. She'll be riding in the front seat with me."

Mrs. Lord said, "Glad to meet you," and reached out a blackgloved hand and shook Abbie's blackgloved hand. It was a surprisingly firm handshake.

"And this is Mr. Angus Lord," Howard said. "Deacon Lord's brother."

"My compliments," Mr. Angus Lord leaned forward, bowed. Then he sat back and sucked his teeth.

Abbie sat in the front seat of the car, close to the door. She was waiting for Mrs. Lord to start that weird wailing sound again, the back of her neck cold with waiting, her hands in the longfingered black gloves clenched into fists, hands tense with waiting. Howard started the car, pulled off, following close behind the hearse. Silence in the back seat.

Then Mrs. Lord said petulantly, "Angus, I can't remember whether I locked my back door."

Mr. Angus Lord said, "I locked it. It don't matter anyway.

That big dog would keep anybody out ceptin' a blind man, who was a deaf man, too. A deaf blind man wouldn't be robbin' nobody's house." Pause. "A lot of folks at the funeral."

"I didn't see his cousin. Was she there?"

"I dunno. I ain't seen her in years." Pause. "By the way, I'd like his gold watch. For a keepsake."

"I'm keepsakin' it myself." Reproof in Mrs. Lord's voice. "I figure to keepsake it the rest of my life. Hubborn never give me nothin' while he was alive and now he's dead, he can start in. I aims to keepsake his gold watch and his diamond stickpin."

"He ain't in his grave," Mr. Angus Lord said, voice scornful. "You can wait awhile before you start puttin' bad mouth on him."

Abbie wondered if the scorn was due to disappointment or to fear of disparaging a dead man, fear so old no one really knew its source. Mrs. Lord had criticized the deacon, "Hubborn never give me nothin' while he was alive — " Speak no evil of the dead.

She turned her head to look at Mrs. Lord. The heavy black veil still concealed her face, but she had removed the black gloves, had rolled them up into a ball, and was kneading them with one hand, just as though the gloves were a ball of black dough. Mr. Angus Lord was staring out of the window, watching the traffic.

When they slowed down in order to turn in between the gates at the entrance to the cemetery, Abbie found herself thinking about the Major again, and his story about Aunt Hal who had ridden to a funeral astride the hearse, and how the rest of the Crunches, shouted, "Whip up them horses! Ride her down! Ride Hal down!"

Then the Reverend Ananias Hill was intoning, "Ashes to ashes — " voice sorrowful, voice sad, voice old, and Mrs. Lord wailed again, "Hubborn, come back, come back to me," and Reverend Hill went right on intoning, "Dust to dust — "

About five minutes afterwards, Howard was helping Mrs. Lord into the long black car, the nurse was hovering close by. Howard said, "Here, drink this — no — drink it right down — and you'll feel better — it's brandy." Then they were off, leaving the cemetery, going faster and faster.

Mr. Angus Lord said, "I'll have a little of that likker, young man." He sucked his teeth, waiting.

Howard stopped the car, reached in the glove compartment, got out the flask, a package of paper cups, handed them back to Mr. Angus Lord, and then started the car, driving even faster now.

Mr. Lord said, "Ah!"

Abbie turned, saw that he was drinking out of the flask, and that he was apparently emptying it; he paused for a moment in his drinking, and then said "Ah!" again.

"Now what might that have been, young man?" he asked.

Howard glanced at Mr. Angus Lord in the mirror. "Hennessy's Five Star brandy."

"Five stars. Stars. Thought so," he said. "Tasted like it." He smacked his lips. "Was that a colored cemetery, young man?" he asked companionably.

"No," Howard said. "But in another ten years or so we'll have that, too. We've got two practically colored schools and we've got a separate place for the colored to live, and separate places for them to go to church in, and it won't be long before we'll work up to a separate place for the colored to lie in after they're dead. It won't be long, brother. Then you'll feel right at home here in Monmouth. It'll be just like Georgia except for the climate."

Howard must be angry about something, Abbie thought. That's no way to talk to a customer. Customer? The customer was dead. They'd just left him there under the hemlocks. Well, it was no way to talk to the customer's family. Surely Mrs. Lord would resent the reprimanding, sarcastic voice Howard had used. Howard. What was his last name? How many people have I ever known that I called by their first names? What's his last name? I'll ask Frances. Maybe he didn't have one. Maybe he came into the world, broad of hips, fullgrown, fullblown, in his cutaway coat and striped trousers, with his flask of brandy and his derby hat and his gray gloves, and his feather moustache, above that delicatelyshaped, moistlooking, thirstylooking mouth. What had made him angry? Why, the brandy, of course. The late Deacon Lord's brother had drunk up every drop of Howard's Five Stars. Then she thought, This whole thing has made me lightheaded, because she was rhyming again, saying over and over, Stars in his crown, to his renown, stars in his crown, to his renown.

The late Deacon Lord's brother must have been mellowed by the brandy, warmed by it, slightly intoxicated by it, because just as Abbie turned to look at him, he laid his hand on Mrs. Lord's large wellfleshed knee and said, "I spose you'll be lookin' around for another man — "

Mrs. Lord snorted. "Another man? Me? Another man? I could tell you things about Hubborn that would make your hair straighten out just like white folks' hair." Pause. "And I'll thank you to take your black hand off'n my leg."

Howard said smoothly, "Mind if I turn on the radio?" Music filled the swiftly moving car, jazz music, loud, strongly accented.

By the time they pulled up in front of Mrs. Lord's house, on the edge of Monmouth, a one-story shingled affair, glassed-in porch across the front, she had removed the black veil and the black gloves. She got out of the car, unassisted, handed Howard a white box edged with black.

Abbie thought, That's where she put the veil and the gloves.

Mrs. Lord said, "Goodbye, Mrs. Crunch, and thank you. Tell Miss Jackson everything was fine," and walked heavily toward her front steps, the late Mr. Lord's brother trailing along behind her.

Howard turned toward Abbie. "Drop you at Number Six?"

"No, thank you. I'll go back to the funeral parlor with you. I want to see Miss Jackson. She said she'd be back after the service."

She wondered what J.C. and Miss Doris were doing. Something intractable about Miss Doris. Even the way she used the word "were," pronouncing it as though it were "wear," and using it constantly. She was short but not stout, bulky, bulk of a statue. Her face and body looked like wrought iron, both as to color of skin, and an almost metallic hardness of the flesh. Flesh on the face, flesh on the forearms, like iron. Thin legs. Splay feet. She planted her feet flat on the ground when she walked. Even the voice hard and cold.

J.C. and Miss Doris? He'd be all right. If he could survive Mamie Powther and Shapiro and Kelly, he'd survive Miss Doris too.

"Tell me," she said to Howard, raising her voice against the sound of the radio. "Why did Mrs. Lord call Deacon Lord 'Hubborn.' I thought his first name was Richard."

"She couldn't say 'husband.' Hubborn was the nearest she could come to it in that loosepalated, liverlipped speech of hers." He turned the radio off.

He's still angry about his Five Stars, she thought. "Was she really upset? She seemed so calm, and then all of a sudden she was shrieking like a banshee."

Howard said, "Yes and no. She didn't want him back. If by lifting a finger she could bring him back, she'd tie her hands together, bind them, so the fingers couldn't move, even by reflex action. He was an old devil and she'd been married to him for forty years, married to a little black man who was mean and stingy and malicious. That was Hubborn. Mean.

"When her old mother died, a few years back, he wouldn't pay for the funeral. The city buried her. He knew a couple of ward heelers and he hollered poor mouth so Mrs. Lord's mother was dumped into what amounts to an open lot. The old lady had insurance. All these old folks have enough insurance to give 'em a pretty good funeral. They save pennies and nickels to pay for their insurance, pay for it by the week. Well, anyway, Mrs. Lord's old mother got a pine box, no extras, just a box. The city paid for it and we took care of the arrangements. That's how I know about it. The old lady got a plain pine box and the box was put in potter's field. Hubborn took the five hundred dollars from the insurance and bought himself a diamond and had one of the local jewelers set it in a gold stickpin.

"He was a great man for gold, Hubborn was. He was a thirty-third-degree Mason, too, and he kept the colored Masons in such a state of confusion and muddlement that they've never been able to buy a home. They rent one of those storefronts one night a week, and on the other nights the members of the I Will Arise and Follow Thee Praise the Lord for Making Me Colored and Not White Church sing hallelujah in it.

"No, she wouldn't bring him back. But he was alive one minute with his gold teeth flashing, and his gambler's cufflinks gleaming, ten-dollar gold piece in each one, and his diamond stickpin glittering, and his bright yellow ties shining and the next minute he was dead. So Mrs. Lord now has his gold cufflinks and his undeaconly diamond stickpin and his gold watch tucked in her black bosom — for keepsakin'."

He stopped talking, lit a cigarette, and Abbie thought he had finished. Then he said, indifferently, "Maybe she screamed because she was afraid she was dreaming, afraid that she would wake up and find that Hubborn was still alive. Or perhaps she saw herself as she would ultimately be, very dead, very cold, lying in a coffin, a satin-lined one, of course."

He gave her a sly sidewise glance, and she thought, This is an assumed callousness and I shall ignore it. He is trying to give me the impression that he is so accustomed to the idea of death that he can speak of coffins and satin linings, and go on smoking, and looking around him as he drives, as though none of it really mattered, as though it had nothing to do with him.

They were going down Franklin Avenue. The street was still filled with people, mostly women, all of whom were carrying bundles, or packages. They had finished their Saturday shopping, had finished exchanging a week's wages for clothes, groceries, liquor.

When he stopped the car in front of the F. K. Jackson Funeral Home, she got out quickly, before he could help her, deliberately ignoring his outstretched hand.

"By the way," she said abruptly, "what is your last name?"

"Thomas. Good old Anglo-Saxon last name. All of us black sub rosa Anglo-Saxons are named Stevens, Jackson, Williams, Smith, King."

"I'll tell Miss Jackson how well you managed everything, Mrs. Thomas." Heavens, what kind of a slip of the tongue was that? She started to say, What could I have been thinking of, I mean Mr. Thomas; but he appeared not to have noticed. He was kicking one of the front tires, trying to dislodge the mud that had spattered on its white walls.

"Muck," he muttered. "Graveyard muck."

Then he opened the door of the car, reached deep inside the glove compartment, took out a package, tore off the green paper wrappings, then the thin white paper underneath, clawing at it in his haste, got a corkscrew out of his pocket, pulled the cork out of the bottle.

"Can't do this on the job," he said, "but if you'll excuse me." He gave a slight shudder and poured half the contents of the bottle down his throat in one great swallowless draft. She walked away from him so that she would not see the second great draft go down his throat, the draft that would unquestionably empty the bottle.

14

● FRANCES JACKSON leaned over and kissed Abbie. Then she said, "Abbie! Come in, come in. Are you all right?"

"Why, of course. And you? Are you all right?"

"Never been better. Come in the living room. Let me take your coat and your cape. And your hat. Take off your hat, Abbie. Here, give it to me." Holding the coat, the cape, the muff, under one arm, she took the hat in her hand, turned it around. "You know, this outfit makes you look like a duchess."

"The Ugly Duchess?" Abbie said, and laughed.

"No. The Duchess of Kent. But older and mellower. Don't sit there, Abbie. Sit in the armchair near the fire. It's much more comfortable."

Abbie watched her quick, nervous movements, and thought She's wound up like a spring from the hustle and bustle, the ordering around that she experienced in South Carolina. She's even dressed to suit this ordering-around mood. Straight black skirt. White blouse. The blouse cut almost like a man's shirt. French cuffs on the blouse. Cufflinks in them. And the gray hair brushed back, away from her forehead, the pince-nez set perfectly straight on her nose. President of the corporation. An austere face. Bony, distinguished. The eyes behind the glasses looked small, shrewd, very wise. Tall bony body. Unrelaxed body. She keeps walking up and down because she's still traveling, still managing the family, offering advice, remembering all the details, the insurance papers, the will.

Frances placed the coat, the cape, the muff, the hat on the horsehair sofa. "I feel just like a world traveler," she said. "I flew down and came back on the train. Do you know, I enjoyed it? It was like a twenty-four-hour holiday, a vacation spent in a different part of the world. Everything different. The customs. The people. The language. On the train, coming back, I began to wonder whether it's a good idea to read as much as I do, to see as many plays, because I don't think I really saw the city of Charleston, even though I was there. I kept seeing Crown and Porgy and Bess and Sportin' Life and Catfish Alley. Isn't that funny?"

I wish she'd stop walking up and down, Abbie thought, she'll never unwind if she doesn't sit.

"And if I ever go to London, I know I won't see the English people as they really are. I'll see Oliver Twist and Fagin, and David Copperfield and Little Nell," Frances said, still pacing.

"What about Monmouth? What do you see in Monmouth, Frances?" She'll have to sit down to answer that. I keep seeing Link as a little boy, keep hearing the Major talk, keep using his phrases. Bulletheaded. Meriney. "When I mourns, I mourns all over."

"Monmouth?" Frances said, and sat down in the wing chair on the other side of the fireplace. Wing chair upholstered in a velvet that reminded Abbie of the dark green plush used on trains.

"Monmouth?" Frances repeated, and leaned back in the chair. The light from the fire was reflected in her glasses. "I see my father. I see myself walking down Franklin Avenue, holding on to his hand, and he's saying, 'Frank, you know you've got a man's mind.' Anywhere I go here in Monmouth, I can always see myself — too tall, too thin, too bony. Even at twelve. And too bright, Abbie, and unable and unwilling to conceal the fact that I had brains. When I finished high school I went to college, to Wellesley, where I was a kind of Eighth Wonder of the world because I was colored. I hadn't been there very long when the dean sent for me and asked me if I was happy there. I looked straight at her and I said, 'My father didn't send me here to be happy, he sent me here to learn.' I have always remembered the look of astonishment that came over her face. Then she said, 'I would like to know your father.' "

Abbie thought, We're both getting old. We tell the same stories, over and over again. We've influenced each other in the telling. Shared experience, I suppose. Tell it and retell it. And finally act on it. Happiness not important. It's the learning, the education. Magic wand. Golden key. I thought it would be that for Link, too. And he works in a bar. And stays out all night. Playing poker. And doing what else? Where does he go?

"Twenty-two, and I was back in Monmouth. A college graduate. All hung over with honors and awards and prizes. And I knew I'd never get married, never have any children. So I was going to be a doctor." She laughed, and the pince-nez trembled on her nose, glittering and trembling there. "But by then my mother had been dead for three years. My father was alone here, and I couldn't bear to leave him, and there was the business that he had built up so slowly and so carefully. So I became an undertaker too. What do I see in Monmouth, Abbie? I see myself, lonely and a little bitter until I met you," a barely noticeable pause, and she added, "and the Major. I see myself at twenty five going to the casket company to pick out my father's casket and I hear the Irishman who owned the place saying to his pimplyfaced clerk, 'That nigger woman undertaker from Washington Street is here again, see what she wants.' At the time it happened I found it unbearable. Now I feel indebted to the man because the sound of the word nigger has never bothered me since then, though I have never been able to share your enthusiasm for the Irish."

Abbie knew that story, too. She thought, On how peculiar, and accidental, a foundation rests all of one's attitudes toward a people. She loved the Irish. Part of her faith, her belief, came straight from the old Irishwomen she had known, in those early years on Dumble Street. Their faith, unwavering, firm, unmoving, despite drunken husbands, drunken sons, wanton daughters, despite idiot children who crouched, hunched over in rocking chairs, always in the kitchen near the big black iron stoves, babbling endlessly, having to feed, diaper, croon to, a fullgrown human being. She, too, like the Irishwomen, had made it a habit, when she was downtown, to go in the cathedral, saying her Protestant prayers humbly in the dim cool interior, sitting there afterwards, refreshed, her faith renewed. When she left, walking slowly down the aisle, it was with the sure knowledge that death is only a beginning.

Frances hears the word Irish and thinks of her father and hears the word nigger. I hear the word Irish and I think of a cathedral and the quiet of it, the flickering light of the votive candles, the magnificence of the altar, and I see Irishwomen, strong in their faith, holding a family together. Accident? Coincidence? It all depended on what had happened in the past. We carry it around with us. We're never rid of it.

Dumble Street, she thought, remembering a Sunday morning, years ago. She had met Mrs. Abe Cohen, weeping, and there was a wail in her voice, as she told Abbie that her little boy had been to the Christian Sunday School, and came home, reciting, Matzos, Matzos, two for five, that's what keeps the kikes alive — wail in her voice, overtone of despair, as she said, "Mrs. Crunch, what kind of people is that to be teaching him a thing like that, to be telling him to come home and say it to his own mother, what kind of people — what kind of thing is that to be teaching my Abie in the Sunday School?" What kind of people — she tried to convince Mrs. Cohen that no one could possibly have taught Abie to say that — not in Sunday School. Hopeless.

Frances said, "Here I've been babbling like a brook, Abbie, and I never once thought to ask you about Deacon Lord's funeral. Was everything all right?"

"Yes, indeed. Mrs. Lord asked me to tell you that everything was fine."

Should she mention the shrieks and screams? The cold sweat that broke out on her own forehead? Talk about the spattering sound of earth on the coffin? Speak of the artificial grass used to conceal, conceal, cover up, the earth that could never be covered up, the earth where what was left of the deacon would slowly disintegrate? No. Frances would lean forward in that wing chair that looked as though it ought to be on a train, thrust her legs straight out in front of her, gesture with her bony hands, and talk of immortality, of hysteria, of selfpity, of overidentification, of catharsis. Frances could be unnecessarily voluble on the subject of death and all that it meant. She would be even more disturbing than Howard Thomas: Probably she saw herself as she would ultimately be, very cold, very dead — satin-lined coffin, of course —

Abbie said, "Your assistant, Howard Thomas, seems quite self-assured. Very capable."

"Howard's a fool. He's half educated. And there's no bigger fool in the civilized world than a half-educated colored man. He was going to be a lawyer and he ended up an undertaker. From law court to mortuary is a long jump. Anyway, he drinks brandy to keep from thinking too much about how and why he made the jump. I'm always afraid he'll show up at a funeral so far gone in drink that he'll do something outrageous."

"Is he married?"

"Married!" Frances snorted. "Good heavens, no! He doesn't like women. But women respond to him on sight. They want to rub up against him. Just as though he were catnip and they were cats."

Including me, Abbie thought, remembering how she had leaned toward him. But never again. And I wouldn't have described it like that.

"He makes a good assistant." Frances got out of the wing chair. "You make yourself comfortable while I go and see about tea." She was going out of the room, and she turned back, and said, "Sometimes I wish his behind didn't wiggle quite so much."

Abbie wondered why Frances thought the jump from lawyer to undertaker was any longer than the jump from doctor to undertaker. We all take these jumps. I went from schoolteacher to coachman's wife, from wife to widow, from widow to needle-woman-landlady. Accident? Coincidence? No. It all depended on what had happened to you in the past. And as you grew older, the sharp edges were rubbed off, rounded, blurred, so that the big things that happened to you were finally reduced to stories that you told, and the stories became fewer and fewer. Even though it was a commonplace, ordinary, story, enough of the emotion you had felt, came through to make it a good story. Frances talks about her father. I don't talk about the Major because I trained myself not to. Selfdiscipline. But I think about him. I talk about Link. Link talks about Bill Hod.

The fire crackled in the fireplace. Fortunately Miss Doris liked fires in fireplaces. She must have liked brass fenders, too, because she saw to it that Sugar kept this one polished so that it shone like gold. Miss Doris must have approved of Frances' living room, because she hadn't changed anything in it, same heavy draperies at the windows, same massive furniture, same Turkish carpet, all dark red, horsehair sofa still against the far wall. A highceilinged room. Dark woodwork. Dark floors. Sugar, who was Miss Doris' husband, waxed the doors and the floors and baseboards. A tall thin man. Face of a Brahmin. Look of hauteur. He talked exactly like Miss Doris. Miss Doris. Where was J.C.?

Frances came into the room carrying a tray.

Abbie said, "Where's J.C.?"

"I was wondering when you'd remember him. He's in the kitchen with Miss Doris. They've been making cookies."

"Really?" They must somehow have declared a truce. "I'll take a look at them while you're pouring."

She went through the dining room, bowl of artificial flowers in the center of the dining room table, because Miss Doris refused to "mess with fresh flowers," straw matting on the dining room floor because Miss Doris said colored people didn't know how to eat, and were always spilling food, Frances' mother's silver tea set on the lowboy, looking as though it had just come out of a jeweler's window because it had been lacquered because Miss Doris said she couldn't spend all of her good time polishing silver, because — and then pushed open the kitchen door, and looked in.

Miss Doris was saying, in that hard cold voice, "And were I surprised? He were coming right through all that traffic, hand over hand, and I told Sugar afterwards, Sugar, he were the nearest thing to the ape I have ever saw in human form."

Miss Doris was sitting by the kitchen table, her hands in her lap, talking to J.C. J.C. was quite close to her, perched on a high stool, his feet twisted in the rungs. Nothing had been changed in the rest of the house, but in the year that Miss Doris had been working for Frances, the kitchen had been radically changed. It now looked like a model kitchen in an advertisement, even to the plants on the long window sill under the battery of windows that had been placed over the sink — and the long counters on each side of it.

J.C. said, "Is them cookies done yet?"

"Well, I picked up that umbrella, the one with the long handle, and I give him a poke, and that took care of him."

J.C. said, "Miss Doris, ain't it time to take them cookies out?"

It would be a shame to disturb them, Abbie thought. I'll stand here long enough to find out whether Miss Doris ever answers him about the cookies.

Miss Doris said, in her cold hard voice, "Another time, I said to Sugar, Dressin' gown? Mr. Orwell ain't never owned no dressin' gown, what color is it? And Sugar said, It's a kind of light tan color and it's kind of tight on him, it's kind of squeezin' him in the shoulders and arms. And I said, Sugar, you go right up there, he's done put that woman's new spring coat on, that's what he's done, you go right up there and get it off him, Mr. Orwell

ain't never owned no dressin' gown; and Sugar went up and he
come back down to the kitchen and he said, Sugar, you were
correct, he were layin' up there in that bed dead drunk wearin'
that woman's new spring coat that come from Carnegie and cost
two hundred dollars, that's just what he had on. There's nothin'
worse, Jackson, than a multonmillionaire who is far gone in
drink."

"Miss Doris — " J.C. started.

Miss Doris said, "Mr. Orwell were a old devil, Jackson. One
time he come in my kitchen and he et up all the lemon meringue
pies I had fixed for the dinner dessert and I told him, I said, Mr.
Orwell, when my menims is fixed for the day I can't start in
fresh at seven o'clock at night for no seven-fifteen p.m. dinner
and make no new dessert. It were in the summer and with that
daylight time it were still like afternoon and the sun were right
in his face and he were a terrible sight in that strong sun, he
were all red-eyed from drink and his skin were full of little small
broken veins so that he were purplefaced. And Mrs. Orwell were
sittin' right close by on the sunporch and he went right out there
and I heard him say, What is the matter with old Doris, she's
out there in the kitchen just as black and evil.

"And I were mad, anyway, Jackson, so I picked up one of them
long thin meat-carvin' knives, and I went right out there on that
sunporch and I said, Excuse me, Mrs. Orwell, for breakin' up the
peace like this but I got something to tell Mr. Orwell and there
were strong sun on the porch and I said, Mr. Orwell, I been
workin' for multonmillionaires all my life and I were never insulted by any of them up until right now, and I were holding
this long thinblade meat-carving knife behind my back and I
snatched it out and I held it right under his nose, and moved
it back and forth and that strong sun made it shine like a switch
blade, and I said, You come in my kitchen with your drunken
self and you et up all my pies and then you come out here and
insult me and I'm goin' to stand right here and take this knife
and cut your nose off even to your face, I mean that, Mr. Orwell.

"Mrs. Orwell she let out a little scream and she said, Miss
Doris, don't, put it away, don't do that to Mr. Orwell. And
Mr. Orwell, he said, Miss Doris what have I done, what have
I said, I didn't mean it whatever it was, and I will never do it
again, I will never eat all your lemon meringue pies up again,
Miss Doris, I promise, and I will never go in your kitchen again,

Miss Doris, I mean that, just move that shinybladed butcher
knife away from my nose, Miss Doris. And he never did either,
Jackson. He would stand in my kitchen door, his face all purple
from drink, and say what he had to say, but he never set his
drunken feet in my kitchen again."

J.C. said, firmly, "Miss Doris, them cookies were done now."

Abbie thought, Why he hasn't been with her two hours and
he pronounces "were" the same way she does, as though it were
"wear."

"No, they were not, Jackson. I were cookin' thirty or forty
years before you were born and I know when cookies is done."

"Where were I before I were born?"

Miss Doris gave him one of those hard appraising stares. "You
were sittin' around under a rosebush waitin'."

"Waitin' for what, Miss Doris? I ain't never sat under no
rosebush. I sets under The Hangman."

"In that case, Jackson, you were settin' around under The
Hangman waitin' to be born."

Silence in the kitchen. They both seemed to be meditating.
Abbie knew the tea must be cooling in the cups, but —

J.C. said, "Miss Doris, is all printhesses white?"

"How's that?"

"Is printhesses always white?"

"I ain't seen one recently. Last one I seen was black."

"Powther say they're white."

"Who's he?"

"My daddy."

"Well," Miss Doris said, "maybe your pappy's only seen white
ones. Folks only see what they want to see. I see black ones. He
sees white ones. If there were a law about it either way the law
would be wrote down in a book somewhere."

"Is them cookies ready now, Miss Doris?"

"Not yet. Now there were another time when Mr. Orwell — "

"Is there a thin shinyblade knife in this one?"

"No. This one's about the time Mr. Orwell seen a buffalo on
the train goin' Pullman to New York. And I were ashamed to be
with them, it were just like travelin' with a zoo because Mr. Orwell
didn't have no decent suit to wear so he put on his tuck, everything else were et up by the moths and covered with gravy drips
and Mrs. Orwell were wearin' his beaver hat, and they both smelt
like moth balls and likker and they were goin' dressed like that to

Mr. Orwell's brother's funeral and Mrs. Orwell had on a diamont necklace and had practically took a bath in Guerlain's and what with her havin' on Mr. Orwell's beaver hat I said to Sugar, Well, Sugar, I just hope they'll let us get on that train. Well anyway, just outside New Haven Mr. Orwell got up and went in the gentlemen's rest room, and he come out real quick, all purplefaced, and he let out a high scream, he came out fast, and he kept lettin' out this high scream, and he said, Miss Doris, come quick, Miss Doris, there's a buffalo in there. And I said to Sugar, Sugar, he's lost his mind, I always knew he were goin' to and here he's gone and done it while he's ridin' on this Pullman of all places. And I said real firm but not loud, Mr. Orwell, you come and sit down. And he said, Miss Doris, where are you, come quick, Miss Doris and get this goddamittohell buffalo out of the toilet. And he let out another one of them high screams, and he said, Please come quick, Miss Doris, before I lose my mind.

"So the ladies and gentlemen on the train were all lookin' at him standin' up there in his tuck in broad daylight and kind of murmurin' to each other, and the porter were not around, they are just like policemen if you need one you cannot lay hands on one, so I got up and I said to Sugar, Sugar, you get Mr. Orwell sat down while I go and see. And Mr. Orwell said, That's right, Miss Doris, you go in there and scare the shit out of that buffalo, and I said, Mr. Orwell, you stop usin' that bad language, you're not at home. You go sit down and be quiet. And he turned more purple and went and sat down when Sugar told him to.

"And I went in the gentleman's rest room and there were a woodchuck in there. And at first I though I had stayed with Mr. and Mrs. Orwell too long, I were always telling Sugar, Sugar, we must not stay here too long or we will lose our minds, too, just like these crazy rich people, but we are poor and so they would put us in confinement, but if you are rich and crazy, you can run loose.

"But that woodchuck were so big and so fat and he looked at me so fresh and made a noise, a kind of a big grunt noise, that I knew he were real, and I were mad anyway, goin' Pullman to New York with them Orwells lookin' like they had just been let loose from a zoo or a circus, so I snatched that woodchuck up by the tail and by the neck, and I come out of the gentleman's rest room, holdin' him and somebody had sent for the porter and he were one of them little wiry old black men been a porter so long he thinks he owns the Pullman and he come sloofootin' it up to me and said, What you doin' in there, woman, and I said, I'm Mrs. King to you and to everybody that ever knew me, and you can call me that. Here, I said, this is your Pullman so this must be your buffalo, too, and I tried to hand him that fat sassy woodchuck, clawin' and gruntin', and he let out a high scream just like Mr. Orwell and jumped back and Mr. Orwell yelled real loud, That's right, Miss Doris, you scare the shit out of him, too, and I said to Sugar, Sugar, put your hand over Mr. Orwell's mouth, and I went and opened up the train door and turned that woodchuck loose."

Silence.

J.C. frowned. "How did de buffalo — " He paused, appeared to think. "I mean, how'd he get down in de toilet?"

Abbie thought, I was wondering the same thing. And the tea must be cold, stone cold, by now, and Frances will be wondering where I am, but Miss Doris hadn't said the buffalo, that is, the woodchuck was down in the toilet — She held the swinging door open a little wider.

"Mr. Orwell he were so drunk and so scared he couldn't tell a woodchuck from a buffalo. Some of them fresh Yale boys had put that woodchuck in the gentleman's rest room while the train were waitin' at the New Haven station, where they changes over the engines, for ten minutes."

She let the door swing to, gently, and went back to the living room.

Frances said, "Were they all right?"

"I should say so. Doris was talking about the Orwells, and J.C. was talking about his princess, and asking when the cookies would be done, and neither one was really listening to the other. That's the way all conversations, really satisfying ones, are carried on."

While they drank their tea, they talked about Link. They always talked about Link. Abbie thought of all the conversations, the discussions, the endless arguments, they had had about him. They had to explain to him, somehow, about his being a Negro, and there was the awful business of sex, and religion, and the problem of where to send him to college, and the more complicated problem of how to finance his education, and that job with the Valkills. It seemed as though he were always making too much noise, and he played football and went swimming in the river. Both equally dangerous. So many things to be explained and avoided

and circled around. And he survived. He survived Bill Hod and
pneumonia, and the redlight district, and the Navy. Tall, now,
Shoulders broad, now. Speaking voice like the low notes of an
organ. If only —
"I wish he'd get married," Abbie said, "and settle down."
"Isn't he settled down?" Frances asked.
"He isn't really settled down until he's married. No young
man is. Lately, well, he stays out half the night and I don't dare
ask him where he goes or what he does. And it worries me. He's
always in New York. He stays there two or three days at a time.
I suppose he has a girl. I'd like to see her, to meet her. I don't
know how to ask him about her, to tell him to bring her home
for tea. I'm afraid he'll think I'm interfering."
She had picked out a house for him, a brick house, on the
other side of town. The instant she saw the For Sale sign on it,
she'd managed to marry Link to a nice girl, and get them moved
into the house, all in her mind. There were lilacs in the dooryard,
big old lilacs, and orange lilies, great clumps of them, in bloom
there, last August. And a fence across the front, one of those
iron fences that you rarely ever see any more. She didn't know
who Link's girl was. She was sure he had one. All young men
had girls. But she'd never seen him with a girl, never heard him
mention one. He seemed to have skipped the girl-crazy stage they
go through in their teens. When he was seventeen and home from
Dartmouth for the summer, he saw girls every Sunday after church,
and sometimes he talked to them, briefly, laughed with them,
briefly, and turned away from them quickly. She didn't know
that she blamed him. They fidgeted so, and their heads seemed
to have been turned out by some kind of machine, all exactly
alike, all slick with grease, and they used too much perfume, apparently the same kind of perfume, so that they smelled alike;
most of them had pimples under the powder and rouge. They
perspired easily, their dresses darkening under the armpits, beads
of perspiration appearing on their wide, bridgeless noses, as they
teetered toward Link on their highheeled shoes, shoes that made
their thin straight legs look brittle, teetering toward seventeen-
year-old Link after church, and perspiring as they talked to him.
But those were the good girls, the ones who went to church,
the ones who wanted husbands and homes and children. And
they were absolutely all wrong for Link. The ones who didn't go
to church were the ones with the shapely legs and the smooth

brown skins that didn't need any heavy concealing layers of powder, the ones with the artfully curled hair, the ones who didn't want husbands and children and wellkept homes. They wanted boyfriends, an endless succession of boyfriends and a perpetual good time. And they were absolutely all wrong for Link too.

"He'll get married one of these days," Frances said easily. "Most of the things we worried about never happened. Now that he's grown-up, we have to remember that he is grown-up. He'll be all right."

Link had said that Frances was right, ninety-nine point nine times out of a hundred. She could be wrong, though, one one-tenth of the time. That afternoon she had hurried to tell Frances that she couldn't have Mamie Powther living in her house, Frances had laughed at her. She couldn't make her understand how shocked and frightened she had been when Mamie Powther told her that Bill Hod was her cousin, couldn't make her understand that moment of pure terror she had known because Bill Hod came down the back stairs, no sound of footsteps, but the sound of a whistled tune, the tune of the song that Mrs. Powther had been singing when she was hanging up clothes in the backyard, the whistled tune coming down the stairs, high, sweet, down, down the stairs, no sound of feet descending, just the whistle, so that it seemed to descend by itself, and then Bill Hod went past the back door, went around the side of the house, still whistling, the same Bill Hod who had supported the Major down the street, who for a space of sixty seconds, probably less time than that, had glared at her, shouting as no one had ever shouted at her before, "You fool — you goddam fool — get a doctor!" His face, so contorted, his voice, so furious, that she had picked up a poker, with the intention of striking him with it if he came any nearer, and his face had changed, and he shrugged and walked away. Cold, cruel face. Face of a hangman. Frances either couldn't or wouldn't understand why she was so disturbed by the knowledge that Bill Hod was Mamie Powther's cousin.

Frances had listened, that afternoon, and said, impatiently, "Sooner or later, Abbie, you'll have to make up your mind to accept defects in your tenants or else stop renting the place. You'll never find a perfect tenant. There's no such thing. If you stop renting the place you'll cut off a big important part of your income. It's unfortunate that Mr. Hod should be Mrs. Powther's cousin, bad for your peace of mind, but there isn't anything you can do about it."

Mamie Powther. Just listening to her, not seeing her, but listening to her voice, you could tell what kind of woman she would be, the big soft unconfined bosom, the smooth redbrown skin, the toosweet strong perfume, it was all there in her voice. Emanation of warmth, animal warmth, in her voice.

Abbie sighed. "I can't tell you how much I wish Link would fall in love and get married."

Lately his getting married had taken on an urgency in her mind. Because of Mamie Powther. She was afraid of Mamie Powther. Afraid of Bill Hod. She had always been afraid of Bill Hod but at least there had been the street between them; now it was just as though he had moved into her house. "Hi, Mamie, what's the pitch?" Didn't this fear of Mamie Powther suggest a doubt about Link? Why should she expect him to succumb to the blowsy charms of a married woman, mother of three children, a big young woman, a careless young woman, who went gallivanting off, with never a thought as to who would look after her children?

"It's getting late," she said. "I'll go and get J.C."

In the modern, lightfilled kitchen, Miss Doris was wrapping up a package. J.C. stood watching her. He had a cooky in each hand. The kitchen was filled with the fragrant, delicate, buttery smell of freshbaked cookies.

Miss Doris said, in that cold hard voice, "Now here you is, Jackson. This here's your midnight snack. If'n you should wake up in the middle of one of them night horses you were tellin' me about, you eat one of these cookies. And you carry this package, careful."

"Yes, ma'am, Miss Doris," J.C. said.

Abbie said, "I forgot to tell you, Miss Doris, but his name is J.C."

Miss Doris gave Abbie a swift, hard stare. "Yes, Mrs. Crunch. I know that. He told me. But I don't plan to have no children around me without no Christian names. So I named him. When he's here with me, he's Jackson."

She woke up, suddenly. Pitchdark in the room. She felt cold. No covers over her chest, her arms. And an outing flannel nightgown, even a longsleeved one, was no substitute for blankets. Wind blowing, too.

It must have been the sound of the metal screen banging, back and forth, against the window that had awakened her. She pulled the covers up, way up, under her chin, remembering how the

Major slept, on his side, a big man, a Teddy bear of a man, so that the covers were lifted by his shoulders, forming a tent, and drafts blew about her shoulders, her neck, all night long.

She ought to get up and put the window down. But she couldn't sleep in a room that was all shut up, but then, neither could she sleep with that ventilating screen rattling, banging, moving back and forth against the window. She wondered if it was still foggy, if J.C. was awake and eating his midnight snack. Thought of Deacon Lord's funeral, remembered that fog was just beginning to drift in from the river when she and J.C. left Frances' house. Thought of Frances' New Year's Eve party. She gave it every year, a kind of mass entertainment that took care of all her social obligations, a big buffet supper, set up in that dark gloomy dining room, and Sugar, who was Miss Doris' husband, did the carving, served the plates, and Miss Doris carried trays, too, and managed to convey her disapproval of the proceeding just in the way she walked, slapping her feet down on the floor, slap, slap, slap. "Coffee?" Slap, slap, slap.

Thought of Mamie Powther, appearing suddenly at the back door, two weeks ago, with a fruit cake, "Missus Crunch, you been so nice to J.C. I thought it bein' New Year's Eve, and all, you know, if you was havin' friends in, this'd be nice to have in the house," smiling, affable, easy-voiced. Mamie Powther had been wearing another new coat, a purple coat, fitted, with brass buttons in a double row down the front, the big bosom making the buttons look as though they were ascending and descending a hill. She had so many coats. Not a badlooking woman. But so much bosom, always so unconfined, even under the coats you knew it was there. Taller than little Mr. Powther. How had he ever come to marry her? The past. The answer in the past. Miss Doris and the Orwells. Frances and her father. Howard Thomas went from lawyer to undertaker because of his past. Abbie Crunch went from schoolteacher to coachman's bride to widow to landlady-needlewoman, now able to go to funerals, to smell liquor without shuddering, to be tolerant of the occasional, unexpected vulgarities that crept into Frances' conversation, "Rub up against him just as though he were catnip and they were cats." "I wish his behind didn't wiggle — "

She had the queer disconcerting feeling that a hand, or hands, had come at her out of the dark. Vague, directionless, groping hands were pulling at the blankets, at the sheet, at the woolfilled comforter. She edged away, thinking, I always knew this would happen, all my life I've been afraid of this, waiting for this, always known that something would come at me out of the dark, feeling, groping, for me. It's my imagination. I'm always picturing disaster.

King of England. King of England. He said it on the radio at Christmas, a few years ago. What was it? I saved it. I never can quite remember it. Safer than a known way. Better than a light. Anonymous. Put your hand into the hand of God. Reach out your hand. Into the darkness.

She put her hand out, reaching out, into the darkness. Something brushed against it. She jerked her hand back, away from whatever it was, and tried to scream, and couldn't. She said, "Oh," and it was like a sigh.

J.C. Powther said, "Missus Crunch —"

For a moment she couldn't answer him, still thinking, I always knew — always in the back of my mind was the fear, formless, shapeless — that something dreadful would come at me, out of the dark. I was certain that that small hand, J.C.'s hand, was the —

"Yes?" she said.

"She's here, Missus Crunch."

"Why aren't you in bed?" Abbie asked.

"Not sleepy."

"Of course not. You don't get up until noon. What kind of way is that to bring a child up? Up all night. In bed all day. It's bad enough for grown people."

J.C. ignored her. "She's here," he repeated.

"Will you please go back upstairs and get in bed and go to sleep. Why do you walk around all hours of the night? Why does your mother allow it? You walk in and out of here and most of the time I don't even know you're in the room."

"Mamie's out," he said.

"That's no excuse. Aren't Kelly and Shapiro in bed?"

"Yes," he said, something very like impatience in his voice. "Missus Crunch, the printhess is in Link's room."

"I've asked you not to tell lies. It's wrong. It's a bad thing to do. I don't know why you make things up."

"She's all gold," he said, his voice dreamy. " 'N she and Link walk gumshoe when dey come in through de door. Dey gumshoe in, through de door."

"Have you got to go to the bathroom?" He didn't answer. "J.C., have you got to go to the bathroom?" That woman didn't have sense enough, or was too lazy, to get up and take him to the bathroom. It was the only way to keep them from wetting the bed when they were that young, and it was probably why he walked around at all hours of the night. He was uncomfortable.

"I just wet. I don't need to."

"Very well. Now go upstairs and go to sleep."

"It's dark in here," J.C. said. "You want a light on?"

"No, I don't. Don't you touch that lamp! Go on, J.C., go on upstairs." Silence. But he was still there, right by her bed. She could hear him breathing.

"Missus Crunch," he said.

She didn't answer. If she didn't answer, he'd go.

"Missus Crunch," he said softly. "I gotta go to de bathroom."

"You haven't. You told me you just went." Oh, dear, she thought. I'm sure he hasn't got to, he's just saying so to get me out of bed, and yet, he might have to.

"I gotta go to de bathroom, Missus Crunch," he whined.

She turned the light on by her bed. He was wiggling, standing first on one foot and then on the other. And he must have dressed himself in the dark. He had his overalls on backwards, the pockets in the back, the stubbed brown shoes were on the wrong feet. She reached for her heavy gray bathrobe, put on her slippers, and then looked at the clock. It was four in the morning.

In the bathroom, J.C. said, "I had to," triumph in his voice. "You hear dat?"

She looked away from him, down the hall. It was better to ignore some things. The night light was still burning. Link wasn't home yet. Where did he go? Four o'clock in the morning. Oh, dear, if it isn't one thing, it's another. She'd turn the light out. It would be daylight soon, and there wasn't any point in wasting electricity.

"I'm going to turn this hall light out, J.C. You go up the stairs before I turn it out so you can see where you're going."

J.C. followed her obediently. He stopped and sniffed. "It's her smell," he said. "It's the printhess smell."

Smell of perfume in the hall, faint, sweet, lingering there.

"Run along before I turn the light out."

"Mamie said don't tell," J.C. said. "Mamie's a robber. Her

took de pretty-pretty. It was all gold and her took it and wouldn't give it back. I'm goin' to tell. Her's in dere," he said, pointing at the door of Link's room.

Abbie was suddenly angry. "There's no one in there. Link's not home yet." Where does he go? What is he doing? "There's no one in there. I don't know what's going to become of you if you don't stop making things up." There were times when J.C. was absolutely unintelligible, she doubted if his own mother knew what he was talking about. Cold in the hall. She'd never get rid of this bulletheaded little boy.

"Here," she said and flung open the door of Link's room.

And stood still. Light on. Link in bed. In that bed that didn't look like a bed, the one the decorator put in there when he did the room over, and threw out the walnut bedstead, this bed just some kind of rubber mattress that stood on legs, no headboard, no footboard, and when she said, "How perfectly dreadful," Link had said, "But try it, Aunt Abbie. It's comfortable. It's the most comfortable bed I've ever slept in," and even now whenever she looked at it, all these years afterwards, she felt resentful, to think of the way in which her perfectly good furniture had been tossed out as though it were —

A girl there in bed with Link. Both naked. The girl's head, the hair yellow, head on his chest, yellow hair on his chest, his shoulder. A white girl. How dare he? In her house, her house, "Abbie — the house — the house — " speech thickened, light gone out of the Major's eyes, as though he were blind, and inside she had already started to cry, a faint smile about his mouth, the effort, desperate, to sit up and Frances helped her prop him against the pillows, and then that awful, horrible-to-watch struggle to talk. "The house, Abbie, the house — "

For a moment she could not speak, could not move.

Then she was shaking the girl, shaking her, shaking her back and forth, trying to talk, no control over her tongue, her throat, having to talk, having to let the girl know, let Link know how she felt. Something seemed to explode inside her head. Spots dancing before the eyes. Heat and heat. Pressure, unbearable pressure, up and down the back of the neck, the head, pressure behind the eyes, the ears, the face. Ringing in the ears. A roaring, a pounding, inside her head.

"In my house," she said, "in my house, hussy, plying your trade, get out, get out of my house."

She looked for something, anything, grabbed a newspaper, not even knowing what it was, brandished it about the girl's head. "Get out before I kill you."

Hands aware of the newspaper. Mind remembering the newspapers under the chair where the Major sat. *Monmouth Chronicle.*

"Abbie," Link protested. Asleep, she thought. He was asleep. He sat up, then reached for the sheet, and pulled it over himself. "Don't," Link said.

She pushed and pulled the girl out of bed, pushed her into the hall. Went back in the room, picked up the girl's clothes, picked up a coat, a fur coat. Coat soft, silky. Her hands aware of it, and her mind ignoring it. She flung the coat at the girl. She opened the front door. Fog outside. She threw the girl's clothes, dress, slip, stockings, out on the sidewalk. Hall filled with fog.

The girl stood in the hall, bending over, trying to pick the coat up, trembling with rage or fear or shame. Abbie pushed her, so that she stumbled, half fell down the steps.

Fog outside. Fog obscuring the sidewalk. Fog billowing up from the river. Lean over and see what was written on the sidewalk. Cesar the Writing Man. Moment of confusion in which she stood in the doorway, lost, not here, not anywhere. Don't let him die. Fog cold against her face.

Fog billowing up from the river. Where am I? She heard laughter. Someone was laughing, outside, standing in the street, laughing.

J.C. said, "Was she a bad printhess?"

Abbie turned toward him, waved the newspaper about his head. "Go upstairs. Go to bed. Go away." The girl was taller, younger, stronger than she was, but she could have strangled her, killed her.

"Go before I kill you," she said to J.C.

He scuttled up the stairs.

Someone was laughing, outside, on the street. Dumble Street. She slammed the front door, banging it shut. Where am I?

She went back into her room, closed the door, still wanting to shout at the girl, even though she was gone, How dare you, dare you, in my house, tramp, in my house, yellow hair on my pillowcases, the bridal ones, the ones that I made with my own hands, as part of my trousseau, with lace edges, filet lace, that I crocheted, smiling, dreaming about my wedding day. Schoolteacher, teaching at the Penn School, children of the Gullahs, beautiful, the first time I knew that black people could be beautiful, the fathers and mothers and the children, and I teaching, and dreaming of my wedding day, fifty years ago, dreaming of the white brocaded satin that cost three dollars a yard, and that I didn't make up because I decided that we didn't need a big wedding, the Major and I, it would be too expensive, and it is still wrapped in black paper, thin black paper between the folds, black tissue paper, rustles when you touch it, wrapped up, in the back of the middle drawer of my bureau, and I thought if I had a daughter, she would have it made up, we would make it up together, for her wedding, and then later, that the girl Link would marry would have it made up.

Girl Link would marry. Harlot. In my house. I put the pillowcases on his bed by mistake. Saturday morning. Change the beds. I always have, and I had pillowcases for my bed and his bed and I started in his room and I had the bridal pillowcases with the others because I had washed them and ironed them, I do it every three months, linen, kept and not used, yellows, and gets stains on it, hard to get out, sometimes impossible, and I was going to put them back in the linen closet.

And J.C. was underfoot, he always is and I wasn't paying any attention to what I was doing because he kept wandering around, as though he were looking for something, and he kept watching me, and it made me nervous, he weaves back and forth like some kind of little animal, in a cage, always under my feet, or he comes and stands and leans against me, all his weight, as though I were a wall or a tree, and he leaning against it for support or protection and so I tried, was hurrying, trying to finish quickly, and he came and leaned against me, almost knocking me down, and then he started wandering around again, and he kept watching me with those inscrutable black eyes, and it made me nervous and he said, "It's her smell."

He'd been saying it for days, and I said, "Whose smell?"

He didn't answer me. He said, "You smell it, too?"

"No."

"It's the printhess. It's her smell."

That made me hurry even faster, not paying any attention to what I was doing, and I must have put the bridal pillowcases on Link's pillows without noticing, then later I couldn't find them, and I spent most of the morning, Saturday morning, yesterday morning, looking for them, looking everywhere, and J.C. following me around, and finally I accused him of taking them.

"I did not," he said, "you got 'em yourself."

"You must have taken them."

"Yeah," he said, finally, and he laughed, and I never saw a young child before who had malice in his eyes and in his laughter. Malice. He said, "I ate 'em all up. I put on season' and butter and ate 'em all up. Yum-yum," and made that humming sound he makes when he's eating, and rocked back and forth just as though he were eating, "I ate 'em pillowcases all up."

How do I know he's in love with her, I knew it the moment I went into that room and saw them lying there naked, because I saw the immorality, the license, the wantonness, but I saw and remembered, just that quickly, their bodies, the perfection, he on his back, one arm extended, so that it was around her shoulders, and she turned toward him, curving toward him, and the young rounded breasts, and he lying there, and the big curve of her hips and the long line tapering down to the knee and then curve again from calf to ankle, small feet, arched feet, with the toenails painted, I think it was not so much the white nakedness of her, not just the shock of finding them there like that, it was the hair, pale yellow hair, not tousled or tangled, but curling about the bare shoulders, pale yellow hair, under his chin, it was the sight of her hair, that pale yellow hair, yellow hair, and Link — Link —

Yellow hair. Yellow chalk. Writing on the sidewalk early in the morning. Pink, yellow. Decorative, elaborately patterned writing, an adornment and a decoration on the sidewalk. Fog coming in.

Up until the time of the Major's death, no situation ever too much. In her what the Major laughingly called the benign persistence of the Jew, laughed, and meant it, though he laughed. She knew the phrase wasn't his, it came straight from the Governor, who probably laughed when he said it, and meant it, too, just as the Major did. The Major's death had been too much for her, vanquished by death, beaten by it. Then surmounted it.

Emptiness. For years afterwards. Sometimes the feeling that he is very close. Nearby. That if I reached out my hand I would find his big strong warm hand. Never again, in anyone, anywhere, that total acceptance, the adoration.

Dumble Street. What kind of people, Mrs. Cohen crying, Matzos, matzos, two for five. Dumble Street. Christian Sunday School. That nigger woman undertaker from Washington Street.

See what she wants. I sets under The Hangman. You fool. You goddamn fool. Get a doctor.

Fog coming in, blowing in from the river, sidewalk obscured, light from the hall, on the steps, swallowed up by the fog, and somewhere someone laughed, somewhere outside on the street, laughter. Someone standing there, watching and laughing, ripple of laughter, vaguely familiar sound, not the laughter, the tone, the pitch of it, laughing, laughing, laughing. Fog undulating up from the sidewalk, in waves. She had closed the front door, slammed it. Thick sound. Lid on a coffin. Final sound. Deacon Lord's funeral. A man who loved God. Mean . . . that was Hubborn . . . a great man for gold.

Link? She would ask him to leave, to live somewhere else. A white girl. In my house. In bed with Link. Tramp of a white girl. Pale yellow hair on the bridal pillowcases. Sweet smell in the hall. In Link's room. He would bring a tramp into my house I am a fool. Frances, "Howard's a fool." You fool. You goddamn fool. Get a doctor.

15

• He was so damn tired, so damn tired. He never got enough sleep any more. And now someone was trying to wake him up, kept trying to wake him up. The room was full of confused movement, senseless movement. He thought at first that he was in The Hotel in Harlem with Camilo, The Hotel where the elevator jerkrumbled outside the door, all night, where the street music of New York, cacophony of pneumatic brakes, of gears, of sirens, played all night, eight floors down, on 125th Street.

Then he decided that they weren't in that suite, on the eighth floor, they were in the lobby, and he was signing the register, Mr. and Mrs. Lincoln Williams, Syracuse, New York, and all this movement, confused, violent movement, was due to the arrival and departure of the hasbeens and the wouldbes who were The Hotel's patrons. He was signing the register in The Hotel and nobody believed what he wrote, the clerks, the elevator boys, the bellhops. Nobody. Male and female certainly. But not Mr. and Mrs. Anybody. Not from Syracuse, either. New York markers on the car, so from somewhere in New York State. Not Syracuse. From Rabbit Hollow or Sycamore Creek. En route to Shangri-La. Heaven bound.

But they weren't in New York. They couldn't be. He had told her he was too damn tired to drive down and back in that fog and she had said, "I'll drive. I just drove up. It took me about an hour and a half. Even in the fog."

"Not me, honey. You won't drive me to New York. You drive too fast."

"I do not," quickly, impatiently, blue eyes darkening with anger. Hair-trigger temper all set to blow. Then, "Don't look at me like that," imperiously.

"Like what?"

"As though you wanted to bite my head off."

"It's a lovely head. I wouldn't bite it off, ever. I have occasionally wanted to knock it off." Like right now. When you sound like the lady of the manor ordering a poacher off the place. "In fact, every time I've watched you tear off in that crate I have wished that I could get my hands on your head, or some other perhaps more appropriate part, for about five minutes."

"For what?"

"For to teach you not to pass stop lights when they are red, honey. For to teach you to hang on to your temper, too. It would be a very pretty kettle of fish if we both lost, couldn't find, dropped our tempers, at one and the same time. One of us would get hurt and it wouldn't be me."

"You — " she said, "you — "

He had kissed her, not letting her talk, pressing his mouth hard on hers, feeling her mouth moving, still trying to form words, trying to protest, and he kissing her, holding her and kissing her, until she stopped trying to talk, and relaxed against him, leaned against him, put her arms around his neck.

Later, in his room, mouth on his chest, mouth moving against his chest, she had murmured, "Don't ever leave me," hair with a shimmer, perfumed hair, under his chin, "I can't live without you, I love you, love you, love you, oh, Link!"

They must be in The Hotel because almost every weekend, since sometime in December, they'd been in The Hotel in New York. Except that Sunday when he waited and waited at the dock, and she didn't show up, staying away for a week, and then the following week she was there, and he, by then, ready to kill her, swearing to himself that when he saw her again he would throttle her for making him wait, for not calling up, or writing, and when he saw her crossing the street, saw the long lovely legs, the ballerina's walk, the innocent lovely face, he didn't even ask her why she stayed away, and she didn't bother to explain, they were both hellbent on one thing, the same thing, fast, because they couldn't wait, couldn't wait. She had said, "Link, put your arms around me. Put your arms around me, hurry," shivering. Ecstasy.

There was confused violent motion, in the room, all around him. He couldn't wake up enough to protest against this unseemly disturbance, whatever it was. Abbie was in the center of the confusion, creating it. She was standing by the bed, leaning over, pushing and pulling at the bed, arms violent, short stout body, violent, long white braids downdangling, violent, too. She's gone crazy, he thought. I have, too. I'm eight years old again and the Major is dead and Abbie is wearing that Aunt Mehalie dressing gown, not a brack or a break in it, wearing slippers all day long, not brushing her hair any more, letting it hang in two long braids. But the braids should be gray. And they are white.

So he was dreaming this. She was leaning over the bed, shouting, pushing and pulling, glaring, shouting, not really shouting, her voice was hoarse, muffled, but the effort she put into it, the energy, was like that which produces a shout, it was a kind of hoarse, furious talking, something about her house, and she was waving a newspaper, the black eyes that he had described to himself as valorous, were the eyes of a virago, a termagant.

"Get out of my house," she said.

He sat up, said, "Abbie — don't." He thought she was about to attack him, with that rolled-up newspaper, and he pulled the sheet up for protection, because he was half asleep, and moving with the illogic of a dream.

New York. Had they gone to New York? Where was Camilo? Nightmare. Abbie went out of the room, and then she was back again, still talking in that hoarse muffled voice, which could not produce a shout, she picked up something, bundled it up, and went out into the hall. He caught a glimpse of Camilo. Abbie was pushing her.

Oh, damn, he thought, what's the matter with Abbie? What has happened to the censor that sits in her brain, controlling her actions, directing her thoughts. If she were anyone else I would say she was drunk. He found a T-shirt, put it on, pulled on a pair of slacks, stuck his feet in his slippers. The night light was still burning, in the hall. No sign of Abbie anywhere.

He walked toward the dock, never enough sleep, life filled with crazy women, one back there in the house, and he out here chasing another one through the fog, cold out here, why hadn't he stopped to put on a jacket, no socks on, feet cold in the slippers, fog in Dumble Street, cold in Dumble Street.

Camilo had turned on the headlights of the car. She was trying to put on her clothes, shivering, furious, frightened. He
helped with stockings, helped with shoes, with slip, with dress,
she still shivering, eyes blazing, not saying anything. All cats bee
gray? All cats bee crazy.

They sat there, in that car with its smooth, coldfeeling uphol-
stery, he talking to her, trying to apologize, thinking, Explain
Abbie? Impossible. Queen Victoria turned shrew, turned virago.
Turned. Changed. Why the fury? Why the violence?

"It was my fault," he said. His fault? Whose fault? Why anybody's fault? How his fault? "I'm awfully sorry."

No answer.

Cold in the car. Fog outside. Fog in the car. He had no coat
on. Dumble Street was silent, asleep, closed up for the night. Fog
in the street. Fog in him. He was asleep, closed up for the night.

"I'm awfully sorry," he repeated. He would have to explain
Abbie. But he couldn't. He'd never been able to explain her
even to himself, how explain her to someone else.

He said, irritably, "Say something."

She kept staring straight ahead, hands gripping the steering
wheel, refusing to look at him. He thought, You're in the doghouse, Bud. You're in the doghouse. Why not stay there? Why
not stay there for keeps? He put his hands on her shoulders,
forced her to turn so that she was facing him.

"Camilo, listen to me," he said.

"You bastard," she said, "you knew — you — knew, leave me
alone," turning and twisting under his hands. "That woman,
laughing at me, laughing at me," twisting, turning, pushing him
away, "Get out of my car," voice imperious.

They all carry eviction notices around with them, typed up,
ready to use. Abbie: Get out of my house. Mr. B. Hod: Get the
hell out of my face. Camilo: Get out of my car.

"Let's fix it up for keeps," he said savagely. Cold in the car.
In love with love? In love with Camilo Williams? Wait for you
on the dock, two weeks ago, on a Sunday night, and you not
come, when you do show up, you not say anything, you not explain, you not apologize, you bitch, you, you keep me on a seesaw,
now up, now down.

Camilo said, "Let go of me."

He tightened his grip on her shoulders.

"You black bastard," she said, voice furious. "Let go of me."

Something exploded inside his head. I never understood, he thought, I never could quite understand Mr. B. Hod. But I do now. I never could figure out what happens to him, what goes on inside him that turns him into an executioner. But I do now. It is just this. It is an explosion inside his head. Will you marry me? Yes, come spring, and the time of the singing of birds, you black bastard.

He held her hands, soft hands, usually warm, cold now to the touch, he held the cold hands in his left hand, and slapped her, with his right hand.

If we were not here, in this car, on Dock Street, I would kill you. Just this way, just by slapping you, just by working on your face. Love. Hate. No one in the USA free-from, warfare, eternal war between the male and the female. Black bastard. White bitch.

She tried to bite his hand, and he kept slapping her, slapping her, remembering a conversation out of his past:

Dr. Easter: You're okay, eh?

L. Williams: Yes, sir.

Dr. Easter: Let's have a look. (pause in the examination and then the sudden question) Who did it?

L. Williams (unprepared for the question. Dr. Easter had been treating him for three weeks and had asked no questions): Did what?

Dr. Easter: Beat you with a rawhide whip until he very nearly killed you.

L. Williams: I don't know.

Dr. Easter: I see. I suppose it was a dark night and you were waylaid by four or five total strangers and you can't identify any of them because you couldn't see their faces. Or did they wear masks? Where did it happen? Here in The Narrows?

L. Williams: I don't remember anything about it.

Dr. Easter: "Don't know." "Don't remember." You must have been studying those gangster trials. You mean you're not telling.

L. Williams: I don't know what you're talking about.

Dr. Easter: A man capable of doing this sort of thing to a six-teen-year-old boy ought to be put in prison. If I were Mrs. Crunch, I would have him arrested. He's a mad dog. He ought to be locked up.

Weak Knees (quickly): Sonny's comin' along fine, now, ain't he, Doc?

Dr. Easter: So we talk about something else, eh?

Kill you, he thought, just by working on your face. Face that he had dreamed about, held between his hands, kissed, rubbed his cheek against, traced the line of the eyebrows with his fingers. Expressive face. Gay, laughing face. Innocent face. Ruin it.

He let go of her hands. Got out of the car, slammed the door.

He stood on the dock, thinking, Bill Hod: I'll cripple you for life. It was, somewhere, in everybody. It was in Abbie, which shocked him. It was in Link Williams, which didn't shock him at all because he had always known it was there. It was in Camilo Williams. You black bastard. Fury rose in him again, and he thought, I ought to go back to that car where you sit shuddering and slap you and keep on slapping you until I have killed you. I can't live without you. You black bastard.

Far down Dock Street he heard the putt-putt of Jubine's motor-cycle, like a series of small explosions, coming nearer. Fog over the river, fog over Dumble Street, lapping of the river under the piling, and over it all the sound of Jubine's motorcycle. The red car was still there, fog obscuring it, but he could see the head-lights. Putt-putt of the motorcycle, nearer and nearer. It would be daylight in another hour or so, or what would pass for daylight in this fog.

He heard her start the motor, and then the grinding sound of a car not in gear, was now though, roaring down the street in first, she'd forgotten to shift, now in second, now in high, she must be doing eighty. "I'll cripple you for life." He thought the fury had died in him. It hadn't. Because he kept thinking, You'll have to explain it, you're going to have trouble explaining the way your face looks, to whoever it is you have to explain things to, to whoever it was you were with that Sunday night when you didn't show up. I wish I had not stopped. Come spring, and the sing-ing of birds. You black bastard. Who did it? I don't know.

The putt-putt of the motorcycle stopped. Headlight turned off. Footsteps on the dock. Jubine. Any other night, any other time, but not now. Face of a snoop. Stand still, don't say anything, and the bulging eyes and the cigar will go away. Hear all, see all, smell all will go away.

A long beam of light cut through the fog, sweeping the length of the dock, beam of a flashlight, moving, Oh, goddamn him, he thought, the light now directly in his eyes. Then it was turned off.

"Sonny!" Jubine said. "Jesus, what're you doin' here at this hour?"

For a moment he didn't answer, couldn't. Then he said, angrily, "I don't know." Who did this to you? I don't know. Where did it happen? Here in The Narrows? I don't remember anything about it.

Jubine was peering at him, trying to see his face.

"I've missed you, Sonny. Where've you been? No poker game. Nobody to talk to. Nobody who speaks my language. Mr. Hod and Mr. Weak Knees and I have been desolate. For a thousand Saturday nights. How come you've divorced us?"

Link was silent.

Jubine said, "Why do you no longer sit out the late watch at The Last Chance? It disturbs all of us. Mr. Hod tries to kill his customers, nightly, instead of just once in three months, as was his wont. Mr. Weak Knees keeps brushing Eddie away, pushing him away. And I, Sonny, I watch for you, wait for you." He lit a match, held it in front of his cigar, too far away from the cigar, held it high, staring at Link, and said, "Did the canary get out of the cage?"

Sound of the river lapping against the piling. Fog. Girl running, running, running down the dock. It began here. It ended here. Fury dying in him now. I want her back, I want to hold her in my arms again, I want her, I want her. Smell of stock. Walk like a ballerina's. Long neck of a ballerina. Blue eyes, innocent, candid. Warm, sweet mouth. What made me —

Jubine said, in his soft, compassionate voice, "Was it your canary, Sonny?"

I like him, Link thought, I like his snoop's face, and his jeering talk, but if he doesn't move off — I, executioner. The river. What more appropriate than Jubine and his cigar, and his inquisitive eyes, his snoop's face, placed finally and irrevocably in his river. Abbie: Out of my house. Camilo: Black bastard. Bill Hod: I'll cripple you for life. And Mamie Powther? Sure. She hung little Mr. Powther from the sour apple tree, a long time ago, and keeps him there, not only refusing to cut him down, but rehanging him, three or four times a week, so that he will dangle, in perpetuity. China? Sure. Stand in a doorway and pull a curtain aside, watching and licking her lips while Mr. B. Hod tries to break my spine. Executioners, all.

Jubine turned the flashlight on. The sudden light blinded him, and he thought, Got to know, got to see what I look like, got to find out. Was it your canary? And how does a man look, what can you see in his face, what would you have had if you could have taken a picture of him at the moment when he lost his canary? Recording angel with a camera? Hangman with a camera.

He headed straight into the long blinding beam of light. "You son of a bitch," he said, "I'll throw you in the river."

The flashlight went off. Jubine turned and ran. Thud, thud, of his feet in the GI shoes. Then the putt-putt of the motorcycle.

He did not go back to Abbie's house to live. He stayed at The Last Chance. He tried not to think about the girl. He could sit in the kitchen of The Last Chance, drinking a cup of coffee, listening to Weak Knees talk, hear what he said, and see, not the stove, or the copper hood, or the bare whitish wood of the table, or the pots and pans like a decoration on the wall, but see, instead, Camilo lying next to him, light from the street, even that far up, eighth floor of The Hotel, powerful enough so that the room was never completely dark, see her lying next to him, wearing a thin thin nightgown, pale pink stuff like gossamer, like cobwebs, pale pink ribbons at waist, at neck, at wrists, longsleeved cobweb, sleeves an artful accentuation of nakedness, like Olympia, with the shoes and the ribbon tied around the neck, seeming more naked than without them, Camilo like Olympia in this pink cobweb of a nightgown, see right through it; and the feet perfect, toenails painted with pale pink polish, hair tied back with a black ribbon, tied back in a kind of horse's tail, pale yellow horse's tail.

Night after night he sat in the kitchen of The Last Chance and listened to Weak Knees, and saw Camilo in his mind's eye.

End of February and he was doing the same thing.

Finally, on a Friday night, Weak Knees said, caution in his voice, curiosity, too, "Sonny, you had a rumble with somebody or somep'n? Not that it's none of my business, but I couldn't help noticin' you don't never go anywhere no more at night."

Link put his feet up on the kitchen table, tilted his chair back against the wall, consciously assuming Mr. Bill Hod's favorite position. "I guess you'd call it a somep'n." It sure to God wasn't a fight. "I don't know exactly what it was."

"You goin' to be here for the game, tomorrow night?"

"Yeah." I have let Mr. Hod bait me, four Saturday nights in a row, while we played poker, I have let Mr. Jubine photograph me with his eyes, watched him record in his mind's eye how a man looks who has lost a canary, while we played poker; both

gentlemen seem quite aware of the fact that I have lost something, though only one of them is certain that it was a canary.
Tomorrow will be the fifth Saturday night, in a row, that I have
let Hod wave red capes under my nose, and ignored them. By
the sixteenth or seventeenth Saturday night, in a row, I will stop
feeling as though I had lost an arm or a leg, the sickness will
have gone out of me. Sickness, anger, regret, fury, ebb and flow
of all four.

Weak Knees poured coffee into a mansized white mug, "Here,
Sonny," he said, not moving away from the stove, "lay your lip
over this."

"Don't make me move, Weak. I'm too damn comfortable.
Bring it over and put it on the table."

"Name-a-God, Sonny, I got a sauce cookin' on this stove. I
can't leave it. Come and git this coffee. Wassamatter with you,
anyway?"

Bill attacked the swinging door, announcing his arrival in the
kitchen.

Weak Knees said, "Boss, make him git up off his can and come
and git this cup of coffee. Wassamatter with him anyway?"

Bill put the coffee cup down on the table, in front of Link.
"You in some kind of trouble?"

"No, Mr. Boss."

"What's the matter then?"

He didn't answer that one. He watched Weak Knees turn
away from his sauce, turn away from the stove, to stare at them.
He's always afraid of trouble, afraid he'll be an eyewitness to
trouble between me and Mr. Hod. But Mr. Hod and I are at
peace, for the moment. I can tell by Mr. Hod's face, by his eyes.
No warfare tonight.

"Are you broke?" Bill asked.

"Thank you, sir, I am not. My funds are ample for my modest
needs. At the moment. I hasten to add that qualifying phrase
because I never know when they may run completely out. Funds
have a way of doing that at the most — "

"Don't talk that crap to me. If you're not broke and you're
not in some kind of trouble, whyn't you go out at night any
more?"

"I have no place to go, friend. I got an eviction notice." And
now we'll end the audience, we'll switch over to you. "Did you
ever get one, pal?"

Bill said, "Yeah," and walked out of the kitchen.

"Ain't no way to fight a eviction," Weak Knees said, relief in his voice. "Man says he wants his property why he's got a right to it. Ain't nothin' nobody can do about it 'cept let him have it."

"Yeah," he said and thought, At night, in The Hotel, in that queer, reflected light that reached into the room, she looked like something out of a store window, dreamed up by an artist who quit painting and took a job decorating store windows before he got so hungry he started eating grass in Central Park, grazing like a horse in Central Park, and the starving boughtandsold talented painter transformed what had been a dummy in a window, breathed life into it, created a female to haunt a man's dreams. Haunt his dreams? Haunt him for the rest of his life, waking or sleeping, in his bloodstream like a disease.

"Girls?" he had said. "Other girls?" They always wanted to know, who they were, were you in love with them —

"Only you. You only," he had said.

"Really and truly? Link, I don't believe you."

"You shouldn't. I had 'em by the hundred. I had 'em by the thousands. I had 'em by the millions, millions and millions of 'em, honey, round ones, square ones, triangular ones, up to and including the octagonal — "

She had poked him sharply, in the side, with her elbow.

"Ouch! That hurt."

Male and female horseplay.

"It was supposed to." She had traced the line of his torso, with the tips of her fingers, and he thought he could feel the blood pulse down his side, in the wake of her fingertips. "Hey, you're tickling me. Stop it!"

"You are the most beautiful color," she said. She kept running her fingers up and down his side. "I remember the first time I saw a colored woman. When I was a little girl. I wondered if the color would wash off, and then I wondered if she was that color all over. Or was it just the face and hands."

"Yeah," he said. "All the missionaries who come back from Africa or India tell that same story, in reverse. I used to listen to 'em, on Sundays, in the colored Congregational Church, and us dark folks whose black souls had been saved practically at birth, would titter when we heard about those ignorant black Africans, those ignorant brown Indians, who were hellbent on finding out if the missionaries were white all over, or was it just the face and hands, we rocked back and forth tittering when we heard how those heathen dark folks peeked at the white missionaries when they took their baths." Silence. "Even a missionary, a fisherman of souls, is aware of, and proud of, his white skin."

"I'm not."

"You're not a missionary. Or are you?" He remembered that he had turned over on his side, remembered that The Hotel's too-soft bed had been long since replaced by a kingsize bed, the suite changed, from week to week, in subtle ways, comfortable, then positively luxurious. He had turned over on his side so he could look at her. "Did some beneficent Board of Missions send you into the jungle to save me from perdition?" She didn't answer. He said, "What are you thinking about?"

"I wish I was colored, too."

"Why?"

"I've begun to be afraid — "

"Afraid of what?"

"I'm afraid that sometime you'll fall in love with a colored girl."

The wheezegroan of the elevator was an overture, a prelude, a finale, playing on and on, outside in the corridor.

You black bastard.

He remembered thinking, She sleeps like Bill Hod, like a cat, all of her relaxed, stretched out, remembered Hod walking barefooted, in a room full of sunlight, full of cold air, Hod, making no sound as he moved, air-borne, creature from another planet, Mars, perhaps, looked at her and thought of Bill Hod.

Weak Knees was no longer talking about eviction notices. He was talking about people — religion — but he was still stirring the sauce: "When they're young they don't go to church. Then when they gets false teeth and they waterworks run all the time, they gets scared, they think that well, after all, everybody's got to die some time and so mebbe they could, too. It's a funny thing but when they're young, Sonny, they don't believe they can get old or die. Then one mornin' they gets up and looks in the mirror and they got gray hair and a bald spot and they kind of adds themselves up, and they got a full set of uppers and lowers and two sets of glasses and some kind of funny crick in the middle of they backs and they begin to figure mebbe they better start goin' to church. I used to stand out there on that sidewalk in Charleston and watch 'em go by. Sunday mornin'. All them baldhead white Christians."

That first night in The Hotel he had looked out of the window, thinking, Well, yes, the sheets are clean, and there's a view from the windows of these rooms which pass for the royal suite, view at night, mostly neon signs, harsh red, harsher blue, and there's the night music of New York, sound of busses and cars, whine of siren on ambulance and fire engine, and police emergency squad, but it is hardly a place that I would choose to spend much time in. The bed's too soft; and the slipcovers on those chairs and the sofa outside in the sitting room are covered with the grease marks from the heads of the Jacksons and the Johnsons, the kind of place where you put a quarter in the radio, and it plays for exactly a half-hour and then dies on you, without warning, slowing down, the sound fading out, a horrid sound like a death rattle.

Suite on the eighth floor of a downattheheels hotel, hot water faucet in the bathtub dripped, dripped, and when you turned it on you got a gush of lukewarm water, place operated on the principle that noise would serve as a screen for shabbiness, as a cushion for the high prices. Yet he had to admit that the view was, well, it was New York, a crosstown street, extending and extending, lights in the buildings, street stretching away and away, and up, slight rise in the ground, small hill, so that the lights were not only strung out but seemed to rise, ascend, and if you didn't know what the place was like in daylight, saw only that, the lights reaching up and up, you could say it was beautiful. New York at night.

Mr. and Mrs. Williams, Syracuse, New York. Hotel maid came in at six in the morning and closed the windows, turned the heat on in the radiators, and then left. He got up, dressed, and found breakfast for one in the sitting room, and wondered how come in this fifteenth-rate hotel — and remembered that Camilo had slipped Room Service a neatly folded bill the night before, Room Service, with the face of a pimp, face of a whore, a could be bought, could be paid for, all of him for sale, and would see nothing and tell all any time, and Camilo knew how to get service even in a fifteenth-rate hotel, all front and no behind, all lobby and the rooms, rundown. No hot water that night, but the next morning it was damn near boiling when he took a shower.

Weak Knees finished whatever he had been doing at the stove, came and sat down at the table, with a cup of coffee, stirring it with vigor. He said, "You know, Sonny, I get sick of all these whafolks askin' me first thing, first drop of a hat, what do I think about Paul Robeson. The meat man he come in here this mornin', a brokedown dogass white man if I ever see one, all bandylegged from carryin' carcasses, and he come in here with my order, and before he gets the meat put down on the table good he wants to know what do I think about Paul Robeson. So I made him happy, I said I thought he oughtta hightail it back to Russia where he come from, and that softened him up, and I waited awhile and I give him a cup of coffee, and then I says, The reason he oughtta have stayed in Russia, mister, is because over there if he went around talkin' about the changes he wanted made, why'd he get hisself shot full of holes, but nobody over there would be goin' around about to piss in their pants because he was a black man talkin' the wrong kind of politics.

"And if his boy went and married hisself a little white chickadee over there in Russia, the whafolks wouldn't waste their time runnin' to all the colored folks they see askin' 'em what they thought about it. I says over there they wouldn't give a damn, mister, and I don't give a damn over here. Any country where the folks can't marry each other when they got a heat on for each other why — "

On Saturday nights, Link thought, sitting here in the kitchen, you could hear, faintly, far-off, because of the weight of the door between, a murmur from the bar. The only time you could hear it. The rest of the week, nothing at all. The door cut off sounds. Friday nights — no sounds at all, a good night in which to think, to remember, to taste regret, to stand off and look at yourself —

The door opened suddenly. Mr. B. Hod, he thought, the only man in the world who could make a swinging door perform in that fashion, make it erupt, not open, erupt. Bill Hod stood still, just inside the door. What in hell's the matter with him? Murder writ all over his face for any man to see, usually only in his eyes when he's about to sap somebody up, this time, all over his face, what's happened in the bar to make him look like that?

He stood up. It's me, he thought, and I always knew that someday you would look at me like that again, and I would decide, finally, that I could take you apart, piece by piece, and find out whether you're a son of a bitch all the way through, or just in sections.

Bill said, "You're wanted out front, Bud."

"Wanted?" he said, glaring at him, not moving, thinking, Stallions? Bucks. Find the antlers in the underbrush, years afterwards, still locked.

"Yeah." Hod turned, went out through the swinging door.

Weak Knees said, "Old Gruff and Grim's got his habits on. Don't you go lockin' asses with him, Sonny," pleading note in his voice. "You leave him be, Sonny. You hear? He's spoilin' for a fight. You leave him be, Sonny — "

The bar was comfortably full, Friday night crowd, yeasty smell of beer, fruity smell of rye, bourbon, blue haze of smoke, strangely quiet though, no male voices lifted in song, in tall storytelling, in laughter. He looked along the length of the bar, seeking Old Man John the Barber, the barometer, the weather vane. Barber had his back turned to the street. At night the old man always stood near the front window, studying the street (man in his private club, watching the world go by), stood where he could catch the street sounds, see the car lights, movement of people, watch the women's legs, all legs redorange under the neon sign, accept or reject them as they passed, play kingemperormaharajahsultanshah standing in The Last Chance watching the women's redorange legs, estimating their rumps, no good, off with her head, fair to middlin', decision reserved, let her live awhile, this one, but definitely, I will take this one for tonight, you could tell when the old man picked one because his fierce old eyes lit up, he bent forward, the thrust of his jaw accentuated, I will take this one, an old man with shaggy eyebrows playing a game.

Old Man John the Barber had turned his back on the street.

Wanted, Link thought. Wanted for what? What goes on here? Why has Old Man John the Barber quit playing his favorite game?

Then he saw that she was standing at the end of the bar, that she had her back turned, facing the street. He walked toward her, moving quickly, In Moscow, he thought, why in Moscow, because of whatever it was Weak Knees was talking about back there in the kitchen, if I walked along a street in Moscow, street filled with kulaks and Commissars and Robesons and whatever else walks the streets of Mr. Stalin's dream city, and you were standing with your back turned I would know you, and it's not the coat either, if you had on rags, had a bag tied over your head covering the pale yellow hair, I'd still know you, recognize your back.

He said, "Hello," softly.

She turned, "Link — I — "

He said, "Camilo," and held out his hands, both hands, "I — "

As they went out, he was aware of a restless movement, a stir, along the length of the bar, and he looked back. Bill Hod's face had changed. He was behind the bar, way down, near the door, looking at them, face expressionless now but the eyes were hooded, like the eyes of a snake.

16

● WEAK KNEES was sitting at one of the tables in The Last Chance, reading the weekend edition of a New York tabloid. He had it flat on the table in front of him. As he read he moved a finger back and forth across the printed column. His lips moved, too, forming words.

"Name-a-God, Sonny," he said suddenly, voice sopranohigh. He turned toward the bar, holding up the tabloid, arms thrust out as though he were handing it, opened out like that, to someone who was taller than he, someone who was standing armlength away from him.

"Lissen to this," Weak Knees said. His dark supplefingered hands were silhouetted against the pink outside sheets of the feature section. Link thought, That's a shot Jubine would eat up, Weak with that tall chef's hat on his head, and only the top part of the white hat visible behind the newspaper, and the dark hands, holding the paper far away.

"Here's another one of them white boys done robbed a bank, tee-hee-hee." Weak Knees' arms and hands moved as he laughed, and the newspaper made a dry, rustling sound.

Link leaned over the bar, staring, frowning at the newspaper. There was a picture of a girl on the front page of the feature section.

"Say," he said.

"Wassamatter?"

"Let me see that paper for a minute." It felt brittle, dried out, in his hands.

Sunday feature section. Story on American heiresses, one of a series of stories about young women who owned, controlled, were heir to the great American fortunes — vast, unspendable fortunes. Picture of Camilo Williams, laughing. Only that wasn't her name. Her name was Camilla Treadway Sheffield. Internationally known heiress. The Treadway fortune was described as being like that of Krupp or Vickers. Young wife of Captain Bunny Sheffield. Blownup picture of Camilo on the front page. Small picture of Camilo and her husband on the first inside page. Bunny and Camilo at Palm Beach, lounging on the sand in bathing suits. "The Treadway Munitions Company is located in Monmouth, Conn." Yeah, he thought, you can hear the noon whistle blasting all over the place; hear the seven-in-the-morning whistle, every morning, all over Monmouth, everybody says, "She's up, you get up, too," because Mrs. John Edward Treadway ran the plant, the *Chronicle* always carried stories about her, and how she took over the plant when her husband died; and how she'd geared it up, speeding up production, even changing the time when it opened up, used to open at eight o'clock, she changed the time to seven o'clock, "She's up, you get up, too."

Why didn't he know that she was the Treadway girl? How could he? He didn't even know there was a Treadway girl. They inhabited different worlds, you could tell even from this scissors-and-paste-job feature story, this patched together story that wasn't news, story that said Camilla went to a boarding school in Virginia, private school, picture of it, could have been somebody's old Georgian mansion, covered with Virginia creeper; story said she actually worked, had a job on a fashion magazine; story said she had an apartment at Treadway Hall (picture of that, all stone and ivycovered too) but rarely ever used it because she lived in New York and London and Paris; story said her husband was a New York broker, Captain Bunny Sheffield.

Story said the Treadways were the conservative, credit-to-the-country kind of millionaires, no scandals, no divorces; story contained a description of the library, the museum, the concert hall the late John Edward Treadway gave to the city of Monmouth.

Why didn't she tell me who she was — probably got a charge out of the setup, rich white girl shacked up with a dinge in Harlem, in The Narrows. Why not? If you were that rich you could have your cake and eat it too, if you were that rich you could keep all the exits covered. I was just another muscle boy in a long line of muscle boys. Tell by this story. She grew up on the nursemaid, governess, private school, Palm Beach, Hot Springs, Paris, London circuit, and that circuit doesn't normally impinge on Dumble Street — The Last Chance, The Moonbeam, F. K. Jackson Funeral Home, Church of I Am The Master, Get Your Kool-Aid Free — unless you're out hunting for a new muscle boy.

It's not true, he thought. But it was. It was the same girl. Same laughing, innocent face. Pale yellow hair, silky hair, with a shimmer. Visible even in the smoky cavelike interior of The Moonbeam. Beautiful body. The skin luminous. (Will you marry me? Yes, come spring. You black bastard.) Captain Sheffield's young wife.

Dry rustling of the paper, again, as he turned the page. Brittle. Why brittle? Heat did that to paper, dried it out. He looked at the dateline, automatically, looked again, not believing it, last year's paper, January 1951. There's a mistake somewhere. No. The boys set this one up for me. Not Weak Knees. Bill Hod had used Weak Knees to convey this information. Bill set this one up. Bill never forgets a face. How do I know he never forgets a face? Never heard him say so. It's got something to do with a permit for a gun.

In that bedroom of his, front room, full of sunlight, walls painted white, windows always open, no curtains, see the branches of the trees in winter, look down into the greenleaved heart of the trees in summer, hear voices from the street (he's still mixed up in my mind with sun and wind and trees), in that front room, pile of old tabloids on the table by the bed, a telephone on the table and a gun and a pile of old tabloids, dating back three or four years, and in the kitchen on top of the radiator, radiator big enough to heat all of Grand Central, and what with a coal fire going in that chef's range, and the steam in that big radiator, could be cold as hell outdoors in winter, and the kitchen like the inside of a boiler room, B. Hod wearing nothing but shorts, torso completely naked, can see him now grabbing up a couple of old newspapers from the radiator, then sitting at the kitchen table, reading them, newspapers dating back three or four years, not reading, looking at the pictures. "He don't never forget a face." Careful search through old newspapers until he found this one because Mr. Hod knew he'd seen the face before. How do I know he never forgets a face? Weak Knees said so.

It was about a permit. I was a knowitall, home from Dartmouth for the summer, just finished my sophomore year, so I knew everything, biology, sociology, history, psychology, math, everything, and I could outrun, outjump, outski, outshoot, outswim anything on two legs my own age, and damn near anything any other age, too. I was on the track team. I was right tackle on the football team. So I was always baiting Bill, still scared to tackle him head on, but always baiting him, always hunting for an opening. I tried it head on before the summer was over and he laughed at me, just before he threw me down that long flight of stairs that leads into the kitchen.

Anyway I was always looking for a weak spot, I knew I couldn't win but I was always giving the thing a whirl, so I said to Weak Knees, "Why does King Hod walk around The Narrows with a gun strapped under his armpit? He's got a permit for these premises but he hasn't any permit that says he can walk through his empire with a gun on him."

"You wanta bet, Sonny?"

"Sure."

"How much?"

"Five bucks."

"Okay. Leave it lay right there on the kitchen table. Because it's mine." Weak Knees went out of the kitchen, came back and waved the permit right under my nose. "What's that?" he said.

"All right. So it's a permit. How'd he get it?"

"He's got a friend high up in the police department who give it to him. He's the one who put all them pansy college boys on the force. They got to pass some kind of tests in Latin now before they can walk a beat in Monmouth."

"Fine. But how'd he get to be friends with a highranking cop? I thought he was the guy you said could smell a cop a mile away, whether he was in uniform or not, and that every time he got a whiff of that cop smell he had to leave fast because if he stayed around he'd try to kill the cop."

"That's right. But one time he was hangin' around New York. And he come through a street and he see a kid being worked over by a couple of cops. It was one of them side streets where the folks strictly minds their own business and they wasn't a soul in sight because the folks always moves off when a cop comes along. There wasn't nobody around but Bill and a priest. He'd a moved off too but this priest comes along. The kid's got blood all over his face and he sees the priest and says, 'Father, help me!'

"Bill's always been interested in folks' religion so he stops to see what the priest is goin' to do. And the priest he looks at the boy kind of dreamylike and says, 'Pray, my son, pray!' And goes on about his business and the biggest cop brings his stick down on top of the boy's head so hard you can hear a crackin' noise for damn near a block. The priest don't even turn his head, he goes shufflin' on down the street, even his skirts movin' kind of pious. Well, in those days Bill never give quarter to no cop. So he pours a little somethin' on the back of the neck of the biggest one, and he starts screamin' and jumpin' up and down and he tosses a little of the same thing on the face of the other one and he starts screamin' and jumpin' up and down.

"They get all mixed up with each other and forget about the kid. The kid, he couldn't have been more than seventeen, nothing but a kid, can just about walk and that's all. Bill takes him to where he's roomin' and gets him fixed up. The kid hadn't had nothin' to eat since God knows when and he had stole himself something to eat, and these big fat cops caught him at it and Bill said the thing about it that made him sore is that there these cops had worked over this kid for stealin' a lousy loaf of bread and every brokedown whore on the block is payin' 'em off, and so are the pimps and the boys who are runnin' a game in the back of the pool hall and the ones who are makin' book. When some of the boys cleaned out Izzie's pawnshop them same fat cops stayed way down at the end of the block where they won't see nothin' or hear nothin' because they're gettin' a cut on the deal. Them was the days, Sonny. These book-readin' cops ain't in it.

"Anyway this white kid is grateful. He's a good kid run into a streak of bad luck. He stays with Bill about three weeks, till he's back on his feet. He writes Bill's name down real careful in a little notebook he's got and just before he leaves he says someday he'll be able to do somep'n for Bill. Well Bill forgets all about it. After he come to Monmouth he was lookin' through the paper one mornin' and there was a picture of this same kid, he's grown bigger, and older, and filled out a lot, but it's the same face. Bill don't never forget a face, Sonny.

"This kid is way up in the police here. Bill goes to see him and he remembers Bill and asks him if he don't need anything, a permit, or anything. That's how Bill got the permit."

Link remembered feeling a vague dissatisfaction with this story. He supposed the story was true but Weak's stories always left him with the feeling that he'd left something out, something important. He remembered asking him what it was Bill had sprinkled on the fat cops, and that he had said, carelessly, "Oh, a little somep'n he used to carry around with him."

And now he handed the pinksheeted tabloid back to Weak Knees, went behind the bar and poured himself a drink and kept the bottle in his hand.

Bill Hod came out of his office, came and stood behind the bar, too. Link thought, You didn't have to come out here to check, Father Hod, it worked, I walked right into it.

"How come you're drinkin'?" Bill asked.

"The weather."

"The weather?"

Bill glanced out the front window, Link did, too. Bright strong sunlight on the snow outside. The kind of sun that you got in March, on a good day. A couple of weeks ago the thermometers at the back doors, fastened outside the north windows, registered zero, today they registered fifty-two and the sun was warm, the street was filled with women pushing baby buggies; water was dripping from eaves, running down gutters, rivulets of water gurgling down the drains, and small boys were floating bits of wood and paper in the water that collected in pools at the street crossings.

Sun on Dumble Street. Sun shining on the brass knocker at Number Six, sun on the brick of Number Six, turning it pink, sun on the dark gray bark of The Hangman, making it lighter gray, sun on the river.

Bill turned away from the window. Link supposed he had confirmed whatever his original impression of the weather had been, couldn't see that it had changed in any way.

"Are you broke?" he asked.

"Broke?" Link said. "Oh, Christ, no! I own custombuilt Cadillacs and yachts. I have them in pinks and blues and yellows and purples. Purple Cadillacs in the morning. Yellow yachts at night. Any time you want to take a cushioned ride from here to hell and back, I'll be glad to loan you one."

What to do now, Uncle George? he thought. Where'd I get that from? One of those kids next door, years back, when the Finns lived next door, before the colored folk, the dark folk, engulfed Dumble Street, in the days when the drunken riotous Finns jumped out of the windows every night, good way to live, from oblivion in the morning to oblivion at night. Money on the table. No complications. One of those kids that belonged to the Finns, weaving back and forth in the strip of driveway next door to Abbie's house, looking for new worlds to conquer, demanding adult direction, adult inspiration, as to the nature of the world to take on next, said, "What to do now, Uncle George?" Yes, indeed, what to do now, Uncle Link? What to do now? How gracefully and tactfully withdraw, retreat, because the position is no longer tenable, it is untenable and ruinous.

Don't ever leave me, come spring and the singing of birds, you black bastard, wait here in the hall.

Why hadn't she told him that she had a husband. The hell with the husband. It was the money. The hell with the money. This was just another variation on the theme. You wait here in the hall. Variation on the theme. Bill Hod and China.

Before I went in China's place he thought, remembering, I used to walk by and sometimes the door opened and it seemed to me that light and laughter and music came out of the door, spilled out into the street, yes and the smell of incense. Incense. China burned incense in the hall, burned it in a bowl under an imitation Buddha, a plaster of paris reproduction, hideous, evil, not peaceful, contemplative, but evil, as though the nature of China's business was summed up there in the hall, summed up in the Buddha. It was the first thing you saw going in and the last thing you saw coming out. The smell of the incense was everywhere in the hall. There was a heavy curtain over the door that led from the hall to what he supposed was the parlor, velvet-surfaced stuff, and while he stood there, waiting, he touched the curtain, inadvertently, and his pants leg must have brushed against it, because when he left he could still smell incense, it seemed to be in his hair, his clothes, and the Buddha became in his mind a symbol of evil, of treachery, indelibly marked in his memory along with the smell of incense. "You wait right here in the hall."

He was sixteen when China told him that. Sixteen, and school was out, and there was a whole long glorious stretch of hot sunny days and hot nights, and the river sparkling in the sun, and the trees in leaf, The Hangman so full of leaves it was like a green roof over the sidewalk, and girls in thin summer dresses everywhere he looked.

He didn't know when he first noticed that Bill was riding herd on him. But he never had chance to linger in the street, never had time to lounge around the dock, to watch, and listen to the girls who went by, walking in twos and threes, arms linked together. Bill always had something for him to do, he sent him on errands in other parts of town, or else he discovered some back-breaking piece of drudgery that needed to be done inside The Last Chance. He was forever saying to do this, or stop doing that, quit brawling in the street, stop hanging out on the corner, get the lead out.

He never had time for anything but work, work, work. And so at night, it was still daylight at eight o'clock, he'd stop in The Moonbeam, the beer parlor on Franklin Avenue; at first he only stopped in there to talk to some of the guys he knew, and to crack jokes with them about the girls who came in without escorts. But two nights running he had some beer and it seemed to him he had never felt quite so adult, nor quite so sick, as when he drank half the beer at one swallow and then laughed too loud with the rest of the guys because one of them said something funny and obscene about a fat girl in a short thin dress who sat at one of the tables with her legs crossed.

Two nights straight he drank beer in The Moonbeam and sneaked in Abbie's house afterwards, the taste of the stuff still in his mouth, bitter, nauseous; sneaked home and called down the hall to Abbie that he was tired and going to bed early, not feeling tired, but sleepy, relaxed, getting in bed early just as he said and lying there drowsing and thinking about girls and wondering what they were really like and if he'd ever have one.

The morning after the second night of beer drinking, of lounging in The Moonbeam, laughing in The Moonbeam, he was polishing the brass rail on the bar, seven-thirty in the morning, and that's what he was doing.

Weak Knees said, "The boss wants to see you."

"To see me?"

"That's right."

"What's he want to see me for? Christ, is he going to send me to the other end of town again to buy a bar of soap or a stick of chewing gum or something? What's the matter with him lately anyway?"

"I dunno, Sonny. But he's kinda mad."

"Where is he?"

"In his office."

Link stuck his head inside the office door, they called it the office, though there wasn't a thing in it but a desk and a chair and a telephone. "Weak Knees said you wanted to see me."

"Yeah," Bill jerked open the drawer of his desk, shoved a pile of papers in it, and watching him Link thought, He always opens the drawer of that desk as though someone had just yelled "Fire" and he was opening an exit door and he shoves it shut the same way, and he jerks doors open and shut the same way.

Bill said, "You stay out of that beer parlor up the street. You go in there one more time and I'll come up there and smack you all over the place just as though you were a twobit whore."

His mind jumped away from the word whore. He wondered if his face had revealed what he had been thinking about. For weeks now he had been wondering what they were like and how much it cost, and —

He said, "Oh, for Christ's sake, Bill, all the guys — "

"All but you, Sonny. You stay out of that dump unless you want to be embarrassed."

He stayed away from The Moonbeam after that though he deliberately walked past the place, slowing down so that he could look in through the open door; after all Bill couldn't very well stop him from glancing inside as he went by. He didn't intend to give Bill the chance to maul him in front of a lot of guys, so he didn't go in. And always there were the girls in the thin summer dresses, laughing and chattering. He eyed them when he passed them in the street, and a kind of yearning would come over him.

It seemed to him that this phase, this stage of his life was impossible, hopeless, and that it would never pass. He was always being told that he was too young for this or that; and too old for certain so-called childish pleasure. It wasn't just Bill either. It was all of them, Bill and Weak Knees and Abbie and F. K. Jackson. They kept him on what Abbie called the straight and narrow path; Bill called it minding your own business; and Weak Knees called it staying away from trouble; and Miss Jackson, who had no handy, easy-to-use categories for right and wrong, spoke in terms of infantile reactions and pulled her glasses up and down on the thin gold chain to which they were attached by a sort of button arrangement pinned to her flat chest.

And all the time he ached for what Abbie called the Broad

Path that leads to Destruction, the Primrose Path. Primroses. Why primroses? He wondered about that, too, and then went back to thinking about girls, girls in thin dresses, whores, whores who sat around in The Moonbeam. Wherein lay the difference? How did you find out about them?

And so finally he went to China's Place, the place the guys talked about, that very respectablelooking house that looked like all the other houses on Franklin except that the lights burned late in the windows, and sometimes the lights went out very suddenly, but other than the laughter and the music and the smell of incense, drifting out into the street when the door was opened, there wasn't anything which told you exactly what went on inside.

He walked into China's Place one evening, fairly early, around eight. China, vast, fat, yellow of skin, opened the door, looked him over, smiled at him, said, "Come on in."

But once inside she studied him, from head to foot, kept looking at him, until he was so uncomfortable that he started to walk out of the place, without saying anything.

"Baby, you're too young," she said, finally. "I'm an old woman," licking her lips, tip edge of her tongue, delicately moistening her lips, tip edge of her tongue going in and out. "I'm an old woman," she said again. "But you wait here in the hall. I'll be right back."

And he believed her. He stood there in the hall, not able to think, excitement mounting in him, excitement and a quiver of fear, and he forced himself to look at the hallway, in which he was standing, right near those dark green velvetylooking curtains behind which China had disappeared, she had pushed the curtain aside, a thick fabric, falling back in place, slowly, deep folds in it, smell of incense, a Buddha on the table, dim light in the hall, and the Buddha right near the curtained doorway, absolute silence, and he believing, waited, not thinking, just waiting.

Someone pushed the street door open, violently, suddenly.

Bill said, "Get out of here."

He didn't move. Bill walked toward him, took hold of his arm, twisted it, kept twisting it, so that he had either to bend toward him or resist him by not bending, and resistance meant the bone in his wrist would snap, he could have sworn he felt it give, and so he bent toward him, and the pain that shot up his arm took his breath away.

He said, "Don't."

Bill said, "Get out of here."

And twisted his arm again, and the pain ran up his shoulder
into his neck, reached into his spine, and he thought he's trying
to break my back, break my spine, and the dark green curtains
moved, and he saw that fat yellow woman standing there watching. He said, "For Christ's sake, Bill."

"What are you waiting for? Get going."

In the kitchen of The Last Chance, he sat down at the table,
touched his wrist, gingerly, with the tips of his fingers.

Bill came in and sat on the edge of the kitchen table, swinging one foot back and forth, and he looked at Link so long that
Link thought, If there was anything around here in reach, I'd
throw it at him.

He had said, finally, still swinging his foot, back and forth, "I
catch you in that whorehouse again, I'll kill you."

Link turned his head away, touched his wrist again, tenderly,
with his fingertips and winced.

"You hear what I said?"

"Yes."

"You better soak that wrist in some hot water," Bill said, mildly,
and stood up.

The war between them started like that, and it never really
ended. He still gave the thing a whirl, now and then. So did Bill.

Bill was giving it a whirl, now. He said, "You got somethin'
on your mind?"

"Just the human race, friend. I have complications to straighten
out with it. In New York. This afternoon."

"Any time you get tired of this job, Bud, all you got to do is
say so. You been playing footsie with it for months now. Saturday night is the night all the Dumble Street punks have to swill
enough liquor to be able to forget their troubles for the rest of
the week. We'd take it kindly if you could bring yourself to stay
around and do a little honest labor some Saturday night."

Complications, he thought. Stevedore and the lady. Prize-
fighter and the lady. Both parties white. Sometimes the rich
white ladies married the big-muscle white boys, the penniless,
body-beautiful white boys. And the marriages wouldn't work,
couldn't work, because the wenches had too much money, and the
penniless muscle men couldn't control them, couldn't keep them
in line because they didn't have anything to keep them in line
with except the good bones and the long smooth muscles, the
fighter's heart and the dockhand's vocabulary, and after a while
the novelty of the whole thing wore off, the rich white lady called

quits, until she ran across another one with bigger muscles, a stronger back.

But if you were a black barkeep, a black barkeep, and the girl was white, and a multonmillionaire as Weak Knees called the very rich, the filthy rich, the obscenely rich, something so wrong with having millions that there must always be the clearcut, clearstated word about money being dirty, if you were a black barkeep: Stud.

"As a matter of fact, pal, and come to think about it," he said, "I will be here for the late watch tonight. It will take longer to dispose of the body than to actually commit the murder."

Part of his mind parroted, I bid two hundred; look at his teeth, make it three hundred; the gentleman says five hundred; look at his muscle, look at his back; the lady says one thousand dollars. Sold to the lady for one thousand dollars. Plantation buck. Stud.

He had been in love with her, wooed her, won her, thought there was between them that once in a lifetime kind of love. He remembered the snow falling on her hair, on her face, on the tip of her nose, and that he had been filled with tenderness, with a yearning tenderness, known once again what complete and utter surrender was like, felt responsible for her, felt protective toward her, standing on that cold windswept corner in Harlem, Christmas lights everywhere, in store windows, in houses, strung across the streets, yellow, red, blue lights, and that he wanted to marry her, thinking of her as the mother of his children, thinking of a home and a continuing, enduring love, not this all at once and clearly, not clearly, incoherently, illogically, but all of it inside him when he kissed the tip of her nose, and asked her to marry him.

Bought and sold, he thought. Bought at an auction, sold again at the death of the owner, part of an estate to be disposed of at the death of the owner, along with his horses and cows. Presents. She was always giving him presents. Lisle socks, English imports, and cashmere sweaters, English imports, too, handpainted neckties, first editions, mint condition. Diamond-studded cigarette case. He didn't even know where the hell it was. Kept man. The wrist watch. Chronometer. Kept man. Stud.

He took the watch off and laid it down on the bar.

Weak Knees got up from the table. "Wassamatter, ain't it workin'?" He leaned over and looked at it. "Hey, Sonny, what's a watch like that cost?"

"A piece of your life." He pushed it toward Weak Knees. "Here, you want it?"

"You kiddin', Sonny?"

"No. You take it. I'm making you a present of it. I've got five more just like it."

Weak Knees hesitated. "You sure you don't want this watch?"

"No. It's contaminated."

"What's that mean?" Weak Knees poked at it with his forefinger.

"It means it's got 'I cost too much' written all over it."

"I don't see nothin' on it."

"Such things are in the eyes of the beholder, old man. If you don't see nothin' on it then I would say there wasn't nothin' on it. So it's yours."

"I can't take it, Sonny."

"If you don't want it, leave it on the bar and let one of the lushes palm it. Then it'll end up at Uncle Abraham's place of exchange. Where it belongs."

He parked the car in front of The Hotel, parked the long red Cadillac, custombuilt, red leather upholstery, a thousand gadgets on it, all polished metal, gleaming car, multonmillionaire's car, right in front of The Hotel.

His distaste for everything, the girl, the car, The Hotel, everything, himself included, was so great that he looked at the doorman and thought, He ought to be in a zoo, with that longtailed dark red coat flapping around his legs and that permanent fixed purchasable grin on his ape's face, grin that only changed the shape of his mouth, did not reach to his eyes, eyes keep estimating the contents of pants pockets, automatically and accurately.

The doorman leaped toward the car, like a kangaroo.

"Mr. and Mrs. Williams," he said, smiling, bowing, opening the door with a flourish. "Let me have those keys, Mr. Williams, and I'll get that trunk open and get those bags out for you. You jus' go right on in —"

Camilo said, "Thank you, Ralph."

The elevator man said, "Good afternoon," the instant he saw them, and pushed the button for the eighth floor without having to be told. Regular customers. You always know where they get off, it flatters 'em to be taken automatically and without being told, to the floor where they hold their assignation, it means a bigger, fatter, juicier tip.

"How are you, John?" Camilo said.

"Fine, ma'am. Just fine. Nice to have you back again."

The elevator creaked and groaned and sighed just as it always did.

Elevator man all smiles. So was the bellboy who practically met them at the door of the suite with all the pigskin luggage, overnight bags and suitcases, that she had bought and paid for, bellboy all smiles, too, all bought and paid for, too.

The bellboy said, "It's good weather to be in the city. Won't be long before it's spring. You both been all right?"

"We're fine," she said. "How about you, Roland?"

"I'm fine, ma'am. Just fine. My mother's all right too. The doctor you told me to get for her fixed her up good. Her back ain't bothered her since she went to him." He was still holding the bags, looking at Camilo with a mixture of awe and gratitude that infuriated Link, his eyes were like the eyes of a setter, soft, liquid, undemanding, humble.

"We can't ever thank you, ma'am. Ain't there somethin' we can do for you?"

Camilo's eyes widened. The incredibly blue, candid, innocent eyes, widening, in surprise. "Why — I — "

"We been tryin' to think of somethin', ma'am, but — "

Link said, "Okay, Bud. Put the bags down and scram."

Roland looked around for the bags, saw that he was still holding them, looked confused and put them down hastily, said, "Oh," and left quickly.

Camilo gave Link a long, direct, meaningful glance, and he thought, I've seen married women give their husbands that same kind of dirty look and you know that as soon as the door is closed, that the gentleman is going to catch hell and when the gentleman has caught all the hell the lady can throw at him, under the inspiration of the moment, the lady would really go to work on him and when she got through, the gentleman was going to wish that the female had never been dreamed up by whatever Machiavellian intelligence had created females as a means of ensuring the propagation of the species.

He picked up the bags, all of them, all the pretty cream-colored pigskin bags, and deliberately slammed them down on the floor of the bedroom, heard the clink of glass, and thought, Well, here we go Miss Multonmillionaire.

"I bet you've broken all my little bottles," she said.

"You can buy some more."

"I can't buy them here in The Hotel, and besides you're being awfully rude. What's the matter?"

She called it The Hotel, just like the rest of Harlem, easily, casually, taking it for granted that you would know that she was talking about this one particular hotel, not needing to identify it by name. She makes everything hers, he thought. Part of that easy adaptability which he had once liked and admired and even envied in her, and which he now found irritating.

She owned everything: people, cars, houses, establishing her ownership quickly; she bought bellboys, desk clerks, elevator men, doormen. Bought 'em up fast. Had bought him, too.

"What's the matter?" she repeated.

He wanted to say, I have thought of myself in many ways, called myself many things, but I have never thought of myself as the toy, the plaything, of a rich white woman. Even if this thing between us were over, ended, finished, long since dead and buried and the grass growing over the grave, even then if I had found out who you are, I would still feel as though I had been tricked, used, played with.

"Link! You're angry. What have I done? Tell me."

"You haven't done anything." He took off his jacket, took off the handpainted Bronzini necktie, the shirt from Sulka. "Come on, get in bed."

"Why are you acting like this?" she said softly.

She put her hand on his arm, and the sweet smell of her perfume seemed to come from her skin, from her hair, smell of nightblooming stock in the moonlight, smell that evoked images of females, roundhipped, globular-breasted, luminous of skin. "Tell me what's wrong," she said.

"I said you were to get in bed."

"What's the matter? Don't let's spoil what we had. It was so beautiful and so wonderful — "

"It's gone down the drain," he said savagely, and then forced her down on the bed, something raging inside him, furious now, and enjoying his fury, thinking, Everywhere, everything, even this bed, that first night we came here, the bed was the one provided by The Hotel for people who thought toosoft mattresses were comfortable, were the last word in luxury, and The Hotel knowing that these rooms would be used for assignations, for the consummation of illicit relations between males, beween females, between males and females, for rape, for seduction, sexes arranged and rearranged, mixed up, mismatched, and so charged Waldorf-astoria prices for thirdrate fourthrate accommodations, but the next night, ah, miracle of wealth, miracle of gun money, miracle of being an heiress, the next night he noticed, only vaguely of course because he was heavenbound, in a state of ecstasy, prolonged and wonderful, the bed was wider, longer, bed with no mounds and hummocks of softness, bed designed by someone who knew what a bed should be like. Kingsize bed. Sheets made to order. Blankets made to order.

Millionaire's bed.

And now, he thought, now, I will get even with you for being rich, for being white, for owning bellboys, for owning one particular bellboy named Roland, Knight of the Bags, for knowing his name, and remembering it, for knowing that the Knight of the Bags had a mother, for helping his mother with your vast unspendable unspeakable fortune.

Rape her? He couldn't.

He got dressed in a hurry, put his shirt on, knotted the Bronzini tie, yanking it, put his jacket on, the jacket she had picked out, made him buy ("We'll both wear gray flannel") in a fancy store on Fiftieth Street, and the clerks had eyed them, speculation in their faces, and word must have been passed around because every time he looked up there was another sheepfaced one standing nearby, staring, eyes round, speculative, astonishment on their faces, bewilderment, until finally, he had roared at the sheepfaced one who seemed to be in charge, "Look, mister, I'm not Public Exhibit Number One. That is not yet. Find something for these flunkeys to do, will you?"

"Where are you going?" she said.

"Don't you know, hasn't anyone ever taught you that you're not supposed to ask a gentleman who is leaving, who is taking a runout powder, where he's going?" He put his hands in his pockets, leaned against the door jamb. "So you won't waste any time hunting for me or worrying about me — would you worry I wonder — I'm going to get myself about five fast drinks, and then get on a train for Monmouth."

He went downstairs to the bar in The Hotel, drank whiskey and soda, not wanting it, kept drinking it though the stuff tasted like hell, and he felt as though he were already drunk and had been drunk for days. But he had accomplished something, he had finally achieved understanding of this bar. You have to be on the

offside of a binge to understand it, he thought. They come in
here to drink, come in here with memory perched on their
shoulders, memory pecking at their vital organs, and after they
drink enough of this amber-colored stuff, pour enough of it down
their throats, they get the critter hooded and chained as though
it were a falcon.

Hooded and chained? That toofat female over there, just five
people down from me, same color as China, same kind of skin,
yellowish, about fifty pounds lighter though, comes in here to get
a hood on the falconmemory, tell by her eyes — the whites blood-
shot, eyes swivel on an axis which eyes should not do, the good
clean line of the jaw obscured by rolls of soft fat.

The woman said, "Mike," to the bartender and pushed her
empty glass toward him.

The bartender reached for a bottle of brandy, filled the glass.
"You getting a head start, Mrs. Cumin."

"I need it."

Her voice was harsh, flat, with a forced tone, unpleasant to the
ear. She emptied the glass quickly, and shoved it toward the
bartender again, and Link thought, Mrs. Cumin, I wonder if you
know what you're doing drinking brandy at this hour in the afternoon, you already have most of the symptoms of a lush and one
of these days they'll call the wagon for you and your spotted dress
and your small shortfingered plumpfingered grubby little hands
and your small and very nice feet will enter the wagon first. Feet
first. He looked at the woman's hair, dyed a queer redbrown,
and thought of Camilo, no spare flesh and yet not bony, the hair
clean, fragrant, silkysoft, the cleareyed innocence of her.

He thought, Maybe I'm wrong. No. I couldn't be. He could
remember exactly how it went. They were going to have dinner
with Wormsley and his wife, and the conversation went like this:

Camilo: I forgot your tie.

L. Williams: Tie? I've got one on.

Camilo: Not that one. This one. I had it made for you. It
matches my dress.

L. Williams: My God! I can't wear that. I've never worn a
green tie in my life.

Camilo: But it matches my dress. And I had it specially made
for you.

Total identification, he thought. I wore white shirts when I
was fifteen because Bill wore white shirts. So I had to wear a

green necktie because she was wearing a green dress — but how could she —

L. Williams (looking in mirror, after the tie was knotted around his neck, she having knotted it): Honey, I sure must love you an awful lot to let you do this to me. I look exactly like a goddamn pansy.

Camilo: You do not.

L. Williams: Well I feel like one. Same thing.

He thought, Necktie, green necktie, made of the same stuff as a fullskirted dinner dress, or wear white shirts because the enthroned one wears white shirts, or put a black man in the family tree, like Lena Wormsley, make him up, and put him in the family tree, because Wormsley is black. Total identification — that's what he thought, then and now — now — kept man — toy — plaything —

Camilo (in the hotel, after the dinner party): I wish I was colored too.

L. Williams (no longer startled, having heard this before): Whyn't you make yourself up a black grandfather like Lena Wormsley did?

Camilo (sitting up in bed): That woman! I could have killed her. She couldn't keep her hands off you. (frowning) How do you know she made herself up a black grandfather?

L. Williams: Wormsley told me so.

Camilo: When?

L. Williams: Why the cross-examination? Oh, I see, you think that at some point Lena and I went into a huddle. No. When we two gentlemen were sitting in the dining room, English fashion, and you two ladies had gone into the good doctor's drawing room, also English fashion —

Camilo: Why did she do that?

L. Williams: Wormsley seems to be just a fat black man but he is an Englishman at heart, an English gentleman, Victorian English gentleman, at that. So after dinner the ladies retire to the drawing room while the gentlemen —

Camilo: I'm not talking about that. I want to know why that woman claims to have a black grandfather, when she's obviously white, obviously French.

L. Williams: Lena Wormsley? A black grandfather? (intoning) "Thy people shall be my people, and thy God my God: Where thou diest, will I die, and there will I be buried: the Lord do so to me, and more also, if ought but death part thee and me."

Silence.

Then he had heard the wheezegroan of the elevator outside in the corridor.

Camilo: Oh, Link! (face buried in his chest; sat up) If she's in love with Wormsley, why did she find you so irresistible?

L. Williams: Doesn't the female always take what she wants and at the same time try to hang on to what she already has? Maybe it's the collector's instinct. I don't know what it is. You tell me.

He had thought of Mamie Powther and Bill Hod. Mamie in The Last Chance at five o'clock, winter, so it was already dark, cold outside, "Bill, mix me a long tall one," warmth of a tropical country in her voice. Same train. Same train be back tomorrer. Same train waitin' at the station. Dusk, not yet dark, the light of the day fading, fading. L. Williams about to leave The Last Chance stopped and watched Powther, a small hurrying figure in his creased pants and shined-up shoes, scuttling through Dumble Street, watched him, convinced that he'd take a watch out of his waistcoat pocket and mutter, "Oh dear! Oh dear! I shall be too late!" just before he disappeared down the rabbithole.

Bill, mix me a long tall one.

Same train.

The female wasn't complicated, it was the male who was complicated. The female was simple, elemental, direct, primordial.

L. Williams: Honey, haven't you ever kept your pretty little left hand on the lead rope you'd put around the neck of one male while you put your pretty little right hand to work fastening a lead rope around the neck of another male?

She had blushed. Deep rosyred color had suffused her face, her neck. He could have sworn that all of her body changed color, turning faintly pink.

Camilo: I love you, love you, love you (silky perfumed hair on his chest, under his chin).

And now Camilo was saying, "What are you drinking?" She put her hand on his arm, and he felt himself assailed, defeated, by the clean lovely line of her, by the smile, by the sweet smell of her.

"Whiskey and soda. Want one?"

The fat yellow woman in the tootight purple dress glanced at him, at Camilo, at him again, and then turned her back, deliberately, and he saw by the motion of her hand, the backward tilt of her head that she had drained the glass in one long swallow. He heard her say, "Mike," and thought, Fat lady in the purple dress you must have had complications, too, at some time in the past, the not toodistant past. Mr. B. Hod and Mr. B. Franklin are in many ways right. There are degrees, however. Degrees.

"Not at this hour, thank you," Camilo said. Then softly, a coaxing note in her voice, "I want to talk to you, sweetie."

Wifely admonition. "Not at this hour." They can't help it. Gentle, wifely admonition.

He shook his head. "If we talk, we'll fight. And I don't, and it's funny, I don't want to fight with you and ten minutes ago the one thing in the world I wanted to do was beat the bejesus out of you. And if we go back upstairs to that, that suite — I am afraid I will forget all the reasons why I shouldn't do it. Because you will say something that will make me forget."

"Come on," she said, and took the whiskey glass out of his hand, set it down on the bar, tucked his arm in hers, and led him, unresisting, out of the bar, into the lobby.

"I see you found him, Mrs. Williams," the elevator man said, grinning, exuding friendliness.

Mountebank, Link thought, bought and paid for, paid to grin, will stand on head, will wave feet in air, will make noises like a human being for one quarter, for one dime, for one penny.

"Well, of course," Camilo said, and grinned back at John-RolandJoseph and his long line of bought and paid for ancestors, as friendly and unselfconscious as though all her life she had been looking for men, black men, big black men — plantation bucks (stud) look at his thighs, look at that back, look at his dingle-dangle — as though all her life she had been looking for colored men to whom she was not married, to whom she would never be married because she was already married to a nice young white man, as though all her life she had told uniformed monkeys who pulled elevators in rundown colored hotels, in Harlem, that she couldn't find, had lost, misplaced, a gentleman of color named Williams.

"They say that if you keep working at it, you'll always find what you want. So — knowing I'd find him, there he was, in the bar, looking into a tall tall glass of whiskey and soda." She laughed. Light, musical, gay sound of laughter. "Besides, you said he'd gone toward the bar."

All of it good clean fun. Lighthearted. Gay. The elevator man JohnJosephRoland, and his long line of bought and paid for ancestors, was still laughing, showing all his teeth, including two gold ones in the lower jaw when he brought the elevator to a stop at the eighth floor, dead-level stop on the first throw.

Having closed the door of the sitting room, he stood with his back against it. Checker game, he thought, it's your move. But there's one thing in all this that puzzles me. How can you look so innocent? How can your eyes still retain that expression of absolute honesty, of purity? Perhaps I wasn't one of a long line of muscle boys, maybe the line is just forming, and I'm only the third or fourth. Or maybe I'm wrong. Maybe you don't live with Captain Bunny Sheffield any more. Maybe you've divorced him. I wouldn't know that either. The checker games they play on the mink circuit aren't likely to come to my attention.

"I'm going to know right now what this is all about," she said.

"It's about you. You and your money. You and who you really are."

"My money?"

"Yeah. The Treadway billions or whatever the total is. I'm running out on it, or quitting, doing whatever it is that a merry-go-round does when it can't be wound up any more."

"There isn't anything I can do about the money, Link. It isn't my fault. It isn't anything I can help or that I planned."

"Of course not. You're just a fashion expert, and you work for a living, don't you? And you're in love with me, aren't you?"

"Yes, I'm in love with you," she said quietly. "As for the money, well, once people find out that I'm a Treadway, they don't see me any more. All they see is money. They either hate the money or love the money but not me. It's just like being covered with a solid gold sheet, nobody cares what's under it, because they can no longer see that there's anything there in front of them but gold."

She waited for him to say something, and when he didn't, she said, "You're doing the same thing. But it doesn't usually make people angry when they find out who I am. They may hate me but they're not angry. I don't understand that. Why are you angry? I'm the same person. I'm really and truly in love with you. I always will be. What's changed? Oh, Link, let's not —"

He interrupted her. He said, "You're not married either, are you? Just for the record, honey, why do you still live with him?

What do you do, take notes on us — for Kinsey?"

"You're horrible," she said.

So she was still married to him, still living with him.

"I haven't finished — "

"Well, I'm not going to listen to you."

"You will — " he said.

But she moved too fast. She went into the bathroom and slammed the door, and he heard the click of the lock.

He went down in the elevator, listening to the asthmatic wheezing, thinking, Even the bathroom, she could fix anything, change anything, buy anything. The water was always boiling wherever they were. The thin worn towels had been replaced by thick big ones. Nobody would believe it was the same place, everything changed, everything fixed up.

Leave it all behind you, the silk pajamas and the brocaded dressing gown, the china and the silver, the pigskin suitcases, and the television set that replaced the putinaquarter and get a neatly, exactly apportioned piece of listening-time radio, leave it all behind, the grinning doormen and the bellboys and the elevator men, the one who peddled numbers and this one of the gold teeth who keeps an apple and a pear on a little shelf, just over his head, this one who was a goddamn fruit eater.

On his way through the lobby, he stopped at the desk, to get one final piece of information.

"Let me take a look at the record for a minute, honey," he said to the girl behind the desk, girl with slant eyes and mascaraed eyelashes, brown girl wearing a crisp white blouse, very white, virginal-looking blouse, girl obviously no virgin, couldn't be.

He stood right beside her and started hunting up the record for himself.

"The guests aren't supposed to go through the account book, Mr. Williams," the girl said, standing up, reaching toward the record book.

"It's okay, honey. Here," he fished a five dollar bill out of his pocket. "You buy yourself some nylons for your lovely legs the next time you're downtown." The girl smiled at him and located the Williams' account in the record book for him, and he smiled right back at her thinking, You can buy any of 'em, they're a dime a dozen.

At the 125th Street railroad station, he had to wait half an hour for a train to New Haven. He stood on the platform, above the street, listening to the foul, noisome racket of New York, car horns blasting, roar of airplanes overhead, rumbling of passing trains, thinking, It's a wonder the people who live here don't have a continual vibration going on inside their heads. They do but they don't know it. Camilo lives here, in New York. So her head is filled with vibrations too. That's what's the matter with her. There's nothing the matter with her. It's me.

Some of Abbie's oldfashioned morality spilled over on me, a long time ago, and I'll never be able to wipe it off. Nuts. It's the husband, it's the continuing continued relationship with Captain Bunny Sheffield and with me at the same time that puts a label on me — MECHANICAL TOY. Put a quarter in the slot and it'll dance for a half-hour.

She paid for that suite in The Hotel by the month. She has been paying for it, by the month, ever since we started going there in December. I thought I paid for it at so much per day. Will stand on head, will wave feet in air. For one dime.

I used to dream about her on the nights when I didn't see her, dream that she was lying beside me, the soft warm naked flesh, the curves, the sweet, sweet curves, within hand's reach. Will make sounds like a human being for one penny.

Captain Bunny Sheffield probably dreamed the same thing, on the nights when he didn't see her.

In New Haven, he had to wait another half-hour for a train to Monmouth, and went in a bar and had three more drinks, one right after the other.

I get a little farther along in it each time I take a drink, he thought. True, Abbie's morality, some of it, spilled over on me, but the portion of it that I retained isn't exactly like the original stuff. It changed a little when it hit me. If I ever get so I really understand all of this, I'll be too drunk to know it. Mr. B. Hod is going to be voluble and vulgar on the subject of one of his hired hands showing up well on the way to being soused to the gills.

He ignored the taxis at the Monmouth Railroad Station. Taxis were for the rich, the filthy rich, the rich who had pale yellow hair and wore mink coats and cheated at cards. He boarded a Franklin Avenue car, the same car he rode on when he worked for the Valkills, those other fine rich people he had known when he was very young. The streetcar put him where he belonged, back with the poor, the peons, the poor, black peons.

17

• "I want de pretty-pretty," J.C., said. "You give me de pretty-pretty. Mamie, you give me dat pretty-pretty."

"What'sa matter with you, J.C.? Come in here waking me up like this." Mamie Powther stretched, yawned, sat up in bed, thinking, Pretty-pretty, he means Link's cigarette case. She looked around the bedroom to see what it was that had made him remember it. Sometimes she could figure out what made him remember a thing, and sometimes she couldn't. Sunlight in the room, on the rug. It was the sunlight. He had been sitting on the floor, in the sun, playing with the cigarette case, when she took it away from him.

"You give me —" he began.

She leaned back against the pillows, sank deep into the pillows. "You don't get out of here and leave me finish my sleep out I'll give you whatfor."

"I want de pretty-pretty," he whined.

"Well, I ain't going to give it to you. See? You go on now because if I have to get out of my bed to make you stop pulling at the cover, I'll wear you out. You go on downstairs and see if Crunch's got anything for your breakfast. You hear? Go on now."

He glared at her and she laughed because he looked just like Bill when Bill was being pure nigger.

"You go on now, J.C.," she said, still laughing.

"You got some Kool-Aid, Mamie?" he asked, not moving, still glaring, holding his round hard head on one side.

"I'll get you some this afternoon. You go on downstairs and get your breakfast."

She listened to the thud, thud, thud of his feet as he went down the hall. He put his feet down hard just like he had planted seeds and was using his feet to tramp them down in the ground. Kids never had any control over their feet. They clumped along just like they were clubfooted. But when he wanted to, he could walk like Bill, just like he was a cat, sneaking up on a robin, and the robin don't know he's coming until the cat's got him between his paws. She pushed the pillows away, lay flat on her back, not asleep, not awake, eyes closed, aware of the sun shining in the room, like something red laid over her eyelids.

She didn't intend to do a damn thing all day, just laze around, not even get dressed, not even bother to fix herself something to eat. She'd get herself some coffee pretty soon. Around five or so she'd go over to Bill's and get a sandwich for herself and have a drink with him. Powther would be home tonight and tomorrow night too.

But I got to get that Kool-Aid, she thought. I promised it to J.C. And when you promise a kid something he would wear you out until he got it. But a kid could promise you something and forget it just as easy. It didn't work both ways. Kool-Aid. Crunch got all upset when she saw J.C. licking something off his hand. Crunch saw him shake some powder out of a package, shake it in his hand, and then lick it off, and she had come out in the backyard, head held up high, "Mrs. Powther," she said, "what's J.C. taking?"

I was hanging up the wash and I didn't know what she was talking about and I said, "Taking?" I thought he'd been stealing some of her things, he don't exactly steal, he just picks up anything that's real shiny, anything that looks like it was gold or silver, on account of them dumb fairy stories Powther's always telling him.

Crunch said, "Does he take narcotics?"

I thought she'd gone out of her mind, and then I started laughing because he was standing there in the yard right behind her licking some of that Kool-Aid powder out of his hand, and she must have figured he was sniffing coke and he only three and a half, and I explains it to her and she looked mad and said, "Well, that probably accounts for his tongue being that peculiar bright red. I thought he had some kind of unusual disease. Anyway I shouldn't think it would be good for him, anything that color couldn't be good for the inside of his stomach."

And I got kind of mad and I shouldn't have and I said, "Well, Mrs. Crunch, I had three children and they all licked up that Kool-Aid and they're all in good health and never had no sicknesses and so I would think that would show that it don't do nothing to the inside of their stomachs. Besides if it did, it wouldn't be sold everywhere all over this country. And besides I imagine I know more about kids than anybody who never had none."

Her head kind of went down, for a minute, and then she held it right up again, and looked at me the way she always does, as though she smelt something bad, and went back in the house. And on the way to the house she must have got mad too, because she banged the door shut.

Crunch is different from anybody I ever come across. But she is awful good to J.C. I hope she never finds out Bill comes over here so much.

She opened her eyes, and laughed, lightly, under her breath. He's a crazy man, Bill is. Two nights ago he come busting in here like all hell was after him, and when he left he looked like an angel, well, a kind of wornout halfgoat angel. He was put together better than any man she'd ever seen, except maybe for Link Williams, and that only because Link was younger.

Link Williams. She still had that cigarette case. She'd forgotten all about it. It was on a sunny morning, just like this one, and she was lying in bed half asleep, just like now, and the sunlight shifted and changed, flashing almost like lightning across her eyelids. When she sat up, leaning on one elbow, looking around she saw that J.C. was sitting on the floor, by the window, the early morning sun shining on him. He's cute, she'd thought. He looked awful clean. Powther must have given him a bath. Powther was always fondest of 'em when they were still young enough to need a lot of care. Or maybe Crunch had washed him. Crunch was always washing him.

J.C. had muttered, "All gold, and the robbers came, bang! bang! You're dead, you bastid."

So he was interested in something that would keep him out of her hair, out of her way, for a long time, and she could lie in bed not moving, half dreaming. The light had flashed again. He was playing with something that glittered in the sun, flashed in the sun. What on earth had he got hold of? She remembered that she had sat all the way up, eyes wide open. He was still talking to himself, turning something around and over, holding it on the palm of his hand, then turning it again so that it glittered and flashed.

"She was all gold, all gold," he'd said.

If she asked him what he had, he'd hide it, behind his back and run out of the room. So she got out of bed and walked right up to him without his hearing her, thinking that when a kid is interested in something he's just like he's blind and deaf too. J.C. was holding the glittering object flat on the palm of his hand, and she had approached him so quietly, had picked it out of his hand so quickly, that he was too surprised to move, just sat there, staring at his empty palm.

When he looked up and saw her, saw that the glittering object was there in her hand, he let out a roar, and threw himself at her, grabbing her around the knees, clawing at her legs, so angry that he couldn't do anything but holler. Then he had said the same thing over and over again, panting, "Give me dat, dat's mine, give me dat, dat's mine."

She had pushed him away, "Stop that," she'd said. "You, J.C., you stop that noise."

She had ignored the noise to study the thing she was holding. It was a cigarette case. There was a monogram on it, picked out in brilliants that caught the light, the stones winking in the sun, flashing red, green, blue, yellow.

"L.W." she murmured. "Some woman musta give this to Link."

How did she know whose it was, right off, like that? Because she had been thinking about him, because she wanted, just once, once would be enough, to try him out. She had turned it over and over in her hands, finally held it flat, on the palm of her hand, just as J.C. had done. Then she opened it, read the fine print, eighteen-carat gold, Tiffany & Co. Not brilliants. Diamonds.

"Great day in the morning!" she'd said. "Diamonds!" What woman — J.C. had dived at her legs again, nearly knocking her off balance and she reached down and whacked him across the seat. "You J.C., you stop that. You better be glad I'm feeling good, you J.C. you, get up from there," and she whacked him again.

"Let me tell you somethin'. You stay outta Link's room. That's where you got his cigarette case."

J.C. had howled and she had leaned over to give him another whack, and missed him, dropped the cigarette case, and had to race toward it, before J.C. got it, a form of exertion in the early morning which she'd resented, and she put the cigarette case down on the bed, grabbed J.C., and held him and cuffed him.

"There," she said, breathing hard from the effort, "that'll hold you."

She remembered how he had sat crosslegged on the floor, silent, his thumb in his mouth, watching her, waiting to see where she was going to put the cigarette case, his glance followed hers as she looked around the room for a good hiding place.

"You had your breakfast, J.C.?"

He shook his head.

"You go downstairs to Crunch's. It's about time she was having herself a second cup of coffee, though it sure surprises me that she should have a weakness like coffee drinking, and she'll be feeling real good and she'll give you some leftovers. You run along now."

She supposed she shouldn't have beat on him like that, but sometimes he looked at her just like Bill, and there were times when Bill made her mad but she never'd worked up nerve enough to let him know it, and she supposed that she took it out on J.C. She had followed J.C. to the door, watched him go slowly, reluctantly, down the hall, heading for the front stairs, then she'd locked the door of the bedroom. Sometimes he moved so quiet that he was right in the room with you, standing behind you, and you never knew he was there till he said something. She didn't intend that he should come creeping back up the stairs and catch her in the very act of hiding the cigarette case. She should have taken it back right then and given it to Crunch but she didn't feel like listening to Crunch being holy that early in the morning.

Instead she had decided that some morning she'd wake up feeling so good or so evil that whatever Crunch had to say on the subject of thievery wouldn't bother her at all. So she had thought, Let's see, where's the best place to keep this until I can get it back downstairs where it belongs. Who could have give it to Link? A woman, yes. But what woman? What made me think he was going to sit around on his can somewhere waiting until I could get around to him? And was I going to get around to

him? Sure. He was ready, willing, and able and his eyes kind
of sparkled whenever he saw her, though he only nodded, very
formal, the formal nod was funny because it didn't match his
face, didn't match the devilment in his eyes when he said, "Good
evening, Mrs. Powther."

She had tucked the cigarette case under a pile of Powther's
handkerchiefs in the top drawer of the tall chest, and afterwards,
stood running her fingers over the fronts, the behinds, of the
cupids carved on the handles, smiling, liking the roundness of
them. Powther didn't like the furniture she'd bought. He
wouldn't. He liked things plain, ordinary, and she liked things
fancy, dressed up. She had glanced in the drawer, still smiling,
at the neatly rolled-up socks, gray cotton socks, black cotton socks,
that he washed himself and when they were dry, rolled them up
in these little balls. He only had two drawers in the chest. He
kept his shirts in the second drawer, shirts done by the Chinaman
and taken to the Chinaman every Monday morning, just like
clockwork, and picked up every Friday. Powther was always carrying packages, under his arm. Had to have everything lined up in
rows, everything folded, even that oldfashioned knit underwear
he wore, what'd they call 'em, union suits, even the union suits
folded up.

She'd tried to get him to wear shorts and undershirts like a
human being, but, no, he couldn't get used to the idea, he had
to wear those funnylooking things. Bill was the only man she'd
ever seen looked good in his underwear, just shorts he wore, and
he looked good in them. Link Williams would look good in just
his underwear.

Powther looked kind of like he belonged in a glass case with
a label on it when he stepped out of his pants and shirts and
stood around in one of those union suits. She always wanted to
laugh, had to swallow the laughter, because she wouldn't hurt his
feelings for anything, he was such a funny, serious little man, so
she always said, "Come on, honey, hurry up and get in bed," because she knew if she kept looking at him, she'd start laughing
and wouldn't be able to stop and men couldn't stand being
laughed at.

She had decided that the top drawer was a good safe place.
J.C. couldn't reach the top drawer and besides there wasn't anything in there to interest him. And she'd give the cigarette case
back to Crunch sometime soon.

Now she traced the outline of a bunch of grapes on the head-board of the bed, round fat grapes, then looked at her hand. I need to do my nails, she thought. Pretty soon I'll get up and do my nails and make myself some coffee, and bring it back to bed and drink it. Wonder if Powther made the coffee before he left. Sometimes he does, sometimes he doesn't. I never ask him about it. He knows I love to laze around in bed, in the morning, drinking coffee, and that I hate to get up and make it, and I got the feeling that when he's kind of mad at me, why he don't make the coffee.

It was late in the afternoon when she got up. She dressed slowly, carefully, spending a long time fixing up her face, study-ing it in the mirror of the dressing table, turning her head this way and that, thinking, I've seen better faces but it's mine and it ain't too bad. Then she took the cigarette case out of the top drawer of the tall chest, put it in the pocket of her purple coat. She liked that coat better than any she'd ever owned. It really showed off her figure, and the brass buttons dressed it up, and at the same time let you know that there were some fine breasts underneath that purple cloth.

If Crunch was out she'd just stick that case somewhere in Link's room and not say anything about it. She was only kidding herself if she thought there would be any time soon when she could hand that case to Crunch and tell her that J.C. took it, because Crunch would look at her as though she thought she smelt bad and her eyes would shoot sparks, and her back would get like she had a bedpost down it. She wouldn't give it to Link Williams because men always got mad when people went through their things, and Link looked as though he could pitch one just like Bill, he looked like Bill, younger, browner, but the eyes and the walk and the stayonyourownside of the street expression ex-actly the same.

She was dressed and ready to go out of the room, and she thought, Powther don't like to have people go through his things either. So she spent about ten minutes lining Powther's handker-chiefs up in neat piles, all the edges even, smiling and humming under her breath as she worked. "There," she said when she finished, "I bet I could learn the Army something about putting things in piles. Powther couldn'ta done a better job himself. Real pretty."

She went straight across the street to The Last Chance with

the cigarette case still in the pocket of the purple coat because she heard Crunch moving around in the kitchen, rattling pots and pans. She thought, Well, I'll get a drink and a sandwich and then go downtown and buy myself a pair of green suede shoes, high heels, open at the toes and the heels, sandals, really, and a red-and-white-striped dress, a silk one, because spring's on its way, I can feel it in the air, it's still cold but the air smells fresh, and I need some new clothes anyway. By the time I get back Crunch may have gone out.

At first glance, there wasn't anyone in the place but Bill. He was standing behind the bar looking as evil as Satan. Then she saw that Old Man John the Barber was in there too, sitting at one of the tables, crouched over a glass of beer looking as though he hated himself. He had a fixed scowl between his bushy eyebrows, and his beard always had a kind of stuckout look, as though he kept thrusting his jaw out, and so the beard stuck out too. She nodded to Barber, said, "Hi, babe," to Bill.

"You want a drink?" Bill said.

"Yeah. A long cold drink."

Weak Knees stuck his head out from the kitchen door. "You want me to put a record on, Mamie? I got a new one that'll send you."

"Sure."

Weak Knees put the record on, and went back to the kitchen.

She didn't pay any attention when the street door opened because the drink was good, cold in her mouth, slow warmth seeping through her veins, and the record on the jukebox was better than anything she'd ever heard, not too fast, not too slow, and the bird doing the singing had a sweet kind of voice, it had a lilt in it, and she wondered who he was because most of them couldn't sing, they messed a song up, but this one was really singing, it was like being in bed, stretched out, waiting, because something good was about to happen, something very good and very wonderful. Like Bill Hod.

She never looked at Bill's customers anyway. They were a rough hungry crew, not good to look at, not good to listen to, dockhands and cooks off the oil barges, hunkies and Swedes and sometimes a foreign nigger off a river tramp, an old tramp loaded down so heavy that she really wasn't safe any more, sitting too low in the water, and the guys looked and sounded as though they'd come right off a tramp, not too clean, wanting to drink fast, get a load on fast, get a woman fast. But she turned and looked toward the door because Bill's expression had changed, not his expression, his eyes, they narrowed down until they were slits, and she felt a funny kind of thrill run all through her, a kind of tingling, because she was afraid of him when he looked like that, afraid of him and more nearly in love with him than at any other time, when he got that got-you-cornered-trapped-beat-you-to-death look in his eyes. And he couldn't cover it up. He could keep his face perfectly still but not his eyes.

She turned to see who had come in through that big door that should make Bill look like that and saw a girl, a white girl in a mink coat. She was looking for someone, not Bill, because she glanced at him and then looked away, looked along the length of the bar, glanced at the tables, at Old Man John the Barber, and then toward the back. Weak Knees had come out of the kitchen and was standing near the jukebox. He started that creepy motion of his hand, and she couldn't hear him say it but she could tell by the way his lips moved that he was saying, "Get away, get away, Eddie. God damn it, get away from me." Then he ducked back into the kitchen.

This was Link's girl, the girl with the yellow hair, girl with a mink coat, the one that Crunch pushed down the front steps, and she felt laughter well up inside her, all over again, and told herself sternly, Don't start laughing again because you'll never be able to stop, you're such a fool you'll never be able to stop. Besides, why should a white girl have Link Williams? When you thought about all the white men there were for this girl to climb in bed with it wasn't fair that she should cheat some colored girl out of the chance to go with him.

The girl acted as though she were going to turn around and go out, she looked around as though she couldn't make up her mind, and then she walked right up to the bar and said, "Scotch and soda."

She drank it fast. She kept turning her head toward the window. Mamie wondered why. You couldn't see nothing out of the window, nothing but Dumble Street, the front of Crunch's house, the knocker on the door, well you knew it was there, you couldn't really see it in this halflight, even though Crunch kept it polished up like it was gold, and the front steps and the iron railing. Those steps made her think of Baltimore where the front steps were painted white, and the housemaids scrubbed them down every morning. That's what she did when she was eighteen, scrubbed down the steps every morning, and a white guy used to be going by when she was down on her hands and knees, she used to know it was him, because he'd start whistling "Yankee Doodle" when he got near that house where she worked, whistling and laughing, and she laughed, too, because she figured she looked like an elephant all turned up to the street like that, scrubbing away at steps that would be dirty before nightfall, and finally they got so they kind of talked to each other and she got tired of doing those same steps every morning, and she went and lived with him and stayed for three years.

She didn't know what made her think about him, it was a long time ago, he was a conductor on some railroad line, and she didn't even remember now how they came to break up.

The girl was still looking out of the window. Nothing to see, except Crunch's front steps and that iron railing on each side of the steps, looking at it from here if you half closed your eyes, it looked like a cock, repeated over and over, though nobody else would probably think of it but her.

"Fill it up, please," the girl said.

Mamie looked at the girl sharply, thinking, She's got half a jag on. I can tell by her voice — sounds like she'd swallowed a lot of fuzz. And she's hanging around here looking for Link. They must have broke up. She reached in her coat pocket for a package of cigarettes and her fingers touched something cold, hard, not cigarettes. What did I put in my pocket, you mean to say I come out without no cigarettes and if there's anything Bill hates it's to have me bum some from him, he's pure nigger about 'em. No, I've got 'em, a full pack. But what else? The cigarette case. She'd forgotten all about it. She was going to put it in Link's room only Crunch was home and it was still in her pocket — and she felt kind of funny about its being there, because this girl must have given it to him — and the girl was looking straight at her —

Weak Knees stuck his head out through the swinging door in the back. The record had stopped playing and he said, louder than he would have, but he must have thought the record was still going, and he had to make himself heard, "Say, Mamie, you wanta ham sandwich, like I make for you and Link, what you say, Mamie, you wanta ham sandwich?"

The girl's face crumpled up. Why she must be in love with

Link, Mamie thought, in love with him, I thought she was just fooling around with him, I ought to say something, I ought to explain about what Weak just said. He talks so dumb sometimes. He made it sound like me and Link are always in here together eating ham sandwiches and it wasn't like that. One afternoon I came over to get a drink and Link was in here, behind the bar, and Weak made a sandwich for me and Link said it looked so good he'd have one and he went out in the kitchen and as far as I know he ate it out there.

"You wanta ham sandwich like the kind I make for you and Link?" Weak Knees repeated.

"Sure," she said, and she knew that her voice sounded funny and that she had a funny look on her face. But the girl was still looking at her, just as though she could see right in the pocket of the purple coat, see that gold cigarette case in there, and Weak talking simpleminded like that.

"How much do I owe you?" the girl said.

Bill said, "Three-fifty."

"Three-fifty?" the blurred, fuzzy sound of her voice was awful. "Why — " The girl didn't finish whatever she was going to say. She laid a five dollar bill down on the bar, a brandnew five dollar bill. Bill laid the change down, almost absentmindedly, and Mamie wondered if he had deliberately selected that dirty crumpled dollar bill out of all the bills in the cash register, anyway he laid it down with an absentminded air, along with fifty cents.

The girl picked up the bill and put it in her pocketbook, her fingers poking at it, as though she really didn't want to touch it, and left the fifty cents on the bar.

She wanted to say, For Christ's sake, honey, pick it up, don't leave a tip, can't you look at him and tell he's not the kind you tip, he's got all the earmarks of being about to pitch one, pick it up, honey.

Bill picked up the fifty cents, put it in his pocket.

She glanced at the girl again. She looks sick. She looks half out of her mind. And she's pretty, she's pretty as a movie star. I never felt that way, not even about Bill. I don't think I could. He's a good guy and all that but, they all got the same thing between their legs and they're all hellbent on handing it around, one way or another, and there's none of them I've ever seen that I'd go looking for, not even Bill.

She watched the girl's slow progress toward the door. There

ought to be something I could say. Well, why don't I say it. I could call her back and tell her it wasn't the way it sounded but did the girl remember me, remember me? Fog. Fog so thick the street lights couldn't cut through it. Dumble Street quiet except for the sound of the foghorn. Crunch's front door open, light from the hall reaching a little way out into the fog, and Crunch pushing this same girl down the steps. Fog outside. Fog. Crunch pushing the girl down the steps, white girl in a mink coat, nothing under it and I laughed because I couldn't help it, laughed because of the look on Crunch's face.

Crunch was standing in the hall, in a nightgown and felt slippers and an old gray bathrobe, hair in braids, white braids, that fell forward as she leaned over to give the girl a final push, saying "Out of my house, get out of my house." And I stood there, laughing, laughing, laughing because Crunch looked the way a person would look if they woke up in the middle of the night and found a tiger in one of the beds, and then Crunch threw some clothes out of the door, and stood there, peering out, looking down at the sidewalk. Then the door slammed and the girl put her shoes on and I stopped laughing because it was cold enough to get pneumonia and the girl was shivering and shaking and I remembered how the girl's face looked there in Crunch's front hall, in the light, and I could tell she'd never been thrown out anywhere, never, not anywhere.

She cleared her throat, "Say, miss — " she began, voice too husky, voice too low in pitch to carry, voice too soft to reach the girl's ears, knowing it, even as she said it, and not raising the pitch, not increasing the volume.

So that the girl kept going straight ahead toward the door, was through the door. I could catch her outside on the sidewalk and tell her that Weak just talks backwards. Girl walking up Dumble Street now, head up, back as straight as Crunch's.

She was hopped up like a cokie, I could tell by her eyes, by the size of the pupils, by the way her mouth was trembling, everything would seem bigger, louder, sounds, smells, the feel of things, everything outsize. Light would hurt her eyes. She probably heard something in my voice that wasn't there, so she's sure I'm gone on Link, and he on me. How do I know that? Tell by looking at her, tell by the way her face crumpled up when Weak was talking about me and Link eating ham sandwiches. She believes Link and I — I ought to go catch her and tell her. Aw, she's white.

It's no skin off my back.

"Give me another drink, Bill. And where's that ham sandwich?"

They'll straighten it out, Link and the girl. A rich white girl. She don't need no help. Link musta laid it on her for keeps. I always heard once a white girl got herself a colored feller she wouldn't give him up, got a perpetual heat on for him, followed him around.

"Where's Link, anyway?" she asked.

"Canada. For two weeks."

"In this weather?" Smell of spring in the air, or maybe she just thought so because she wanted some new clothes, but it was cold out and there was plenty of snow still on the ground.

Bill shrugged. "Maybe he'll get cooled off. In a snowbank."

Canada, she thought. He must have had a heat on, too.

Bill said, "Somebody ought to tell that little white bitch to stay away from here. She's been in here five nights straight now."

"I told him," Weak Knees said. He put the sandwich down on the bar. "I said to him if a man's got to have a piece of white tail then he oughtta go live in some other country, some country where they don't give a damn about such things. Get away, Eddie, get away," he made a nudging movement with his elbow.

Old Man John the Barber gave a prefatory grunt, lifted his head, glared toward the door, "Tell her to go do her huntin' in her own part of town, Bill. Tell her to stop stinkin' up the place with perfume. Tell her to stop haulin' her long hot lookin' legs in and outta that car out in front of here. Who's she think she is?"

Mamie listened, thinking, She's got them talking to themselves just like a bunch of old women. Not one of them is listening to the other. I come in here for a quiet drink, nicest part of the day, and I got to run straight into the tailend of somebody else's hurricane and if there is anything I can't stand it's a whole lot of mess about who is sleeping with who as though it made any difference to anybody.

"What's Link doin' in Canada?" she asked. The place has a creepy feel, like being in the house on a night when it rained and you had to stay home, by yourself, for some reason, and the radio wouldn't work, and you sat around listening to the rain as it hit the windows. Creepy.

"Tryin' to break his neck on some damn ski jump," Bill said, still looking out of the window.

"What's he want to do that for?" she asked, just to keep some talk going about something other than that white girl with her face all collapsed, pretty girl, too. And young.

Barber lifted his head again. "He's just one of them young squirts that's got to try out different ways of breakin' his own neck, got to keep tryin' to find out will it break. Tell by lookin' at him and listenin' to him. Tell by all that fancy talk he does. Talks so you don't know what he means because he's still tryin' to find out will his neck break. If he keeps talkin' that stuff to me I'll help him find out what he wants to know, I'll show him that his neck — "

Mamie thought, Let me get the hell out of here before they start fighting with each other. She said, "Did you ever try breakin' yours, Barber?"

"Not since I was sixteen. You only try out different ways of breakin' it when you're young and the hookworm hustle keeps you runnin'."

"You ain't old, Barber," Weak Knees said.

"Nine years older'n God," the old man mumbled and picked up his glass of beer.

It was Weak Knees who started on the white girl again. He said, "Any brokedown whore'll give a man a better time. No complications. I told him that, I said, Name-a-God, Sonny — "

Mamie left, left before she'd buttoned up the brass buttons on the purple coat and had to button it up outside, standing on the sidewalk, wind from the river blowing around her neck, thinking again, She's got them talking to themselves just like a bunch of old women, I wish I hadn't, oh, well.

Crunch was still home. She heard her moving around downstairs, heard her talking to somebody, heard J.C.'s voice, answering her. I'll leave the case in my coat pocket and put it in Link's room some day soon, when she's out.

Old Man John the Barber had said, Who's she think she is? He came nearer to saying the right thing than the other two. I'll fix Powther something special for his supper, and where are those little devils, Shapiro and Kelly. I bet they're sitting in the movie house. Well, they got to do somep'n to pass the time.

When she lit the oven in the kitchen, she started moving with a deftness and speed that could only have come from long practice. Late as it was, by the time Powther and the boys got home, supper would be ready and the table set, just as it would have been if she had been the kind of housewife who planned her meals long in advance and stayed home working in the kitchen all day.

"Oh, Jesus," she said suddenly, "I gone and forgot J.C.'s Kool-Aid." She put on the purple coat, ran down the backstairs, laughing at herself, moving so fast that the long full skirts of the coat whirled about her legs.

18

● HE INSERTED his key in the front door of Number Six Dumble
Street, put his bags down in the hall. It was good to be back.
Two weeks on a long slope of mountain was enough. After two
weeks of snow, gleaming like mica in the sun, shadows of trees
bluepurple on the snow, wind, coldhot, like a cat-o'-nine-tails
across the face, it was good to be in a house that was warm inside,
that smelt of floor wax and lemon oil; good to be where the gleam
of a goldheaded cane, shine of a silk hat, hung on a hatrack just
inside the door, set the tone, prepared you, for the spitandpolish
look of the hall, the big curve of the winding staircase, smallscale
repetition of the curve in the legs and backs of a pair of Victorian
chairs.

Abbie said, "Who is it?" There was a tremor in her voice.
"Who's there? Is there someone there?"

He thought, embarrassed, I came in here like a homing pigeon.
I just plain forgot that I don't live here any more — not since
that night —

"It's me, Miss Abbie," he said. He went toward the sitting
room, thinking, It's all there in her voice, the fear of robbers lurking under the beds, the fear that hordes of Mongolians (though I
never knew why Mongolians or why they should always attack in
hordes) will appear suddenly at the windows, the expectation of
disaster that makes her hide the silver butter dish, and the silver
cake basket, the one with the grapes on it, if she's going to be
away from home more than an hour or so. It's the thing that

307

makes her check the doors and windows, at least three times, to make certain that they're closed and locked.

Once she lost the front doorkey and sent me hightailing over to Franklin Avenue to get Penfield the carpenter, in the hope that he could jimmy a lock somewhere, so we could get back inside the house. Penfield kept tapping a screwdriver against his overalls, as he walked around the house, trying doors and windows, muttering, "Got it locked up like it was a fort." Then he turned to me and said, "Say are you sure she's married, she's got this place bolted up just like an old maid bolts up a place." He tried another window, in the back. "Christ," he said, "anybody'd think she kept gold bricks in the cellar. Old maids keep the houses bolted up because they're always scared of rape, even when they're ninety, got it on their minds. But you say she's married. Must be she keeps gold bricks."

She was sitting on the narrow Victorian sofa, in the sitting room. J. C. Powther sat beside her. There was a card table in front of them, books and paper, a bottle of ink, and a pen, on the table. She must have been teaching him something, or trying to. What a game old girl she is, sitting there dressed up like a duchess, in that gray dress, darker gray leaves printed on it, white hair piled on top of her head, head up in the air, and a gold necklace around her neck, and that little street urchin right beside her, and she scared out of her wits but it only showed in her voice, no trace of it in her eyes.

"Link!" she said. "You'll never know how much I missed you." There was still a faint tremor in her voice. "I thought I heard somebody come in, but I wasn't certain. Ever since that night — " her voice slowed, faltered, "that night you left," she said, voice firm now, "I've been hearing a key turn in the lock. I'd wake up and think I heard your key in the lock, think I heard you walking down the hall. I'd get up and look out in the hall. But there was never anyone there. It was just my imagination. It was just that I so desperately wanted you back. I never knew how empty a house could be until you left."

She's more than game, he thought, she's one of the last of the species known as lady. She isn't even going to mention the fact that I absolutely outraged her, violated her moral code, offensively, unforgivably.

"I am most awfully sorry," he said, slowly. "Sorry about all of it. I owe you an apology. I somehow overlooked the fact that you had a point of view, too, and that — "

"I don't want you to apologize," she said quickly. "I was more in the wrong than you, or — " her voice faltered again, "or anyone else."

She still can't mention the girl. Well, that's ended too, so it doesn't matter. He leaned over and kissed her forehead, and thought of Camilo, of the perfume she used, of the silky softness of her hair, of the color of it, and didn't know what it was that had reminded him of her. Not Abbie's hair, silkysoft like Camilo's, not the clean, fresh smell of the eau de cologne she used. It's the way she sits, with her back so straight, her head up. Camilo sits the same way.

As he straightened up, he saw that J. C. Powther was staring at him. He said, "How are you, pal?"

J.C. blinked his eyes, and kept on staring. He seemed to be studying Link's throat and neck.

"I've been teaching J.C. the alphabet," Abbie said, and patted one of J.C.'s grubby hands.

"Yeah?" Link said, noncommitally, thinking, As round and hard as his head appears to be, I doubt that even you could teach him anything. He could probably teach both of us things we never knew, or heard of, or dreamed existed. What in hell does he see on my neck that makes him keep staring at it?

"Mamie say you was tryin' out new ways to bust up your neck. Did you bust it up?" J.C. asked.

"Not yet, old man." So that was it. "How did Mamie know that I was trying to bust up my neck?"

"Bill told her. Mamie say that white girl keeps lookin' for you over in Bill's place, and she say that if that white girl had good sense she'd stop goin' in there. Bill don't like her comin' in there and he — "

"J.C.!" Abbie said severely. "That's enough. You must not repeat things you've heard. I've told you that time and time again."

"It's my fault, Miss Abbie. He was working his way around to answering a question." Camilo has been looking for me? For what? Maybe she hasn't found Muscle Boy Number Four yet. God help him. And God damn him.

"I didn't finish yet," J.C. said. "So Mamie asked Bill where you was and Bill said you was tryin' out new ways to bust up your neck. Old Man John de Barber said you had to keep tryin' out new ways to see would it really bust or not because you was young. He say if he had to listen to that funny talk you do all the time he'd bust it for you. He say he can stand it days but if you was in Bill's place nights too, he couldn't stand it."

Abbie looked at J.C. and then at Link because Link was laughing. "There are times when I don't understand a word he says. It's just as though he spoke another language. What did he say that was so funny?"

"He was repeating what was said in The Last Chance when Bill Hod told Mamie Powther that I was up in Quebec, trying out a ski jump." Well now, wait a minute, he said to himself, leave us make a fast switch here because sooner or later Abbie is going to mull this over in her mind, and get on a very high horse because Mamie Powther is a patron of Mr. Hod's sinkhole of iniquity.

"Can you make an 'A,' old man?" he asked.

"I ain't no old man," J.C. said waspishly. "I kin make all de letters. But I didn't finish yet. I ain't told you what Weak said."

"Don't, old man, don't," Link said, hastily. "I'll see you later, Miss Abbie. I'm going across the street to see if I can grab a seat in a poker game."

"All right, dear," she said. "Don't stay out too late."

Come the revolution, he thought. We have blown up on our lines, or else the script's been changed. She should have said: Those poker games, that man, you get in so late, alone in the house, hear noises, someone walks through the backyard, knocks over the ashcan, you ought to wear a coat, Dumble Street not safe, people knifed, held up. So that I could say: Know everybody for blocks around, safe in Dumble Street, safe as a church, my end of town.

He changed his exit line. He said, "Do not worry, honey," and patted her firmskinned, clearskinned brown cheek. "I have few fish to fry tonight. Few and small. And they will fry easy."

He heard laughter from outside in the street, girls' laughter, gay, musical, the pitch high enough to reach into the sitting room. Abbie heard it too, because she looked straight at him as though she were asking a question.

She wants to know what became of the girl, only she wouldn't ask a thing like that. I couldn't answer her anyway. I don't know and I wish I could say I don't care. But I do.

After he left the house he stood outside on Abbie's front steps, looking at Dumble Street. He watched a group of girls walking arm and arm, heard a male voice lifted in song, caught a whiff of perfume, of aftershaving lotion. There were lights in all the houses. He saw the shadows of women, moving back and forth against the lighted kitchen windows, in the frame house next door. Thursday night. The tempo of the street was not as fast as on Saturdays, night music of the street, softer, slower, because this was the maid's day off, cook's day off, handyman's day off, so it was a courting night. Almost eight o'clock so all Dumble Street would soon be en route to the movies. Two by two. Go home afterwards. Two by two. Or like L. Williams, one by one.

The Last Chance was giving off muted Thursday night noises, too. The boys lined up at the bar were drinking lightly, companionably. They looked extra clean, extra scrubbed.

Wertham, the night bar man, a big, dark young man, lifted a hand in salute, when he saw Link. "Hi, Jackson," he said.

"Hi, Johnson," Link answered. They used to say Hi, stud, to each other. But not any more. Not since the night Camilo showed up at the bar looking for L. Williams.

"Where's the boss?"

"In the office, Jackson," Wertham said and grinned. "Peace, it's wonderful."

"Great God Almighty! What's he been eating?"

"I dunno. Could be Weak is sprinkling saltpeter on his food. Anyway, he hasn't whipped a head for six whole days. Maybe he's savin' himself for you," Wertham said, hopefully.

"Leave us hope not, Johnson. Mine doesn't whip as easy as it once did." He turned away and looked at Old Man John the Barber. The old man was playing his favorite game, staring out the front window, watching the girls go by. He said, "How are you, John?"

Barber looked at him, glared, looked away.

"Not yet, Barber," he said. "See?" He held his neck up as if for inspection then leaned over and half chanted, half sang, in the old man's ear, "Oh, de muscle bone connected to de shoulder bone; and de shoulder bone connected to de neck bone; and de neck bone *still* connected to de head bone; cry-in', didn't it rain, chil-lun, mah Lord, didn't it rain?" Saying it so fast that it sounded like gibberish.

"Ah!" the old man snorted in disgust.

Peace, it's wonderful, he thought, as he looked in Bill's office. I bet if I returned in the year two thousand, he would be sitting with his feet up on that desk, wearing a white shirt, the sleeves rolled up, the collar open at the throat, and his hair would still be black, and he'd have on a pair of brown shoes with a mirror shine on them, and the light from that desk lamp would not be on him but it would still be swiveled around so it would blind whoever comes in through this door.

"How are you, Boss Man?" he said. And moved away from the light.

"Jesus," Bill said. "I thought we'd have to use bloodhounds and a posse."

"Thursday, remember? I said I'd be gone two weeks. It's two weeks, pal. On the nose."

"Yeah. But how was I to know you hadn't broken your neck, Sonny."

"You and J. C. Powther and Barber the bastard," Link said, irritably. "Whyn't you make book on it?"

"Because I don't make book on crazy sons of bitches," he drawled. "If I did, I'd be out of business in twenty-four hours." He crossed his legs so that one shined-up brown shoe was higher than the other, shoe practically covering his face.

Clink of glasses from the bar. Voices. Snatch of song. Thursday night quiet. Peace all broke up in little pieces and strewn around the office floor.

"You hungry?" Bill asked, amicably.

"Yeah. I could eat a horse. Stewed, fried, or picked fresh right off the vine." Peace, again.

"Weak's sitting out a movie. But he's got enough filet mignon stacked up in the icebox to even take care of you. Come on in the kitchen and I'll fix it for you."

After they finished eating, he said, "Boss, you're not in the same class with Weak but you're damn good. I haven't eaten a meal like this for two solid weeks."

"I figured you were making noises like a maneating tiger because you had an empty gut."

"You were about eighty per cent right."

"Sonny — " Bill said, and stopped.

Here we go, he thought. Poppa is about to tell Junior the facts of life as they concern white women and gentlemen of color.

He was wrong. Bill reached in his pocket, took out his wallet, and counted out a fairsized stack of very pretty new bills, and laid them on the kitchen table. He watched him, thinking, I forgot that he lets every man bury his own dead unless the other man's dead happens to get mixed up with some of his dead. But he's always willing to drop something in the hat to help out with the funeral expenses.

"Two weeks' pay. I thought you might be broke."

"Thanks," he said. Gentlemen, all. "It isn't necessary, but thanks, anyway. I'll give you a chance to get it back. How about a game tonight?" They all have cures. Abbie's is a cup of hot tea. Weak's is a cup of hot cawfee. Mr. B. Hod's is cold hard cash. Mine is snow on a mountaintop. Cold, too. Maybe Mr. Hod and I are blood brothers. Some like it hot. Some like it cold. Some like it in the pot. All one-shot prescriptions are alike. They don't work.

"Yeah," Bill said, "can you get hold of Jubie?"

"I'll try to flush him around midnight. At the dock."

"Okay. Let me go break the news to Wertham that what he really wants to do is work until closing time instead of laying that nappyheaded high yaller from midnight on."

He said, "Hold on a minute, Bill. Don't do that." Maid's night off. Courting night. The high yaller would be waiting for Wertham. "Tell him to go on home and come back at midnight. I'll take the bar over until he comes back."

"You feel like it?"

"Sure. I'll go take a shower and change and be downstairs in five or ten minutes."

At midnight he was still behind the bar, talking to Weak Knees. The door opened and Wertham came in. He said, "Hi, Jackson, and thanks."

"Don't mention it, Johnson, the pleasure was all mine," Link said. "Come to think of it though I guess it was all yours."

"It was all mine, Jackson," Wertham said, solemnly.

Weak Knees said, "Sonny, you know — " and then his voice hit high C and died away, almost like a siren, the tailend of the wobble of a siren, because the door had opened again.

Link turned to see who it was and saw Camilo walking straight toward him, smiling. He thought, I'll never get her out of my blood. All I managed to do was just forget how beautiful she is. She still walks as though she owned the world, and come to think of it, she does. That's why she walks like that.

"Link!" she said. "Where've you been?" smiling, holding out her hands, reaching across Bill Hod's bar, long mahogany bar that came out of an old New York hotel, the pale yellow hair looked like silk, same kind of gleam and shine, back straight, head up, either unaware of, or ignoring the silence, the stares. Well, of course, he thought, not moving, pretending that he didn't see her hands, if you're a multonmillionaire and white, you don't give a damn what the black peasants think.

Wertham nudged him. "Here's your coat," he said. "Give me the monkey jacket."

"Okay, stud," he said. When Wertham glared at him, he laughed. "Thanks, pal. I'm going to get you over a barrel someday just like this."

He put the coat on, said, "Come on, honey," to Camilo and held the door of The Last Chance wide open. "Leave us go bay the moon."

They walked toward the dock. Both silent.

She said, "Darling, where've you been? I've been looking for you."

Darling, he thought. I've been sweetie, and you black bastard, but — darling. "Quebec. Washing the gold dust out of my hair. Off my skin." Angry again. Sorry again. In love with her again.

She moved closer to him, and he could smell liquor mixed with the old familiar smell of her perfume. You've been drinking, he thought. You're just this side of a binge, lee side of a binge. And I shouldn't have said that business about gold dust but I still react to you, and I don't like the smell of whiskey, smell of The Moonbeam, smell of The Last Chance, smell of the twobit whores, mixing and blending with the smell of your perfume.

"I'm in love with you," she said, softly. "I'm so in love with you that nothing else matters. You can't even insult me."

"Camilla — " he said.

"Don't say it like that."

"Isn't that your name? Camilla Treadway Sheffield? How should I say it? You tell me. Perhaps I shouldn't say it at all. I really ought to call you Mrs. Sheffield. I ought to say, Mrs. Sheffield, you picked the wrong man. Or did your husband, the captain, pick me out to keep you happy? I've heard of things like that being done — only among the very rich, though."

"Don't — " she said. She tried to light a cigarette, and the wind blew the match out. Tried again, and the match illuminated her face. Her eyes were filled with tears. Blue eyes. The innocence still there, intact, the lovely mouth trembling. After the match went out it was darker on the dock. The sound of the river lapping against the piling was louder, more insistent, in the sudden darkness.

"You can't stop being in love with me," she said, voice shaking, voice blurred, as though her throat were filled with tears too, "any more than I can stop being in love with you. I tried it and it doesn't work."

Her hand was shaking, both hands probably, but the one that held the cigarette was shaking because the lighted end was bobbing up and down like a buoy in the river, a warning signal, bobbing up and down.

"Listen, honey," he said carefully. "You keep forgetting that there are two sides to this. From your point of view it was just good clean fun, and it still is. You were shacked up with a dinge in Harlem, or here in The Narrows. You were rich enough to keep all the exits open, to have your cake and eat it, too. But from my point of view — "

She interrupted him and the blur was gone from her voice, there was sharpness in it and something like anger. "You know it wasn't like that," she said. "Why do you keep harping on my money? What's that got to do with it? Everything was fine until you found out — "

"Yeah. Until I found out I was just one of a collection. Back in the eighteenth century I would have been a silver-collar boy. Did you ever hear about them? The highborn ladies of the court collected monkeys and peacocks and little blackamoors for pets. Slender young dark brown boys done up in silk with turbans wrapped around their heads and silver collars around their necks, and the name of the lady to whom they belonged was engraved on the silver collar. They were supposed to be pets like the peacocks and the monkeys, but in the old oil paintings, the lady's delicate white hand always fondled the silkclad shoulder of the silver-collar boy. So you knew they were something more useful, more serviceable — "

"It wasn't like that," she said angrily.

"Wasn't it? Isn't it?"

"No. And if there weren't something wrong with you, you'd know it. We had something wonderful."

"Yeah. You had a platinum collar and a diamond leash and I had a neck. But that kind of collar doesn't fit my neck any better than the imitation-leather ones people have tried to buckle around it from time to time."

"You're just making up excuses."

"No, I'm not. I'm trying to show you how this thing looks from where I sit. You think there's something wrong with me because you tagged me for your collection of muscle boys and I stood up on my hind legs and shook the tag off — "

"Collection?" she said. "Collection of muscle boys? What are you talking about?"

"Stevedores. Prizefighters. Big-muscled chauffeurs. The he-men boys with the big muscles that the little millionaire girls lay up with overnight or for a weekend, after they begin to get bored with their husbands but still don't want to divorce them."

"You don't mean that," she said, slowly.

"But I do. You're not in love with me. You think you are because I ran out on you. And it should have been the other way around. So you're kind of frantic. That's all. Apparently I had the right build for the muscle boy role but my mental equipment's all wrong and, curiously enough, I've got the wrong kind of moral equipment, too. You know, even the white muscle boys run out on the little rich girls, eventually. Even with them the gold finally and awfully sticks in their throats."

"Weren't you in love with me?" she asked.

"Sure." And I still am.

"Well — "

"Look," he said. "Much as I loved you, and may still love you, I'm just not built to be anybody's shack job. Yours or anybody else's. No matter how you slice it, honey, that's what I was."

She put her hands on his arms, hands trembling, body trembling. Anger, he thought. No. Frustration? Perhaps. Love? No. Too much whiskey.

"Can't we go somewhere and talk?" she asked.

"There isn't anything to talk about."

He pushed her away, gently, firmly, thinking, We started here much like this, with me pushing you away. Difference in time, and in degree, of course. We have made love to each other, we have lived together, I suppose you could call it living together in that suite in The Hotel that you turned into a replica, smallscale, of course, but a replica of Treadway Hall, where you footed the bills, creating a silken bower for the silver-collar boy. I lay beside you and thought you were like a pink and white figure straight out of one of those Fifth Avenue store windows, thought, looking at you, that even sleeping was something you did completely, totally involved in it, relaxed all over, as though nothing else existed but you and sleep, you surrendered to sleep. Total involvement.

It would have ended anyway, eventually, not this soon, not this way, but even without the Treadway Gun, and the husband, the poor bastard of a husband, it would have ended because with you love is like sleep or dancing or driving a car, everything you do, you do too hard. You dance as though that was all there was in the world, you and me, the only dancers, the music playing for us, you creating an atmosphere of the dance, just the two of us, so that we had all the fluidity of motion, the matched rhythm, seemingly spontaneous, not rehearsed and worked over and sweated over, but the perfection of rhythm of a professional dance team, so that no one could say who led or who followed. Making love to you was almost like that, too.

He frowned, remembering the warm perfumed skin, the rounded softfleshed arms that clasped him, held him, the slender body arching up toward him, the absolute and complete surrender, the abandonment to surrender. It is at the moment the Treadway Gun and the husband, but it would eventually have been a matter of survival, a refusal to be suffocated, owned, swallowed up. He supposed she inherited this trait from her father, John Edward Treadway, the mild little mechanic, softspoken, dreamylooking, who set up shop in an old barn on the outskirts of Monmouth and tinkered and puttered, and puttered and tinkered with guns, until he perfected and patented the Treadway Gun just before the First World War. The story of the Treadway Gun was drilled into the students at Monmouth High School as an outstanding example of a rags-to-riches success story. American success story. The one goal. The total involvement in it.

Camilo had the same trait. Never give up. In spite of ridicule and insult and —

She said, "It's not really the money, is it, Link?"

"What?" he said, voice blank, face blank.

"It's not just the money," she said.

"I suppose you're right," he said, slowly. "It's not just the money."

"I thought so. The money's just an excuse, isn't it? It's that woman."

"Woman?" Abbie? Did she think that Abbie had ever really had any influence over him. He could see her in his mind's eye, sitting on that narrow little sofa, wearing a dress of some sort of printed material, a tracery of gray leaves on a darker gray fabric, the white hair piled on top of her head. There was something indestructible and wonderful about Abbie, impossible to live with, impossible to please, starchy, prideful, full of fears, afraid of thunder and lightning, of sounds in the night, of wind. Deeply religious and yet as superstitious as an Irish peasant. The week before the Major died, a hoot owl sat high up in the branches of The Hangman, for three nights straight, his repeated who-o-o-o-o like a moan in falsetto. Years afterwards she told him that she lay in bed listening to the owl, for two nights, and on the third night she got up and turned her right slipper over, leaving it with the sole turned up, and that she was ashamed of what she'd done and said a prayer, had not finished praying when she reached down and turned the left slipper over too, leaving both of them with the soles turned up, to propitiate the powers of darkness. Acting like a heather while she prayed like a Christian, because the turned-over slippers were a snare, a trap for the evil spirits evoked by the owl.

"Woman?" he repeated. "What woman?"

"Mamie," she said.

"Mamie?" He threw his head back and laughed.

"I won't stand for it," Camilo said. "You're still in love with me. I know you are. I'll never let her have you — "

He walked away from her, walked slowly, steadily away, and heard her footsteps behind him, heard the lapping of the river, slow, soft, monotonous, against the piling, against the dock. A clear night. Stars hung low, in the night sky. He was suddenly aware of her loneliness, and of his own, and of something else, a feeling of defeat, his, not hers. He still wanted her, but on his terms — not hers. He stopped, under the street light so he could see her face, and he saw despair in it, and in her eyes, in the down droop of her mouth.

"Don't follow me, little one," he said gently. "You get in that pretty red crate and run along home and don't come back. It's all over. Finished. Done with. If I thought it would work I'd say let's start in all over again, clean slate, just as though we'd been reborn. But it wouldn't work. You know it and I know it." I, executioner. Why do it this way? I could say I've just got back, long train ride, need sleep, have to go to work. See you tomorrow or next week or next month or just, see you later. Why this way? I, executioner.

"I'll get even," she said. "I'll hurt you just like you've hurt me." "You couldn't. It was done a long time ago. By professionals. You're only an amateur." He leaned over and kissed her, lightly, on the forehead. "Honey," he said, and he felt something like regret, "you're drunk. Lay off the stuff. It never solved anything. It doesn't even fuzz up the edges good. I know because I tried it, too." You run along now, run along and play, Link.

It may have been the finality with which he spoke, he didn't know, he never would know, whether it was the actual words or his manner of saying them, but it got through to her. She knew either from the expression on his face or the tone of his voice that it was over, ended.

She slapped him, hard, across the face, an attack so sudden and so unexpected that he didn't move, he stood looking at her, too surprised to move, and she tried to slap him again, aiming for his eyes, and he grabbed her hands, pinioning them by her sides, saying, "Not even from you, little one," and shook her and then pushed her away from him, thinking, Defeat? Are they ever really defeated? Don't all of them when it comes to the end decide to scorch the earth, If I go you will, too, if I go down I will take everything with me. Had Abbie's rejection of him been all due to shock, couldn't part of it have been the subconscious urge to destroy everything, the Major gone, she would go too, and she would destroy the eight-year-old Link, as well.

She screamed, suddenly. He looked at her in astonishment, not believing that that fullbodied sound, born of terror, came from her throat, unrehearsed, that it had always been there, waiting to be called forth, terror, outrage, fury, all there in the throat, emerging when needed. He winced, listening to her, thinking, Now I understand all of them, this Dumble Street sound is in all their throats, the potential is there, and when the need arises they emit this high horrible screaming. When the candles bee out, all cats bee gray.

I know so much about them now, he thought, I believe I could convince Wormsley that I was right. They used to argue about women when they were at Dartmouth, started doing it when they were freshmen, and by the time they reached their junior year they regarded themselves as experts, because of their vast knowledge of biology, therefore they always said the same thing:

Wormsley: Aves. The human female has the nesting instinct of the bird.

L. Williams: Felis. The human female has all the characteristics of the cat. The claw technique is congenital, it's there at birth, perfected, ready to use. The human female is a predatory animal like the cat, because the hunting instinct is congenital too. Treacherous, too. Like the panther, the leopard. She always attacks from the rear, without warning, for the sheer pleasure of it.

Wormsley: Aves. The nesting instinct is the strongest instinct in the female. They build nests, first, last and always. The other, the claws, the chase, the immorality — none of that is important. The female is always immoral. Nature makes her that way to assure the propagation of the species. Man is the moral animal. That's what makes the endless trouble between the male and the female. But above all, the human female builds nests.

L. Williams: Felis. Once the cubs, the kittens, are weaned the catleopardpanthertigerhumanfemale rejects them, tries to destroy them. Felis.

Wormsley: Aves. They build nests. It transcends the cat in them. They built nests in caves, in slave quarters, in covered wagons, on barges, in shanties. They will always be builders of nests.

Camilo screamed and screamed. He heard the thud of feet, on the sidewalk, feet running toward them, coming down Dumble Street. He stood, not moving, watching her open the expensive mink coat, watched her wrench at the front of her dress, give it up, reach inside, wrench at her slip, the lovely delicatelooking hands strong from tennis, golf, badminton, trying to tear the fabric, and the fabric not giving, the fabric used in the clothes made for a multonmillionairess not easy to tear, impossible to tear. The hands gave it up, the hands were now rumpling the pale yellow hair. Hair disordered, disarranged, but the clothes intact.

Felis, he thought. And drunk.

"Hey, what's goin' on here?" It was Rudolph, the cop, the colored cop, and Mickey, the cop, the white cop. Not safe for one cop, all alone, all by himself on Dumble Street after midnight. Two of 'em assigned to this beat. A fat white one and a thin colored one. Rudolph and Mickey. Straight from Mack Sennett, except that both of 'em belonged body and soul to M. B. Hod. He wondered what the soul of a cop who belonged to Mr. B. Hod would look like in a photograph. Scrambled like an omelet, no visible design, just scrambled.

"Wassmatter here?" Mickey, the fat, white cop asked.

Camilo was panting. Could pass for fright, he supposed, and not a mixture of spoiled rich girl who lost her mechanical toy, and found John Barleycorn no substitute.

"He — he — " she said, panting, pointing at L. Williams. "He tried — "

Rudolph looked at Link. Mickey looked at Link. "Him?" they said together, staring at Camilo, staring at Link, looking at Link for confirmation or denial, for direction. Tweedledum and Tweedledee. Never around when needed. Always around when not needed, not wanted.

"Arrest him," Camilo said. "I want him — locked — up."

Link still said nothing. Rudolph and Mickey looked confused, embarrassed. Situation impossible. Situation implausible, incredible. How take Mr. B. Hod's boy? How take Mr. B. Hod's right-hand man? How take the junior Mr. Hod to the lockup?

Ah, what the hell, he thought, let's play it all the way out. I, executioner. You, executioner.

He said, "If it will give the white lady any pleasure, boys, and it seems that it would, leave us retire to the Franklin Avenue jailhouse."

He called Bill Hod at three in the morning, and listened to him curse, and held the receiver of the jailhouse telephone away from his ear, far, far away, and said into the mouthpiece, "Okay, Boss. I'm all those things but I'm also in the jailhouse. Come on down and get me out of here. What?" He laughed. "A white lady says I tried to rape her," and he laughed again. "Oh, they did, finally, and with great reluctance, write it down in the book as attempted attack," he said, and banged the receiver down on the hook, still laughing.

It was four in the morning when he and Bill got back to The Last Chance. Bill followed him to the foot of that long flight of stairs that led from the kitchen to the second floor.

"What happened?" he demanded.

"Just as I told you, pal. A white lady said I tried to rape her." He started up the stairs.

"You dumb son of a bitch," Bill said. "The next time you decide to cat around on the dock, and get caught, don't call me up at three o'clock in the morning to get you out of jail."

"Okay, Poppa," he said, over his shoulder.

He was halfway up the stairs and Bill yelled, "Go take a shower.

Quit stinkin' the place up with that white woman's stink — with that jailhouse stink."

He looked down at him, at the white shirt visible under the loose tweed coat, at the black hair, at the young-old face. He thought, This is as good a time as any to find out if I can really knock your teeth down your goddamn throat.

"White woman's stink?" he said softly, and came back down the stairs. "Is Mrs. Powther's any sweeter, friend?"

Bill looked at him with murder in his eyes, on his face, in the thinlipped mouth, and then turned away, went out of the kitchen, toward the bar.

He waited at the foot of the stairs, waited for him to come back with an appropriate weapon, meat axe, or jagged end of bottle, and heard the front door close, and then nothing but silence. Mr. Hod had gone out. He obviously did not intend to come back with knife or gun. Come to think of it, he didn't have to hunt for a gun, he's got one on him. Maybe Wertham was right. Weak's been tampering with Mr. Hod's food.

He sat down on the side of his bed, upstairs, in that big bare-looking bedroom in the back, took off his shoes, held one of them in his hand, thinking suddenly of the Italian shoemaker who used to chalk "Negre" on the soles of his shoes when he took them to be repaired. "Negre" chalked on the old worn leather. He was ten years old then. And he'd go back for the shoes, with reluctance, never mentioning that chalked word to anyone, rubbing it off, once he got outside the shoemaker's shop, hating Abbie for insisting that shoes be resoled when the soles were worn.

Once he took a brandnew pair of shoes to the Italian, to have rubber heels put on them, because Abbie said the rubber heels wore better and when he went to get them, there was the word "Negre" chalked this time on the new yellowbrown soles. He remembered the smell of wax, of shoe polish, remembered the dusty look of the big old machine that the shoemaker used, remembered his bent back, the curve of his back, the lined face, the calloused brown hands, the heavy accent, remembered wondering by what right that bentover man had labeled his shoes, like that, remembered thinking, Even my shoes, separated from the others, clearly marked: shoes of a black.

Not too long after that Mr. B. Hod and Mr. W. Knees, started re-educating him on the subject of The Race. Part of the education of L. Williams.

He finished undressing and got in bed, and lay flat on his back, staring up at the ceiling, thinking, Maybe there's something wrong with me. What did she say? "There's something wrong with you." Something wrong with me. Why wouldn't I take her on her terms? Why did it have to be all or nothing? Muscle boy. Shack job. Mechanical toy. Stud. Fine. Keep saying all those words over and over. Keep saying, Everything she does she does too hard. Keep saying, Total involvement, Swallowed up, Suffocated, Strangled. Keep saying, Would have ended anyway, eventually. Say all of it, over and over. Fine.

Yeah, I can keep on saying all those words and yet I will never be able to forget her, will never get her out of my mind. Any more than I ever was able, wholly, to forget China, so too, I will never forget Camilo. I will be haunted by her. The ghost never laid. Not waiting for midnight. Any hour will do. Not haunting any special place. Any place will do.

I will hear the asthmatic wheezing of an old elevator, or catch a glimpse of a young woman with pale yellow hair, or walk too close to Abbie's border some night in August when the night-blooming stock is perfuming the air, or smell a perfume like it, and the ghost will walk again.

The trouble with me is — he thought, and grinned, remembering the summer he hauled ice for Old Trimble. Old Trimble hauled ice in summer, and hauled junk in winter, and summer or winter, growled and grumbled all day long, sucked on a toothpick, all day long. The summer I worked for him he kept saying, "The trouble with boys is they fathers don't break enough sticks over they backsides — " and I kept thinking, The trouble with me is a man who isn't my father tried to kill me. Because that was the summer I was sixteen, the summer I stole F. K. Jackson's gun because I was going to kill King Hod because he caught me in China's place again, and, justifiably, from his point of view, and, justifiably, according to his theory of educating a young male, damn near beat me to death.

All part of the education of one Link Williams. A longdrawn-out affair. Can now include Camilla Treadway Sheffield as part of the process, the finishingoff process. Can now say that I have taken the advanced course in the graduate school.

No one in the USA free-from — free from what? Leave it lie. No one in the USA free (period period).

Weak and Mr. Hod? Hardly. Hod hardly. Mr. B. Hod *in loco*

parentis. Parents: blank space. *In loco parentis* write Mr. B. Hod. Preliminary course in The Race: under Miss Abbie. I failed that one but got an "A" under Mr. Hod and Mr. W. Knees.

Advanced courses: had had various advanced courses. One of the best under old Bob White, Robert Watson White who taught history in Monmouth High School. He had an absolute passion for history. Passion like a transmitter, always some kind of response to it. Even the dimwits had responded to Bob White. Even a dimwit would respond to Mrs. Bunny Sheffield.

Bob White had a lowpitched voice, and knew how to use it, and so could make you feel as though you had been there when the Stars and Stripes went up over Fort Sumter, because he read an eyewitness account of it: "And then we gave a queer cry, between a cheer and a yell; nobody started it and nobody led it; I never heard anything like it before or since, but I can hear it now."

I felt as though I had been running and couldn't get my breath back when Bob White read those words, one afternoon, in the history class, last class of the day.

"But I can hear it now." Can hear the voice of the gun heiress now, light voice, sweet voice, musical voice, "Don't ever leave me — don't ever leave me." Time passes. The year turns. And the same voice says, "I want him locked up — "

Write it off as part of the education of Link Williams.

L. Williams took the graduate course on the subject of The Race, under Bob White, not meaning to, not wanting to.

I was fifteen then, a junior in High School, Monmouth High School, and one afternoon Bob White stopped me as I was about to leave the classroom, said, "I want to talk to you, Williams," then said, "Pull up a chair," then said, "I've noticed that you wince, fidget, get upset, every time I mention the subject of slavery." Said it suddenly, bluntly, with no warning.

Then he handed me three large books and one small one, and a notebook. He said, "Once a man knows who he is, knows something of his own history, he can rid himself of selfdoubt, of belittling comparisons. This is a special assignment. You have three months in which to complete it. At the end of that time I shall expect a monograph from you on the subject of slavery in the United States."

I picked up the books and they were heavy as all hell and I walked out of the room, and the sound of his voice followed me. He said, "This assignment should cure you of any further embarrassment on the subject."

I walked along the street, carrying those damn books, swearing that I'd never open them, never return them. Instead of going straight to Abbie's house, I stopped in the kitchen of The Last Chance. Weak was sitting at the kitchen table drinking a cup of coffee. Bill was reading a newspaper and Weak said, "Name-a-God, Sonny, what's in them big books? You'll be gradiated from the high schools and finished from the colleges, before you finish 'em."

I said I'd be through in three months and Bill stared at me and said, "Three months?"

Education of one Link Williams rested at that moment on chance, on fate, on the turn of the wheel. And the wheel turned, because I said, "Sure," boasting, trying to impress Bill with my ability, my superior knowledge.

Bill said, unimpressed, "Want to bet?"

So it was cigarettes against a desk. And the payoff date was marked on the calendar, a big calendar, new one sent out every year by some packing company in Chicago, brilliantly colored picture of a couple of heavyweights mauling each other in the ring, same picture every year, hanging on the wall near the stove. Fifteenth of January marked on the calendar, recorded there as the payoff date.

October to January of the year I was fifteen I read all the time, and went to school, and kept up in all the rest of the stuff, played football, and as the fall turned into winter, played basketball. Can remember reading during the lunch hour, gulping the food down, book propped up on the table against the water glass, and Abbie staring at me, frowning at me, finally asked what I was reading and why I was reading at the table.

When I explained that I was making a rather specialized, but very brief, study of slavery and the Civil War, she looked even more disapproving. Her frowning disapproval spurred me on. It was a race against time but I told myself I'd win it. There wasn't literally, wasn't enough time to win in, but I'd win anyway.

And I did. I handed the finished paper to Bob White on the morning of the fifteenth of January. And said, "Could you read this sometime today, Mr. White? And give me a letter or just a note, that I can show to a friend of mine, so he'll know I read these books in three months' time. We had a sort of bet about it."

He still had the letter somewhere, knew some of its phrases by heart because it was the first time anyone, other than Weak, had ever praised him, wholeheartedly, no reservations, no if's: "a flare for history," "What amounts to genius," "you write with eloquence and yet simply and clearly," "heartiest congratulations," and then, "finest monograph ever written by one of my students during the ten years I have taught history in this high school."

All part of the education of Link Williams.

When he returned those books to Bob White, he had felt self-conscious, awkward.

Bob White said, "Did you win your bet?"

"Yes, sir."

"I'm curious. What did you win or rather what were the stakes?"

"A carton of cigarettes against a desk." Bob White had looked blank and he said, "If I'd lost, I would have bought my friend a carton of cigarettes. He smokes Camels." Unnecessary piece of information, and it sounded as though Bill was a chain smoker and he wasn't, and it wasn't what he wanted to say, but he didn't quite know how to put it, and then blurted it out. "I didn't intend to read those books, Mr. White. But my friend was so — well, he said I couldn't do it, not in that length of time. A couple of times I didn't think I'd make it. But I did. And then you wrote the letter and now I've got a desk — a real desk."

And still had it. The same desk. It was that good. He had thought about it, while he was standing there talking to Bob White. The drawers worked like they were oiled, and the top was covered with dark red leather, handtooled along the edge, and the smell of it was wonderful, a clean, new, leathery smell, like new shoes, and he ran his fingers over the surface every time he went near it, sheer pleasure in the feel of it, smoothsoft.

Bob White had said, "A desk," thoughtfully. "I thought you were going to say a tennis racket or a set of golf clubs. But you're too young for golf. A desk. I see."

"Are you going to college?"

"I want to."

"I went to Dartmouth. It's one of the best. Not too big. Not too small. Superior faculty."

"Is it expensive?"

"All of them are," Bob White had said. "But there are scholarships. What do you plan to do after you finish college?"

"I don't know, sir. I'm pretty good at chemistry."

Bob White pushed three more big books toward him. "Don't hurry with these. Take your time."

That winter he lost interest in chemistry. He stopped carrying out the experiments that had made Abbie turn up her nose and say, "Those horrible smells. I don't think it's safe. Anything that smells like that couldn't possibly be safe."

Further education of Link Williams completed by Miss Abbie. King Hod and Miss Abbie. What a combination. Have to include Weak Knees and F. K. Jackson. And Bob White. And an heiress.

Go back to Miss Abbie's final part in the education of L. Williams.

Dust settled on the test tubes and the Bunsen burners and the beakers and the little bottles of acid and alkali, on the packages of chemicals and the filter papers. Abbie complained because he didn't go near the small laboratory he'd set up in the cellar.

"All that expensive equipment," she said. "Don't you use it any more?"

"I haven't had time lately." An evasion. He didn't want to tell her that he was no longer interested in chemistry, that he spent every penny for history books.

"Why not?"

"I've been reading history books."

"They don't have anything to do with medicine."

"I'm going to be a historian."

She was startled into silence. Then she said, "I thought you were going to be a doctor."

"I changed my mind."

"Oh, Link! One minute you're going to be a doctor, and you litter up the house with bandages and splints and borrow books from Dr. Easter and don't return them —"

That was when he was fourteen.

"Then you're going to be a cook, and you waste flour and sugar and butter and eggs and burn things up —"

That was when he was eleven. He had burned things up, sure, but he was a better cook than Abbie would ever be.

"Then you're going to be a chemist and for weeks the house is filled with the most horrible smells and I don't know how much money you spent for all those little tubes and bottles and packages and now it's history —"

Everywhere she looked, in his room, there was evidence of the change in the direction of his thoughts, his desires; the notebooks, the growing line of books on the bookshelves, indicated it clearly. History books. He'd been buying them brandnew until

Bob White found out, and gave him the address of a place in New York where he could get them secondhand for one-third the price of new ones. The shelves were filling up faster and faster. Abbie didn't like the room anyway, never would like it. It was an offensive comment on her taste in decoration, and it was due to Bill Hod's interference, because the room had to be done over to get the desk in. She always looked around with an air of disdain. The black walnut bedroom set had been discarded and the Brussels carpet taken up, and this barelooking room was the result, all bookcases and desk and peculiarlooking bed with no headboard or footboard.

He didn't listen to what she said because he'd heard her preach this sermon before. He caught a familiar phrase here and there: "inability to stick to anything," "Negroes are incapable of concentrating on a long-term objective," "constantly changing jobs, changing moods."

Then her voice went up in pitch, grew louder, caught and held his attention. She said, "Whoever heard of a colored historian?" Head up. Eyes flashing with anger.

He was bewildered and hurt in a funny kind of way. He had looked at her thinking, Why should you who are colored try to destroy me, discourage me, and why should the history teacher who is white, encourage me, keep telling me I can do this thing? Why do you want to hurt me? How can you say that and then turn around and quote your father, "The black man can do anything if he sets out to do it, if he's willing to work at it, night and day, can do anything, can do anything."

All right, he thought, I will do the impossible. I will be the impossible. Because of you. I wasn't certain I could, I had doubts about it, but not any more. It's like those books Bob White handed to me, that I never intended to read, and if it hadn't been for Bill's amused, I-knew-it-all-the-time, gambler-betting-on-a-sure-thing, fifteenth-of-January-ha-ha-ha attitude, I would never have read them, never have written the paper.

When he went to Dartmouth, he majored in history. He thoroughly enjoyed the closed off, artificial, kindly, paternal world that composed that particular college. His faculty advisor approved his choice of a career, praised his ability, took it for granted that he would be what he wanted to be.

After four years of Dartmouth he ended up with a Phi Beta Kappa key, the Major's diamond stickpin and the Major's solid gold watch, and a brandnew Cadillac, special job, that had never belonged to anyone else. "Mark of esteem, Sonny, I didn't think you'd make it."

In less than two months after he graduated, he was in the Navy. After four years in the Navy, Abbie no longer loomed on his horizon like a dreadnaught. Didn't loom at all. When he was discharged, he headed for The Last Chance.

Weak Knees said, "Boss, Boss, Boss, come quick. Sonny's back. Sonny's home," and his eyes were filled with tears.

"Jesus Christ," Bill said. "What'd they feed you? You look like Louis the night he knocked out Carnera," and patted his shoulder, grinning at him.

Not too long afterwards he told Bill that he wanted a job.

"Yeah?"

"Here. Days. Behind the bar."

"Why here?"

"Because like everybody else, I have to earn a living but I don't want to have my mind all cluttered up with somebody else's business when I sign off for the day."

He didn't tell Abbie that he was working on a history of slavery in the United States, and therefore found it convenient to work for Bill Hod because the pay was good, and the hours were short, and that nowhere else would he have so much leisure in which to do the necessary research for the books he wanted to write. He simply said that he had taken a job as day man behind the bar in The Last Chance.

Abbie went off just like a firecracker. He had grinned at her, enjoying the expression of outrage on her face, the crackle in her voice.

"A bartender? What did you go to college for? It was a waste of time and money. A bartender — in that place?"

Off and on ever since.

Everything was fine until that night the fog spewed a girl with pale blond hair smack into the middle of his life. Even now I'm not sure that I was right. Maybe she was in love with me. Maybe I know too much about the various hells the white folks have been cooking up for the colored folks, ever since that Dutch man of warre landed at Jamestown in 1619 and sold twenty "Negras" to the inhabitants, just as though they were cows or horses or goats, to be able to accept a gift horse, even if it was a palomino, without a microscopic examination of the teeth.

Blame it all on China, with her tremendous buttocks, and big breasts, the layers of fat under the smooth yellow skin of the arms and throat, and the skin on the face not the same, swarthy, coarse-pored, and the hair not gray but brown and probably would be until she died. She couldn't say, Run along, kid, or you'll get in trouble. Not even that second time when I went back anyway. It took me about six months to figure out that she called Bill up both times and told him I was there. She couldn't say, Kid, Bill owns a whole string of whorehouses and this is one of them, couldn't say, Bill owns a whole string of whores and I am one of them, so you run along. No. She said, Wait right here, and went and called up Bill and then stood in the doorway and pushed that dark green curtain aside when she heard him come in so she could have a front row seat from which to view the kind of trouble I was in.

Come spring and the time of the singing of the birds, and the Treadway Gun and the black barkeep will be united in the bonds of holy matrimony. I believed that one, too.

You wait here in the hallway.

You black bastard.

I should have laid one on her jaw — for luck.

19

● Malcolm Powther laid a copy of the *Monmouth Chronicle* down flat on one of the long wide counters, under the cupboards in the butler's pantry, placing it there as carefully as if it had been an old illuminated manuscript. Putting on a pair of hornrimmed spectacles, he leaned over the paper, one elbow resting on the counter, and using his forefinger as a guide, went down one column and up the next, in a rapid scanning of the front page.

His posture, the hornrimmed glasses, the quick co-ordinated movement of finger and eyes gave him the appearance of a middle-aged accountant who was rapidly reviewing the financial report of a bank. His clothing would have been suitable for such a role, too: the sharply creased trousers, starched white shirt, carefully knotted black necktie, highly polished black shoes suggested conservatism, neatness. Even though he was alone in the pantry, he was wearing a coat.

When he finished with the front page, he straightened up for a moment, thinking that the news didn't vary much from day to day, from year to year. There was a stalemate in the war in Korea. The Democrats were peevishly blaming the Republicans for the state the country was in; and the Republicans were peevishly blaming the Democrats for the same thing. As far as he was concerned, this was just another case of the pot calling the kettle black; but political parties preferred to hurl the words venal and stupid at each other. Another airliner had crashed in the Midwest, in a mountainous area, which was only to be expected. After all, it was March and high winds and big snowstorms made flying hazardous. And that bony lady manufacturer whom the Madam had entertained at a dinner party last fall, the night Captain Sheffield made a scene at the table, was still waging her private war with the Treasury Department. He doubted that he'd ever get the details of it straight in his mind, but a story about her was always featured somewhere in the *Chronicle*.

He turned the page, slowly, carefully, because this was the Madam's copy of the paper, and he prided himself on the delicacy with which he handled it, intending to go up and down the columns again, just as he had on the front page. But a story far over to the right on page two seemed to come at him, leap at him, so that he began reading it at once, not reading, absorbing it, frowning, not believing it.

He read the story again, his mouth slightly open, the frown deepening between his eyebrows. A mistake, he decided. A stupid mistake. The newspaper had transferred Miss Camilo's name and her New York address, from some other story, so that it appeared here in this short item where it did not belong. Mistakes like this happened so often in newspaper offices that he was convinced they were due to malice rather than carelessness.

Having finished with the first section of the paper, he refolded the whole thing. The second section wasn't worth bothering with. There was never anything in it but sports news and inch-high stories about Ladies' Aid meetings and church suppers, accounts of weddings and funerals that had taken place in the little towns all over the state.

He placed the *Chronicle* on top of the *New York Times* on the Madam's breakfast tray. When the Madam got through with the newspapers they would be carefully folded, the pages all in order, as they were now, but after Rita, the Madam's personal maid, read them, they would look as though they had just blown in from the city dump, crumpled, the pages mixed up.

How could he most effectively annoy Rita on this gray, windy morning? She couldn't keep the resentment out of her eyes, her face, when she saw the Madam's breakfast tray. He enjoyed varying the china, the silverware that he used. Yesterday had been warm, so he'd used the Lowestoft because it had a cool, fresh look. But this cold morning called for warmth. He decided that the English bone china with the rose-colored decorations would offer a cheerful contrast to the weather. And there were just two white roses in the icebox, and he'd put them in a small crystal and silver vase, and he'd use some of that thin finely woven Belgian linen, not white but cream-colored, the napkin and place mat embroidered in white. A combination that should make Rita's nose go straight up in the air, as though she'd received a personal affront.

What a pity that Miss Camilo's name should have appeared in the paper like that, he thought, as he plugged the percolator in. She had been staying at the Hall for the last two weeks, dining with the Madam every night. He didn't think she was very well. She was too quiet, almost depressed, and drinking more than any young lady should. Just recently he had noticed that when she wasn't smoking a cigarette, or holding a glass of liquor, her hands were clenched tight, the fingers enfolding, covering the thumbs. It had startled him when he noticed how her thumbs were enclosed by the fingers, because that was a sign of a depression deep enough to be interpreted as a death wish in a grownup. When he saw the telltale position of the thumbs, he decided that her lover had left her, though he could not imagine how or why it could have happened.

Picking up the *Chronicle* again, he laid it flat on the counter, turned to page two, and reread the story. The Captain was in New York, so he wouldn't see it. The Madam wouldn't necessarily see it, and even if she did, she would recognize it for what it was — a mistake in the name and address.

It was a queer story. Link Williams, twenty-six-year-old Negro of Number Six Dumble Street, had been accused of attempted attack by a Mrs. William R. Sheffield of Park Avenue, New York City. Incident occurred at the corner of Dock and Dumble Street, about midnight. Names of the arresting officers. Link Williams out on bail. That predatory young nephew of Mrs. Crunch's must have been drunk or temporarily out of his senses, to attack a woman, almost on his own doorstep.

Sometimes he and Mamie tried to figure out, just from a short item like this, what had really happened, just for the fun of it. That is, when life was normal and she wasn't on a diet, and the house was a comfortable, warm place to be in, and she was laughing and singing and telling jokes. Though he basked in this after-supper warmth and gaiety, he was uneasily aware that Bill Hod's visits had a direct connection with Mamie's obvious sense of well-

334

being, but not dwelling on it because it was better not to. She didn't do much reading but she liked a magazine called *True Crime*, and she was quite clever about figuring out ways in which a crime might have been committed. She was always saying that the way a detective solves a crime is to make himself think like somebody else, put himself in somebody else's shoes. She knew a lot about it because she was always going to movies that had to do with murder and detectives. She couldn't stand the ones that had to do with love.

He'd try to figure this story out by pretending that he was an average reader of the *Chronicle*, say a bank clerk, riding to work on the Franklin Avenue trolley. Bank clerks were about the only ones who rode on trolleys. What would he make of it?

I'd read it again because I would be puzzled by it, intrigued. How did this woman who lived on Park Avenue, in New York, richest street in the world, most expensive place to live, come to be walking about on Dock Street, at midnight? Park Avenue meant wealth, penthouses, liveried servants, elegance. Dock Street at the corner of Dumble meant poverty, colored people, tenements, whether you called it Dark Town, Little Harlem, The Narrows, or The Bottom.

Perhaps she was driving through Monmouth, en route to New York, stopped to ask for directions, and this young Negro immediately attacked her. But how could he attack a woman sitting in a car, engine running, he standing on sidewalk, woman leaning out of car, window down, "Could you tell me —"

Undoubtedly the woman got out of the car. It's a lonely street, Dock Street, at midnight. It was the kind of street you stumble into in a dream, a street that runs parallel to a river, and you're always falling when you reach a street like that in your dreams, you know there's a river nearby though you can neither see it nor hear it, and you keep falling, falling, falling, toward the river. The lights are so few and far between that they can't penetrate the darkness, they only serve to make the street longer and darker than the inside of a nightmare, and there's never any traffic, nobody walking by.

So this woman, this stranger from Park Avenue, got out of her car and asked directions of the first passer-by, who happened to be Mrs. Crunch's unscrupulous young nephew, and he immediately attacked her.

Nonsense, he thought. Besides I've accepted the Park Avenue

part of this story as being correct. But so would a bank clerk. He would not know that Mrs. William R. Sheffield's name and address appeared erroneously in the story; nor would he know that Camilla Treadway Sheffield and Mrs. William R. Sheffield were the same person.

Having replaced the *Chronicle* on the Madam's tray, he unplugged the percolator and busied himself making toast, squeezing oranges. He couldn't waste any more time puzzling over this conundrum. This was one of his busiest days. They were having a tea, a high tea, in the afternoon, for three hundred young women from the plant.

It would have been understandable if the Madam had said, They're just little working girls, anything will do, just the fact that they're asked out here for tea is enough, no need to fuss, give them some little sandwiches and small cakes and that will do very well. But she didn't. That first year he worked for her, she had told him that this annual tea was to be handled with as much care as though they were having the President of the United States in for tea, well, any of the presidents before Roosevelt.

Under his direction it had become more than tea, it was a kind of open house, which called for the best silver and china and the finest napkins, oak logs burning in the fireplaces, two waiters from the Monmouth Hotel to help keep the service smooth, and honest-to-goodness food: sandwiches with wonderfully flavored fillings — chicken, anchovy, cheese, lettuce, pâté; toasted muffins accompanied by slivers of Virginia ham; bitesize cakes as well as loaves of cake, candies, mints, salted nuts — all of this set out in the dining room.

At seven-thirty when Rita came into the butler's pantry, he was rubbing up the trays that he was going to use that afternoon.

"Good morning, Mr. Powther," she said, yawning, patting her hair, giving the small pleated apron she wore a kind of jerk, as though she'd like to take it off.

"Good morning, Rita." She looked sleepy and so her clothing didn't sit properly on her. The white dress was clean, unrumpled, but because she was sagging with sleep the uniform sagged too. Lately she'd been having an affair with Al of which Powther disapproved. She didn't keep her mind on her work any more. Right now she was leaning over the sink, staring out of the long window, in hope she'd catch a glimpse of Al as he came toward the house for breakfast.

He started to say something to her about the unfortunate mixup in names in the paper, but didn't. She was much too fond of gossip, especially if it concerned the family. She was about twenty-five pounds heavier than the Madam, and so couldn't wear her clothes, always a source of irritation to a personal maid. As a result, she constantly disparaged the Madam. Al did the same thing but he went in for an all-inclusive largescale vulgarity, that not only included the Madam, but the house, the other servants, the garage, the cars, everything. Rita went in for a highly personal, smallscale cattiness directed exclusively at the Madam.

"She's in her bath," she said, turning away from the window. She opened her eyes very wide, as she always did whenever she was about to say something unkind. She had large brown eyes, and the sudden widening of them underlined, pointed up whatever she said.

"She can get in and out of a bathtub faster than anybody I've ever seen. I don't think she's clean. In one minute and out the next — "

"You'd better run along then," he said coldly. "Or the coffee will be cold."

She picked up the tray, and he held the door open for her. He was quite near her when she looked down at the tray, really looked at it, and he saw sullenness, resentment come into her face, changing it, as though a mask had been placed over it.

"Roses," she said, a sneer in her voice. "White roses! I suppose she'll be wanting them pinned on that mink coat when she leaves for the plant."

"They should look very well on it," he retorted, thinking, You'll feel more spiteful than ever when you get your first look at the downstairs part of the house this afternoon. Rita was pressed into service, taking care of coats, under Mrs. Cameron's direction, and he always judged the degree of perfection he had achieved by the quick resentment that came into Rita's face when she looked around.

By eleven o'clock he felt that the entire downstairs had the burnished look of a house ready for a high tea. Rita would not know that a week's work had gone into the making of the gleam and shine that included windows, the fine wood of the furniture, the floors. Rogers had sent his men over with oak logs for the fireplaces, had personally delivered daffodils and tulips from the greenhouse, and had included some of the poets' narcissi because of their wonderful fragrance.

He had persuaded Rogers' men to help Jenkins move a pair of sofas and ten Sheraton armchairs from the morning room upstairs down into the entrance hall, in order to increase the amount of sitting space. The east drawing room was as big a room as he'd ever seen but three hundred people could not possibly find seats in it. There was always a moment, about five o'clock, when all three hundred young women were drinking tea at one and the same time, no matter at what hour they had arrived.

After he finished arranging the flowers, he went toward the kitchen for a second cup of coffee. He would have to drink it quickly because he still had a lot of details to work out with Jenkins, but he hated to miss the midmorning coffee that the Frenchman made especially for him and for Al.

It never failed to amuse him to watch the transformation that took place in Al when Mrs. Cameron came into the kitchen. Al would be lounging in the doorway, coffee cup in hand, chauffeur's cap on the back of his head, and at the sight of Mrs. Cameron, he snatched his cap off and stood up straight. Like any firstclass housekeeper, she could be very sharp on the subject of what she called disrespectful behavior, and could, by a skilful choice of words, make Al take on the appearance of an overgrown schoolboy being sharply reprimanded by the teacher, face red, head hung down.

He pushed open the swinging door between the butler's pantry and the kitchen, and then stood still, shocked into stillness. He was totally unprepared for what Al was saying. It had never occurred to him when he was pretending that he was an average reader of the *Chronicle* that there was still another angle, another way in which people would react to that story about Link Williams.

Al was saying, "You don't believe me, huh? Well, then, what was she doin' on the dock in Niggertown, at three o'clock in the mornin'? Just like she was askin' to be raped by a nigger — " He saw Powther standing half in, half out of the kitchen and he stopped talking.

Powther sipped the scalding hot coffee, wishing that it was cold so that he could drink it fast, and leave the kitchen. He tried to pretend he hadn't heard what Al said, pretended not to see how red Al's face was, or the way his pale blue eyes were blinking. I always forget about race, he thought. I forget that other people think about it. I didn't think of Link Williams the way a white man would think of him. I thought of him as another man, that was all. To hear him spoken of like that hurts me.

He had never given any thought to the way the *Chronicle* identified Negroes. He had never reacted to it, one way or another. Now his reaction was a purely personal indignation, not even indignation, a kind of fretfulness. If they had just put Link Williams' name in the paper without saying he was colored, he, Powther, would not be in this awkward situation, sitting across the table from the Frenchman, who would not look at him, pretending not to see that Al's pale blue eyes were still blinking, that his big face was redder than ever, that he had pushed his cap so far back on his head that the short cropped blond hair was visible, and that the position of the cap emphasized the roundness of his skull.

Silence in the kitchen. He thought, We're all embarrassed. The Frenchman keeps stirring his coffee, the spoon clinking against the cup, stirring it though he doesn't put sugar or cream in it, and I keep sipping mine though it's so hot it burns my lips. Al keeps pushing that cap farther and farther back on his head, and it will soon fall with a soft plop on this brick floor. The Skullery keeps peeling potatoes at the kitchen sink. He must have his face almost in the sink, he was holding his head so far down, revealing his embarrassment by presenting a view of the seat of his bluejeans to them.

The Frenchman said, "Watch it there, blockhead. Watch the peels. Watch the peels."

"Yes, sir. I am, sir," the Skullery said meekly.

Powther thought his face must now be resting on the stopper, his head was so far down in the sink, the rear of the bluejeans so far up.

"You are not. Scrape. I said, scrape. Not peel."

The Frenchman was trying to fill the kitchen with talk again. By himself.

"Coffee's good, Frenchie," Al said.

Al was trying to help out, too.

Then Mrs. Cameron came in the kitchen and Al straightened up, and took his cap off, fast, as though at the unexpected approach of a five-star general.

Well, she should have been a general, Powther thought, watching her, and if she had been a man she would have been. In many ways she reminded him of Mrs. Crunch. They were both short, they had the same erect carriage, and they wore their hair in the same fashion, piled on top of their heads. Mrs. Cameron had a small neat figure, not that Mrs. Crunch's figure wasn't neat, but it was a little more ample than Mrs. Cameron's, and Mrs. Cameron was pink-cheeked, whereas Mrs. Crunch's skin was brown, skin on the face alike though in the firmness of the flesh, and the lack of wrinkles. They both had the same uncompromising manner.

She said, "Good morning. Have you seen the paper?" Brisk, don't beat about the bush, bring a thing right out in the open, don't whisper about it, talk about it, clear it up, straighten it out, all there in those few words.

She kept walking up and down, looking first at Al, then at the Frenchman, then at Powther. She was wearing a longsleeved gray dress, and he decided it was cotton and stiffly starched, because the skirt rustled as she walked. Her expression was so severe and her lips were compressed in such a thin tight line that if she'd had a birch rod in one hand and a book in the other, she would have looked exactly like a caricature of a schoolteacher.

"Well?" she demanded.

The Frenchman said, "Yes."

"I thought we'd talk about it now. The four of us. And work out a point of view, so that when the others — "

The Frenchman held up his hand. "Wait," he said. "Empty the garbage cans, blockhead." As soon as the Skullery left the kitchen, he said, "Now — "

"What is there to discuss, or work out a point of view about, Mrs. Cameron?" Powther asked. "Obviously the Chronicle made a mistake. There's a mixup in names. They transferred Miss Camilo's name from some other story. It's an easy thing to do in a newspaper office. A line of type is picked up and transferred — "

"I thought about that too, Mr. Powther. But there isn't any story in the paper about the family, or about Miss Camilo, from which a line of type could have been transferred to this story. That theory just doesn't fit. I wish it did," she said.

"Then — " he faltered. It's true. But how could it be? What would Miss Camilo be doing in The Narrows at that time of night? Much as he disliked and distrusted Link Williams, he couldn't quite picture him attacking a woman, a stranger. Especially a woman as beautiful and as obviously aristocratic as Miss Camilo. He must have been terribly drunk.

Al said, "She's been runnin' with him for months. Ever since December — "

"That's enough of that, Albert," Mrs. Cameron said. Her cheeks were no longer pink, they were red. "There will be no loose talk about Miss Camilo in this house. If I hear of any, I shall take immediate steps to put an end to it — permanently. I will not allow any malicious gossip about her or any other member of the family."

Powther left the kitchen first, understandable because of the tea that afternoon, and he had so many things to do, and so little time in which to do them. He saw Mrs. Cameron go through the hall shortly afterwards, skirts rustling, head up in the air, the severe expression still on her face. He went into the butler's pantry, pushed the swinging door open about half an inch, holding it like that because he wanted to hear what Al and the Frenchman were saying. He had never listened outside a door in a household where he worked, but he had to find out what Al had been going to say when Mrs. Cameron interrupted him. *Who* had been Miss Camilo's lover ever since December?

The Frenchman was talking. He was always excited, always outraged, screaming and swearing half in English, half in French, a prima donna of a cook. He didn't sound a bit excited now. He sounded cold, matter of fact, and perfectly horrible.

The Frenchman: She's a whore. A whore ought to work in a whorehouse.

Al: Bunny oughtta take her out in the garage and strip her down and beat her every morning.

Powther thought, Why are they saying these things? There is nothing in the newspaper to make them talk like this. Then he remembered Al, sitting behind the steering wheel of the town car, studying Dumble Street, looking down the length of Dumble Street, "It would be just about here — what's down there — followed her — lost her right here in this street — she come up that driveway like a bat outta hell — somebody oughtta tell her, Mal — smash that crate up — if I was the Captain — she looks like an angel — "

So Al has told the Frenchman about Miss Camilo staying out late at night, staying somewhere in Monmouth, he thought. Then too they both know, just as I do, that she stays away from the Captain as much as six months at a time, and has ever since that first year they were married. Six months or a year in Paris or London or Quebec or Chicago, and the Captain always in New York. Naturally they believe that so young and beautiful a woman must long since have found a lover whom she preferred to her husband.

Al: Everybody in Monmouth's goin' to be askin' what was she doin' on the dock in Niggertown, three in the mornin', just askin' for that nigger to rape her.

The Frenchman: She's a whore.

He let the door swing shut, tight shut. He supposed it would never be called attempted attack, though that was the charge. There would always be the suggestion of rape. People would say three o'clock in the morning, when it was midnight. On the dock, when it was not the dock itself but Dock Street, corner of Dumble. It said so in the paper. But when the people in Monmouth told the story, they would always make it sound as though Miss Camilo was held down, flat on her back, on the dock, held down by a Negro, but they would say "nigger." Miss Camilo held down by a nigger.

It made him feel sick inside. That was another thing he forgot when he read the paper, pretending he was a bank clerk trying to figure that story out. He forgot that the staff at the Hall would know instantly that Mrs. William R. Sheffield of such and such an address in New York was Camilla Treadway Sheffield. But other people wouldn't know it. The newspaper didn't know it either. There was no reason why they should. People in Monmouth didn't know the Captain or Miss Camilo. They knew the Madam but not Miss Camilo. But they would. All Monmouth would know it eventually. You couldn't keep a thing like that quiet. The story would spread slowly, slowly, just like ink on a blotter. Mrs. Sheffield is the Treadway girl. Scandal. Story enlarged upon, embroidered, even to the nighttime trips, until Miss Camilo would sound like a common streetwalker, subject to attack, one of the weak ones to be preyed upon.

There wasn't anything that Mrs. Cameron could do to stop the progress of this scandalous story. He could tell by the way the staff avoided all mention of it at lunch in the servants' dining room, that the whole thing had been thoroughly discussed. Al had undoubtedly told every one of them about Miss Camilo coming up the driveway like a bat outta hell, had used the word nigger as though it were his own personal invention, over and over again. Mrs. Cameron, sitting at the head of the table, looked more severe than ever, and Rita, who sat midway, had a sly kind of smile that kept coming and going about her mouth. Al talked pointedly and constantly about cars, and the weather, and how he had spent the morning tuning up the old Rolls-Royce.

Powther contributed nothing to the conversation. He made himself think of something else. The Frenchman was a prima donna of a cook, not a cook, a chef — not a chef, an artist. Better than Old Copper's Angelo, the Italian, because his flavoring was more subtle, and at the same time more unexpected. If Old Copper had ever had the chance to taste the Frenchman's food, he would have kidnaped him. Old Copper always took what he wanted.

The cook at The Last Chance was even better than the Frenchman, his skills seemed to range over a wider area, included a greater variety of foods. He remembered the doughnuts, crisp outside, tender inside, flavor spicy, and not sweet. The wonderful texture had stuck in the roof of his mouth, in his throat, like glue, as he looked at Bill Hod, looked at him once, and not again, but dreadfully aware of him, and afraid of him.

He had never been able to forget that moment when he saw Hod sitting at the kitchen table, across from Mamie, not laughing or talking or caressing her, not eying her, just sitting there in his shirt sleeves, drinking a glass of milk. He had tried to drink a cup of coffee and had put the cup down because his hands had begun to shake, because of that man in a white shirt, sleeves rolled up, shirt open at the neck, not looking at him, but aware of the predatory tomcat look of him, back alleys and caterwauling fights, claw your way up and out, use tooth and nail, knife and gun, written all over his face. Like Old Copper. You looked at Old Copper's face, his eyes, his mouth, the lines about the mouth, and you knew that anything you could imagine about his past would not be as evil or as cruel as it must really have been to write the story on his face like that.

Yet he had liked Old Copper and Old Copper had liked him. That is, before he married Mamie, before Old Copper stared at Mamie. Then he had hated him, been afraid of him. He knew now that he had liked the old man only because he had never before had anything that Old Copper wanted, anything that Old Copper might take away from him.

Perhaps if it hadn't been for Mamie, he, Powther, and the idea startled him, perhaps he and Hod might have been friends. He and Al were friends, incredible as it seemed. Under different circumstances, just possibly, he and Bill Hod might have been friends — could you be friends with a man like that?

Al said, "You put two and two together and it always makes four."

"What do you mean by that, Albert?" Mrs. Cameron asked.

"I mean I got to go to work on Miss Camilo's Caddy. It sure has took a beating these last few months."

Powther watched Al get up from the table. "Put two and two together . . ." Al's voice matched his size, his appearance, his personality. It was a big voice, slightly hoarse, because he smoked cigarettes all day long; an insistent voice, you could tell by the sound of it that once he got an idea in his head, it would be impossible to get it out. "It would be about here . . . I measured the gas . . . what's down there?"

The River Wye was down there, in the direction that Al had been looking. So was the dock. So was Number Six Dumble Street. Oh, no, he thought. Impossible.

Why impossible? Put two and two together. After Al mentioned the nighttime trips he, Powther, had decided that Miss Camilo was in love, she seemed to have come suddenly alive, her face was animated, she was always laughing, her flesh had a kind of gleam. If Al was telling the truth about those trips, then her lover lived in Monmouth. Al had seen her car in Dumble Street. Sometime during the last two weeks, the love affair had ended. Miss Camilo was unhappy about it. She was too quiet, drinking too much. According to that senseless story in the Chronicle, she had accused Link Williams of attempted attack. "She's been runnin' with him for months now." Add all of this up and "him" was Link Williams.

A shiver ran down his spine.

He had forgotten he was still sitting at the table in the servants' dining room. Mrs. Cameron's quiet voice startled him. She said, "Mr. Powther, you're having a chill. Have you caught a cold?"

"It's these sudden changes," he said, shaking his head. "Yesterday was almost like spring, and today is like the middle of January. I've felt frozen all morning."

Attempted attack, he thought. Midnight, corner of Dock and Dumble, no traffic, no passers-by. They would have heard the lapping of the river, and the street would have been dark all around them, in spite of the light at the corner. They were within sight of that red neon sign in front of The Last Chance, but they wouldn't have been able to see the pink light in that upstairs bedroom at Number Six, and The Hangman would simply have been a dark bulk against the night sky, not really distinguishable as a tree.

Miss Camilo and Link Williams, painful to think of those two being connected in any way, stood on that corner, quarreling. Miss Camilo with her young trusting eyes, innocent face, pale blond hair, he wondered if she wore that ring with the diamond in it like the headlight of a car, a ring that said she had no business anywhere near Dumble Street, standing near Link Williams, who would have been hatless, probably coatless, too. The street light should have thrown a shadow across his face, a shadow like a scar, to emphasize the way in which his face with its thin-lipped cruel mouth resembled the face of a pirate, of an outlaw.

They must have quarreled to the hurting point. Miss Camilo was the hurt one. So it was about another woman. She probably threatened to ruin him, to get even, and he laughed, and then she stood there under that street light that could not dissipate the deadly darkness all around them, and screamed. The police came and she made the accusation and they arrested him. But he was already out on bail. The paper said so. Even if the charge was proved, and he doubted that it could be, he and Mamie had read so many of these cases in the papers, a charge like that, attempted attack, no witnesses, late at night, was too flimsy to hold up in court, and with Bill Hod's influence, he wouldn't even get a suspended sentence or a fine. Nothing.

I don't believe it, he thought. Even now I don't believe it. There's some other explanation. Link Williams couldn't have been her lover.

Al had said to the Frenchman, "You don't believe me, huh? Well, what was she doin' on the dock in Niggertown — "

Sweat broke out on his forehead.

He reached in his pocket for a handkerchief, mopped his forehead, asking himself why he kept refusing to believe that Link Williams had been Miss Camilo's lover, why he so desperately wanted it not to be true, and remembered the feel of old, soft, worn handkerchiefs, handkerchiefs that he kept at the bottom of the pile in the top drawer of the chest, in the bedroom that he shared with Mamie.

He could see that tall imitation-mahogany chest, with grapes and tendrils, and roundbottomed cupids glued on the front of the drawers, chest he didn't buy, didn't pay for, see himself reach in the drawer. His hand had struck something cold, metallic, square, shaped like a box.

L.W. The initials picked out in small flawless diamonds. Even when he held the cigarette case flat on his hand, the stones had quivered, as though the blue-red-yellow sparks they encased were trying to free themselves, and so were never still. The gold of the case was beautifully worked, obviously made to order, by a master goldsmith.

"Put two and two together."

Miss Camilo had given that cigarette case to Link Williams. Link had handed it on to Mamie. Monogrammed. Obviously his. He didn't care if the husband saw it, the husband who didn't count, didn't matter, and never had or would; because he was a fool, and a coward, and everyone who ever saw him immediately recognized him as such, even Old Copper, a lecherous old man, knew that the husband would stand for anything, telling the new husband to his face, "If I was younger I'd give you a run for your money."

Link Williams knew that the husband would put up with anything. So he told Miss Camilo, I've got another woman, a better woman. Powther supposed that Mamie was a better woman than Miss Camilo. Then he thought, appalled, This thing has already changed me. It would never have occurred to me to compare them, because Miss Camilo moved in a separate different world. But Link Williams had made these separate worlds coalesce, collide. The princess of the fairy tales, all gold, was not gold at all, was flesh, human flesh, all too human, all too weak, capable of jealousy, of vengeance, capable of being ruined, like any other woman.

He was overwhelmed by a sudden sense of urgency. If Miss Camilo could fall in love with Link Williams, then Mamie — Mamie would run off with him. They might already have gone. He had to find out. Now. Tea or no tea. Nobody had as much at stake in this dreadful business as he had.

He went straight to the garage, leaving the table so abruptly that Mrs. Cameron frowned.

"Al," he said, "would you do me a favor?"

"Sure. Just you name it, Mal."

"I've got to go home in a hurry, home and back so fast that

I still have everything ready for the tea this afternoon. The Madam is having the office girls in for tea." Al knew that but he was much too upset to be able to think clearly. "And I have to be back, right away, but I've got to go home right now. I've got to go home."

"Sure, Mal. Any time. You know that."

"I'll tell Mrs. Cameron that I'm going — "

"Ah," Al said, and waved his hand, back and forth, dismissing Mrs. Cameron. "You ain't got to tell that old bag nothin'. Just hop in one of them crates. Come on, I'll use one of them goddamn convertibles. You can run like hell in 'em for the first fifty thousand miles. After that the motors ain't worth a good goddamn."

"No," he said quickly. "She'll have to keep an eye on Jenkins for me while I'm gone. It's a big tea. We've quite a lot of people coming. It won't take me a minute to tell her — "

He almost ran down Dumble Street, and up the back stairs, and into the kitchen. Just inside the kitchen door he stood still, astonished. Mamie was ironing a small blue shirt, either Kelly's or Shapiro's, humming under her breath. Just like any other wife, housewife, mother. She had a brilliant red scarf tied around her head, so she must have washed her hair. He had never seen her look quite so beautiful, so young, so appealing. She was wearing a green-and-white-checked dress, a fullskirted dress, that made her waist look very small, and made the curve of her breasts something to stare at in disbelief. A sigh rose in his throat.

"Pow-ther!" she said, smiling, mouth curving over the white even teeth, the smile enhancing the dewy look of her skin. "How come you're home?"

"I forgot my keys," he said, and gulped. "I went off without my keys. The keys to my wine cellar."

"Now ain't that a shame. You want me to help you hunt for 'em?"

"No," he said, hastily. "I know where they are. They're in my other pants." He felt humble and apologetic. It seemed as though he ought to say so, to explain how he'd been falsely accusing her in his mind, picturing her as a destroyer of other people's love affairs, tell her how he'd expected to come home and find the house cold and empty because she'd run off with another man. Instead here she was ironing in a warm clean kitchen, no dirty dishes in the sink; and she had mopped the linoleum, and waxed it afterwards, because the blue and white squares had a sheen, a kind of luster; and she had made ginger-bread, he could smell it baking, spicy, fragrant, and over the smell of the gingerbread there was the strong, toosweet smell of her perfume.

He lingered in the kitchen, watching her, loving the big-bosomed look of her, thinking, I used to take it for granted that a married woman who has an affair with another man will have a depraved, wornout look. But they don't. They grow younger and there is an emanation of happiness from them that can be sensed and felt by other people, and it makes them more beauti-ful. Like Mamie. Like Miss Camilo before Link Williams left her.

Then he remembered that Al was waiting for him over on Franklin Avenue, in the Lincoln, remembered the tea, and all the last-minute business of fireplaces, be sure about enough spoons, get the candles lighted, and the pianist had to be fed when he arrived, he was coming from New York.

He went into the bedroom, and opened the top drawer of the dresser, to make certain that that damnable, expensive, worth-a-king's-ransom cigarette case was still there. After that night he discovered it, he had forced himself to stop thinking about it, stop conjecturing about it; he had never once permitted himself the luxury of finding out if it was still there.

It was gone. Mamie, who never bothered to put anything straight in a drawer, had lined up his handkerchiefs when she removed the cigarette case. It couldn't have been anyone else.

Perhaps it had never been there. Of course it had been there. Nobody could dream up the existence of a golden geegaw that looked like a crown jewel.

He shoved the drawer shut with a blow of his hand, trying to smack as many of the cupids as he could. A childish thing to do. But they seemed to be leering at him, mouths open, eyes sunk deep in their heads, and he struck at them again. If furniture could talk, these fat hideous little figures could tell him what Mamie had done with that cigarette case. Perhaps she had re-turned it to its owner. Perhaps she hadn't. Perhaps she kept it tucked inside the front of her dress, so that she would have some-thing that belonged to Link always near her.

When he went into the kitchen, she took one look at his face, and laid the iron down. "Aw, Powther, you didn't find 'em, did you? I'll go look too."

For one incredible moment he thought she was talking about the cigarette case, and he felt as though his face and neck had been enveloped in steam. Heat was rising all about him.

Then he remembered. "I've got them," he said and pulled a bunch of keys out of his pants pocket. Her voice had sounded exactly like Drewey's voice, like the voice of that big fat woman, sitting in the creaking rocking chair, in a rooming house in Baltimore, doing what she called hum-a-byin', voice as soothing as a warm bath — now, now, now, everything is all right.

"I've got to hurry," he said. He had to get back to the Hall, and check the number of napkins, make certain about the brand of tea — one of the smoky dark ones — and yet he wanted to stay here, to put his head down in her lap, to —

"You feel all right, Powther?"

"A little indigestion. It's just that I came so fast." And that ever since Bill Hod came into our lives, I have felt as though I were stumbling around in the dark, in a strange house, hunting for a door, fumbling for a door in an unfamiliar house that has no doors. More and more, of late, I have wished that Old Copper's lust for women had not infected me, because it did, finally, so much so that I could not stop, would not stop, would not heed the warnings of my common sense, but went ahead and married you anyway. Because of that old man, who sat huddled in a red leather chair, licking his lips, staring at his paintings, oil paintings of bigbosomed, softfleshed women. And yet — I would really never have lived if I hadn't married you because I would never have known what ecstasy is like.

"I'll fix some soda for you."

"No, no. I haven't got time. Really. I've got to get back."

"Okay, sugar."

He couldn't leave like this. He ought to say something else, but he didn't know what. She had picked up the iron, was moving it back and forth, across another small shirt. "Where's J.C.?" he asked.

"J.C.?" she laughed. "Crunch took him to the liberry with her. I think she's educatin' him but I bet it's goin' to work out the other way. Time she listens to that jaybird jabber of his, especially walkin' right along the street with him for a half-hour, she'll be talkin' the same way he does. He come runnin' up the stairs, tellin' me Crunch said for me to change his clothes because he was goin' out with her, and for me to put his new shoes on him, and that Crunch said for me to hurry up because she couldn't wait. I told him, I said, Listen, J.C., I'll change 'em this time, but you come up here just one more time tellin' me what Crunch said I got to do and I'll fix your seat so you won't be able to sit on it for a week. He looked real cute when he went back downstairs."

She laughed again, head thrown back, round brown throat pulsating with laughter; and kept on laughing as though she were enjoying the rich mellow sound bubbling up in her throat. But she gave him a queer, sharp glance that made him wonder if the laughter were a screen for whatever she was thinking.

"Oh, my God!" she said suddenly, and put the iron down and hurried toward the stove. "I'm cooking with my ass again." She took the gingerbread out of the oven. It was just beginning to singe along the edges. "I guess I got up off it just in time. Them two starvin' Armenians are always looking for something to eat when they come home from school. So I stirred this up in a hurry, and then plum forgot about it."

As he went down the stairs, hurrying again now, almost running, he heard her singing, not that song he hated about some kind of train her mother took, the words of this one didn't make much sense but the tune was lovely and so was her voice, slow, clear, true, and he could hear the slap thump of the iron:

> Tell me what color an' I'll tell you what road she took.
> Tell me what color an' I'll tell you what road she took.
> Why'ncha tell me what color and I'll tell you what road
>   she took.

When he got in the car, Al looked at him queerly, too.
"Is there somep'n the matter, Mal?"
Without thinking, he said, "It's my wife."
"She sick?"
"Well —" he hesitated, "not exactly."
"What'sa matter with her?"
He shook his head, frowning. "It's — it's her heart."
"She probably runs too fast, Mal. Just like you do. Probably works too hard. People got to give themselves a break, you know. Ain't no rich bastards standin' around handin' out new tickers when the one you got quits on you."

On the way back to the Hall, Al talked about cars, about heart trouble, about the Madam and how mean she was to Rita, about Mrs. Cameron and how mean she was to Rita.

Powther ignored Al's conversation. He was trying to reorient himself to the atmosphere of the Hall, trying to forget about Mamie and Link Williams and Miss Camilo and a Tiffany cigarette case, with which Mamie was playing hide-and-seek, so that he could think about the tea, concentrate on the tea. If he didn't, he might drop a tray, step on someone's foot, do any of the hideous, awkward things a butler could do when he didn't have his mind on his work.

He succeeded fairly well, too. By five o'clock, when the east drawing room was filled with young women, all wearing print dresses and little hats with flowers on them, some seated, some standing, all talking and laughing, drinking tea, eating, thoroughly enjoying themselves, he was able to admire the scene in front of him, to the exclusion of any private worries.

Mischoff, the pianist, had arrived on schedule and was now playing the Steinway grand, so that under the talk and the laughter there was music. There was a wonderful blend of smells: tea, faint smell of cedar from the fires where he'd sprinkled cedar chips, the girls' perfume, the poets' narcissi. As he looked about him, he thought, if you stood in the doorway of this white and gold room, and took just one hasty glance, at the lights over the oil paintings, at the flickering light from the candles, and from the open fires, listened to the sound of the piano, watched the constant movement of the girls, you would want to go inside and share the warmth, the gaiety, the hospitality.

The Madam belonged in this room. She looked like a *grande dame* because of the pearl choker around her neck, because of the soft smoky blue of the afternoon dress she was wearing. The girls' faces lighted up, glowed, as she talked to them, and the glow lingered even after she'd moved away, to speak to someone else. Her hair was almost as pretty as Miss Camilo's. From a distance she seemed to be a platinum blonde, but when you got close to her, you saw that it was because the pale blond hair was mixed with gray. She was as erect and as slender as Miss Camilo. They had the same deep blue eyes but there was a difference in the expression. Miss Camilo's eyes were very young, very innocent. The Madam's eyes were the eyes of a woman in her late fifties, a little tired, eyes of a woman who had played a man's role for years. She actually managed the plant, and when you studied her eyes you saw that sometimes she had achieved the things she wanted, and sometimes she hadn't; but you also saw determination in the eyes, and the face, and you knew why she was so successful.

As he was crossing the room, to pick up some empty teacups, she came up to him, put her hand on his arm. She said, "It's perfect. Everything is perfect. Thank you, Powther."

He was tremendously pleased. She paid him to see that everything was perfect, and it would have been understandable if she took perfection for granted. She never did. She was always thanking him for doing his job, as though he were an old friend who had done a favor for her.

There's a glow in me now, he thought, just as there is in these girls. She has restored my confidence, made me believe in myself again. I can look at this room and feel sorry that the weather will soon be too warm for lighted candles, for fires in the fireplaces, and that we won't be entertaining on a scale like this until next year.

There was the summer picnic though. But that was handled by an outside crew. He had nothing to do with it, and he disapproved of it, anyway. Every Fourth of July, the Madam invited workmen from the plant, and gave a kind of mass entertainment for them and their families. It was more like an invasion than a party. The men wore T-shirts and their fat wives came in shorts and slacks and bathing suits. The men and women and their stickyfingered, badly behaved children ate hot dogs and crackerjack and ice cream, drank Coca-Cola and beer and lemonade, and shot off fireworks. Even the children drank beer, so that he referred to all of them, contemptuously, in his mind, as the beer drinkers.

The Madam hired special guards for the occasion, but they didn't have the family's interest in mind, weren't ever really on their toes. He was always afraid that some of these undesirable people would wander into the house, tracking it up, fingering the tapestries, smearing the upholstery.

Last summer, an unshaven young man who smelt of beer and sweat, actually got as far as the front door. When Powther opened the door, the young man said, in a loud, truculent voice, "Just wanted to see if the inside of the palace stinks like the plant."

Fortunately, one of the hired guards came up just then and led the young man away. That beer-soaked young man would always epitomize the summer picnic in Powther's mind, just as these attractive, perfumed girls in their spring dresses epitomized this late-winter tea.

Ah, well, he thought, as he crossed the room to tell Jenkins to collect the empty teacups piled up on one of the mantels, you can't make a silk purse out of a sow's ear. He paused, just behind the sofa, in front of the fireplace, to admire two girls who were sitting close together on it, watching the fire. The mandarin red silk of the sofa formed a striking background for the yellow-orange tones in the print dresses they wore.

One of the girls sitting on the sofa said, in an undertone, "Don't you know who she is?"

"No." The other voice went down, lower. "Who?"

He started to move away, and the prettier of the two girls said, "Mrs. Treadway's daughter. Camilla Sheffield."

His attention was caught, held.

"I didn't know she had a daughter."

"Sure. Mrs. William R. Sheffield is Mrs. Treadway's only child. Camilla Treadway Sheffield. Now isn't that something?" The voice went up.

"How did you know?"

"I heard my boss say so. I heard him talking to somebody about it just this morning, over the telephone."

"Mrs. Treadway's daughter? What was she doing in The Narrows at that hour?"

"That's what he said, too. My boss, I mean. He said, 'What was she doing on the dock with a nigger at that time of night?'"

"She wasn't really on the dock with him, was she? I mean it didn't say that in the paper. Wait a minute," relish in the voice, curiosity, "do you mean she was — "

"Shhh!"

The Madam was coming toward them, and both girls turned toward her, smiling, faces glowing, and then stood up, to talk to her.

Powther thought incredulously, That fast! By night, all Monmouth would be asking the same question. Now he looked around the room with distaste. These girls smelt of perfume, their hair was curled, they were wearing their new spring dresses, but they were exactly like the sweaty, beer-drinking workers who invaded the park in July. They, too, resented the fact that the Madam belonged to the millionaire class.

The beer drinkers expressed their hostility in vandalism. Rogers said that every year, after the picnic, it took a crew of men a whole month to put the park back in shape, what with the mutilation of trees and shrubs, and the empty beer bottles and crackerjack boxes, and Coca-Cola bottles, and exploded firecrackers, thrown into the lake, despite the fact that he put the biggest refuse cans he could find less than ten feet apart all through the grounds.

"I finally got smart," Rogers said. "It took me three years to get smart. I move the swans back in a place where they can't find 'em. I made another little lake for 'em. For three years I found my swans with their necks wrung, or their crops so bloated up they died two or three days later. And I string an electric wire all around the rose gardens. Used to be I'd go out there and find it stripped, and some of the bushes dug up. But I got it fixed now so they can't get at it."

The beer drinkers wrecked the grounds, or tried to. And the tea drinkers, as he now called these girls from the office, were just as hostile. They welcomed the fact that the Madam's daughter was mixed up in a scandalous situation. By the time this tea was over, they would have reduced Miss Camilo to the level of a prostitute, simply because her mother was a millionaire. They couldn't take the Madam's wealth away from her, but they could destroy her daughter, just by whispering about her, while they drank a smoky dark tea, out of the Madam's best teacups, while they clinked the Madam's Versailles spoons against the saucers.

20

● PETER BULLOCK, editor, owner, publisher of the *Monmouth
Chronicle*, was drinking a glass of milk, in The Swiss Steak, a small
restaurant on Centre Street. He watched Rutledge, head of Monmouth's police department, who sat across the table from him, as
he worked his way slowly, steadily, through a steak, French fried
potatoes, Parker House rolls; watched him wash his food down his
throat with beer, big drafts of beer.

He tried to keep his eyes away from Rutledge's plate, and
couldn't, any more than any other starving man could keep his
eyes away from food. He told himself that this was unappetizing
unhealthy fried food that Rutledge was stuffing in his mouth, and
the beer he was pouring down his throat was little better than
poison; and the smell of the steak, smell of the beer, the vast
growling emptiness in his stomach made him feel as though his
head were going around and around, revolving on a private Ferris
wheel of its own.

"That Treadway girl sure messed herself up," Rutledge said,
chewing steak. "Couldn't have done a better job if she'd been
paid to do it. She was drunk when she accused Link Williams of
attempted attack. Drunk again this afternoon when she ran that
kid down." He signaled the waiter with his fork.

There was a big piece of steak speared on the end of the fork,
and Bullock wondered what Rutledge would do if he should lean
forward, mouth open, and snatch the meat off with his teeth.

"Maybe she's competing for the title," Rutledge said.

"Title? What title?"

"The rich bitch title," Rutledge said, grinning. He turned to the waiter, said, "Two pieces of apple pie. No, not for him. Just for me. And cover the whole thing over thick with ice cream. Put about a pint of vanilla on it." He popped the hunk of steak in his mouth and grinned at Bullock, chewing and grinning, and talking, "Damn if I know why I eat so much. Maybe it's because I was hungry when I was young. So hungry once that I stole a loaf of bread and — " he started in on the pie " — I've been filling my gut up ever since so I won't ever be able to remember what it felt like when it was empty."

Bullock grunted.

"She'll be in to see you."

"Who?" he asked, thinking, It's easier to be hungry when you're young. He was too old for it. Forty-nine and hungry all the time. Forty-nine and an emptiness in his stomach, a burning emptiness in his stomach, all the time.

"Mrs. Treadway. She came to see me, right after the accident. Funny thing. I felt kind of sorry for her. Imagine me feeling sorry for a billionaire. She wanted me to wipe the record off the blotter. But there wasn't a damn thing I could do about it. Hell, the girl was drunker'n a coot, passed a stop light, street crawling with witnesses — "

"What'd you say to her?" Bullock asked. He knew all the details of the accident, the story was already dummied in, already set up. Happened about five-fifteen, on Dock Street, child knocked down.

"I tried to sound as dispassionate as a judge. 'Mrs. Treadway,' I said, 'the laws in Monmouth are all written down. There are no unwritten ones. These laws apply with equal force to every resident. This is a serious matter. The child was badly injured. There is always the possibility that the child may die. There is nothing, absolutely nothing, that I can do about it.' " Rutledge paused, swallowed more beer. "She'll be in to see you," he repeated, maliciously.

"For what?"

"When the rich folks can't fix the cops, they do the next best thing, they keep the details of the mess out of the public print. You're the public print in this town, Bullock."

He shrugged. "So what good would it do to keep it out of the paper?"

"The label of rich tramp wouldn't be written down, permanently fixed on paper. It could stay where it is, up in the air, a matter of hearsay and rumor." Rutledge lit a cigarette. "What're you going to do when the old lady comes in to cop a plea?"

Casual question, he wondered. Hardly. Rutledge didn't ask casual questions. He had the cold eyes of a cop, eyes the color of lead, had the professionally expressionless face of a cop, face like a mask, only Rutledge's mask never slipped, so it was impossible to say where he stood on anything, how he felt about anything. But he didn't ask idle, casual questions.

"I don't know," he said, and pushed his chair back from the table.

The smell of steak, of French fried potatoes, of beer, accompanied him as he walked along Centre Street. It went right into his office with him, he still hungry, and the good smell of food, moving on into his office with him, tantalizing, maddening, making his head reel.

His secretary said, "Mrs. Treadway is waiting for you. I told her that you'd be right back."

"You're so goddamn efficient," he said, and let the dizziness, and the irritability born of hunger, turn into anger, and let the anger explode in the face of this old maid who was his secretary, watched her face crumple, redden. "I suppose you've got your headstone already marked, haven't you? And the coffin picked out," he said, glaring at her, and went in his office, and shook hands with Mrs. Treadway, acting as though he were pleased to see her, as though he thought this was an informal call she was paying him.

He was surprised at himself because he felt sorry for her, just as Rutledge had. She had grown older, more gray in her hair, new deep lines at the mouth, around the eyes. Not that he saw her very often. He and Lola dined with her at Treadway Hall, once a year, largely a matter of business courtesy on her part, though Lola always managed to create the impression that it was a social gesture, when she told her friends about it.

Mrs. Treadway said, "I have come to ask you not to print anything about this unfortunate accident of Camilo's."

"I can't do that," he said, just as bluntly, just as quickly. "It's on the police blotter. The child is in the hospital. There were witnesses."

"Camilo has been under a tremendous strain," she said. "That's why I am asking you not to print anything about this."

"I will make it a small story, bury it on an inside page. But it has to go in."

"There must be no story at all. On an inside page or an outside page," she said insistently.

He could understand why, anybody could understand why. That case hadn't come up yet, it had been less than a week ago, that Camilo Sheffield had charged a Negro with attempted attack. The Negro was out on bail, very low bail, and no date had been set for the trial. This accident wasn't going to help Camilo's reputation, would, in fact, polish off what was left of it.

"I'm sorry," he said, gently, and meant it. "But it will have to go in."

She stood up, and so he stood up, too, trying to think of a way to express his regret, his sympathy.

"Mr. Bullock," she said, the eyes no longer sad, the eyes determined, cold, the face grim, and the voice implacable. "If the story goes in, our advertising comes out. We have no contract with your paper."

After she left, he kept pushing a blotter around on the top of his desk, thinking, Oh, damn the woman anyway. Why couldn't she keep her tramp of a daughter under control? It was a nasty business. The girl was drunk, driving as though the devil was riding with her, sidesaddle on a fender, and she was trying to outride him, outrun him. She passed a red light. In Niggertown. On Dock Street. Why Dock Street? How did she come to be in that narrow, dingy, street composed of warehouses and stinking little factories, and old frame buildings, street that ran parallel to the river, and smelt and looked like what it was — a waterfront street.

These things were always bad. The priests and the rabbis, the jackleg nigger preachers, the union leaders, the ward heelers would holler and scream about a bought press for months afterwards. You couldn't prevent people from knowing about a thing just because you kept it out of a newspaper. It had happened shortly after five o'clock, and the streets were filled with dock workers and factory hands, going home. He had tried to tell Mrs. Treadway that, but oh, no, if the story went in, the advertising came out — permanently. And he couldn't afford to lose it, and she knew it.

So he personally pulled the story, and even as he did it knew that word of what he'd done would be all through the building, five minutes after he left the pressroom.

Back in his office, he tried to shift the blame, the responsibility, for his action. Rutledge could have wiped the thing off the police blotter. Why did Rutledge have to be so goddamn moral, or rather, he thought, why should Monmouth's leaden-eyed Chief of Police be in a position where he can afford to put his morality into practice, and the editor of the *Chronicle* shouldn't be? Is it a matter of morality? No, it's a matter of what will people say — what will people think — public opinion.

The original error stemmed from that numbskull who had picked up the story about young Mrs. Sheffield accusing a Negro of attack. He was one of those knowitalls from the Columbia School of Journalism, complete with crew haircut and more lip than John L. Lewis, and a sophomoric belief in his own judgment.

"So I didn't know she was the Treadway girl," he said, when Bullock got after him about it. "But any woman from Park Avenue on the loose in the Dumble Street area at midnight is news. Because of the sheer incongruity of her being there at all."

"You're supposed to know who people are. It's part of your job. That's what you're paid for. Or don't they teach that at — "

The crew haircut had interrupted him. "Who'd recognize her by that name? It got past the desk. It got past you. Did you know who Mrs. William R. Sheffield was? So I was supposed to know anyway, huh? That's what you pay me for, huh? All right. Even if I'd known who she was, I'd of picked the story up. A stranger could have got in that section by accident. The Treadway girl must have gone there deliberately. She's been commuting between Monmouth and New York for months now. So she wouldn't be apt to lose her way. If you ask me, that line of hers about attempted attack is absolute rot. It was a lovers' quarrel."

"What?" he roared. "Why you — "

"Listen," the crew haircut said calmly, "I looked the man up. My girl works in the plant and she told me that Mrs. Sheffield was the Treadway girl. So I got curious and looked up his record. He's a Phi Beta Kappa from Dartmouth, majored in history, honor graduate of Monmouth High School, football star, basketball star in high school and at Dartmouth. Was in the Navy for four years, censor, Navy installation in Hawaii. There's nothing in his background to make the charge believable. If you want to know what I think, I think they were in love and — "

"You goddam fool," he shouted, and his throat constricted, just as though he were choking. When he was able to talk again, his voice no longer contained the surface irascibility of the ulcer victim, it was an outraged furious voice, because the idea, the possibility that the Treadway girl could have had a nigger lover, that any rational white man could contemplate such a thought without — "You're fired," he shouted, "I won't have any irresponsible bastard like you on my payroll — "

The knowitall with the crew haircut said, cheerfully, "It's okay, pops. I felt the same way about you the first time I saw you."

He had watched him go toward the door, saw him hesitate, turn back, and thought he was going to say, I need the job, I got a wife and four starving kids, and a dying grandmother; and instead, he offered advice.

"You better get your ulcers taped up, way up out of the muck," he said, "otherwise you might get 'em mired in this Treadway case."

At eight o'clock, that night, the phone on his desk rang, and the girl at the switchboard said that Jubine wanted to see him.

"Tell him to go drown himself."

"He has a picture that — "

"Tell him to drop it in and pull the chain and — "

"He says — "

Jubine interrupted. "Bullock, you better look at this picture. See this picture."

"No."

"You'll be sorry, peon, sorry, sorry — "

"Get the hell out of my building before I call a cop."

"You'll be sorry, sorry, sorry."

Jubine's soft reproachful voice singsonged the words in his ear again and he banged the receiver down, cutting the sound off, thinking, Yes, eight o'clock at night, that's all I need is to have that bastard come in here and start yapping that line he talks, unlit cigar in the corner of his mouth, beady eyes roving all around the room, looking, looking, looking, as though he were estimating the cost of everything, putting a price on it, cost of the desk, cost of the dark red carpeting, cost of the mahogany paneling on the walls, price you paid, Ha, ha, ha, you got gypped, look at the price you paid. Restless, inquisitive eyes, moving over and around the editorpublisherowner of the *Monmouth Chronicle*, examining him, cataloguing him, summing him up by saying, "You're a type, Bullock. A state of mind. And you'll never recover from it."

He kept remembering the sound of Jubine's voice, Sorry, you'll be sorry, sorry, a singsong, tuneless, reiterated, like some brat of a child baiting another brat of a child. He stayed in his office until the presses started to roll, and he thought he could hear that singsong under the rumble and roar of the press. Heard it off and on all night, even after he got home, got in bed.

At six o'clock in the morning he woke up, feeling uneasy, worn-out, as though his subconscious had been trying to get a message through to him all night, and so he had slept restlessly, aware of something wrong, but too obtuse to recognize the signal, to answer it. Pictures, he thought, what about —

He reached for the telephone by the bed, dialed Rutledge's number.

"Listen," he said, when he heard Rutledge's voice, thick with sleep; though he already knew the answer to the question he was going to ask, he asked it anyway, "Were there any pictures taken of that Treadway girl's accident? Who? Oh — Christ!"

Lola sat up in bed, not yawning, not sagging with sleep, wide awake, face as fresh as the morning, hair curling over her forehead. "What's the matter?" She watched him dress, frowning. "Where are you going at this hour? Pete, answer me — "

He was gone before she could ask him again. He backed his car out of the three-car garage, attached garage, station wagon in it, Lola's brandnew convertible in it, his slave ship, as Jubine called it, also housed in it. Why'd they need two cars and a station wagon? Because he was a sucker, he was a peon, he was a poor peon trying to act like a rich peon because he was in love with an expensive beautiful redheaded female peon, and somewhere in the twentieth century they'd both lost the use of their legs, and their minds, and their will power. So they couldn't walk any more, they couldn't —

The loft where Jubine lived, across from the Commerce Street Police Station, was empty. Door wide open. He yelled, "Jubine, hey, Jubine!"

No answer. He went inside. It was just a big, bare, practically unfurnished room, not even a room, a loft, so big that the walls couldn't define it, give it form, just unfurnished space, with a roof over it. Pictures everywhere, all the litter of photography, everywhere. Not even a bed. Probably sleeps on the floor. No, there was a cot, but no sheets, an army blanket rolled up at the foot took the place of sheets, bedspread, blanket, all in one; could serve as pillow, too, if one put one's head on it.

An old man's voice said, "You want something, mister?"

He turned toward the direction of the voice, and saw that there was a chair in the loft, and that a thin old man was sitting in it. Wrinkled face. Something satirical in his eyes, or it may have been the effect of the toobig gray cap he was wearing, peak of the cap threw a shadow over the eyes. He was sucking on a corncob pipe. His face seemed to consist of the peak of the cap, the pipe, and the wrinkles.

"Where's Jubine?"

"New York."

"New York? Jubine?" The *Chronicle* was piled on the news-stands by now, it was being distributed in the post offices of all the little towns all over the state, it was in the big bundles being tossed off trucks in front of drugstores and candy stores, and in another hour it would be on the doorsteps of the houses, boys would be hawking it on Main Street. He used to think of this hour with pleasure, with satisfaction, because his paper was being read over the breakfast tables, on the trains and busses, his personal creation, brandnew, eagerly awaited, every morning. And now —

"That's right, mister. He's been gone all night. He said ye'd be here, lookin' for him. Said ye'd be here last night. It's morning though, ain't it. Ye're later'n he said." He paused. "He left a message."

"Well?" How did this old man in his mismatched pants and coat, his toobig cap, know him. Jubine would have left a description of him. Camel-hair coat. Rich peon's coat. Of course. "Well?" he repeated.

The old man took the pipe out of his mouth, licked his lips. He spoke slowly, deliberately, as though he had been rehearsing this speech for hours, and was now enjoying the opportunity to deliver it before an audience, blinking his eyes, cat fashion, in approval of his own performance.

"He said to tell ye that he was sorry ye was goin' to get more of them little sore places in ye belly but ye would."

Curse him, Bullock thought, curse all his ancestors, curse — little sore places in your stomach. You want to be a middle peon, neither rich nor poor, and there's no such thing. That's why you swear so much, that's why you wear that rich peon's coat, that yellow camel-hair coat. All poor peons who try to be middle peons, ache to be middle peons, get those little sore places. Sure I set 'em up. I tell the poor peons you stand here, you go without food so you will look hungry, for three days you go without food. I tell the rich peons, Jubine is here with his camera, stand on your head, ride a horse up the courthouse steps, jump in your swimming pool with your clothes on. Sure, I set 'em up, Bullock.

He sat in his car on Commerce Street, waiting for the newsstand on the corner to open up, watched the slowmoving owner of the stand rip open the big bundles of newspapers, and then heave them into position on the stand.

After the papers were lined up on the stand, he crossed the street, thinking he'd have to buy all the New York papers, and hunt, until he found — But he didn't have to. The first thing he saw was Jubine's goddamn picture.

He must have mailed it in, oh, who the hell cared how he got it there. Perfectly evident he'd gone to all the trouble, taken the pains, wasted the time, to deliver it in person, speeding through the night, on that motorcycle of his, speeding, speeding, to get even, straight to New York; and one of those halfbreed mongrel newspapers that had little or no advertising, certainly was not dependent on any from the Treadway Munitions Company, one of those New York tabloids, published it.

It must have been a dull night for crime in New York, because the picture had been blown up and put on the front page. The legend under it was short, clear, concise, easy to understand. It implied, in a few, carefully chosen, easy-to-read words, that the Duchess of Moneyland, young Mrs. Moneybags, of the gun empire, while drunk on a long life of lewdness, drunk on black beluga caviar and pink champagne, drunk on mink coats and Kohinoor diamonds, while driving her golden coach (he thought, Cinderella, pumpkin coach, papers in the pumpkin, Chambers, Hiss), accompanied by eighteen outriders wearing crimson velvet, trimmed with gold braid, had ridden down a child of the poor, in the streets of Monmouth, a city which belonged body and soul (since when do cities have bodies and souls, he thought) to the dowager Duchess of Moneyland. While the child of the poor lay helpless in the street (It would have to be a female child, he thought), the outriders had beaten her with blacksnake whips.

The Duchess of Moneyland, young Mrs. Moneybags, had laughed, her lascivious lips had curled as she pulled her sable coat about her slender shoulders, shouting, "Lay on, Macduff; and damn'd be him that first cries, 'Hold, Enough!' "

It didn't actually say that though the implication was there. But the tabloid's caption writer forgot to coach Mrs. Bunny Sheffield for the role she was to play. True, she was wearing a mink coat, and you could see that on one hand she wore a ring with a diamond in it so fiery that even on the cheap grayish impermanent paper of the tabloid she seemed to be wearing a spotlight on her finger. But her face was white, eyes haunted, mouth slack, one hand lifted, as though to ward off a blow. She was leaning against one of the fenders of the car, and she was looking up, no beauty in the face, nothing human about the face, just emptiness, and the drunkenness showed in the awful slackness of the mouth.

The child of the poor looked the part, might have been dressed by an imaginative stage designer for the part. The clothes were worn handmedowns, the coat sleeves too short, revealing thin wrists and thinner arms, shockingly nakedlooking wrists and arms. The coat and the dress so short that the legs were grotesque, too long, the knees knobby, the leg bones twisted; twisted from lack of food, but one leg twisted at an angle that was painful to look at, even in a photograph, because it had been twisted from contact with that big powerful shiny car, part of which could be seen.

And in the background, surrounding the car, the girl, were people, a great crowd of people, with angry, hostile faces; women with their arms akimbo; men frowning, shaking their fists, mouths drawn back in a snarl; and a policeman taking notes, two more policemen, arms uplifted, threatening the crowd; the child of the poor, dead center in front of the car, eyes closed, face deathlike.

Lest some careless reader miss the details, it said, just above this picture, See story page 3.

"Holy Mother of God!" he muttered. There wasn't a word about this in the Chronicle, not a word, not a line.

He flipped the page and read the story, quickly. Goddamn Jubine, anyway, he thought, may he burn in hell, he not only took pictures, he also played reporter, slick reporter, able to convince a sonofabitching city editor that one of his pictures was front page news, and that it deserved a story, a story longer than a tabloid normally uses.

It was one of those easy-to-read feature stories, padded with local color about Jubine, the photographer (called the recording angel), about Monmouth (that beautiful, rich, conservative, typically New England city), located in Connecticut (that neat, small, rich, conservative state, unlike any other in the Union), about Cesar the Writing Man, who was poetically referred to as the city's conscience. Detail about Cesar: how he chalked verses from the Bible on the streets of Monmouth. Samples of same: "For where your treasure is, there will your heart be also," in front of the banks. "Therefore all things whatsoever ye would that men should do to you, do ye even so to them: for this is the law and the prophets," in front of the courthouse. "Physician, heal thyself" in front of the professional building. "For wheresoever the carcase is, there will the eagles be gathered together," in front of real estate offices, insurance companies, churches. "For they that take the sword shall perish with the sword," in front of the armory.

Fine. And then he cursed again, felt a spasm of pain that twisted his stomach. "Thirty pieces of silver." Chalked in front of the building that housed the *Chronicle*, Monmouth's one big newspaper. Jubine made that one up. Nobody had ever written that there. Son of a bitch, he thought, skunk, bastard.

The pain in his lower abdomen was no longer a spasm, it was a twisting, turning, spreading horror that reached into his throat. He had to sit down or he'd vomit.

He sat in his car and waited until the pain eased off into a burning sensation, hateful but bearable. Then he went on reading what he now knew was Jubine's story. Jubine said that Cesar had prophetic powers, that if one of his quotes appeared in an unusual place, he, Jubine, knew that a crime would be committed on that spot. It had happened that way many times.

So, earlier on the afternoon of the accident, Jubine had seen Cesar chalk a verse at an intersection, on Dock Street: "Like the driving of Jehu the son of Nimshi; for he driveth furiously. II Kings 9:20."

Jubine had hung around, waiting. He was there when Camilo came roaring past the red light, slammed on the brakes, too late. The street was filled with factory workers going home — Poles, Italians, Negroes formed a mob around the car. The vagueness of her manner, her halting speech, the mink coat, the delicate shoes, the manicured hands, the big diamond were like a personal insult to these people.

Camilo murmured, "I lost — I can't find — I lost — "

Jubine said, "Camilo, ah, Camilo, what have you done?"

She looked up, eyes wide, horrified, and Jubine got his picture. Even the quotes there in the tabloid. And then the story of

Camilo's charge of attempted attack against Link Williams, Negro. Photograph of Link Williams on the same page. Bullock studied the face. You couldn't trust Jubine's pictures. He waited and waited until a building, a church or a bank or a school, or a human being, a man, woman, or child, assumed the aspect, momentary, fleeting, that he wanted, and then clicked his shutter. The result was not truth but a distortion of it achieved by tricks of light, by special circumstance, surprise or shock.

So here was this Negro standing on the dock, lordlylooking bastard, leaning against the railing, head slightly turned, profile like Barrymore's, sunlight concentrated on his left side, so that the head, the shoulders, the whole length of him had the solidity of sculpture, the picture damn near had the three-dimensional quality of fine sculpture. There was an easy carelessness about the leaning position of his body, controlled carelessness, and the striped T-shirt, the slacks, the moccasins on the feet suited his posture.

Every woman who saw this nigger's picture would cut it out, clip it out, tear it out, drool over it. Every white man who saw it would do a slow burn.

He crumpled the mongrel tabloid newspaper between his hands, tossed it out of the car window. Jubine had tried the case, handed in a verdict, with his goddamn pictures. He'd made the Treadway girl look like a whore and made the nigger look like Apollo.

It was planned, deliberate. Jubine waited three hours before he brought that picture around, waited that long so I wouldn't connect it with the accident. Even if I'd had it, he thought, I wouldn't have used it.

Not a word, not a line, in the *Chronicle*.

Those same words were thrown at him, spat at him, later in the morning. He was sitting at his desk, not thinking, not doing anything, just sitting there, when the door was flung open.

"What the hell kind of newspaper you think you're runnin' here?"

He didn't answer. He stared at the man who had invaded his office, a big angry, unshaven man, thinking, Well, well, well, I always wondered what Public Opinion would look like in the flesh, and here he is: hatless, drunken, odoriferous, brandishing a New York tabloid about his head as though it were a weapon.

"No fear, no favor, huh? That goddamn woman don't own this town yet, see? There ain't a word, not a line, in the *Chronicle* about it. Anybody'd think it never happened. Things is in one hell of a shape when you got to read a New York paper to find out what's goin' on in your own home town."

Bullock opened his desk drawer.

Public Opinion shouted, "I don't hold for niggers rapin' white women but I don't hold for no drunk rich women runnin' down poor folks' children in the street, either, see?"

Bullock said, "I don't hold for no drunken bums in my office either, see?" And took an automatic out of the desk drawer, and aimed it at the chest region of Public Opinion's dirty white shirt, and watched him deflate like a balloon, even to the hissing sound of his breath, just before he yelped and ran out, bumping into the door in his haste to get away.

Right after that he called in the city editor, and they planned the details of the story of the accident for the next day's paper, a reporter was to interview the child's parents, and another one was to get information from the hospital on the child's condition. The finished story was a smooth minimization of the accident, but it contained new information: the child had a broken leg, and a mild concussion, and was enjoying the special nurses, the flowers, the toys that Mrs. Treadway had provided for her. The parents of the child were grateful for the many kindnesses and the special attention that their child had received at Treadway Memorial Hospital.

He thought that was the end of it. But it wasn't. He was sitting in the dining room, eating breakfast with Lola, at eight o'clock the next morning when the telephone rang. He let it ring awhile, irritated that his normal-morning grumpiness should be disturbed by a telephone bell, feeling a curious kinship with his father, thinking that you had to get to be near fifty before you arrived at understanding of a male parent. His father had always performed like this at the breakfast table, and his mother had been as silent and as unobtrusive as Lola, not speaking until he downed his second cup of coffee.

Shrill ringing of the telephone again.

Lola said, "Pete — " softly.

Hush in her voice, just as though she were talking to an old and delicate invalid. He looked straight at her for the first time since they'd sat down at the table. She had on a white negligee, thin, silky, long. At eight in the morning she smelt good, looked good, red hair curling all over her head. Damn near forty and she could have passed for eighteen, with that handspan waist, and her breasts rising up out of that thin white pleated stuff, soft to the touch, delicately perfumed, ah, what the hell, he thought, she didn't do anything else but work at looking like that, just like an actress, whose appearance is an investment to be protected.

"Aren't you going to answer it?"

He sighed and got up from the table. The telephone was behind a screen, in the corner of the dining room. All dining rooms either eighteenth-century reproductions, or Swedish modern, theirs was Swedish modern, probably because it was more becoming to a redhead, and had cost enough to buy a house, just this modern furniture where he sat down to drink the skim milk and eat the mashed potatoes at night, and to drink the two cups of coffee in the morning, coffee that he wasn't supposed to drink, but had to — like that stuff they shoot into a hasbeen racehorse, jazz him up so he can keep running.

He went behind the screen, eightfold screen of thin blond wood, with drawings or paintings of wheat or rye on it, the thin curved blades a pale green, and the grains of wheat or rye painted a deeper color than the wood; both sides decorated like that, the bend and sway of the wheat or rye suggesting wind blowing through it, and the goddamn thing had cost enough to have been a Picasso, and after he'd stared at that grain blowing in the wind for as much as two minutes, his stomach began to heave, it made him seasick, cost as much as a Picasso and it made him seasick.

He said, "Hello," and stared at the wheat, and said, "Yes, all right," voice stiff, sounding rude, and not caring because he was thinking, What the hell do you want now, have I got to let you ruin my paper, or is it just a small matter of a Chinaman you want murdered, or a simple case of blackmail or arson?

"Yes, I'll be here," he said. "Very well." And hung up.

"Who was that?" Lola asked, holding a thin white coffee cup in both hands, the scarlet fingernails like an exotic decoration on the thin china.

"Mrs. Treadway." He wondered what his mother would have thought of Lola, wondered what he really thought of her himself. Unproductive. Good in bed, sure, but aren't they all? Wouldn't it have been cheaper to set her up in an apartment, and just go on from there? "She's coming here. This morning."

"Pete," she said, face thoughtful, eyes thoughtful. "Don't do it. Whatever it is she wants you to do, don't do it."

"Why?"

"It's gotten too complicated. She's still trying to save Camilo's reputation. And she can't. It's shot to hell. She wouldn't be coming here this morning, if she didn't plan to use you. Pete, you're not listening."

He grunted his refusal to commit himself. Did she think he was a simpleton? Well, wasn't he? Lola'd seen Jubine's pictures in the tabloid, she knew the *Chronicle* hadn't mentioned the accident. She must have heard the jokes, the salacious stories being told about Camilo, on every street corner, in the markets, on the busses and trolley cars. The flavor of the stuff being mouthed in the beauty parlors and the department stores, the special domain of the female, would be subtler and nastier than what was said in the bars and the barber shops.

He'd heard a fair sample of the barber shops' opinion of Camilo when he went to get a haircut yesterday afternoon. The barber behind the chair, right next to him, said to his customer, "Rich women got some funny tastes. I've heard that some of 'em got to go with colored fellers, just like they believed — "

"I don't think — " the customer started to say.

The barber slapped a hot towel firmly over the customer's face, and said, "So what was Camilo doing up in Niggertown at that hour in the morning when she said that the colored feller raped her? My wife says someone told her Camilo'd been to a dance, or somep'n, and she got out of the car to take the air, and kinda cool off. Now we got air all over Monmouth but Camilo's got to go breathe the stink up at the Dumble dock. After I see that picture of the colored feller, I figure he's been layin' her right along."

He had wondered if Mrs. Treadway knew what was being said about Camilo, and when he opened the door in answer to her ring, and she said, "Good morning, Mr. Bullock. I want to thank you for seeing me at this hour," he knew by the strained, tired note in her voice, the weariness in her face and eyes, that she probably knew more than he did of the stories being told about her daughter. Inside forty-eight hours, her face and voice had become that of an old woman.

He ushered her into the library, a pinepaneled room, that he rarely ever sat in, let alone used. The walls were lined, floor to ceiling, with shelves filled with books that had belonged to his father, his grandfather, his great-grandfather. The worn bindings were a shabby anachronism in the artful brightness of this mod-

ern widewindowed room, with its white linen draperies and its
handwoven offwhite nylon rug. A woman's room. A pretty room.
Except for the dark grimy leather bindings on the old books.

It was a room in which Mrs. Treadway in her fur cape and
dark gray tweed suit, small fur hat on the hair that once had
been pale yellow and was now streaked with gray, should feel at
home. A pretty woman in a pretty room. A woman's room.

"Won't you sit down?" He indicated an armchair near his desk,
chair upholstered in some kind of nonsensical whimsical geranium-
red fabric.

She sat down, but she leaned toward him, and her manner was
urgent, unrelaxed.

"These stories about Camilo," she said. Then the tired voice
died, came to life again. "You've got to help me put a stop to
them. You've got to help me, Mr. Bullock. She's disintegrating,
emotionally, psychologically, because of them."

I could tell her about the monkey and his friend, the cat, and
the roasted chestnuts, he thought. I could say, These are not my
chestnuts, Mrs. Treadway; and I will not thrust my paw into the
fire to pull them out for you. But if I plan to keep, hold on to,
that thirty thousand a year she pays out for advertising in my
paper, then I will pull rabbits out of hats, I will stand, sit, beg,
charge, sic 'em, and pull her hot chestnuts out of the fire — as
ordered.

"They are saying horrible things about her. I didn't know
people could be so cruel. Nobody believes — they're saying that
she — " the tired voice faltered, stopped, refused to put in
words the accusations against Camilo. "I never knew that people
could be so cruel," she said again. "My own servants believe these
dreadful stories. I have been to see the Judge, and he will not set
a date for that man's trial. He was evasive, full of excuses. He —
he managed to express doubt of Camilo's innocence — " Her face
changed, still haggard, old, but the expression was angry, ruthless,
coldly determined.

He thought, Juggernaut. I'm in the path of a juggernaut. It's
more serious than that. He remembered having seen this same
expression on his mother's face. He was ten years old, hair always
hanging down over his eyes, because he would not have his hair
cut, and a trip to the barber shop entailed assault with intent to
kill on the part of his parents; so they postponed the necessary
violence until he began to look like Rip van Winkle or a buffalo,

or both. He was in that shaggyheaded state one night, at supper, and there were candles on the table; and he stood up, bent over, long unkempt hair falling forward over the lighted candles. His hair caught on fire. His mother reached out and smothered the fire with her hands, bare, unprotected hands. As she bent toward him, reaching across the table, beating the fire out, just with her hands, the expression on her face had frightened him, so that he cried out in alarm. Years afterwards he saw a painting of The Furies, and there was the same expression that had been on his mother's face as she thrust her hands straight into his blazing hair — a ruthlessness, and a fury, and a cold determination. Same expression still on Mrs. Treadway's face.

"You've got to help me," Mrs. Treadway said. "I want — "

After she left, he wondered how it was that he came to be in a position where he couldn't say no. It was the rising cost of newsprint, it was the cost-of-living increase in wages that he had paid because it was requested, open threat behind the request. Most of the people who worked for him belonged to the Newspaper Guild, and it was perfectly obvious, though he had done everything he could to prevent it, that sooner or later his newspaper, the newspaper that had belonged to his father and to his grandfather, The Monmouth Chronicle, started as an abolitionist newspaper, started by that erratic highly moral definitely crazy man, his great-grandfather, would soon be run as a closed shop.

Yes, and it was the payments on that modern horribly-expensive-but-absolutely-necessary rotary press; it was the real estate tax on the building; the interest on the mortgage on the building, and on this ranchtype completely modern and unjustifiably expensive house that Lola had had to have. Now that she had it, she was not one whit happier than she'd been when they lived in that oldfashioned three-story affair that had belonged to his father — or maybe she was, she could spend more money living out here. There was the upkeep and the payments on the two cars and the station wagon, and the income taxes, and the Social Security payments. There was Social Security to be paid for the maid, and the laundress, and Social Security to be paid for the three-times-a-week heavy cleaning woman, whom Lola facetiously called the work girl; work horse would be a better name, he thought.

Social Security for maids. Blah! People didn't want to work any more. He could remember when maids saved for their old age, worked and saved, just like anybody else, and now they didn't have to, the State would take care of them, just like in Russia.

But what of a man named Bullock? Who was going to take care of Bullock in his old age? Not the State. Just Bullock.

If Mrs. Treadway took that institutional advertising with the American flag at the top, advertising that consisted of editorials on democracy, hymns of praise to the United States, out of his paper, it would just about fold up.

Lola would have to give up the green Buick, and the maid, and the laundress, and the cleaning woman, and the new fall clothes and the new winter clothes, the new spring clothes, the new summer clothes, and the annual cruise to Bermuda. She would have to do her own washing and ironing. What the hell did she do all day anyway? There was always extra help brought in for dinner parties, for luncheons, for bridge parties.

He could remember, how well remember, that his mother had had one girl, Swedish, name of Jenny, who stayed with the family until she died, and not only had his mother's house been a pleasant, orderly place, but she'd had five children and — But Lola had to have someone to do the cleaning and the dusting, someone to do the washing and the ironing, someone to do the cooking, and they had no children, yet there were always the most terrific, the most unexplainable and unexpected bills.

Take this house, this big mortgaged completely modern house that they'd built in the most exclusive section of Monmouth, on the outskirts, near Treadway Hall, and Lola still said they were lucky to be able to buy the land because after all, only millionaires lived out here. Monmouth's tradespeople knew it, so it cost them three times as much to live here as it had to live in his father's oldfashioned house in the center of the city.

Suppose I'd said no to Mrs. Treadway. Would Lola, could Lola, do her own washing and ironing and cooking? Would she? Could she? No. Well, he supposed she could, there were women who did. Lola? Why blame it on Lola?

Mrs. Treadway had said, again, "We have no contract with your paper, Mr. Bullock."

So that night he sat in the pinepaneled library, in the mortgaged ranchtype house, and thought about Mrs. Treadway, and then about his maiden aunt, who used to say, "A lie will be all over Providence while Truth is getting his boots on," salt of the sea in her speech, on her tongue, so that she looked and sounded as though she had been pickled in brine, remembering her house with its three chimneys, and a fireplace in every room, captain's house, double house. He'd lived with her in that house during the four years he went to Brown, thought of the city of Providence, lowlying city, and yet hilly, and of the graduation exercises and the baccalaureate held in the Baptist Meeting House, long hill to go down, and the caps and gowns descending, moving slowly, might have been a procession of blackrobed priests, except for the mortarboards, except, too, for the Baptist Meeting House, sacred to the memory of Roger Williams.

"A lie will be all over Providence," he said to himself, "or Berlin, or Rome, or MonmouthConnecticut, or any other damn place, while Truth is getting his boots on."

But this that he had agreed to do, and he reminded himself that he had agreed, was simply a matter of selecting one or two stories about crimes committed in The Narrows (Why not Niggertown? Because there is in me somewhere a reluctance. Then call her up and say you won't do it, say you changed your mind; and thought, Social Security, income tax, interest on mortgages and the amortization thereof, and payments on cars, and all the different kinds of insurance) and giving them a front page spot, in the *Chronicle*, every morning. Simply a matter of emphasizing, spotlighting, underlining these stories about crimes committed by Negroes. Simple. Uncomplicated. Neither truth nor lie. But truthlie. Lietruth.

Then he thought, But the mind of man being what it is, I know, and Mrs. Treadway knows, that if the *Chronicle* keeps saying that The Narrows breeds crime and criminals, a new set of images will be superimposed over those pictures that Jubine sold to the goddamn tabloid. The face of that nigger (Why not Negro? Because of the arrogance) Apollo will change first. It will almost immediately be transformed into the face of The Criminal, and will be remembered as such. Camilo's slackjawed face, face of the eternal whore, will be changed, transformed (more slowly, of course), until it becomes the face of The Victim, and she will be remembered and spoken of as such. Truthlie? Yes.

Is this possible? Of course. And quite necessary because that highly moral man, Judge Doan, has thus far refused to set a date for the trial. Someone must have got to the Judge, must have tampered with the Judge. He suddenly remembered Rutledge's seemingly idle question, "What're you going to do when the old lady comes in to cop a plea?" Thought of Rutledge's face, the way he talked, the lack of expression in his lead-colored eyes, and decided that he had the corrupt look of a man who had been born with a dollar sign where his soul should have been.

Then thought, Who am I to appraise, evaluate, another man's soul?

But if Rutledge got to the Judge, then who got to Rutledge? Who persuaded Monmouth's Chief of Police to intervene, interfere, in this case? A person or persons unknown. Person powerful enough to push a judge and a chief of police in the direction he wanted them to go, just as though they were pawns on a chessboard.

Jubine? Hardly. He is a simpleton with a monomania, a monomaniacal simpleton, and therefore powerless. Not really powerless. He has already tried the case and turned in a verdict. With his camera.

It doesn't matter who controls the Judge and the Chief of Police. What really matters is that Monmouth has a venal judge, and a venal chief of police. What of Bullock? Man named Bullock? Venal, too. The purchase price for all of us is low. We're bargain basement stuff. Marked way down.

These days people make that nasty counting gesture with the fingers, whenever my name is mentioned, whenever the Chronicle is mentioned. They say I sold out to the Treadway interests. Truthlie. Lietruth.

At midnight Lola came into the library, slender, redheaded, perfumed, wearing a dress of some kind of pale green brocaded stuff. Emerald earrings in her ears. He'd given them to her at Christmas.

"Whatever are you doing?" she asked. "You've been in here for hours."

"I am paying the piper," he said slowly. "I met him just the other day and he told me that I've been dancing to the tune he plays for a long time. Therefore I must pay him."

"What do you mean by that?"

"Just what I said. My business is, at the moment, inextricably mixed up with the piper's business." I wish she'd go away, leave me alone. She looks like a wood nymph.

"Have you been gambling?" she said, sharply.

"No. Nor wenching. Nor drinking. Nor contracting bad debts. Wait a minute," he said, thoughtfully. "Maybe it's the debts.

No. That's not true." Lietruth. Truthlie. "I'll be goddamned if I know how my path crossed the path of the piper." He thought of Jubine, saying, "The price you paid," of Jubine, saying, "You're a poor peon and you ache to be a rich peon."

Lola said, "Pete, has this got something to do with Mrs. Treadway?"

"Sure, it's got something to do with Mrs. Treadway," he said, glaring at her, thinking, All marriages are like this. The component parts are contempt and irritation because we know each other by heart, by rote; we're all graduates of the blab school for double harness. Then he looked at the redgold hair, the sweet curve of the mouth, and thought, Truthlie, because marriage is more than that. It's part hate, part love. It's remembered agony, and remembered delight.

"Sure," he repeated, leaning forward, lowering his voice, "Didn't you know that I raped Camilo? But I wore a black mask and used a bow and arrow instead of Popeye's corncob."

He leaned back in his chair, watching her, waiting for her to say, "I don't know why I go on living with you," because that's what she always said when she was angry. This time she didn't say anything, simply turned away from him, and went out of the room. He sat still, for a moment, listening to the rustling sound of her brocaded skirt, thinking of the way she looked when she first woke up, how the freshness of the morning seemed to be reflected in her face, in her eyes, and he got out of the chair quickly, and followed her out into the hallway, and put his arms around her.

Two weeks later, he sat in his office, frowning. He had been looking at copies of the *Chronicle*, all the issues, for the past two weeks, trying to determine why this crusade (If you could call it that, he thought) against crime in The Narrows had influenced his own thinking so that he had done something, finally, that he was ashamed of. His secretary had stacked the newspapers on his desk, in a neat pile, and he had crumbled them up, one by one, and tossed them on the floor.

He searched through these crumpled papers until he found Tuesday's paper, and reread the story about Miss Eleanora Dwight. On Monday night, Miss Dwight, an old maid schoolteacher, retired, was walking toward the rooming house where she lived. It was dusk, and the street was filled with shadows. She saw a man, a Negro, emerge from an areaway. She said it was as though a part of the night came toward her, a moving piece of darkness. The man knocked her down. Before he could harm her, she was rescued by a passer-by. Her assailant disappeared. Miss Dwight said, "He seemed to vanish, seemed to go right back into the blackness of the night."

This story, which had nothing to do with the dock or The Narrows, had been placed on the front page. Bullock's orders. No good reason for putting it there (a thirty-thousand-dollar reason). No good reason for not putting it there (a thirty-thousand-dollar reason). It should have been buried on an inside page where it would have been read with amusement, and dismissed as the wishful thinking of an old woman, and so forgotten. Instead — he shrugged. There was something poetic and disturbing and unforgettable, about that phrase, "a moving piece of darkness."

Wednesday's paper was of no importance. He didn't bother to look for it. It had the usual front page story about a crime committed in The Narrows. A robbery.

But Thursday's paper was very important. So was Friday's. He found both papers, smoothed them out, put them on his desk. On Wednesday night, a prisoner escaped from the State Prison. Thursday morning's paper said that all Monmouth knew about his escape. Because of the wail of the siren that stood atop the gray stone walls, because of the lights, the searchlights, because of the sudden frenzied activity of the guards, who were stationed along the length of the wall. The siren sounded about six o'clock. There was a dense fog and so the foghorn was sounding at the same time. The sound of the siren and the bray of the foghorn mixed, mingled, but the siren was always louder, stronger, more terrifying, symbol of disaster, of death.

The convict, a big heavily built Negro, knocked a man down, and took the man's clothes, and thus was able to leave his prison garb behind, on the road. He headed toward Monmouth, straight toward Monmouth, running with his head down. Dogs sensed his passage and barked, and he kept going, almost unseen, because of the fog. A dangerous man, a brute, a murderer. He disappeared.

Bullock read the story twice, thinking, There's nothing to be ashamed of here. It's overly dramatic but it is all true.

He picked up Friday's paper, with reluctance. He was ashamed of this one. This one told the story of the convict's end, and it carried his picture, a front page, blownup picture of the Negrovillianconvicthero.

He thought, I did this myself, no one told me to. It had nothing to do with Mrs. Treadway or that goddamn institutional advertising. The headline is bad enough. It ought to be on a billboard. They use the same kind of type on 'em. The picture is infinitely worse. But it's been done before. It's an ugly, senseless thing to do but not unforgivable. It's the story itself. It is the outrageous lie that I deliberately put in there.

But by next week, the convict would be forgotten. People would be talking about something else. Besides it was the kind of story that didn't harm anyone. It couldn't.

He started reading Friday's paper. It said the convict disappeared. The next day hunger drove him out into the open. He circled around a solitary farmhouse, waited outside for half an hour, crouched down in the shrubbery near the house. There was no car in the barn that was now used as a garage.

He went nearer, looked in through the kitchen windows, saw a woman, alone, fixing food, and opened the kitchen door.

"Food," he said. "I want food."

The woman screamed and he put his hand over her mouth, grabbed a dish towel, and made a gag, stuffing it in her mouth, snatched up some food, and was gone. The woman was lying on the floor when her husband found her, and when the gag was removed, she began screaming, and couldn't stop.

They caught the brute, the murderer, the escaped convict, the Negro, on the edge of the city. All the roads leading into and out of the city, leading to and from the prison, were patrolled.

Though why, Bullock thought, rereading this story that he had written himself, why any sane escaped convict would head toward those gray walls from which he had emerged, after God-knows-what struggle, God-knows-what weeks, probably months, of planning, nobody would know. But the readers of this story would not stop to question a matter of phrasing, they would shiver with horror and fright, and there would be, also, a certain delicate enjoyment, pleasure, mixed with it, because the convict was dead.

The policemen, detectives, guards from the prison, National Guard, had patrolled the roads, the streets of the city, so that everywhere you went you saw armed huntsmen, peering, walking, patrolling.

Ah, what the hell, he thought, as he threw the newspaper down on the floor of his office. He wasn't responsible for this. This had happened all by itself. Or had it? How did he know whether this man, this convict, had not somehow been influenced by the stories in the *Chronicle?* How did he know what word had seeped back inside the walls of that gray stone prison, so near the city that you could see it, yet so far away that you could easily forget that it was there, except when the siren sounded. Anyway, the man was dead. He'd been shot, riddled with bullets, the story said.

It had damn near backfired, too. Because that thin, grayhaired, overworked housewife had refused to say that the convict had tried to attack her.

The *Chronicle's* reporter said that she had stubbornly repeated the same words, over and over again. "He didn't do nothing to me. I hollered because I didn't know he was there in the kitchen. He spoke up and I didn't know there was nobody there but me until he spoke up and it scared me and I hollered. I didn't know he was no convict. He was a big black man and the sight of him there so sudden and so unexpected in my kitchen scared me. I'da hollered the same way if he'da been a big white man showing up so sudden and so unexpected in my kitchen. He didn't do nothing to me except stuff the dish towel in my mouth, and then stuffed some food in his own mouth, and grabbed up some more food and run out the door. He didn't do nothing to me."

Her husband kept saying, "Shut up, you're nervous, you're upset, you don't know what you're talking about — "

The wife, the thin overworked past-middle-age wife, said to the reporter, "Young man, don't you write down that he bothered me. He didn't do nothing to me. All he done was — "

So Bullock wrote down simply, and untruthfully, that the black convict, the brute, the escaped murderer, had attacked the frail housewife when he found her alone in the big farmhouse. And put the convict's picture on the front page.

It was a picture which showed the convict not as a man but as a black animal, teeth bared in a snarl, eyes crazy, long razor scar like a mouth, an open mouth, reaching from beneath the eye to the chin, the flesh turned back on each side, forming the lips of this dreadful extra mouth. Bullock knew that everyone who saw that picture would remember it, and wake up in the middle of the night covered with sweat, because this terror, this black terror, had a shape, a face; and they would remember the headline NEGRO CONVICT SHOT in boldface type, headline that took up the center half of the paper, and they'd think Yes, the crazed black animal with the mutilated face is dead, but what about the others, there are others who are still alive, who are just as dangerous. White women not safe. Not safe in Monmouth.

What the hell, he thought, if it hadn't been this it would have been something else. No matter how you looked at it, it was a nervous time in which to be alive, a nervous year, what with high prices, and all the little wars that threatened to become big wars; what with people fumbling for, reaching for security, and looking over their shoulders at insecurity.

Even the State Department was acting like a harried housewife, searching out the hiding place of mice and cockroaches and bed-bugs, any of the vermin that from time to time invade a house, searching carefully under beds and in bureau drawers, and on closet shelves, in cellars and in attics, peering inside ovens, and sugar bowls, looking in every likely and unlikely place for commu-nists and socialists, for heretics and unbelievers, and uncovering so much dust, so much of what Bullock's maiden aunt, the one with the sharp vulgar tongue, called slut's wool, so much of the dirty traceries of moths, so many cobwebs that the whole country shuddered.

So what difference does it make, he thought, whether we here in Monmouth hunt down Negroes or whether we hunt down Communists. We? You mean you and Mrs. Treadway. And there is a difference, though at the moment it escapes me.

That picture of the Negro with the mutilated face — that wasn't, I shouldn't have. It is the one thing I regret. The rest of it isn't important. But I had to. I had to offset that other picture, Jubine's picture of that arrogant nigger with the Barrymore profile. I had to. I had to offset, counterbalance, outweigh that dirty counting gesture made with index finger and thumb that had be-come an unspoken byword, a symbol for the *Chronicle*. I had to.

But on Monday he was going to tell Mrs. John Edward Tread-way to take her goddamn advertising and stick it because he was going all out in another direction. He would —

But by Monday it was too late.

21

● MALCOLM POWTHER sat in the back seat of Captain Sheffield's car, on Dumble Street, and listened to the soft sound of the motor, soft sound of the motor, and the windshield wiper kept saying, Scupper, scupper, scupper, scupper, just the one word, over and over, and it made a sound in the car, which was good, and the foghorn was sounding at intervals, Whodid, whodid, on two notes — and it made a sound outside, which was good, because they were sitting there silent, all of them, waiting.

The Madam, and that had surprised him, was in the car too, sitting in the front seat with the Captain. And the two young men, who were friends of the Captain's, were in the back seat. Waiting.

He wouldn't let himself think about why they were waiting. Though bits and pieces of the reason would float up to the surface of his mind. He approved of the rain. The early dark. Otherwise there would be more people on the street, and they would have turned to look at that parked car, people sitting in it, seemed to be a lot of men in it, and the engine running.

Last winter Al kept saying, "Whyn't she divorce Bunny?" That was before any of this had happened. He had told Al, "It's kinder. What she's doing is really kinder. When a man, all of him, is involved with a woman, I don't think the man really cares whether she has affairs with other men. So long as she doesn't leave him. He cares, yes, that is, he doesn't like it. It hurts him. But it would hurt worse if she left him. And Miss Camilo is a very kind person. A lovely person. She knows that it would ruin the Captain if she left him. It's not a perfect situation for her or the Captain. But Miss Camilo is a very great lady and perhaps she feels it's her fault that the Captain is so dreadfully in love with her, so she stays with him. She can't bring herself to hurt him, the way it would if she left him."

That was before all this other business. The Captain must have known he would have rivals. Yes, but had he been able to foresee one the size and shape — and color — of Link Williams?

Scupper. Scupper. Scupper. Link Williams. Mamie tore that picture of him out of that New York paper. It was on the kitchen table, one night when he came home. He said, "What's that there for?" not wanting to ask, but having to, afraid to know, but having to know, actually believing that she would say, "Because I got a heat on for him, sugar."

She never talked about love, always about somebody having a heat on for somebody else, and he expected her to say that, standing there in the kitchen, wearing a new red-and-white-striped dress, with no sleeves in it, and the neckline cut so low you could see the dividing line of her breasts. And the kitchen filled with the toosweet smell of her perfume, and J.C. standing there barefooted, looking at both of them, licking raspberry Kool-Aid off the palm of his hand, no expression on his face, just that bovine licking of the palm of his hand, and his tongue a brilliant poisonous red, and the acidulous smell of the stuff competing with the smell of Mamie's perfume.

Mamie laughed. She said, "That's one goodlookin' nigger, Powther. Look at him standing there on that dock, just like he owned it, and would throw anybody in the river who said he didn't. That's why I cut it out. Because he looks like he owns everything in sight. That's why."

She didn't say a word about Miss Camilo's accident with the car, and that dreadful picture of her on the front page of that New York tabloid, and the talk, the talk, everywhere, so much of it, and so filthy, that he finally asked Al to drive him home nights because he couldn't bear to listen to what people said on the Franklin trolley. Listening to the servants at the Hall was bad enough, but it was worse, infinitely worse to have to listen to strangers bandying Miss Camilo's name around, just as though they knew her and had the right, had been given the right, to discuss her. He tried to figure out why people were so malicious, why they showed such delight in saying horrible things about a young woman they'd never seen. He supposed it was the same thing that had, for years, sent thousands of people to championship fights when Joe Louis was fighting. Sure they all thought he was wonderful, was a great fighter, had the heart of a champion, but they wanted to see him knocked out. People like to see a king uncrowned, like to see a thoroughbred racehorse beaten when he's running at the top of his form and has outrun everything in sight. They wanted to see demonstrated right before their eyes that there was no such thing as invincibility, wanted to see that the king, the top dog, the best man, has a flaw, can be beaten like them, is vulnerable like them, can be defeated, unfrocked, uncrowned, knocked down, and thus brought right down to their level.

Scandal in a wealthy, important family like the Treadways served to bring the Treadways right down to the level of the trolley car conductor, the bootblack. It showed they could be hurt, wounded, ruined, just like other people.

He sighed, impatient with the waiting, wishing that some one of them would say something. As soon as he got out of the car, he would hurry across the street, go in through the front door, up the carpeted staircase, ears straining with listening, trying to determine in that dark upstairs hall whether Mamie was home, still there, or did the darkness and the silence mean that he had been too late, that she had gone off somewhere. He didn't use the outside back stairs any more, hadn't since all this crime had been going on in The Narrows, couldn't bring himself to walk around the side of Mrs. Crunch's house, head into the darkness at the corner of the house. He'd tried it and it seemed to him that his shoulder blades started to itch, in anticipation of a knife blade plunged into his unprotected back. He explained to Mrs. Crunch why he came in through the front, and she had said, "Mercy, yes, Mr. Powther. I keep expecting we'll all be murdered in our beds. I move a bureau in front of my bedroom door every night, and I've got new locks on the windows, and I still wake up frightened. What ever has happened to these people? Why are they acting like this?"

Someone came out of The Last Chance, and he leaned forward. No. It wasn't. How much longer would they have to wait?

Sunday and a quiet rain, April rain, falling in the street. Umbrellas, rubbers, raincoats. And the interminable swish of the windshield wiper, a mechanical thing, but it ought to be tired. Not time for evening church services to start, dinner mostly in the early afternoon, this was a kind of winding down of the day, of Sunday. Very few people on the street, an occasional passer-by, intent on his or her own business. No sound of voices.

He became aware of the beating of his heart, unpleasant, wanted to count it, noticed that it was not synchronized with the whodid of the foghorn, the scupper, scupper of the windshield wiper, his heartbeat faster, than the other two, and the windshield wiper faster than the foghorn, irritating, listening to, waiting for three different sounds occurring at different intervals. A car passed, and then another one, and they all shrank back, drew back, the sudden illumination of the headlights disturbing.

A man turned into The Last Chance, a man who shambled, shuffled when he walked, shapeless felt hat pale redorange under the neon sign. Weak Knees. He stood still in front of the door, looking up and down the street. Powther thought, He knows there's something wrong, he senses it, smells it, like an animal recognizes the presence of danger without knowing what it is. "Weak made 'em. He's the cook in Bill's place" — doughnuts, wonderful texture, sweet fragrant flavorsomeness sticking in his throat —

Weak Knees went in The Last Chance. Another car went by. This one going slowly, not the sudden flashing brilliance, there one moment and gone the next, this one slowmoving, so that he saw the back of the Captain's head, saw each reddish hair, the cleanlooking neck, thought he must have had a haircut in New York, before he came up yesterday; saw the back of the Madam's head, her shoulders straight, held stiffly under the tan-colored raincoat, the hair looked white in the slowmoving unfocused car lights, disturbed by it too, because she lifted her hand, beautifully manicured hand, in a vague, purposeless gesture which reached for and never touched the whitelooking curls.

Never until now had he thought of her as a person, with feelings, with emotions, always vaguely as a fine, generous, kind, great lady, a kind of separate and apart person, living and breathing, yes, but not as ever having known anger or hate or fear, not as a mother. She and the Captain didn't like each other. Or rather, the Madam didn't like the Captain. He wondered why the Captain called her Mrs. Treadway, never having had a mother-in-law he couldn't hope to figure out all the delicate posturings and nuances and half-formed vague resentments that such a relationship might entail. The Copper boys' wives all called Old Copper "Pop" easily, naturally. This formality between the Captain and the Madam was a strange thing.

He watched the doorway of The Last Chance. Nothing. Another car, and that sudden swift illumination revealing the Captain's head, the Madam's whitelooking curls. He wished someone would say something.

Two people walking past. Talking. He listened, glad to hear voices.

The man (querulously): I don't know where he is. What you keep askin' me that for? I told you - - I ain't seen him for two weeks.

The woman: What kind of fool you take me for? If you don't know where he is, how come you got his wallet?

The man: He give it to me. He give it to me before he left.

The woman: 'Fore he left for where? You ain't said nothin' bout his leavin' for nowhere.

The man: You ain't give me chance. You been sayin' nothin' but where is he. I don't know where he is. He told me he was goin' away and he's gone. I don't know where he's gone.

The woman: You always been a son of a bitch. He ain't give you no wallet of his and you know it. What you done with him? You answer me that. Where is he? He's your own brother and you gotta know where he is —

A quiet April rain, just enough fog to blur the edges of buildings, to destroy the clean outline of The Hangman. Hangman's buds beginning to swell. No one would really be aware of the coming of spring in Dumble Street, except for The Hangman. Thought of Old Copper, "Got the goddamndest climate, in the whole United States." Old Copper and his paintings, Mamie coming down the steps, walking slowly, bigbosomed, firmfleshed, brown skin translucent, like there was a light under it, redbrown, even the smile, the expression, just like the women in the paintings. The nudes. Outsize. Pinkfleshed.

Dreadful to watch Miss Camilo, to see Miss Camilo. Unbearable. He would collapse just like that if Mamie should leave him. Sound of the foghorn, Whodid? Whodid? Whodid? Why wouldn't she go away from Monmouth? Go into the country. Country. Cows. Cool. Spring. Could remember that bellowing, that moaning mooing of a cow, night after night, day after day, nerve endings right at the surface of the skin, the sound tearing the nerves, and his grandmother finally yelling, Whyn't somebody go git a bull, whyn't somebody, nerve ends frazzled, exposed, jumping. Miss Camilo.

Wish again for voices. Scupper? Scupper? Scupper?

Then a blast of sound in the street. He jumped. And felt the men, the two men, the friends of the Captain's, the two big young men that were like a blanket on each side of him exuding heat, warmth, jump too.

The Madam said, "What was that?" in a whisper, desperate, tense.

Then a voice, magnified, huge, all about them, said, "In the beginning God created the heaven and the earth."

Then a whirring sound. Powther sighed. It was that new loudspeaker they'd installed in Reverend Longworth's church — Masters University, healings of mind and body, I am the Way, the Truth, and the Life, and then the minister's name, Dr. H. H. Franklin Longworth, F.M.B. Minister, Psychologist, Metaphysician. Everyone Is Welcome. That's about what it said on the sign.

Mamie had told him about the loudspeaker that Reverend Longworth had had installed, had said they were going to try it out this Sunday, using a record. She said, "Now ain't that goin' to be a bitch, to have to listen to that pansy preachin' and prayin', just like he was in your house."

The lights came on in the church, or rather the building that housed Reverend Longworth's followers, came on suddenly, all over the building, spotlights on the sign across the front. Powther thought, It's just as though he said, Let there be light. He could visualize Longworth's face, his figure. He was a tall thin man, and his skin should have been brown but it was a sickly yellow, pallid yellow skin, like a plant whose leaves should have been dark green but because it was untouched by the sun, the leaves were pale yellow. He had a pointed beard too, and the beard was luxurious, thick, glossy, and didn't match his face.

Well, I didn't really bring the Madam here, he thought, that is, it was her idea, not mine; but I hate to have her listen to that charlatan perform. Then he couldn't think any more because the blasting sound of the Reverend Longworth's voice not only filled his ears, it filled his mind too.

Longworth (in a highpitched, rhythmical, hypnotic voice): And the Lord said unto Cain —
Then there was music, a choir composed of male and female voices began to hum, the sound rising, falling, rising, increasing in volume, and then an organ accompaniment in the background.
Slight pause. Organ music again. So loud it hurt the ears. Then the choir picked up the pitch of Longworth's voice, uncannily, preposterously, so that the singing voices seemed to be answering him, or questioning him.

Choir: Oh my good Lord, Show me the way,
   Enter the chariot travel along —

Longworth (voice louder, slower): And the Lord said unto Cain —

Choir: Noah sent out a mornin' dove
   Enter the chariot travel along —

Longworth: Where is Abel thy brother?

Choir: That dove came bearin' a branch of love
   Enter the chariot travel along —

Longworth (voice sonorous, slower and slower): And he said, What hast thou done?

Choir: Oh my good Lord, Show me the way,
   Enter the chariot travel along —

Longworth (voice faster, louder, voice blasting): The voice of thy brother's blood crieth unto me from the ground.

Choir (faster, louder, volume increasing):
   Oh my good Lord, Show me the way,
   Enter the chariot, travel along —

There was the loud whirring sound of the record. And then the voice of Reverend Longworth filled Dumble Street again. There was a caressing note in it this time. He said, "The service starts at seven o'clock tonight. Everyone is welcome. In the beginning there was the Word." Long pause. "I am the Way, the Truth, and the Life." Then the whirring sound again. That's what he said but the cajoling, caressing voice suggested that he was saying, Come unto me, I understand everything. Come. Be Saved.

Silence in the street now. Just the soft April rain. No cars. No one walking past. Idling sound of the motor. Scupper of the windshield wiper. Foghorn. Whodid, whodid, whodid. Red-orange neon sign in front of The Last Chance. Then the clang-clang of a trolley car over on Franklin.

He was unpleasantly aware of the two big young men on each side of him, unpleasantly aware of the warmth from their bodies. Two big young male animals.

The mateless cow, bellowing.

Where is thy brother? Lost somewhere between the whodid of the foghorn, and the scupperscupper of the windshield wiper. He wasn't my brother. I have to prove he wasn't my brother. Prove to these people in this car, that all Negroes are not criminal, some of them are good, some of them are selfrespecting, some of them are first class butlers named Powther.

He had looked at that picture on the front page of the *Chronicle*, picture of a black man with a livid living scar across one side of his face, picture of an escaped convict who was dead, but who lived again in that nightmare photograph. Looked at it and shuddered.

Then he had seen the same newspaper on the Madam's desk, the same picture, when she said, Will you point out, point at, point? Looked at it and started to shudder again, thinking, Why should the face of this animal be permitted to enter my world, expected to hear the Madam say, You have been satisfactory, done a good job here, but you might become, you might, after all, you belong to the same race, there must be in you whatever it was in this man that made him — and instead she said, Will you point out. Point at. Point.

Sunday morning. This morning. It seemed a long time ago. He had gone up the stairs, slowly, wondering why he was being summoned to the morning room at ten o'clock. The Madam was sitting at her desk, turning over some papers. She said, "Powther, I need your help."

"My help, madam? I'll be glad to — "

"Wait," she said sharply. "Don't say that until you know what I want you to do. Do you know the man named Lincoln Williams?"

"Lincoln Williams?" he repeated. "You mean Link Williams?

Why, yes — " and he was embarrassed because he did not want
to discuss Miss Camilo with the Madam.

"You see, I — that is, we, Captain Sheffield and I want to talk
to him. And we do not know him when we see him. I thought
you might be willing to go into that area with us, and point him
out to us."

Link Williams, he thought, Link Williams, point him out,
point him out, what did she mean, point him out for what, point
with your finger, but why? For what? Then he thought, "That
area." It sounded like a compound. Dumble Street. She doesn't
know, she has forgotten that I live there.

"You undoubtedly know about the troubles we've had of late.
And if you could help us, I would be extremely grateful, Powther."

In the early morning sunlight she looked old and tired and
there were new fine lines around her eyes that he hadn't noticed
before; and her hair was drylooking, brittlelooking, that light
blond hair that had gray in it, but it didn't show up at first
glance because of the color of the hair, same color hair that Miss
Camilo had; most people thought Miss Camilo dyed it but she
didn't, it was naturally that color. And the Madam's eyes, funny,
and he didn't quite believe it, seemed to plead with him for help.
He thought, Why, she's really all alone. There isn't anybody to
help her. Miss Camilo is walking around in a trance, drinking too
much, taking sleeping pills, Rita said the Madam had gotten after
Miss Camilo about the sleeping pills, had asked Miss Camilo to
go back to New York, and Miss Camilo had refused to leave Monmouth. Or so Rita said.

What did she want him to do? Point at, point to, point out.
Point.

"You will do it?"

"Certainly, madam. It's a small enough thing to ask. I'll be
glad to."

So here they sat, in the Captain's car, waiting, and the windshield wiper kept making that talking sound, Scupper, scupper,
scupper. Sometimes he thought it was in the form of a question:
Scupper? Scupper? Scupper?

The door of The Last Chance opened again. Powther leaned
forward, "That's him," he said, pointing at the man who stood
for a moment under the redorange sign, bathed in redorange light,
redorange from head to foot, hatless, coatless.

They all watched him, waiting, to see if he was going to cross the street, move away from the door. He stood there, motionless.

Powther kept willing him to move, thinking, End the agony, the jealousy, the pain, the hurt, the outraged cries that bubble up in one's throat at night, and the nights, the dark, pitiless, endless nights, I know what it's like and so does the Captain. Link Williams and Bill Hod, mixed up in his mind, had become one and the same person in his mind.

At this moment, if it works out right, because they only plan to frighten him, make him leave Monmouth, I am helping to get rid of this creature who is worse than thief, worse than murderer, this wife stealer, and here and now in this thing the Captain and I are equals, both outraged, both victims, and so we have achieved a kind of togetherness, and in this way I have restored a little of my own long lost selfrespect.

The two young men were leaning forward, watching, too, waiting, too, and Powther thought he could feel the tenseness in them, thought of the badges they had, nickel badges that would shine just like real ones, under an electric light, thought of that white paper they carried, that could at just a glance appear to be a warrant, paper with a picture pasted on it, smooth paste job, so that it was almost like print, and that official-looking type, cut from an old newspaper and pasted on so that that, too, at first glance seemed part and parcel of a real warrant, only it said:

Life is a mysterious and exciting affair and anything can be a thrill if you know how to look for it, and what to do with opportunity when it comes.

Rain misting the windshield, and the wiper talking to itself, it was a statement now, Scupper, scupper, scupper.

He thought, Why am I here? Why me? They couldn't trust anybody else. They can't tell one colored person from another. Link Williams and I look alike to them. They couldn't pick him out of a crowd, let alone on this street, this rainy street, at almost night, because all colored persons look alike to them.

Suddenly he said, "There."

Because Link Williams was moving away from the door of The Last Chance, walking away, toward the dock, with that easy effortless walk. He said, "That's him," again, louder, emphasizing it, with a large wide gesture of his hand.

The two big young men got out of the car. Powther saw Link

Williams hesitate, saw the flash of the badges under the street light, saw the whiteness of the paper they held out toward him, warrant for his arrest, official-looking warrant.

Then he slipped out of the car, got out on the side next to the road, a little man indistinguishable in the dusk, just a small anonymous figure, moving fast, moving away fast, hurrying away from the sound of the windshield wiper, Scupper, scupper, scupper.

Once inside the kitchen, in the heat, and the light, and the smell of the food cooking, and the yelping of the boys, the sound of Mamie's singing, he started to tremble, to shake, it was more than shaking, it was a jerking of his body.

Mamie said, "Sugar, what's the matter? You look awful," and put her arms around him, pulling his head down on her big soft breasts, cushioning his head there.

22

● THE MOMENT Link Williams sat down in the back seat of the
car, handcuffed, he knew that these men, sitting on each side of
him, were not policemen, not plainclothesmen, knew that this
new black Packard was not a police car. The motor was running,
and the man behind the steering wheel put the car in gear, pulled
off, before the doors slammed shut, in the back.

They went down Dock Street, car going fast, faster. He thought,
Kidnaping? Ransom? Have I somehow got mixed up in one of
Mr. B. Hod's private wars?

He leaned back against the seat, relaxed against it, and the
trenchcoated gentlemen, on each side of him, stiffened, tensed,
very nearly jumped, he could feel their bodies tighten up. He
wondered what they had expected him to do, a man handcuffed,
sitting between two men not handcuffed.

They turned off Dock Street and went east for a block, turned
again, and went down Franklin Avenue, following the trolley
tracks. Couldn't be a kidnaping because the driver was staying on
this through road. Yet the lady on the front seat doesn't like light.
He could see the outlines of her shoulders, see whitelooking, curly
hair. She doesn't like the pauses for the stop lights, she stiffens,
shoulders get rigid; and these gentlemen in the back seat don't
like the stop lights either, they shrink back as though they were
trying to escape into the steel framework of the car. Not kidnaping. Some other dark midnight deed.

Going faster and faster, still following the car tracks. He used to ride this route, on the trolley. If they stayed on Franklin he would recognize the place where the tracks ended, just disappeared in the black of the macadam road. End of the line. Used to ride the trolley, going to work for the Valkills, an almost-but-not-quite-middle-aged, childless couple, who wanted someone just for the summer, someone to set the table and wash-wipe a few dishes. Abbie found the job for him when he was twelve years old.

He used to get on the trolley about eight-thirty in the morning, and the air was clean and clear and fresh, and still cool, at that hour. He liked the clang of the trolley, liked to watch the people get on and off, most of them knew the motorman, and everything was friendly and the people all looked early morning clean and brisk. He rode the car to the end of the line, and got out and walked a quarter of a mile to where the Valkills lived, and as he walked along, the nearer he got to the house, the more the early morning cleanness seemed to evaporate, diminish, begin to slide down into the hot tired dreary part of the day.

The Valkill house was on the edge of the river, a small weathered gray house filled with an indescribably stale, old, shutup river smell; it seemed to come from the wood, the walls and the floors. He finally got so he thought he could smell the house before he saw it, thought he could see the Valkills before he caught a glimpse of them.

They were always outside the house, lying on a narrow strip of gravelly rocky shore which constituted a beach, a mere separation of the river from the land. Mrs. Valkill wore a black bathing suit and Mr. Valkill wore khaki shorts. Even at nine in the morning, even when he was on a three-week vacation, Mr. Valkill had his eyes closed, as though he were too tired to look at Mrs. Valkill's meaty underside-of-a-flounder-white thighs. Mr. Valkill was very tanned. His eyes were blue and very wide open — when he wasn't looking at Mrs. Valkill.

Abbie said they were fine rich people. He thought they were fine slave drivers. He hated them.

He rebelled against this job that Abbie had picked out for him, rebelled against doing housework that was never finished. There were the breakfast dishes, and the last night's dinner dishes, more or less skilfully tucked around here and there, but he recognized them, knew that two people could not possibly use all those dishes just for breakfast. And he was supposed to sort of help with lunch, and while they ate in the dining room, he sat on the small porch off the kitchen, on the railing, watching the river, and wondering about these people he worked for, the Valkills.

After lunch he cleared the table, washed the luncheon dishes, swept and dusted, and dusted and swept. He'd been there about two weeks when Mrs. Valkill gave a tea, and had him wear some kind of Japanese kimono and the kimono was all peculiar colors, made of a sleazy thin material that smelled like the house, and the old tired musty river smell that clung to the material made his skin crawl.

Mr. Valkill strolled in at the tailend of the tea party, and his eyes were filled with laughter whenever he looked at Link in the kimono, and he followed him out to the kitchen and watched him as he washed the cups and saucers, and said, "Mrs. Valkill is a genius. I never would have noticed — never would have known how attractive a Japanese kimono could be — "

Mr. Valkill called him Cassius, and when Mrs. Valkill asked him why, he said, " 'Yond Cassius has a lean and hungry look,' such men are dangerous," and Mrs. Valkill laughed and laughed and had to wipe her eyes. They talked about him, right in front of him, just as though he weren't around.

He hated the job, and told Abbie so, and Abbie wouldn't listen to him. She folded her mouth into a thin straight line, and said in that refusingtolisten voice, "Every boy should know how to keep a house clean. There aren't any easy jobs. You might as well find it out now while you're young — "

After he wore the Japanese kimono, Mr. Valkill took to appearing suddenly in the kitchen, watching him, leaning in the doorway, or practically lying down on one of the straightbacked kitchen chairs because he lolled on the end of his spine, but his bright blue eyes were wide open, bright blue eyes always filled with laughter.

Now when he approached the house, Mr. Valkill greeted him, from the beach. "Good morning, Cassius, what's the weather like? You want to go back to sleep? There's plenty of room." Bright blue eyes very wide open, one hand indicating the beach, the rocky little beach, hand extended in invitation.

Mrs. Valkill said, "Stop it, Henry."

Mr. Valkill ignored her. "The rocks aren't bad once you get yourself in the right position."

Shortly after that they went away for the weekend, a long weekend. He had all of Monday off, and spent it in the kitchen of The Last Chance, except when he went swimming off the dock with Bill. He told Bill about the Valkills, and Bill kept looking blank, completely blank, except when he came to the part about the Japanese women's clothes they had him wear when they had people in for tea, and his face changed. "Holy Christ!" he said. "Listen, you go out there tomorrow morning and you quit. You hear? Quit. Just like that. And if your aunt don't like it, tell her to see me and I'll spell it out for her, in two words."

Tuesday morning he went back to the Valkills. Just as he opened the kitchen door, Mr. Valkill came sauntering into the kitchen, wearing khaki shorts, his long hairy legs, his knobby knees, thick blond hair on his tanned chest, something not to look at, to avoid looking at.

"Well, well, well," he said. "If it isn't Cassius just in time to fix the morning coffee." His eyes looked more alive than Link had ever remembered seeing them.

He made the coffee and Mr. Valkill lingered in the kitchen drinking it, and talking, and when he finished he sat on the end of his spine, delicately balancing the cup on his fingertips. He said, "Madam Valkill won't be home until late this afternoon."

He stopped listening to the soft drawling voice because Mr. Valkill seemed to be talking to himself. He supposed he'd have to wait until Mrs. Valkill came home, tell her he was quitting, because she was the one who hired him, who paid him, and Abbie said you always told your employer when you resigned from a job, or if you had any complaint. You had to take the direct approach, never the indirect approach, because colored people invariably avoided unpleasantness, they would lie, they would laugh, but they never faced right up to a situation, head on.

He wondered what he ought to do when he finished the dishes. These were the Friday morning breakfast dishes, really stuck with food, like it was glued on, eggs on the plates like yellow oil paint, crusted black stuff in the bottom of both coffee cups, two sticky glasses that had contained orange juice, both of them had had toast, and there had been marmalade on Mr. Valkill's toast, because the leftover portion had little fine red ants on it. Mrs. Valkill didn't eat marmalade on her toast for fear of getting fat — no, she said because of her hips.

There was a change in Mr. Valkill's voice. It was softer, gentler. Link turned and looked at him.

"Did anyone every tell you you were goodlooking?" he said, idly, not moving, still balancing the coffee cup.

"What?"

"You're a goodlooking boy, Cassius."

Link said Yeah, yeah, yeah, thinking of Weak Knees: Some things is natural and some things is against nature. Don't you never spend no time listenin' to any man who starts sweet talkin' to you. You hear me, Sonny? You always move off. If you ain't got no place to move off to, then you holler.

He hung the dish towels on the rack, carefully, taking his time about it, his movements slow, his thoughts fast, remembering Weak Knees kneading bread, one Saturday morning in the kitchen, thump thump of the dough, "Any time you smell trouble, and you kind of all alone some place where can't nobody hear you if you was to holler, why it ain't never no disgrace to turn tail and run. Even the Boss has had to hightail it a coupla times anyway. Ain't never no disgrace to turn tail and run."

The black Packard was going faster and faster. Nobody spoke in the car. Good advice. If you smell trouble. I smell trouble. How do you go about running, in the interior of a car, with handcuffs on your wrists, how do you run then?

But he'd run that other time. Mr. Valkill put his hand on his arm, Mr. Valkill's hand reminded him of Bill Hod's hand, firm warm wellcaredfor clean hand, the nails filed, but the forearm was thickcovered with blond hair, like blond fur on the forearm, forearm of a blond ape, and revulsion made him move. He'd been standing there half fascinated, half afraid, curious, too — wondering what and how —

He said "Yeah" again and moved fast, so fast, that Mr. Valkill's hand was left outstretched, reaching. He went toward the kitchen door, out on the porch, down the steps, fast, not running, but covering ground without wasting any time, so that he was outside the house, going down the road, before Mr. Valkill could possibly overtake him.

He heard him shouting, "Hey, what's the matter? Where are you going?"

Then he ran. He ran all the way to the car line, to that place where the tracks, the trolley tracks, appeared suddenly in the black of the macadam road. When he reached Dumble Street, he went in The Last Chance, and when he came out, he had a job for the rest of the summer, working in the kitchen there. And told Abbie so. Abbie said, "I won't allow it. You're going straight back to Mrs. Valkill tomorrow morning and tell her that I sent you back."

"I won't," he said, flatly, stubbornly.

He heard Abbie and F. K. Jackson discussing it.

F. K. Jackson: He can't go back to the Valkills, Abbie.

Abbie: I've already sent him back. He is not going to work in the kitchen of that place across the street.

F. K. Jackson: It's most unfortunate. But Mr. Valkill is abnormal. He likes little boys. He —

Abbie: I don't see anything abnormal about liking little boys. Most people do. I think it's wonderful that a man like Mr. Valkill should take an interest in a mere boy.

F. K. Jackson (sharply): Listen to me, Abbie. Mr. Valkill is a pervert, a sexual pervert. He will corrupt Link.

Abbie: Corrupt him how? What are you talking about? A pervert — you mean — oh — Link — oh —

F. K. Jackson: That's why he can't go back there. That's why you will have to get used to the idea of his working at The Last Chance. Mr. Hod is using this as a stick over our heads, a threat. He sent for me, summoned me, just as though he were an emperor, couldn't use the telephone or write a letter but sent his servant to tell me that he wanted to see me. When I went over there he said, "Link will be here for the rest of the summer, helping Weak Knees in the kitchen. When school starts he will be here after school and on weekends. If you can't convince his aunt that it's a good idea, I'll be glad to." He actually smiled at me, Abbie, and he looked just like a wolf, baring its teeth. He said, "There's a juvenile court in this city."

Abbie: The nerve of him. I don't care what he said. Link is not going to work there. It's against the law anyway. He's a minor. And the state liquor law says that a minor cannot be employed in any capacity on the premises of a place —

F. K. Jackson: It doesn't cover a private kitchen. He would be working in their private kitchen. Not in the bar. I'm afraid you'll have to get used to the idea. Mr. Hod claims that Mr. Valkill has a most unsavory reputation. If Hod wanted to make trouble, I think he could. He has considerable political influence and he might be able to get himself appointed as some sort of guardian for Link, on the grounds that you were no longer a suitable person, that you had placed Link in a position where —

Abbie: They seemed like such fine people and Mr. Valkill had the loveliest manners, and his wife was so sweet and they were wealthy. Fine rich people. It was Link's first real job —

F. K. Jackson (slowly): I honestly believe that he will be safer over there. There are a great many things that they know more about than we do.

Abbie: Oh, dear!

They were on the outskirts of the city now, still going fast. Used to be nothing but fields and open lots and woods out here, now all neat lawns and forty-thousand-dollar houses with attached garages. The Major used to tell him stories about when there were farms in this part of Monmouth, and people kept goats and cows and horses. Used to tell about Gleason's goat, a diabolical male animal, complete with beard, and what he now recognized as the naturally foul disposition of the male animal in a state of perpetual and unappeasable rut, who worked and worked and worked until he made an opening in Gleason's fence, and then would appear suddenly in the dooryard of one of the houses.

The cry would go up, from house to house, "Gleason's goat is out, Gleason's goat is out!" and women would run out of the houses, armed with brooms and mops and pokers and shovels, emerging from the back doors like arrows hurled from a catapult, intent on working over Gleason's goat, looking forward to the attack with a kind of furious pleasure, because the goat could destroy a prize rosebush in less than thirty seconds, because the goat headed straight for clotheslines and preferred the clean white shirts and the white dresses which represented a whole morning of backbending labor over a washtub.

The Major described the uproar and the excitement, with relish, telling how the goat would be ducking, butting, charging, retreating, silent, malevolent, intelligent, and the middle-aged women would duck and butt and retreat and advance too, but not silently, emitting an unholy screeching as they mauled the goat and then retreated.

He laughed now because he thought it wasn't the clean clothes or the rosebushes that infuriated the women. It was the goat, the sheer maleness of the goat, that they were butting, charging, mauling with intent to kill. It was the old old war between the male and the female. Laughed again under his breath, and felt the men on each side of him stiffen again, saw the woman's head turn, ever so slightly.

He could smell perfume, the woman's perfume. Perhaps because of that slight movement of her head. Woman in the front seat. Why? Woman with a straight back, shoulders held rigid. Something in his mind said, Even with a bag tied over your head, even on the streets of Moscow, I would know — would recognize — your back.

Then he lost the thought, the nudging memory, looked out of the opened window, past the trenchcoated figure on his right, watched the landscape, the houses were smaller now, postage-stamp size, matchbox size, houses of war veterans, man spend the rest of his life paying for one of these chickencoops, one right on top of the other, no *lebensraum*, no garages, park the car right near the house, near the front door, but television aerials on all the little rooftops, a tangle of wire against the dark night sky.

Car going faster and faster. What the hell is this, he wondered. Relax, Bud, and wait and see. So they went along and they went along, Henny Penny and Turkey Lurkey and Ducky Lucky and Foxy Loxy. Now which of us, he wondered, is Foxy Loxy. Most logically the lady in the tan-colored raincoat, because otherwise why would she be here, riding in this car, riding through the fine misty rain with a handcuffed man in the back seat.

The car slowed, turned off to the right, entering a driveway, not a driveway, a long wide private road with a pair of gates at the entrance, gates studded and decorated and gilded like the gates of Victoria's summer palace in the south of France, pair of stone lions, couchant, emphasized the entrance, dramatized it, guarded it. The car picked up speed again. A rabbit bounded across the road, white cottontail going hell for leather, suddenly there in front of the headlights, and as suddenly gone. The car swerved to the right, and then as abruptly to the left, straightened out. Nerves all shot to hell, he thought, even from where I sit in this back seat, he wasn't anywhere near the damn rabbit, rabbit probably in a thousand cabbage patches or briar patches at the moment when he jerked the wheel like that.

The woman sitting on the front seat said, "Bunny!" protest in the voice.

And it all fell into place. He thought, No one in the USA free from prejudice, shows up somewhere, finally got all these male and female people into this black Packard. Finally. Why after all this time? Or did she in the back of her mind know when she stood under that street light on Dock Street, corner of Dumble, screaming her head off, that it would end like this, even to the handcuffs?

He thought of that picture on the front page of the tabloid,

Jubine's picture, and how he had looked at it and cursed Jubine, because the canary, the little lost one, the palomino, had the face of a drunk, a lush, mindless, insentient, slackjawed, one hand lifted in an atypical cringing. He had laid the tabliod flat on the bar, Bill Hod's mahogany bar, the wood smooth, polished by the slow motion of elbows, of hands, by the wool of coats, sliding motion of bare forearms, until the wood responded to the warmth, the friction, the oil from the skin, and acquired a patina, not a surface slickness, but a glow that came from deepdown in the wood. The bar served as a frame, polished frame for Jubine's picture. It reminded him of something. It was the cringe in the shoulder line, there because the hand was raised, it was the way the hair fell forward, the awful jaw line. If he covered the eyes, lowered the hand but left that shoulder line intact, what would he see? He'd see Toulouse-Lautrec's Harlot.

He had thought he didn't love her any more, didn't hate her any more, and felt an ache inside him, a loss, an emptiness, thought it was like losing an arm or a leg, thought it was the kind of ache you got from an old wound when it rained, dull, monotonous, and studied the face again, the horrified eyes, the pale blond hair. He had stared across the bar at the telephone booth in the corner, near the front. Could drop a coin in the coinbox, and dial a number, and the light musical voice would answer, and he would say, Let's begin again, my fault, I am a fool, let's begin again. Shack job. Stud.

And so didn't do anything. But stand still. Then started cleaning the bar, cleaning out the beer pumps.

Remembered that headline in milehigh type, NEGRO CONVICT SHOT, strung across the front page of the *Monmouth Chronicle*, remembered that blownup picture of the escaped convict who had had one side of his face practically destroyed because someone had slashed him with a razor, years back.

Could hear Old Man John the Barber, when he came for his morning beer and looked at the picture. Barber would start to drink the beer and then put the glass down, and stare at the convict as though he were hypnotized, and say, "The bastards"; start to drink the beer again and put the glass down and say, "The bastards," just as though he were a nickel-in-the-slot automaton and someone had dropped a nickel in a slot somewhere inside him, and the two words emerged from his throat, automatically, no emphasis, just the two words.

So it was Jubine Lautrec's Harlot and The Convict by Anonymous that got me in this black Packard. That is one-quarter of the explanation. The other three-quarters reaches back to that Dutch man of warre that landed in Jamestown in 1619.

And they went along and they went along and the house was a stone pile, pile of stone, huge, formless, so few lights in it that it would be impossible to guess at the architecture, nothing to define its shape to the eye, no indication of windows, doors. The car stopped.

One of the trenchcoated gentlemen said, "Come on. Get out." His voice tense, excited. The GrotonHarvard accent blurred with fear.

They went in through a side entrance. He saw ivy on the walls, wet, slicklooking on the walls, rippling in the wind. Then they were standing in a hallway, hesitating there, uncertain.

The woman said, "This way."

It was a small room, no rug on the floor. Seemed to be a small sitting room, with a stone fireplace across one end. There was a moment, awkward, fleeting, during which they looked at him, and then looked away, and then looked again.

He dismissed the three men as unimportant, all of them out from the same tree, perhaps elm, a soft wood no good for burning. But the woman. The woman is dangerous. It's in the face, the eyes, the mouth — determination, intractability. Danger in the shaking. There's a tremor running through her that she can't control, running all through her body. Not fear but hate.

I know because I once shook like that myself. I watch this woman shake and I am standing in that dark little corridor outside Bill's office, holding his gun, and I am shaking so that I can hardly stand up, I have to lean against the wall, because I am remembering how he caught me in China's place again. We walked back to The Last Chance together and he said, Go in my office and he closed the door and locked it and picked that rawhide up, it was on top of his desk, and when it landed I gasped, and went on gasping because he kept hitting me with it.

When I got so I could walk again I tried to kill him, was going to shoot him with his own gun, and stood, shaking and trembling, not even able to point the gun, let alone hold it up, because I kept hearing his voice, seeing his face, when he bent over me, with that rawhide in his hand, "Get up, you bastard, or I'll kick your guts out — " I went down that long flight of stairs, leading into the kitchen, stood outside his office door, shaking and trembling, because I saw him sitting there, feet up on his desk, his back to the window, sunlight on the black hair, on the white shirt, the clean starched white shirt that he put on every morning, and that F. K. Jackson said was a fetish.

L. Williams: Bill!

B. Hod (looking up, voice deceptive, mild): So you're feeling better. What's the gun for?

He lifted his arm, tried to aim the gun, and his hand was shaking so that the gun went back and forth, back and forth, as though he had reverted to infancy and was waving byebye with it, his hand shaking and trembling so violently that the gun began moving in wide loose circles. Bill got up, walked toward him, hit his arm, one short sharp blow, and the gun went out of his hand, landed on the floor.

B. Hod: I suppose you're sore because you got a licking. What're you sore about?

L. Williams: You tried to kill me.

B. Hod: I told you not to go in that whorehouse again. And you did. So I took some of the hide off your back.

L. Williams: You tried to kill me.

B. Hod: So as soon as you can walk down those stairs again, you come in here and pull a gun on me. My own gun. Get the hell outta my face.

L. Williams: You bastard. You beat me until I couldn't stand up, couldn't see, couldn't hear. What do you call that?

B. Hod (voice ugly, voice furious): I ever catch you in China's place again, I'll cripple you for life. Get the hell out of my face.

The trenchcoated gentlemen, his escorts, keepers, bodyguards, said, together, in their GrotonHarvard voices, only GrotonHarvard had not prepared them for the handcuff technique so that they sounded solemn and dimwitted at the same time, "We'll wait outside. If you want us, just call."

Just call, gentlemen. On call. Call house.

The man with the reddish-blond hair, the goodlooking face, the poor bastard of a husband, closed the door behind them, waited a moment, hesitated, and then said, "Do you know who I am?"

He didn't answer, thinking, I could have predicted that you would start off that way, at an angle. You've chosen this tortuous, adumbrative approach, out of embarrassment. Because you've been horsed into this and you don't know what to do with it. So keep on circling around it because it's still your move.

Silence.

The man said, "I think you know who I am."

The woman said, "Why don't we sit down?"

That's right, lady, he thought, because if you don't, you'll fall down. I know how that feels, too, to hold oneself up, keep forcing oneself to stand up when the bones the muscles the nerves won't co-operate, and signal their lack of co-operation by shaking, shaking, shaking, and the shaking says, Sit down, lie down, or you'll fall down.

The woman sat down but the man stayed on his feet. The man said, not looking at him, "We don't want to harm you, to hurt you in any way. We just want to talk to you — to — " and his voice stopped, died.

"Suppose we stop playing tag with it," he said. He sat down in an armchair, directly across from the woman. "What do you want to talk about, Captain Sheffield?"

The woman tried to get up, almost managed it. What did I say that caused that change in her expression? If she'd had a gun, she would have shot me, right then, at that moment. But why? Voice. It's the sound of your voice, Bud. You hadn't spoken before and she took it for granted you would sound like Amos-AndySambo, nobody in here but us chickens. And it has for the first time occurred to her that you and Camilo were making the beast with two backs. An old black ram has been tupping her white ewe. She will never let you get out of this room alive, and how will she manage to keep you from being alive. She has the shakes. These gentlemen that she is depending on to help her in the blood sacrifice are weak sisters, sad sacks.

Silence again. The man was leaning against the mantel now, staring at him. He looked at the woman, she was breathing at a faster rate, and the trembling had not increased, but somehow, the expression on her face, the outrage in her eyes, had changed the feel of the room. It was like a change in the tempo of a song, faster now, the woman had made it go faster.

She said, "We want you to sign a confession."

He kept watching her face. "A confession?" he asked, slowly. "Mea culpa?" He thought, I have no weapon, I have nothing to attack you with but my voice. I will make you wait and wait and wait and wonder what I am going to say, and finally tell you — tell you —

"How far back shall I go?" he asked. They were both staring at him, fear in the woman's face, tension in the man's, fear and tension, building.

He began to use his voice as though it were an instrument, playing with it, reminiscent now, speaking deliberately, letting his voice range around. "I stole a lollipop when I was five, stole it in a candy store run by a man named Mintz. I ran away from home when I was eight. I went a long ways, too, just across the street." He stopped again, thinking, well, I might as well at some point name the complication, the inflammatory complication that the choreographer rang in on the old rigadoon of adultery and cuckoldry, because The Race with his deathshead face unmasked walked right in here with us, with me. "But the distance that I went was farther away from where I had been living than if it had been the coast of Africa where your rapacious Christian ancestors went to kidnap the Guinea niggers who were my ancestors."

He paused again, watching the uneasiness, the fear, the hate. "When I was sixteen I tried to kill a man. Between then and now, well, I have not always loved my neighbor as myself. I have, on occasion, looked on the wine when it was red, looked too long, and with too tender and yearning an eye." He grinned, remembering Old Man John the Barber, If I had to listen to that funny talk he does — "I have been guilty, also on occasion, of running swiftly with the hares, gamboling with the hares, and at the same time running swiftly with the hounds, baying the moon at midnight, with the hounds." Pause again.

"How about you two people?" he said, conversationally. "Do you want to join me in the confessional? All of us culpa?"

Captain Sheffield moved farther away from the mantel. "You raped my wife," he said, "there on the dock. You — "

"No."

Captain Sheffield said, "You raped my wife, you — "

He watched the woman, though he addressed the man, speaking softly, taunt in his voice, "What was she doing on the Dumble Street dock at midnight? Why don't you keep your wife home — at midnight? Why don't you keep her home — at night, Captain Sheffield?"

He watched the woman. She opened her mouth, tried to say something, and she couldn't control the trembling of her lips. She tried to get out of the chair, force herself to stand up, and couldn't make it, sat down again.

Shared experience, he thought. I know about that, too. Know how it feels. After Dr. Easter's last visit I tried to get out of the chair, sat back down again, tried again, and made it. I walked across the hall, went in Bill's room, and got the gun from under his pillow and went down the stairs, slow, because I couldn't go fast because of the shaking and the trembling. I used the wall for support, leaning against it, going down that enclosed staircase, no railing, stairs went straight down, no turn, walls were pine, they call it knotty pine these days, but to me, at sixteen, it was just wood, dark brown wood, and I leaned against it, going down three steps and then standing with my back against the brown wood of the wall, waiting until my heart stopped trying to jump out of my chest, and the damn gun was so heavy I was afraid I'd drop it.

There was a tremor in the woman's voice. She said, "Bunny, there's no use talking to him, there's no use, don't let him — "

He watched her try to get out of the chair again. This time she succeeded but the effort she put into it made the shaking worse. She walked over to the sofa, bent over, fishing for something under the cushions, hands shaking, groping, reaching for something. Gun in the shaking hand.

It was a forty-five. He stared at it in disbelief. Tribal law, he thought. Man who breaks a taboo must die.

One for the money. Two for the show. Three to make ready. "It wasn't rape, Captain Sheffield."

The woman tried to point the gun, and couldn't lift it. It kept slipping down, and she tried to hold it with both hands, and the weight was too much, still couldn't raise it, muzzle kept pointing down at her own feet, downdangling. A forty-five.

You'll shake like that for the rest of your life, he thought, watching her. Like you had palsy. He knew. He'd had the tremors too, that time after Bill beat him up. He hauled ice for Old Trimble, in the belief that if he got his body rockhard he wouldn't shake and tremble every time he caught a glimpse of a man in a white shirt. Stole F. K. Jackson's gun because once he got rid of that shameful trembling, he was going to kill Hod. He hadn't succeeded the first time. He was going to try again. Because he hated him. Was afraid of him.

When Abbie found she couldn't make him quit hauling ice, she froze up, refusing to speak to him, turning her back on him, acting as though he had cut off his right arm and were peddling bits and pieces of it on the corner of Franklin and Dumble.

But he wouldn't stop. He went on hauling ice, grimly, despairingly, stubbornly returning to the job, day after day, lived with an icecold woman at home, and handled ice at work, hauling it into dirty kitchens, walking through dark foulsmelling hallways, up long flights of filthy stairs. At night he collapsed into bed, and slept as though he were dead, not moving, not dreaming. Sometimes he woke up in the middle of the night, sweating, cold sweat from head to foot, shaking again, because he'd heard a sharp cracking sound outside in the street, and cringed because he thought Bill was standing over him with that rawhide in his hand, cursing him. And he'd get out of bed and reach up in the chimney, one hand braced against the marble mantel, reach up where he'd put F. K. Jackson's gun and take it out and heft it in his hand, and find he still couldn't hold it, that the trembling got worse, somehow, just from the feel of the gun.

"I want the truth from you," the man said. "We brought you here to tell the whole story of what happened there on the dock. And I want the truth."

He isn't geared for this, isn't geared for violence. But the woman is. Unfortunately, or fortunately, she's geared up so high she's practically paralyzed.

"If you won't talk, we'll make you talk," the woman said.

"I thought you said you wanted a confession," he said politely. "Sometimes there is a difference. The truth. Confession. Not always the same thing." Fight back. With what? Sitting duck. A forty-five. Never get out of this room alive. And how will she manage it? Do the boys from GrotonHarvard know what a forty-five can do?

The woman sat down. She laid the gun on a table. Too heavy for her to hold. She sat there staring at him, and shaking.

He finally got his shaking under control. After six weeks of hauling ice to those stinking airless top floors in the tenements on Franklin, on Dumble, always to the top floors, he finally stopped shaking. And Abbie got colder, and more unbearable. He began to forget that he was going to try to kill Hod — to try again.

One morning he almost bumped into Weak Knees, right at the corner of Dumble and Franklin. And was ashamed because if he had seen Weak first, he would have crossed over on the other side of the street, pretended he hadn't seen him. Weak said, "Sonny, Sonny, Sonny," over and over, and his eyes filled with tears and he patted his arm and then went off down the street, shambling worse than ever, weaving from side to side as though he were dead drunk. He saw Weak stop and brush that imaginary figure away and knew that he was muttering, "Get away, Eddie, get away!"

Weak hadn't done him any harm. Neither had Bill. Not really. They had balanced that other world, the world of starched curtains and the price of butter, the world of crocheted doilies and what will people think, the world of white bedspreads and pillow shams and behavior governed by what The Race did or did not do.

He went home and ate lunch and Abbie looked down her nose at him. When he finished eating he went straight across the street, went in through the open door of The Last Chance.

Bill was behind the bar, reading a tabloid, the clean white shirt open at the throat, the clean white apron tied tight around his lean waist.

When he looked up his gaze was as impersonal as though Link had been down the street, trotting around town on those thousand-and-one errands they were always sending him on. Impersonal and penetrating. He didn't know that he'd ever been looked at quite so thoroughly.

B. Hod: Well?

L. Williams: I came over to tell you I think you were right and I was wrong. I thought —

B. Hod: What'd they do, put you out across the street?

L. Williams: No.

B. Hod: You get tired of playing horse?

L. Williams: No. It's just that I'm not mad any more.

B. Hod: So? (reading the paper again)

He had waited, not knowing what to say next or what to do.

B. Hod: Now that we've kissed and made up, whyn't you go in the kitchen and kiss Weak, too. (not looking up)

He stood there wishing he hadn't come. There didn't seem to be anything he could say that would make Bill get over being sore. Why should Bill be sore? Then Frankie came from somewhere in the back, old then, but he jumped up on him, snuffing around him, licking his hands, slobbering on him, panting, acting like a puppy half crazy from the joy of seeing him. He hugged him and patted him and turned toward Bill, grinning.

Bill said, "Yeah. Even Frankie's been acting droopy since you quit us. And Weak has been looking as though he just came back from his mother's funeral, if he'd ever had a mother who had a funeral." He paused and then said, "I've been wearing full mourning myself."

So the next Sunday morning when the smell of Canadian bacon, yeasty smell of freshbaked rolls, drifted up into his room from the kitchen, along with the sound of Weak singing, "Give me a girl with a curl, give me a girl I can furl," he ducked under the shower, got his clothes on, and when Weak yelled, "Come and get it," he let Frankie get a head start down the hall, and then ran down the hall, sat down on the top step and kicked his heels against the riser, drumming, drumming, drumming with his heels, and then sat motionless, waiting and listening, and then drummed again, and Bill's voice, deep, outraged, furious, assailed his ears.

"For Christ's sake cut out that goddamn racket what the hell you trying to do wake up the whole goddam neighborhood," in one breath, on the same note of absolute rage.

He kicked the stairs again, drumming, drumming, drumming, and Bill came tearing out of his room, came down the hall, roaring, "What the hell's the matter with you?"

He laughed and choked and went on laughing and had to lean against the wall, choking and laughing.

Bill leaned over, "Sonny, are you all right?" concern in his voice. Bent all the way over him, put his hand on his shoulder, "What's the matter with you?"

"I just wanted to hear you carry on like a crazy man again. I missed the sound of it for six weeks."

Bill said, "You — all that goddam noise — " hauled him to his feet, lifted his hand as though he were going to clip him, drew his hand back and laughed. He said, "Go on. Hightail it down those stairs, Sonny, before I change my mind and lay one on your jaw."

The woman got up, handed the gun to the man. The man held it, gingerly, as though it were a hardshell crab, a big one, and it might turn on him.

He thought, The gutless bastard. She's using him, just as though he were a hired gunman. Let's see what he'll do with it. Gambler. You're gambling with your own life. So let's see what he'll do with it.

"We were in love," he said, casually, conversationally.

The man's face stayed the same, just the same. The woman sighed, or at least there was the sound of the exhalation of her breath. Then the man's face did change, slowly, it became still, stunned. He's gone into shock. I don't think he even knows he's standing there. He's out on his feet, not lifting the gun, not doing anything just standing there with a forty-five in his hand.

"Four to go," he said. "The black barkeep and the Treadway Gun were in love."

The woman said, "Bunny!"

He thought, It's just as though she were a steeplechase rider, and something's gone wrong with her hands and her knees, and he's the horse that's got to take the jump. She's trying to make him jump, just with her voice.

She said, "Bunny!" again.

Then, he thought, amazed, Why he's going to. He doesn't know what he's doing, he's out on his feet, knocked out, but he's taking the jump anyway.

He heard the explosion. It was in his ears, his chest, his head, at one and the same time. There was one split second in which he thought, Legacy, I have to leave a legacy, for this multonmillionaire white woman who has the tremors, the shakes.

"The truth is," he said, and felt the great engulfing thickness in his chest well up into his throat, and talked through it, in spite of it, "we were in love."

He heard the woman say, "Bunny, what have you done?"

He tried to laugh, and pitched forward on the floor.

23

● WHEN SHE OPENED the door of the sitting room, the two young men were walking toward her, moving swiftly, their hard heels hitting the polished floor in unison, as though they were marching. They were still wearing their raincoats.

"He — " she said, and heard the gun go off again, and put her hands over her ears, and heard the explosive sound of it again and again. Then silence. "He — " she repeated. "The Negro confessed — and Bunny shot him."

"Is he — "

"Yes," she said and turned back into the room. Bunny was still holding the gun. She took it out of his hand and laid it down on a table. Though he looked at her, his eyes were fixed, unseeing.

One of the young men said, "I think you ought to take him into another room, Mrs. Treadway. Let him sit down somewhere — but not in here."

She guided him into the dining room, turned on a wall switch, and the Gainsboroughs on the walls, the crimson draperies at the windows, the long polished table, the chairs seemed to move in the sudden light, and then were still.

"It's all right," she said. "Everything will be all right." He lifted his hand, shielding his eyes with it, as though the light were painful. "Sit here. You'll be all right in a minute. We'll take care of everything. Bunny, do you hear me? It's all right."

Back in the sitting room, she said, "We'll have to hurry. The servants are all off this evening. There's no one here. But we'll have to do something quickly because Mrs. Cameron, the house-keeper, will be back very soon. She always goes through the house, just to see that everything — " And then she said, "The blood. There's so much blood. I can't — "

One of the young men said, "I tell you what you do, Mrs. Treadway. You get us some rope. If we had some rope we could tie the body up, use old sheets, get it away from here, in the car."

"Yes," she said. "In the garage. I think there's some out there. We had a runway for Camilo's dog. There must be some in the garage."

It was still raining outside. Quiet, gentle rain. She walked to-ward the garage, fumbled for the lights, turned them on. There was a coil of rope on a bench, near the back wall. She carried it to the house.

One of the young men met her at the door of the sitting room, blocking her view of the room. "If you'll turn the car around, Mrs. Treadway, we'll be right out."

"Captain Sheffield — Bunny is — he's very much upset, of course." She could see bloodstained towels on the floor. The gun was still there on the table. "I think he'll be all right in a few minutes." She took a deep breath. "There's so much blood," she said again, staring into the room. "I didn't know — "

"If you'll go and turn the car around, Mrs. Treadway," the young man repeated firmly, "we'll be right out." He closed the door.

She kept looking at the door. "But these new cars," she said. "The shift is on the steering wheel. I've never driven one of them. I couldn't — I can't turn it around. And Bunny is prac-tically unconscious. He can't drive." She went out through the side entrance, went into the garage.

She backed the Rolls-Royce out of the garage, drove it to the side entrance, and waited with the motor running, listening to the quiet sound it made, watching the rain, falling in myriad slanting lines in front of the headlights.

When she saw them coming out of the house, their backs bent, struggling under the weight of that roped heavy bundle, she got out of the car, opened one of the doors in the back, got in and closed the side curtains and the curtain across the window in the back. Then she got out and held the door open for them.

"We found a thin old rug in one of the rooms in the back of

the house," one of the young men said, panting a little from the exertion of lifting that bundle into the car. "It's better for this than sheets." Then he frowned, looking at the car, "Why are we using this ark? What's the matter with the Packard?"

"I can't drive the Packard. I'm not used to the shift — "

"But you're not going to drive — you're not — "

"Yes," she said. "Yes, I am. You can't be involved in this. Not any further. I can manage alone."

"Take Bunny with you," the other one said quickly. "The air will help bring him to. He mustn't stay there, knocked out like that. If anybody showed up, the housekeeper or anybody they'd wonder — "

"All right."

They brought him out of the house, and he staggered along between them, like a drunken man. They helped him get in the front seat.

One of the young men got in the car beside Bunny. "We decided you couldn't possibly manage alone. Rick'll clean up while we're gone."

"Oh," she said. "I couldn't remember. I've been trying to remember what your names were. The other one is Rick. I see. But you're — "

"I'm Skipper. Rick and I were in the Air Corps with Bunny. Remember now?"

"Yes. Yes, of course. It's just since — there was so much blood — " her voice died.

She seemed to be listening to the idling sound of the motor.

Then she said, talking faster and faster, "The Judge wouldn't set a date for the trial — he wouldn't bring the Negro to trial — and Camilo was going to pieces — we thought if we could get him to sign a confession it would end these dreadful stories about her." She sighed and her voice slowed, "We never intended to hurt him — we just wanted him to confess — that was all — and then when he did — when he confessed — "

"I know."

"I've stopped shaking," she said. "You know I was shaking so that I thought I'd never stop. But it's gone now. See?" She held out both hands.

"Good," he said. "Everything will be all right now. Just hold the car to the same pace. Not too fast and not too slow. Steady pace."

When she drove down the long driveway, not too slow, not too fast, out through the gilded, decorated entrance gates, past the stone lions, couchant, the rain was still falling in long slanting myriad lines in front of the headlights.

"Where do you plan to go?" he asked.

"To the river."

24

● ABBIE CRUNCH was waiting for Frances Jackson to come out of Davioli's market. She had not gone into the market because she did not want to see the look of sympathy that would come over Davioli's face, did not want to hear the sound of heartbreak that would come into his voice, when he spoke of Link, as of course he would.

Suddenly impatient with this waiting, with standing still, she started walking down Franklin Avenue, going slowly, turned into Dumble Street. Most people were home eating supper at this hour, though there were still a great many children playing on the sidewalk, calling to each other, their voices high, shrill. The Hangman was in bud, early this year. It was a pale green, not all over, just lightly brushed with it at the top and on the sides, like a prime coat on an old house, color daubed here and there, over the old weatherbeaten wood, not a finished job, but a visible freshening.

In this fading afternoon light, light going, fading, dying, her house, Number Six, was a deep dark red; and the river was diminished in size, narrower. It looked like a band of tarnished silver, depthless, darkly gleaming, at the foot of the street.

This river, she thought, this one river, and this street, Dumble Street, and this city, Monmouth, are famous now. Or infamous. Not just The Narrows. The entire city. Famous or infamous because of Mrs. Treadway and Link and that girl with the pale

412

blond hair, and that oldfashioned car, a Rolls-Royce, with its curtains down. I keep going over it in my mind, over and over it, and I still do not understand it.

I can see it, I can picture it. An oldfashioned car with the curtains down, side curtains and a curtain in the back. A patrol car started to follow the Rolls-Royce, and the Rolls went faster and faster, and the patrol car relayed a message to two motorcycle policemen. Then the men on the motorcycle pursued the Rolls-Royce, and finally shot at the tires. A woman was driving that carefullycaredfor oldfashioned car. There were two men sitting on the front seat. But the woman was driving. There was a body on the floor of the car in the back, a body wrapped up in a thin worn rug, tied with heavy rope.

But she had omitted that exchange of words that had taken place between the woman who was driving the car and the policeman:

Motor Policeman: What's in the bundle, lady?

Mrs. Treadway: Old clothes for the Salvation Army.

Motor Policeman (to his confrere): You better check.

The Chronicle had reported that the policeman who opened that roped bundle wished that he hadn't.

She thought, I mustn't begin thinking about this again, going over and over it in my mind. It doesn't do any good. And instantly thought of that picture on the front page of the Chronicle, a picture of Captain Sheffield and Mrs. Treadway, sitting on the side of the road, near the dock, waiting, already under arrest, but waiting to be loaded into a police car, and people all around them, behind them, and there was horror and disbelief on the faces of all those people in the background; kept remembering the girl, the Treadway girl, Mrs. Sheffield, and the pale blond hair curling, the delicately arched feet, and could see the girl lying beside Link, her head on his shoulder, both of them naked. And even now could feel rage at the memory of them in her house, and thought again, as she had ever since that night when the telephone rang and Frances told her, bluntly, almost rudely, what had happened to Link, that she could almost understand, could almost understand how Mrs. Treadway came to be driving that car.

Shock, yes, pain, and a sense of loss, and infinite regret, and the familiar feeling that if she hadn't failed Link when he was a little boy none of this need have happened. She had experienced these things when the Major died. There was nothing new in any of these reactions. But she had behaved differently this time. Because she felt as though something inside her had congealed, frozen, and that it would never thaw again, as long as she lived, as long as she remembered that question and the answer to it: What's in the bundle, lady? Old clothes for the Salvation Army.

She turned and looked back toward Franklin Avenue. Frances wasn't in sight. What was keeping her so long? Frances had been so kind, always been so kind. I'll stand here and wait for her.

Frances had no family of her own, so she adopted us, adopted Link and me, looked after us as though we were her family. We were an outsize family, or at least we had outsize problems.

We all adopt each other, or marry each other. Miss Doris has apparently adopted Frances. On the day of Link's funeral Frances sent Miss Doris to look after me. Miss Doris looked exactly like a stone monument with a black straw hat on its head, gray gloves on its hands, but in motion, moving majestically down the steps, across the sidewalk, into the car.

She supposed that all of them were shocked, Frances and Miss Doris, and Sugar, Miss Doris' husband, and Howard Thomas, because she didn't collapse into weeping. But she couldn't. She simply felt cold and furious and indomitable. She was impervious to the stares, the comments, the photographers, getting out of the car in front of the church, unaided, going up the aisle of the church, head up, back straight, coming out of the church the same way, watching the service at the grave, as though she were a stranger who had paused for a moment to watch a group of people who happened to be listening to the burial service. She no longer cared what people thought, or what they said, she, who all her life had been governed by the fear of other people's thoughts, had acquired an armor of indifference.

On the way back from the cemetery, she talked about the murder, discussed it, tried to find the reasons behind it. She rode on the back seat of the car with Miss Doris and Frances. She had said, "It was that woman. That Mamie Powther. I should never have allowed her to stay under my roof. A woman like that starts an evil action, just by her mere presence. She doesn't have to take part in it — just her being in a place — she's a — " She had stopped talking, thinking, That isn't true. This all started long ago. It started when the first married woman whoever she was took a lover and went on living with her husband, and the husband discovered the existence of the lover and so killed him. It has always been done that way. Why do the women always go free, as though they were guiltless?

Howard Thomas murmured, "Catalyst," loud enough for her to hear him.

"It were everbody's fault," Miss Doris said in that cold menacing voice.

"It were — " Frances said, paused, corrected herself, "I mean it was the girl's fault, the Treadway girl. She seemed to forget that she was white and Link was colored, so when she made that silly charge against him — "

"It were everbody's fault," Miss Doris' hard metallic voice interrupted. "It were purely like a snowball and everybody give it a push, that twocent newspaper give it the last big push. The morning I seen that picture, that big black convict picture, with half his face gone from a razor, just a long hole where one side of his face should have were, all strew across the front page, I said to Sugar, Sugar that picture were pure murder, and this white folks twocent newspaper ought to be took out and burned, didn't I, Sugar?"

Sugar said, "That's right," automatically.

When Howard stopped the car in front of Number Six, Miss Doris gave him a cruel jab in the back, and when he turned around, she handed him the doorkey, "Go open the door," she ordered.

Sugar stayed behind to help them out of the car. They went up the steps, slowly, all of them. Inside the hall, they stopped. Because Howard Thomas was standing quite still, and as they looked at him, puzzled by his lack of motion, he started backing away, backing toward the door.

Abbie looked past him and saw that there was something squatted down on the staircase. She thought at first it was some kind of animal, the kind of thing you half expect to see materialize in the middle of a nightmare. The creature on the stairs seemed to have a body, small and partially clothed, but it was faceless. No face. It didn't have a head, either, where the head should have been there was simply a black shiny surface, smooth, rounded, and very sleek.

Howard kept moving away from it. There was a tearing sound, and Howard said, "Oh — " and his voice was as highpitched as a woman's voice, "it's laying an egg. No, it's a foetus emerging from the womb. See?" he said, still backing away, as a round head emerged, kept emerging, and making sounds like an animal, "It's fighting to get out of the womb, and tearing the flesh."

She remembered letting her breath out in a long sigh. Because J. C. Powther's round hard head had appeared, and there was something black around his neck, almost like a bracelet, and something black and shiny far back on his head, and she had thought, Haile Selassie reduced to midget size but crowned, with a black and midnight crown.

Miss Doris said, "You, Jackson, you," in that flat toneless perpetually threatening voice.

"The Major's hat." Abbie could hear her own voice, the sound of it, again. Because there was a note of mourning in her voice at that moment, note of mourning and the sound of tears, for the first time since Link's death. They had stared at her, and she had looked right back at them, not caring what any of them thought. "It's the Major's silk hat," she said.

The round hard head, the dark brown small face, had ducked back under the tall crown of the hat, as though sensing disaster.

Miss Doris had lifted one of those powerful hands and struck the crown of the hat a resounding blow, jamming the crown down, way down, covering the round hard bullet head, the domed forehead, the black inscrutable eyes that were not a child's eyes, covering the small mouth that had opened in protest.

"You, Jackson," Miss Doris had said, in that cold metallic voice, "You set there now. That hat's yours now. You set there under it. Sugar, you stand right there and see that Jackson sets with his hat." She waited until the tall dark man said, "Yes, Sugar," in an obedient voice, and then she said, "Come, ladies, the tea were about ready, come right in the setting room."

And now Abbie thought, aimlessly, The tea were about ready, and then, What's in the bundle, lady? Old clothes for the Salvation Army.

Midway in the block she stopped and looked back toward Franklin Avenue, wondering why it should take Frances so long to buy three lemons. Then she stood still, waiting for Frances. She glanced toward the river, then at the redorange neon sign in front of The Last Chance.

While she was standing there, a man came out of The Last Chance. She got the impression that he had been backing out. When he reached the sidewalk, he headed toward the dock and the river, moving quickly, and then turned around with such speed that he almost lost his balance, and came toward her. He wasn't running but he looked as though he were. He kept mopping the back of his neck, his forehead, with his handkerchief, and he was constantly turning his head, glancing hastily behind him, as though he expected to be followed, or thought he was being followed.

As he came nearer she recognized the striped pants and cutaway coat of Howard Thomas, Frances' assistant. She assumed that he was intoxicated, and, not wanting to listen to the meandering conversation of a drunken man, she continued to stand still, confident that he would pass her without recognizing her.

He went past her, muttering to himself, "Chinaman's chance. Not a Chinaman's chance," and then turned around again, looked back over his shoulder, then hastened on his way, almost running toward Franklin Avenue. Either he didn't see Frances, or if he saw her he couldn't control his movements, anyway he walked right into her, almost knocking her down.

Abbie heard Frances say, "Well — really — "

"Oh — " he said, "Sorry, Miss Jackson. I didn't see you — wasn't looking — "

Frances peered at him through the thicklensed glasses. "How funny you look. What have you been doing?"

"I have," he said, "I did," he said. "I'm going to — What am I saying anyway?"

"I really don't know. Have you been drinking?"

"No, no, no, Miss Jackson. I just came out of The Last Chance but I haven't been drinking. Ha-ha-ha, but I'm going to. If I live that long, what am I saying? I'm going straight home and drink three lunches and four dinners, in fact, ha-ha-ha, all my meals for the week, all at once, right now."

There was a tremor in his voice, and Abbie, listening, thought, It's as though his voice, too, was constantly looking behind it, mopping its forehead, its face, the back of its neck. And his fear, his terror, whatever it was that was making him perspire and tremble, communicated itself to her so that she, too, looked back over her shoulder, half expecting to see someone behind her, threatening her, looked back over her shoulder and saw only that redorange sign, vivid now in the dusk. She thought of Bill Hod's face and shivered, and turned and watched Howard's progress, rapid, erratic, as he went on up the street, watched him go in a drugstore at the corner of Franklin Avenue. The door had barely closed behind him, when he was out on the street again, then he turned around and came back down Dumble Street.

Abbie said, "Frances, what on earth's the matter with him? Why he's gone back in the same drugstore he just came out of. Do come along. I can't bear to stand here and watch him."

Frances didn't move, didn't answer. She was staring at the front door of The Last Chance, staring and frowning.

Abbie said, "Did you get the lemons?" and touched her arm, lightly.

"Of course. It took forever. Mamie Powther was in Davioli's doing some last-minute shopping, and I thought she'd never finish. Davioli was in there by himself, so I waited." Frances cleared her throat, hesitated, said, "Here, you take the lemons. I'll be along in a minute. I think I'd better go in that drugstore and see what's the matter with Howard. You can start the tea. I won't be gone very long."

"All right," she said, and took the little paper bag, three lemons in it. As she walked along the bag made a rustling sound and she thought, Bag, bundle, what's in the bundle, lady. How they must have hated him. She shook her head, remembering the pictures in the newspapers, picture of Mrs. Treadway sitting near the dock, face immobile, pictures of the dock, of the car with its curtains drawn, of that bundle, open on the dock and its awful contents revealed, exposed, and pictures of the crowd of people that collected there, the bobtail, ragtail, flotsam and jetsam from The Narrows and the waterfront.

When she opened the door of Number Six, the little paper bag rustled because she pushed the door open with it in her hand. She turned the hall light on, stood still for a moment listening, wondering if Mamie Powther were home yet. She wished they'd move. She couldn't bear having them in the house any more. A woman with that kind of blowsy face and figure, all that toosoft flesh, didn't belong in any wellkept home. When Mrs. Powther walked down the street men turned to look at her, turned to watch the rippling movement of hips and thighs. She was always half smiling as she walked, as though she experienced some inner pleasure from the motion of her own hips.

As she stood there in the hall, she felt old and defeated, because she started thinking about Link and the Major, remembering the fog in the street that night she pushed the blond girl out into the hall, down the front steps, remembering the sound of

Link's laughter when he said, "The female fruit fly," and then went out of the house whistling that tune of Mamie Powther's, I'm lonesome, I'm lonesome.

It was Mamie Powther's fault, she thought. I'm sure of it. Mamie Powther in that purple coat with brass buttons down the front, a double row of them, coat selected to accentuate the grossness of her bosom, could and would upset the pattern of anybody's life. It wasn't her fault. Not really. It was that girl with the blond hair, and her mother, and her husband. She wondered what it was like inside that great stone mansion now. Milelong driveway. Lake with swans in it. And a park. And a picnic every Fourth of July. Perhaps it was little Mr. Powther, too. The Treadway butler. Perhaps it was his entry into my house which precipitated this, perhaps he was the one who out of some awful hideous weakness set the wheels in motion. Then she thought impatiently, It was all of us, in one way or another, we all had a hand in it, we all reacted violently to those two people, to Link and that girl, because he was colored and she was white.

Why should Link be dead, and that girl, that girl with the pale blond hair, be left alive? It didn't have to end that way. The girl was here in my house with him, lying beside him, naked, obviously in love with him, and then two months later, not much more than that, she accused him of attacking her. Why?

She took off her hat and coat, turned on the lights in the sitting room, and in the kitchen, and set about getting supper. She filled the big nickelplated teakettle with water, lit the stove, started to set the table in the kitchen, and decided that it would be pleasanter to eat in the sitting room, and so put a white cloth on the Pembroke table. While she was arranging the silver, she thought about Howard walking at that hurried erratic pace, looking back over his shoulder, mopping his forehead, his face, with a wadded-up handkerchief; thought of that blond girl, intoxicated, and driving a car too fast, running over a child; and then thought of J. C. Powther sitting on the stairs, of his round head emerging from the wreckage of the Major's silk hat.

The teakettle made a hissing sound and she went into the kitchen, turned the fire low under the kettle, rinsed the big brown teapot with boiling water, then sat down at the kitchen table, waiting for Frances, and thinking of Link and that girl. Warmth and affection when her thoughts turned toward Link. A coldness and a fury when she thought of the girl.

Who would ever know what happened between them, or why it happened. Then she thought, But I can guess, conjecture, because of that house next door, that old frame house, where the Finnish people used to live. They were the only white people on Dumble Street, for five or six years. It was a rooming house then, just as it is now, and the men who lived there were almost always intoxicated. On Sunday mornings she saw them staggering home, and there was an iron fence, an ornamental iron fence, in front of the house, and the men would lean on the fence, clinging to it, and from her windows, upstairs, they looked as though they had been impaled on those iron pickets.

During the course of the years, she got to know the Finnish woman who was landlady and janitor in that rooming house. On winter mornings, the woman emptied the ashcans, pouring the contents in the driveway, wind blowing the fine gray stuff back into her face, wind blowing strands of rough uncared for gray hair across her face, and she thrusting it away with impatience. Even on the coldest days her arms were bare, reddened from the cold, and she wore no hat.

Abbie got to know most of the tenants, just by watching them come and go. She knew what time they got up, and what time they went to work. A thin young man, and a thin young woman, occupied the front bedroom on the second floor. In the summer when the windows were open, Abbie could hear them quarreling, and toward dusk she would see the young man stumbling home. Sometimes late at night, she could hear him say, voice thickened, "Aw, I got a right, what's the matter with you," could hear the girl crying, and then the man's voice, again, "Aw, shut up, whatsamatter with you, I got a right."

The girl worked in the Five-and-Ten on Franklin Avenue. Abbie went in there once to buy something, saw the girl standing behind one of the counters, wearing a white blouse, open at the neck, revealing the bones in her neck, the hollows at the base of her throat, and felt embarrassed, and hurried out of the store, because she knew so much about this girl, yet had never seen her closeto before, though she had heard the nighttime quarrels, heard the sound of her weeping.

The thin young man did not work at all. He got up about noon. Abbie could see him moving back and forth in that front room, whose windows were so near her own bedroom windows, looking at himself in the mirror, knotting his tie, putting on his jacket, adjusting and readjusting his hat brim, finally lighting a cigarette, turning to study his profile, making another minute adjustment of his hat brim, and then a few minutes later, she would see him outside on the sidewalk, moving at a slow, leisurely pace.

One day she noticed that the girl no longer lived there. She never saw her coming home whitefaced, exhaustedlooking, any more. The woman who ran the rooming house began quarreling with the thin young man. She was always shouting at him, shaking her fist, as she said he was no good, no damn good, that he didn't work, that he had never worked, no, she wouldn't give him any money, all he'd ever done was sit on his can all day, day in day out.

His clothes got shabbier. The widebrimmed light gray hat was streaked with dirt, lost its shape. Late one afternoon, Abbie saw him coming home. It was raining but he had no coat on. He couldn't get in the house, and he stood on the steps rattling the door, then he kicked against it, then he stood outside on the sidewalk, looking up at the windows, and finally walked away.

Finally, she had asked the Finnish woman about the girl. The woman said the boy, she called him the kid, half contemptuously, was no good, he lived off the girl, and the girl was crazy about him, so crazy about him that it would make anybody sick to watch her, to listen to her, and the girl believed in him, stood behind a counter all day, stood on her feet, earning a little bit of money the hard way, and the kid was always drinking up and gambling away the money the girl earned.

Abbie, puzzled, had said to the woman, "But if she was so crazy about him why did she leave him?"

The woman had stared at her, the blue eyes, hard and cold, the red roughened hands on the hips, the mouth compressed as she said, "She find out he got another woman. Nobody stay after that. Nobody. If I find my man got another woman, I leave, too. But I got strength, see? So I break up everything first. Everything. This girl got no strength. She just go."

Abbie thought, That's what that girl with the yellow hair and the beautiful feet and hands, that's what that girl did. She had strength and so she destroyed Link. Because he had fallen in love with someone else. But he hadn't. Then she thought, How do I know? How would anyone know?

She stopped thinking about it because she heard Frances knocking at the front door, knew it was she because the knocker sounded against the door quickly, lightly, three times in succession and then there was a pause and the knocker hit the door twice. Frances always knocked like that so she would know who it was, had been doing it ever since the Major died, ever since those days when the thought of a stranger at the door filled Abbie with a senseles fear, afraid to open her own door.

She opened the door with a flourish. "I've got everything ready for supper," she said. "You might as well eat here and have tea at the same time."

Frances said, "I'd love to. But I'll have to phone Miss Doris."

While Frances used the telephone, Abbie heated the soup, a thick meaty soup, practically a meal in itself, and then made a salad, fixed the tea, and then filled the soup plates.

Frances came into the kitchen, "Can I do anything?" she asked. "Just sit down at the table."

They ate slowly, and when they had finished, they stayed at the table, talking.

Abbie said, "Was Miss Doris angry?"

"Oh, no. It took her forever to answer the telephone. She was listening to a news broadcast, so she didn't say much of anything, sort of grunted, and then said, 'I were listening' — and hung up." Frances stirred the tea in her teacup, vigorously, and then said, "Abbie, why don't you come and live with me? Rent out this place. I've got that great big house and there's nobody in it, really, or at least not enough people in it to fill it up."

She toyed with the idea for a moment, Miss Doris would look after both of them, there would be no more household cares, never come home to a dark house, people always around, yes, and Miss Doris didn't like cats, especially didn't like tomcats, and there would be no comfortable cushions for Pretty Boy to lie on in a house which Miss Doris managed, no house plants, so the geraniums and the cyclamen and the African violets, would be left behind, or given away; and Frances was just as dictatorial as Miss Doris, and between them one Abbie Crunch would rapidly disintegrate into a doddering old woman.

She said, "Thank you very much. But I'm not that old, or that feeble. I'll be all right. If the time ever comes when I feel I can no longer live here alone, why I'll let you know."

"You've been wonderful."

Abbie thought, She's trying to find out why, and changed the subject. She said, "By the way, what is a Chinaman's chance?"

"A Chinaman's chance? What on earth made you think of that?"

"Well, when Howard Thomas passed me, fairly running along the street, he muttered something about a Chinaman's chance. That reminds me, did you find him? And what was the matter with him?"

"I don't think he knew himself. Or if he did he didn't tell me. He said he'd lost his wallet, and then proceeded to take it out of his back pocket right in front of me. I said, Why there it is, and he said, Why so it is, ha-ha-ha, Miss Jackson, why so it is. So I walked off and left him."

"But a Chinaman's chance," Abbie persisted. "Whatever was wrong with him must have had something to do with that. He kept repeating it, 'Not a Chinaman's chance,' and looking back over his shoulder as he said it."

Frances was sitting in one of the Hitchcock chairs, and when she leaned back in it it made a creaking sound, and she moved again, farther back, and said, "Ha!" and smiled and her glasses glittered as the light struck them. "That's the chance a Chinaman has when he's wrapped up in a burlap sack, tied up, with the stones, the necessary stones to weight him down, when he's to be smuggled across the border, in a boat. I have heard it said that Bill Hod used to bring them in over the Canadian border. Years ago. At a thousand dollars a head. If the border patrol stopped him, challenged the great god Hod, why he dumped the Chinese overboard. That is a Chinaman's chance."

Abbie thought that Frances was waiting for her to say something, at least she was looking directly at her. Abbie avoided her gaze. She glanced at the African violets blooming in the bay window, at the Boston rocker, and the marbletopped table, at the little Victorian sofa by the fireplace, and the card table drawn up in front of it, books and magazines on it, ready for the evening of quiet reading, saw none of these things, saw instead Bill Hod's face, the hooded eyes, the cruel thinlipped mouth, as plainly as though he were there in the room. She experienced a moment of prescience, in which she foresaw that Bill Hod would never permit that girl with the blond hair to stay alive, unscathed, in the same world in which he lived. And Howard Thomas —

"Well?" Frances asked. "Have you figured it out?"

"No," Abbie said, lying, deliberately lying. "And I don't want to."

I could be wrong, she thought. Perhaps Hod's face is deceptive, perhaps I have always misjudged him. Impossible. He has always taken an eye for an eye, and a tooth for a tooth. It is written all over him. There is no reason to believe that he has changed, or would, or could change. Miss Doris said, It were purely like a snowball, everbody give it a push. So Bill Hod must have arranged to give this dreadful business a final push. And Howard Thomas knows it. Has somehow discovered it.

Shortly afterwards, Frances went home. Abbie went to the door with her, patted her arm, kissed her lightly on the cheek. She stood in the doorway watching Frances' tall bony figure until it was out of sight, and not meaning to, not wanting to, she glanced across the street at the brilliant neon sign in front of The Last Chance.

She could go to the police and say — say what? Say that a man who appeared to be frightened came out of The Last Chance, that he went into a drugstore, that she believed he wanted to telephone to the police, meant to, but he was too frightened, too afraid of Bill Hod, therefore she had become convinced — and they would laugh at her, not laugh, they would listen politely but they would not believe her. She had no evidence to offer.

Stepping back into the hall, she closed the front door quickly, shutting out the sight of that vivid neon sign, thinking, Even if I knew, even if I could offer irrefutable evidence that Bill Hod was planning to destroy that blond girl I would not do anything about it. I would not try to stop it.

She caught her breath, appalled by the changes that had taken place deep inside her. During this last week she had lost part of herself, irretrievably lost the part of herself that had been composed of honor and integrity, lost the ability to distinguish between right and wrong. Not lost it. It had been seeping away ever since she read those words: What's in the bundle, lady? Old clothes for the Salvation Army.

In the sitting room, she sat down on the Victorian sofa, put on her glasses, and began to read the Chronicle, and finally laid it aside, because no matter what she read, she kept seeing that front page picture of Mrs. Treadway sitting on the side of the road, near the dock, surrounded by policemen, her son-in-law beside her; kept seeing that signed statement of Mrs. Treadway's: "We were helping the law. Camilo was going to pieces, and we had to do something. We didn't mean to harm the Negro. We thought if he confessed it would put a stop to those terrible stories about

Camilo. Then when the Negro confessed, Bunny seemed to go out of his mind, and he shot him."

We didn't mean to harm the Negro, Abbie thought. The Negro confessed. The Negro.

To them, all of them, he's the Negro. And to me —

She could remember when he was the most important player on the football team at Monmouth High. Though she was proud of his ability, pleased at the acclaim he received, she had never gone to watch him play. She'd always been too busy. Finally he persuaded her to attend one of the games.

That morning, before he left for school, he took a pencil and a piece of paper, and drew a rough diagram. "See," he said, "these are the teams, here in the center of the field, eleven men on each side — "

Men, her mind had echoed the word. Men. Link was only fifteen. True, his shoulders were broad, and he was taller than she, but he was a boy. His bones not really hardened yet. When he finished talking she said, "Is that all there is to it? Just running with a ball?"

He had seemed disconcerted. "I suppose so. It really isn't quite that simple. But you'll see." Before he left the house he said, "I wear number twenty-one. That's how you'll know me."

She had smiled, thinking that she would know him anywhere, with or without a number. Yet that afternoon, when the boys ran out on the field she couldn't tell one from another. The padded pants and the helmets made them look exactly alike. She wouldn't have known which of them was Link if it hadn't been for that big printed number on his back.

When the game started, she was dismayed by its roughness. The players were always piling up in mounds, their arms and legs every which way. She wondered if they didn't sometimes tug at a leg or try to move an arm and then discover that it was another boy's arm or leg.

Toward the end of the half they piled up again — a mass of seemingly headless bodies, the arms and legs askew. When they struggled to their feet, she saw that Number Twenty-One was flat on the ground, not moving. Her first thought was, I knew this was going to happen, I knew it. Number Twenty-One can't move. Number Twenty-One is Link.

She said, "I'll stop the game." Said it out loud. The woman sitting next to her looked at her, in surprise.

Link got to his feet, slowly, and stood up, shaking his head back and forth, leaned over and felt one of his knees. A short stout man came waddling from the sidelines, carrying a pail, and a towel, and what looked to be a sponge, and he poked at Link, prodding him here and there, and made him take off his helmet and Link kept waving him away. There was a little group of players around Link, and then they all seemed to wave their arms at once, and a whistle blew and they were running back and forth on the field again, running headlong into each other, piling up in those horrid mounds, arms and legs twisted.

Number Twenty-One seemed to be all right. He ran and fell down and got up. Her mind was full of thoughts of concussion, of fractured skulls and cracked ribs and broken legs and elbows, and she had found herself rhyming again: Twenty-One is my only son. Son and one. Over and over.

Then they all seemed to move faster, to fall down oftener, to run into each other with greater violence, and suddenly Number Twenty-One had the ball, and was running down the field, evading those other fastmoving figures. Her heart started hammering in her chest, as though she were running with him, and she was filled with pride, at the sight of that swiftfooted strong young figure moving so fleetly across the green field. She didn't know enough about the game to know exactly what he was doing, but all around her people were standing up, shouting, calling out his name, chanting his name, "Link! Link! Link!" It was a deep-throated roar that increased her own excitement, made her breath catch in her throat, as though she were the one going swiftly down the length of the playing field, while a great crowd cheered her on.

Then from somewhere in the back of the stadium, an angry voice rang out, "Get the nigger! Get the nigger!"

She sat down, suddenly, on the hard concrete seat, sat down without ever having been aware that she had been standing, and the abruptness with which she sat jarred her entire body. She sat there, trembling, thinking, I will never let him play football again. Never.

When she left the stadium she went to see Frances, told her about Link's being knocked down, about that loud furious voice, calling, Get the nigger, get the nigger, told her that Link could not play football any more.

Frances had said, "Nonsense. You're not to say a word about

it. You may have forgotten that he was an orphan adopted by
people who were strangers. But he hasn't forgotten it. And you
may have forgotten that you rejected him, completely, totally,
when the Major died. But he hasn't forgotten it. He never will.
Football is good for him. Every time he hears a crowd of people
roar their approval of him it helps him build up a reserve of belief
in himself as a person. As for the word nigger —"

It was then that Frances had told her, for the first time, that
story about her father's death, and why she was never again the
least bit disturbed when she heard someone use the word nigger.

And now she thought irritably, That's fine. For Frances. It
doesn't help me a bit. Link and that girl, girl with pale yellow
hair, girl here with him so often that she left the smell of her perfume in my house. Link running down a football field, carrying
a ball, eluding all the other strong young figures. Link walking
down Dumble Street with her, on Saturday mornings, carrying her
market basket, swinging it back and forth, looking up at her.
Adoration, devotion in the young face, in the eyes.

He was in love with that girl. In love with her —

She got up, put on her hat, her coat. She was going to the
police. She was going to tell them that she believed the girl was
in danger. They would not believe her over there at the Franklin
Avenue Police Station. But if she used her most emphatic manner, some one of those policemen would be sufficiently impressed
to suggest that special guards be assigned to that blond girl.

She was ready to leave, when J. C. Powther sidled into the
room. She had not seen him since the day of the funeral, the day
he had demolished the Major's hat.

He stared at her then put his thumb in his mouth, took it out,
said, "You goin' out, Missus Crunch?"

"Yes."

"Kin I go with you?"

"No. You run along upstairs."

"Ain't nobody home but Powther. He's just settin' around
holdin' on his head. Mamie told him it would drive a body crazy
if they had to keep lookin' at him settin' around holdin' on his
head like that. 'N she went out. 'N then Kelly and Shapiro went
out. That's why they's nobody home. Kin I go with you?"

"No," she said firmly. "You run along now —

She heard an echo out of the past, heard Frances' voice saying,
Run along now, Link, run along and play, and saw that small des-

olate figure leave the room, slowly, reluctantly, and tried to call him back and could not form the words, could only huddle under that shawl with Frances and weep because the Major was dead.

"All right," she said, and patted J.C.'s shoulder. "You can come with me." Though she couldn't imagine what they would think at the police station when she arrived with this bullet-headed little boy by the hand.

"Get your hat and coat. But you go to the bathroom first. You go right now," she said. Because he was wiggling, standing first on one scuffed brown shoe and then on the other, holding his knees together.

"Where we goin'?" he asked suspiciously. "Ain't they got no wee-wee chairs dere?"

"I really don't know," she said. "I've never been inside a police station before."